Crow-Omaha

Amerind Studies in Anthropology

Series Editor John Ware

Trincheras Sites in Time, Space, and Society
Edited by Suzanne K. Fish, Paul R. Fish, and M. Elisa Villalpando

Collaborating at the Trowel's Edge: Teaching and Learning in Indigenous Archaeology
Edited by Stephen W. Silliman

Warfare in Cultural Context: Practice, Agency, and the Archaeology of Violence
Edited by Axel E. Nielsen and William H. Walker

Across a Great Divide: Continuity and Change in Native North American Societies, 1400–1900
Edited by Laura L. Scheiber and Mark D. Mitchell

Leaving Mesa Verde: Peril and Change in the Thirteenth-Century Southwest
Edited by Timothy A. Kohler, Mark D. Varien, and Aaron M. Wright

Becoming Villagers: Comparing Early Village Societies
Edited by Matthew S. Bandy and Jake R. Fox

Hunter-Gatherer Archaeology as Historical Process
Edited by Kenneth E. Sassaman and Donald H. Holly Jr.

Religious Transformation in the Late Pre-Hispanic Pueblo World
Edited by Donna M. Glowacki and Scott Van Keuren

Crow-Omaha: New Light on a Classic Problem of Kinship Analysis
Edited by Thomas R. Trautmann and Peter M. Whiteley

Crow-Omaha
New Light on a Classic Problem of Kinship Analysis

Thomas R. Trautmann and
Peter M. Whiteley, Editors

The University of Arizona Press

Tucson

The University of Arizona Press
www.uapress.arizona.edu

We respectfully acknowledge the University of Arizona is on the land and territories of Indigenous peoples. Today, Arizona is home to twenty-two federally recognized tribes, with Tucson being home to the O'odham and the Yaqui. The university strives to build sustainable relationships with sovereign Native Nations and Indigenous communities through education offerings, partnerships, and community service.

© 2012 by The Arizona Board of Regents
All rights reserved. Published 2012
First paperback edition published 2025

ISBN-13: 978-0-8165-0790-0 (cloth)
ISBN-13: 978-0-8165-5557-4 (paper)
ISBN-13: 978-0-8165-9931-8 (ebook)

The series formerly known as Amerind Studies in Archaeology has been renamed Amerind Studies in Anthropology.

Publication of this book is made possible in part by a grant from the Amerind Foundation.

Library of Congress Cataloging-in-Publication Data
Crow-Omaha : new light on a classic problem of kinship analysis / Thomas R. Trautmann and Peter M. Whiteley, editors.
   p. cm. — (Amerind studies in anthropology)
   Includes bibliographical references and index.
   ISBN 978-0-8165-0790-0 (cloth : alk. paper) 1. Crow Indians—Kinship. 2. Omaha Indians—Kinship. 3. Crow Indians—Social networks 4. Omaha Indians—Social networks. 5. Kinship—Great Plains—History. 6. Social structure—Great Plains—History. 7. Social evolution—Great Plains—History. I. Trautmann, Thomas R.   II. Whiteley, Peter M.
   E99.C92C77 2012
   978.6004'975272—dc23   2012006699

Printed in the United States of America
♾ This paper meets the requirements of ANSI/NISO Z39.48-1992 (Permanence of Paper).

Contents

Preface   vii

Kinship Notation   xi

Linguistic Note   xiii

1   A Classic Problem   1
Thomas R. Trautmann and Peter M. Whiteley

Crow-Omaha in Theory

2   Crossness and Crow-Omaha   31
Thomas R. Trautmann

3   Tetradic Theory and Omaha Systems   51
Nicholas J. Allen

North America

4   Omaha and "Omaha"   69
R. H. Barnes

5   Crow-Omaha Kinship in North America: A Puebloan Perspective   83
Peter M. Whiteley

6   Phylogenetic Analysis of Sociocultural Data: Identifying Transformation Vectors for Kinship Systems   109
Ward C. Wheeler, Peter M. Whiteley, and Theodore Powers

Africa

7   A Tetradic Starting Point for Skewing? Marriage as a Generational Contract: Reflections on Sister-Exchange in Africa   135
Wendy James

8 Crow- (and Omaha-) Type Kinship Terminology:
The Fanti Case   153
David B. Kronenfeld

9 Deep-Time Historical Contexts of Crow and Omaha Systems:
Perspectives from Africa   173
Christopher Ehret

South America

10 The Making and Unmaking of "Crow-Omaha" Kinship in
Central Brazil(ian Ethnology)   205
Marcela Coelho de Souza

11 Schemas of Kinship Relations and the Construction of Social
Categories among the Mebêngôkrê Kayapó   223
Terence Turner

Australia

12 Omaha Skewing in Australia: Overlays, Dynamism,
and Change   243
Patrick McConvell

13 "Horizontal" and "Vertical" Skewing: Similar Objectives,
Two Solutions?   261
Laurent Dousset

Afterword

14 Crow-Omaha, in Thickness and in Thin   281
Thomas R. Trautmann and Peter M. Whiteley

Notes   299

Glossary   303

References   309

About the Contributors   335

Topics Index   337

Peoples Index   344

Persons Index   347

Preface

This volume has grown out of a conviction that the time is ripe to make real progress on one of anthropology's oldest and most obdurate of problems: that of Crow-Omaha. It is the result of an Amerind Foundation Advanced Seminar held early in 2010, bringing together fifteen scholars engaged with the Crow-Omaha problem. Participants were chosen for wide regional expertise in places where Crow-Omaha and related kinship systems (especially Iroquois and Dravidian) are prominent—North and South America, Africa, and Australia—and to represent contrasting theoretical approaches—linguistic and structural, formalist and evolutionary, historical, and agentive. The Crow-Omaha seminar had generous support from the Amerind Foundation and the National Science Foundation, here gratefully acknowledged.[1]

The Crow-Omaha seminar was inspired directly by the 1998 volume emanating from a conference held in France, the 1993 Maison Suger roundtable organized by Maurice Godelier and his associates. The book is called *Transformations of Kinship*, and it was coedited by Godelier, Thomas Trautmann, and Franklin Tjon Sie Fat. That conference was directed toward explaining how transformations occur among different types of kinship systems, whether these are reversible, and "whether there is an overall directionality of change, or an evolutionary drift that cumulates transformations in a particular way" (Godelier et al. 1998:vii). In pursuing this question, the conference sought to reinvigorate the originary core of kinship study, the formalist study of categories as logically integrated sets. In doing so, it sought to restore a balance between the "hot" kinship of practice, "kinship red in tooth and claw," and the "cool" kinship of categories and terminologies, and more generally between the new and growing literature on "cultures of kinship" and the long tradition of formal analysis and comparison of systems. The present book continues in the aspirations of the *Transformations* volume and extends its results, descending both "lineally" and "collaterally" from the earlier conference.

The Maison Suger roundtable announced its interest in Dravidian, Iroquois, and Crow-Omaha systems (Godelier et al. 1998: viii), and it elicited some contributions to Crow-Omaha, notably by Trautmann and Barnes (1998) and Kryukov (1998). But the main thrust was on Dravidian, Iroquois, and structurally similar forms; we could say that the *Transformations* volume had become a major contribution to the study of crossness in all its variant forms, including Dravidian, Iroquois, and many others, but leaving Crow-Omaha a live problem. While postponing the question pro tem, the Maison Suger group always intended to return to it at some point (Tjon Sie Fat personal communication to Whiteley, 2007). The "Crow-Omaha problem"—at base, why some kinship systems equate relatives of different generations—has intrigued anthropologists throughout the twentieth century, and indeed earlier, since the times of Morgan, Kohler, and Durkheim. As one contributor to *Transformations* noted, "the interpretation of Crow-Omaha terminologies has been one of the most puzzling problems in the whole field of kinship studies" (Kryukov 1998:312). Subsequently Godelier (2011:199 [2004:218]), in his recent big book on kinship, reemphasized the need for sustained analytical attention to Crow-Omaha.

In the meantime, Peter Whiteley, a coeditor of this volume but not a member of the Maison Suger group, was working on a deep history of the Hopi social system. His work discerning structural patterns in this classically Crow system drew significant benefit from comparative work, including the analysis of some North American cases by Trautmann and Barnes (1998), and the notion of "semi-complex alliance" developed by Claude Lévi-Strauss and Françoise Héritier (Whiteley 2008:40-41, 829). Whiteley also became interested in how the concomitants of Crow-Omaha systems might be identified through comparative study, especially with the enhanced techniques developed by phylogenetics, a specialty of his colleague at the American Museum of Natural History, Ward Wheeler. Whiteley and Wheeler forged a plan to compare Crow-Omaha systems worldwide, using Wheeler's phylogenetics program, POY. In late 2007, inspired by contributions to *Transformations*, they enlisted the advice of Tjon Sie Fat and Trautmann. The ensuing discussions evolved into the seed of a plan for the Crow-Omaha seminar.

Godelier registered immediate enthusiasm and graciously agreed to co-chair the seminar, though in the event he was unable to attend, as was Tjon Sie Fat. In serial back-and-forths, Trautmann, Whiteley, and Godelier formulated a list of participants who would cover the important global concentrations of Crow-Omaha and related systems and would also bring differing theoretical perspectives to bear. In some instances, other Maison Suger participants led us to new specialists in their respective fields. Eduardo Viveiros de Castro, whom we invited, gave us an immeasurable gift in his recommendation that we invite instead his student, Marcela Coelho de Souza, who had written a doctoral dissertation on Crow-Omaha systems in Amazonia.

The Amerind Foundation in Dragoon, Arizona, proved an ideal setting for the Crow-Omaha seminar. The Amerind Advanced Seminars are usually on archaeological questions, but director John Ware has long promoted the intersection of archaeology and ethnology. Ware's and Whiteley's common interest in Puebloan kinship and social organization had brought them together before, in intense conversations that left a lingering sense of unfinished business when they parted. Ware greeted Whiteley's proposal for the seminar warmly and set the table for us with the hospitality for which the Amerind is famous.

The seminar went well, generating among the participants a sense of real progress on one of the longest-standing problems of anthropology, and it was agreed we should turn the papers into a book.[2] The University of Arizona Press set a strict word limit that required considerable rewriting and shortening of the papers, and they instructed us to ensure that they were student-friendly. It was a challenge to make one of the most difficult-to-comprehend problems of anthropology accessible to students and to do so without dumbing down the analysis. Students reading this book will judge the extent to which we have succeeded. For our own part, we believe the press did us a great favor in forcing us to be as clear and brisk as we could, editing down intelligently to reach the essentials, so we could bring this classic problem to the widest audience possible.

For institutional and academic support at various stages, Whiteley is most grateful to Barbara Green, Sue Ng-Maresco, Theodore Powers, Jennifer Steffey, Merrily Sterns, Ward Wheeler, and Nathan Woods at the American Museum of Natural History; Deborah Winslow at the National Science Foundation; Franklin Tjon Sie Fat at the University of Leiden; and Sander van der Leeuw at Arizona State University. He most especially wishes to thank Thomas Trautmann and Maurice Godelier, without whom the project could not have come together. Both editors thank Dianna Downing for her indispensable editorial work in rendering the chapters into the appropriate format and keeping all the loose ends tied together.

Kinship Notation

M	mother
F	father
D	daughter
S	son
W	wife
H	husband
Z	sister
B	brother
P	parent
Ch	child
G	sibling
E	spouse
Xc	cross cousin
//c	parallel cousin
N	nephew or niece ("nibling")
e	elder, for example, FeB = father's elder brother; e(FBS) = father's brother's son, older than ego
y	younger
♂	male's, male speaker's, for example, ♂ZS = a male's sister's son
♀	female's, female speaker's
ss	same sex, for example, ♀ss//c = a female's same-sex parallel cousin
os	opposite sex
G^{+2}	grandparents' generation
G^{+1}	parents' generation
G^{0}	ego's generation
G^{0e}	ego's generation, older than ego
G^{0y}	ego's generation, younger than ego
G^{-1}	children's generation
G^{-2}	grandchildren's generation

LINGUISTIC NOTE

An asterisk * prefixed to a word form, sound, or meaning represents the reconstructed form in the proto-language (common ancestor of a family or subgroup of languages).

Crow-Omaha

1

A Classic Problem

Thomas R. Trautmann and Peter M. Whiteley

Anthropology began with kinship. To be sure, kinship is everywhere and did not need to be discovered like some hidden continent; but everywhere kinship is found it is specific, and what anthropology did was to recognize this variety and try to account for it.

The anthropological analysis of kinship was comparative from the start. It started from the decentering encounter with the variety of kinship. L. H. Morgan, studying the Iroquois in the middle of the nineteenth century, was surprised to find that they had matrilineal clans, something new and strange to him. He also found, as he put it, that for the Iroquois the father's brother is equally a father, and the mother's sister, a mother. This principle carried through the kinship terminology. If my father's brother is also father to me, then my father's brother's son and daughter are my brother and sister, and the same goes for the mother's sister's children. If I am male, my brother's children are also son and daughter to me, but my sister's children are nephew and niece; if I am female, my sister's children are son and daughter, and my brother's children are nephew and niece. These last classifications are logically entailed by the first ones, because father's brother and a man's brother's child are reciprocals (correlative relations, as Morgan called them) of one another, as are a mother's sister and a woman's sister's child. Morgan considered this a kinship *system*, coherent and logically integrated due to "the consistency of reciprocals" (Lounsbury 1964a:366).

Figure 1.1 maps the pattern of Iroquois just described, translated into English terms. The three columns, from left to right, are the parents' generation (G^1), ego's generation (that is, my own generation, G^0), and the children's generation (G^{-1}). (If the figure is difficult to read, try rotating it a quarter turn clockwise, and it will have the more familiar look of a downward-flowing genealogical diagram.) The translation is only possible because what is different about Iroquois reconfigures and redefines a distinction that is familiar to English speakers. We may call

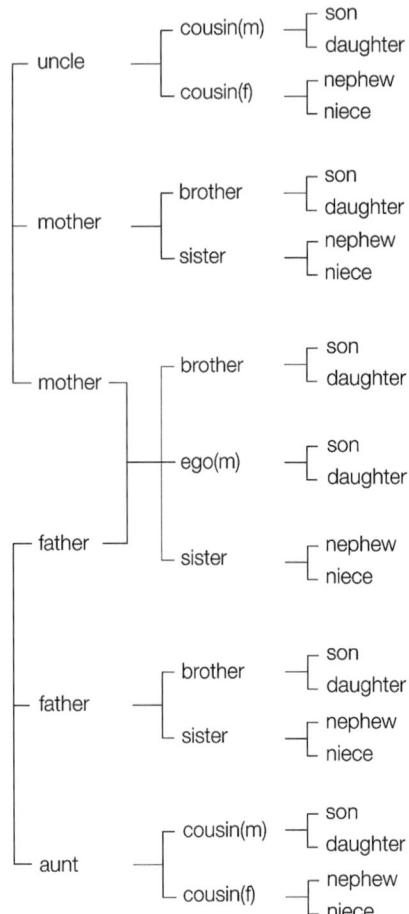

Figure 1.1 Iroquois crossness. English terms are redefined such that *mother, father, sister, brother, son,* and *daughter* are parallel kin, and *uncle, aunt, cousin, nephew,* and *niece* are cross-kin.

this the distinction between lineal and collateral kin, the lineal kin being father, mother, sister, brother, son, daughter; the collateral kin are aunt, uncle, cousin (male and female), nephew, niece. In English terminology the actual contents of the lineal kin will be limited and the collateral kin numerous and potentially unlimited. The Iroquois pattern, by contrast, has instead a distinction between what anthropologists call parallel kin (father, mother, sister, brother, son, daughter as redefined in figure 1.1) and cross-kin (aunt, uncle, cousin(m), cousin(f), niece, nephew as redefined in figure 1.1). In moving from English to Iroquois we have merged some collaterals with some lineals, and the resulting classes of cross and parallel kin are in principle of equal size. We call this the distinction of crossness. It is crossness that gave Iroquois its qualities for Morgan of being both strange and logical.

The enigma of crossness provoked Morgan to find an explanation for it, first in the matrilineal clans of the Iroquois. When that proved unsuccessful he launched a worldwide comparison of kinship terminologies, collecting material by extensive questionnaires of kinship categories sent to missionaries, U.S. consuls, and scholars around the globe and undertaking research journeys to the American West. Out of these efforts he compiled massive tables of kinship terminologies that became the first data set for comparative study, published in his great work, *Systems of Consanguinity and Affinity of the Human Family* (1871). The difference between English and Iroquois kinship was mapped globally onto the two mega-classes, Descriptive (containing English) and Classificatory (containing Iroquois). By "classificatory" he meant the classification or *merging* of father with father's brother and the like, found in crossness. Morgan's ultimate explanation, which involved a supposed evolutionary sequence of marriage rules, is not persuasive, but he had elicited a mass of data on phenomena that had never before been subject to comparative and global investigation, and he identified some of the major types of kinship terminology. Anthropology as a discipline largely took shape around kinship as a problem for comparative analysis.

Morgan anticipated that the Iroquois pattern of crossness would be found throughout North American societies, and his collection of kinship terminologies in the western territories abundantly confirmed this hypothesis. His survey also found crossness in the Old World, notably in Dravidian-speaking south India.

In the course of his western journeys, Morgan encountered another kind of terminology that has since come to be called Crow-Omaha. Crow-Omaha systems have a further increment of strangeness for English speakers. In terminologies of the Crow type, which are matrilineal, the cross-cousins on the father's side are called aunt and father, and on the mother's side son and daughter; in the Omaha type, which are patrilineal, the cross-cousins on the mother's side are called mother and uncle, and those on the father's side nephew and niece. Both apply terms across generations, and this cross-generational merging is called *skew-*

ing. Skewing applies to the cross-cousins among others, and it applies in opposite ways on the father's and mother's sides, *raising* the generation level of one and *lowering* the generation level of the other.

In figures 1.2 and 1.3, the effects of Crow-Omaha skewing are mapped. When we compare these with the Iroquois terminology in figure 1.1, we see that the first column (parents' generation) is identical, but the second and third columns (ego's and children's generations) show generational skewing, unlike Iroquois. This skewing occurs among what in Iroquois would be the cross-kin but not among the parallel kin, who are brothers, sisters, sons, and daughters. (The figures illustrate

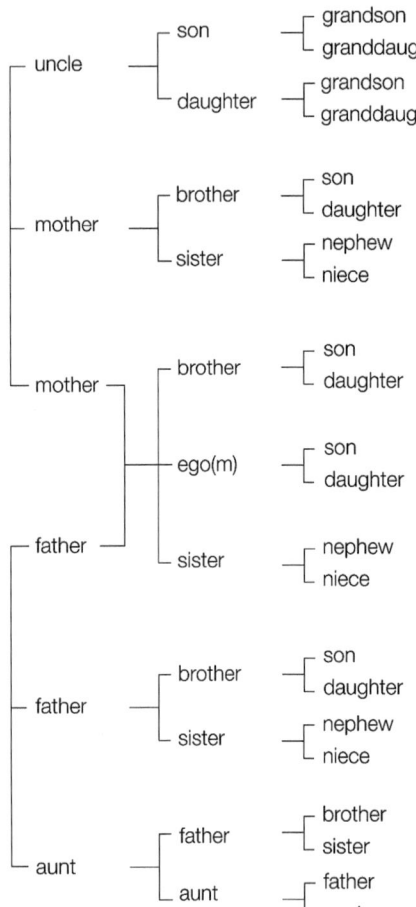

Figure 1.2 Crow skewing. English terms are used as in figure 1.1 but have been subjected to skewing or the merger of kin categories across generations, or columns of the diagram. This can be seen where English terms appear to be in the wrong generation and occur in more than one generation.

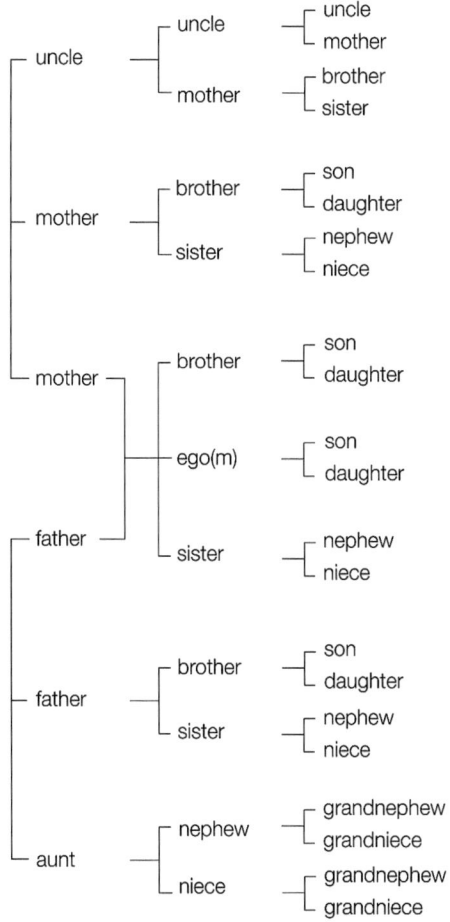

Figure 1.3 Omaha skewing. This pattern of skewing, associated with patrilineal transmission of statuses, is the opposite of the Crow pattern of skewing in figure 1.2, associated with matrilineal transmission of statuses.

only one pattern for Crow and Omaha. Lounsbury [1964a] identified four different structural types each for Crow and Omaha, details of which may be found in his important article on the topic, from which we have adapted the diagrams of what he calls Type I of Crow and Omaha.) Explaining this strange patterning that reconfigures the generations in an asymmetrical and yet internally consistent way has been a classic problem for the anthropological analysis of kinship, virtually from the beginning.

Morgan gives us a vivid record of his initial encounter with skewing:

> I first discovered this deviation from the typical form while working out the system of the Kaws in Kansas in 1859. The Kaw chief from whom I obtained it, through a perfectly competent interpreter, insisted upon the verity of these relationships against all doubts and questionings; and when the work was done I found it proved itself through the correlative relationships. Afterwards in 1860, while at the Iowa reservation in Nebraska, I had an opportunity to test it fully, both in Iowa and Otoe, through White Cloud a native Iowa well versed in English. While discussing these relationships he pointed out a boy near us, and remarked that he was his uncle, and the son of his mother's brother who was also his uncle. (Morgan 1871:179, n1)

This discovery of what has come to be called skewing applied to all those Native American societies of the Prairies Morgan called "Missouri Nations"—Omaha, Ponca, Iowa, Otoe, Missouri, Kaw, Osage, and Quapaw—and to the Winnebago on the shores of Green Bay. In time, after Morgan's work, the system as such came to be called Omaha—after one of the nations who exhibited these kin term equations and distinctions. However, "Omaha" as a type quickly superseded its use to refer to a particular Native American society. Just as the Ojibwa word *totem* was expanded by anthropologists into "totemism," a general category of behavior found among unrelated societies across the globe, Omaha kinship systems soon became detached from their original ethnographic context.

Morgan discovered the inverse correlation, assimilating father's sisters to father's sister's daughters (all "aunts"), among the Crow and Hidatsa of the Plains, the "Prairie Nations"—Pawnee, Arikara, Wichita, and others—and the "Gulf Nations" of the Southeast: Choctaw, Chickasaw, Creek, Seminole, and Cherokee. Subsequent analysts grouped these initially as "Choctaw" systems, but in time the preferred label became "Crow." As for Omaha, Crow became a general type, with limited connection to the actual society of Native North Americans named Crow (or more properly, Upsaroka, the name Morgan derived from indigenous usage). He hazarded the suggestion that the line of development was from Crow to Omaha to Iroquois, but this has not been upheld by subsequent research.

Morgan's two decentering discoveries—that the father's brother is equally a father (crossness) and that the uncle's son is equally an uncle (the skewing of Crow-Omaha)—have had a very different afterlife in the anthropological study of kinship. In a word, crossness has proven easy to analyze and immensely productive for the further analysis of kinship, whereas Crow-Omaha has proven a tough nut to crack.

Crossness, which is widely spread in the world, was quickly found to be associated, at different times and places, with dual organization or unilineal exogamous moieties, marriage classes, the rule of cross-cousin marriage, and other things. As many as five actually existing variant types of crossness have been identified, and the structural relations among the variants have been mapped. Crossness was the principal object of study in a conference at the Maison Suger in Paris, convened by Maurice Godelier and subsequently published in the volume *Transformations of Kinship*, edited by Godelier, Trautmann, and Tjon Sie Fat (1998). This book is conceived as a successor to that one, taking up the Crow-Omaha issue left by that conference for a future moment and for which it implicitly prepared the way.

To understand why Crow-Omaha kinship has been such a refractory problem for kinship analysis, we must trace the main events in the history of scholarly treatments of it. That history is readily divisible into two quite different periods, from Morgan to Lévi-Strauss and from Lévi-Strauss to the present. In the first period, analysis of Crow-Omaha largely addressed its relation to unilineal descent. Lévi-Strauss's book *The Elementary Structures of Kinship* (*Les structures élémentaires de la parenté*, 1949; revised English version 1969) reoriented kinship analysis by directing it to the study of marriage alliance, understood as a social solidarity–making form of exchange. Crow-Omaha was increasingly seen as a particular pattern of marriage by Lévi-Strauss and others influenced by his arguments. As we shall see, this interpretive move was very fruitful, but it also made the Crow-Omaha problem more refractory by redefining the object of study in such a way that some systems with skewing were excluded, as we shall shortly explain.

Beginning with the first period, in which Crow-Omaha was explained by recourse to features of unilineal descent, we note that the Crow-Omaha question was taken up for study very soon after Morgan published his *magnum opus*. Two early events that were fateful were the detailed ethnography of the kinship and social structure of the Omaha nation itself by Dorsey (1884), and the analysis by the comparative jurist and early theorist of kinship analysis Josef Kohler (*Zur Urgeschichte der Ehe,* 1897; English translation 1975). Kohler, a professor of law at the University of Berlin, developed from Morgan's materials an explanation of the problematic, generation-skewing terminologies, which he labeled "Omaha" and "Choctaw." Kohler argued that each type always went together with societies that practiced patrilineal and matrilineal descent, respectively. Social emphasis, for inheritance of property or offices, organization of corporate groups like "clans," lineages, and so forth, on a patriline—the line encompassing father, father's father, and father's father's father—tended to correlate with those systems that had Omaha terminological equations. Conversely, a society that emphasized the matriline—that is, keyed to mother, mother's mother, and mother's mother's mother—tended to correlate similarly with Choctaw terminology. In a famous review of Kohler's work, Émile Durkheim (1898) emphasized these aspects of Kohler's analysis, and it gained in prominence. Attending to the kin term equations and distinctions in a manner that precedes formalist analysis, Kohler also showed clearly that each of the two systems was in effect a mirror image of the other, skewing down opposite lines in identical ways. Thus, the two systems were logically paired.

Since Kohler there has been a general consensus among anthropologists that Crow-Omaha kinship terminologies are connected with unilineal descent. Indeed, it is virtually a matter of definition. If kinship categories descend from father to son, such that an uncle's son is an uncle (MBS = MB) in Omaha, or from mother to daughter, such that the daughter of an aunt is an aunt (FZD = FZ) in Crow, we see that unilineality of both kinds has an integral place in the terminology, although the same is *not* true of Iroquois matrilineal descent, which cannot be read from the terminology, much as Morgan had tried and failed to do.

Within the scholarly consensus, however, disagreements developed over exactly how and in what mode unilineal descent and skewing are connected. Radcliffe-Brown (1941) emphasized the signature principles of his structural-functionalist approach to social organization: namely, that unilineal descent groups acted collectively as jural corporations, which received a stronger emphasis with Crow or Omaha terminology, and that siblings were functionally equivalent within corporate groups composed of unilineal kin. This would explain both features that Morgan found at the beginning of the tradition of comparative analysis of kinship—that the father's brother is a father and that the uncle's son is also an uncle. Is the *corporate unilineal descent group* the key to Crow-Omaha skewing? Or is it *unilineal succession* to roles and rights (Lounsbury 1964a)? Or *residence patterns*, whether matri- or patrilocal (Murdock 1949; Titiev 1956)? Murdock and Titiev hypothesized that Crow systems derived from matrilocal residence, Omaha from patrilocal. However, unilateral residence could not be a sufficient condition, because there are plenty of cases without Crow or Omaha terminologies. Leslie White (1939) was cognizant of a problem implicit in unilineal theories of Crow-Omaha, namely, that there are many societies with unilineal descent but only a small proportion of them have Crow-Omaha skewing. He argued that Crow-Omaha arose as unilineal descent grew stronger and formed a "mature" clan system. White rightly recognized that unilineal descent is necessary but not sufficient to account for Crow-Omaha skewing, and he offered an explanation turning on the degree of its strength. But there is no very definite way to calibrate this notion of strength of unilineality, and one would be hard pressed to say in what way the matrilineal clans of the Iroquois are less strong than the Crow ones. Tending against the strong unilineal descent group kind of argument, however, Tax showed that the Central Algonquian Fox have an Omaha terminology but lack unilineal descent groups (Tax 1937). Then there were the Yuchi of the Ohio Valley, an Omaha system with matrilineal descent groups (Lesser 1929). More recent analyses of Amazonian Gê societies (Maybury-Lewis 1979; see Coelho de Souza, this volume) and some West African societies (e.g., Muller 1997) have shown variant combinations of unilineal descent with Crow or Omaha terminologies. In spite of this disagreement—the range of which is limited—the debate was predicated on the prevalent sense that Crow-Omaha has *something* to do with unilineality, even if, as in the Fox case, this may be apparent only in the terminology itself and not overtly in the present social structure of groups with this terminology.

Other proposals have included that both Crow and Omaha derive from a rule of matrilateral cross-cousin marriage, that is, that male ego should marry his mother's brother's daughter (MBD) (Lane and Lane 1959). From comparative survey, this was rejected on its face, but arguing for a unidirectional (quasi-evolutionist) variation, it was proposed that matrilateral cross-cousin marriage emerged from a prior conjunction of bilateral cross-cousin marriage (i.e., marriage for male ego with either MBD or FZD) with matrilineal descent. Under certain social conditions, this conjunction might transform directly into either a Crow or an Omaha system (Eyde and Postal 1961). A more recent proposal (Kryukov 1998) to derive Crow-Omaha systems from asymmetric prescriptive marriage rules is a variant on this theme, but it conflicts sharply with Lévi-Strauss's formal distinction of asymmetric from "semi-complex" systems (discussed later).

Over the course of the twentieth century, the body of ethnographies on which the Crow-Omaha question was based grew larger and richer. In North America there was the Omaha ethnography of Dorsey, already mentioned, which improved on Morgan and corrected errors in the record he had formed (see Kronenfeld 1989; Trautmann and Barnes 1998). Lowie began sustained ethnographic studies of Crow Indian social organization in 1911 that proved particularly influential. Lesser (1929) published a brief but important analysis of Plains Siouan groups with their Iroquois, Crow, and Omaha kinship variations. Eggan (1937c) brought together several focused analyses of Native American Crow-Omaha systems (including Tax on the Fox and Gilbert on the Eastern Cherokee) and published a new analysis of Choctaw kinship (Eggan 1937b). Building on Lowie's important work on Hopi kinship (Lowie 1929a, 1929b), Eggan (1950) also developed a landmark analysis of Crow systems among the western Pueblos (see also Whiteley's chapter in this volume). Partly in response to Eggan, Fox (1967) produced a key critical analysis of Keresan Pueblo kinship. Regarding comparative classification, Leslie Spier (1925) produced a benchmark study organizing kinship terminologies into a distinctive typology. It was Spier who effectively replaced Kohler's "Choctaw" type with "Crow." Crow and Omaha systems, discovered in Morgan's great comparative researches and first effectively characterized by Kohler, acquired the name that has attended them ever since.

While the ethnographic record was improving, explanatory methods grew apace, providing more rigorous forms of description and analysis. Kinship terminologies, comparatively examined, hold out the promise of formal analysis based on mathematics of some kind, which has proven fruitful in the natural sciences since the time of Pythagoras.

Malinowski was moved to speak of "kinship algebra," though it was not meant as a compliment. But not everyone is algebra-phobic, and it is hardly an intellectual distinction to be so. A signal development for our purposes was the "formal account" of Crow-Omaha by Floyd Lounsbury (1964a). The goal was to rigorously describe the structure of Crow-Omaha terminologies in themselves and apart from questions of marriage rules and social structures. The means was a set of equivalence rules that, applied to a stock of primitive terms (F, M, Z, B, S, D, W, H), generated models that should replicate empirical terminologies more or less closely. Kin types were reduced to primary terms (for example, FB → F) or, what amounts to the same thing, primary terms were expanded to more distant kin types (F → FB); equivalence could be written in the form of reduction rules or expansion rules with perfectly identical results. Of the three rules for Crow-Omaha, the most diagnostic one was called the skewing rule, which crossed the generations and produced the generational skewing of cross-kin we saw in figures 1.2 and 1.3. A stronger reading of this procedure is that kin categories contain focal kin types and more distant ones, the latter linked to the former by rules modeling the operations of the mind. But one does not have to embrace this bolder version to find formal semantic analysis to be an excellent tool by which to make clear the structural properties of the terminology. Lounsbury's classic article made a notable advance on that front by identifying four distinct types of Crow terminological structures and four of Omaha. Because this analysis addresses only terminologies, it applies to "whales" and "fish" alike (see later discussion)—skewed terminologies that accompany semi-complex marriage structures and those that accompany asymmetrical cross-cousin marriage. Linked in some respects to Chomskian transformational grammar (or, for that matter, the transformational grammar of Panini), formalist approaches emphasize the "generative" impetus of logical reciprocals in a specific culture's kin terminology. Formalism as a methodology has continued to prosper in certain quarters, perhaps most notably with the recent work of David Kronenfeld (2009, and see his chapter herein), Per Hage (e.g., 1999, 2001), Sydney Gould (2000), and Dwight Read (e.g., 2001).

At the same time, the ethnographic record was thickening in other parts of the world that proved significant for the Crow-Omaha problem. Australia was a region that Morgan reached in his kinship studies only at the end of his life, but it quickly became a privileged terrain for the field. In focusing on the family social life in Australian aboriginal societies, Bronislaw Malinowski (1913) refuted evolutionary explanations of classificatory systems. The same year, influenced by W. H. R. Rivers's correlation of kinship terminologies with social organization, A. R. Radcliffe-Brown launched a series of studies of aboriginal kinship, culminating in *The Social Organization of Australian Tribes* (1931). In an Australian context, Radcliffe-Brown developed his sense that terminological merging of lineal and collateral relatives functioned toward unity and coherence of "lineages" as operational social groups.

In 1949, another benchmark was reached by George Peter Murdock's *Social Structure*, a sweeping comparison of kinship systems and their social-structural and socio-evolutionary contexts. Murdock's typology divided Crow and Omaha (as well other systems) into subtypes based on residence and descent rules and proposed multiple theorems for the classification of kin, involving lineality, descent groups, marriage rules, and postmarital residence. This survey originated his later comparative work and evolved into the *Ethnographic Atlas* (e.g., Murdock 1967, Gray 1999), the *Standard Cross-Cultural Sample* (Murdock and White 1970), and the Human Relations Area Files—the most important comparative databases of sociocultural features, albeit attended by much anthropological dissensus. Murdock is also largely responsible for the latter-day entrenchment of ethnonyms to refer to kin terminologies. Lowie (1928) had recognized four structural types: "generational, bifurcate-merging, bifurcate-collateral, and lineal." Murdock effectively replaced these with the names they most often bear in anthropological discourse: Hawaiian (generational), Iroquois (bifurcate-merging), Sudanese (bifurcate-collateral), and Eskimo (lineal). This in effect left Crow and Omaha as subtypes of Iroquois. However, Murdock used only the cousin terms of a single generation, ego's, as a diagnostic of the terminology type as a whole for societies in his databases. This gives only coarse-grained and sometimes incorrect or misleading information that is of limited value for comparative study of terminologies (see Barnes 2005).

Meanwhile, in British India, Tibeto-Burman-speaking tribes of Burma and Assam, especially the Kachin, became the objects of ethnographic studies that played a central role in the second major phase of the history we are reviewing (Gilhodes 1913, 1922; Hanson 1913; Hertz 1915; Hodson 1925; Leach 1945; Wehrli 1904). That second phase began with the great book by Lévi-Strauss, *Elementary Structures of Kinship*, which was dedicated to Morgan, honoring his pioneering work and the American school of anthropology that he founded and with which Lévi-Strauss was associated during the war years, "recalling that this school was especially great at a time when scientific precision and exact observation did not seem to him to be incompatible with a frankly theoretical mode of thought and a bold philosophical taste." In so saying, the author implied a criticism of the Boasian refusal of theory while signaling the mode and taste that would govern his new work. Lévi-Strauss did not destroy the consensus about Crow-Omaha, but he reframed the issue around the idea of marriage alliance. The effects of this reframing were mixed: it made Crow-Omaha generative of new interpretations and at the same time less coherent as an object of study. For this reason we need to look closely at this interpretive move.

Marcel Granet had developed a theory about the kinship system of ancient China, in which Australian marriage classes—especially of the Kariera, four-class, type, and the asymmetrical cross-cousin marriage of the Kachin tribe of Burma—were heavily used as resources to model what Chinese kinship may have been in ancient times. Lévi-Strauss devotes an entire chapter to Granet's theory, acknowledging that he pioneered the concept of marriage as forming a system of exchange and distinguishing two types of exchange (which Lévi-Strauss names *direct* and *generalized*).

The central spine of *Elementary Structures* is what Lévi-Strauss calls the Burma-Siberia axis, with Kachin at one end and Gilyak at the other, running through China, and continuing on the southern end through the islands of Indonesia. For Lévi-Strauss, the eight-section Murngin system of Australia (rather than the four-section Kariera) and Kachin of Burma are keys to elementary structures of kinship and the asymmetrical cross-cousin marriage rule they both embody. Like Granet, Lévi-Strauss brings marriage rules, understood as constituting systems of exchange, to the fore—without canceling the importance of descent, unilineal and otherwise. Marriage rules activate modes of exchange by which families create bonds of alliance by marrying their children to other families. Kinship systems are elementary (meaning simplest) if they have a prescriptive rule of marriage, that is, a rule that prescribes a specific category among a limited number of categories in which a spouse must be found. By and large this means cross-cousin marriage in some form, so that the notion of elementary structures proposed here is linked to kinship systems containing crossness. Lévi-Strauss deals mainly with two kinds of cross-cousin marriage. *Symmetrical cross-cousin marriage* directs one to marry one's mother's brother's child or one's father's sister's child. If this prescription is regularly followed, it often happens that a prospective spouse is related in both ways at once, as the mother's brother and father's sister will have married one another. This rule expresses what Lévi-Strauss calls *direct exchange*, direct because *two* units (families, exogamous moieties, clans, lineages) can form an alliance by marrying their children to one another (see figure 1.4). Quite different is the effect of *asymmetrical cross-cousin marriage*, under which a man marries his matrilateral cross-cousin, the mother's brother's daughter, and a woman, her father's sister's son, but is prohibited from marrying the other cross-cousin (FZD or MBS). This expresses what Lévi-Strauss calls *generalized exchange*, in which marriage partners move in one direction only; to complete a marriage circle one needs a minimum of *three* exogamous clans or lineages. Figure 1.5 shows that effect. Murngin and Kachin marriage is of this kind. The

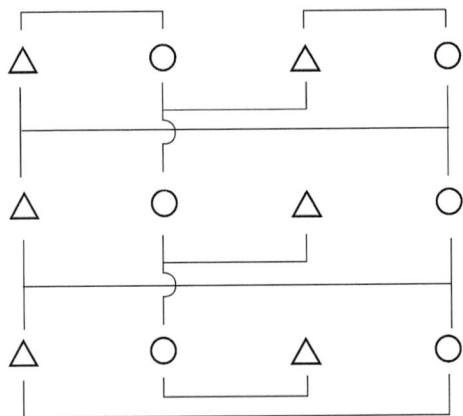

Figure 1.4 Symmetrical cross-cousin marriage

A Classic Problem

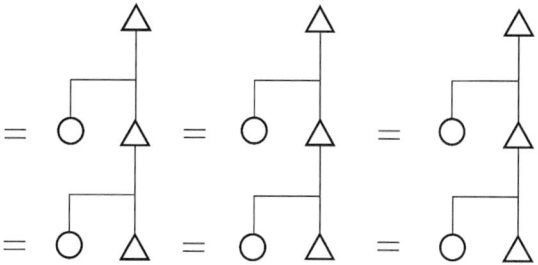

Figure 1.5 Asymmetrical cross-cousin marriage

Kachin kinship terminology, in addition, is skewed in the Crow-Omaha fashion.

Nevertheless, Crow-Omaha kinship is barely mentioned in the first edition of the *Elementary Structures*, and the skewing of Kachin terminology is not framed in that book as a problem to be solved; what is foregrounded instead is marriage alliance of prescriptive type as the key to elementary structures of kinship. After the publication of the book, however, Lévi-Strauss addressed Crow-Omaha directly in a lecture on the future of kinship studies. In that lecture, Crow-Omaha is conceptualized as a form of *marriage* rather than a form of kinship terminology (i.e., lineal merging or skewing): it is conceptualized as *semi-complex marriage alliance*, standing between elementary and complex forms. *Complex marriage alliance* is the form of marriage rule in which the only rule is to forbid the marriage of a close circle of consanguineous kin, and the category of permitted marriage therefore enlarges to encompass the whole of society or, indeed, the entire human species. Semi-complex marriage alliance is a system in which there are only negative rules, forbidding marriage within the father's and mother's clans and perhaps others, that is, prohibiting one from repeating the marriage alliance that brought the mother and the father together but allowing marriage in other clans. "Crow-Omaha provide the connecting link between elementary and complex structures. They relate to elementary structures in so far as they formulate preventions to marriage in sociological terms, and to complex structures in so far as the nature of the network of alliances is aleatory, an indirect result of the fact that the only conditions laid down are negative" (Lévi-Strauss 1969:xxxix). By the very name Lévi-Strauss identifies as a problem for the future of kinship studies to resolve: the passage from elementary to complex marriage alliance via the semi-complex form, which is his way of defining Crow-Omaha.

Newly coined as "semi-complex alliance structures," Crow-Omaha systems were thus redefined as inseparable from marriage rules. But they differed from both symmetrical and asymmetrical exchange systems—both "elementary" in Lévi-Strauss's terms. In symmetrical exchange, Group A gives spouses to Group B and receives spouses in return. In an asymmetric system, of the type found in numerous Australian aboriginal societies, Group A gives women as spouses to Group B; Group B gives to Group C, Group C to Group D, and Group D to Group A, thus forming a circle of exchange groups. In contrast, in a semi-complex system, Lévi-Strauss (1966, 1969) and his student Françoise Héritier (1981) argued, there is no unidirectional exchange and no orderly circle of transactions; rather, spouses of both sexes may be exchanged with a large (though limited) number of like groups, without repetition from one generation to the next. But then, what of the Kachin? Lévi-Strauss rules them out of the newly redefined Crow-Omaha. Semi-complex alliance structures (Crow-Omaha) and structures combining skewing with asymmetrical cross-cousin marriage as the Kachin do are alike as "fish and whales" (1966), the former operating to turn kin into affines, and the latter affines into kin (Lévi-Strauss 1969:xxxix). As a result of this move, the Crow-Omaha concept has been split into two variants. On one hand, in the inherited sense Crow-Omaha means kinship terminologies containing skewing; on the other hand, in the Lévi-Straussian sense it means semi-complex structures of alliance. This has been a source of advances and also an often unnoticed source of confusion and speaking to cross purposes.

As the "bridge between elementary and complex structures" (Lévi-Strauss 1969:xl), Crow-Omaha alliance must be explained, Lévi-Strauss argued, as a necessary precondition to understanding complex structures. His inquiry (into both semi-complex and complex) was famously abandoned, however (ibid.:xxxvi), as a result of the "tremendous difficulties" presented by Crow-Omaha alliance permutations. For societies like the Hopi, with more than thirty matrilineal clans and prescriptive exogamy from three descent lines (mother's clan-set, father's clan-set, and mother's father's clan-set)—statistically permissible "marriage types" were preliminarily computed in the 300 million range (ibid.:xl). Although "still quite convinced" that a general theory of "complex kinship structures" could not be had without accounting for Crow-Omaha systems (ibid.:xxxvi), Lévi-Strauss retreated in the face of these difficulties. Nonetheless, his sense that Crow-Omaha kinship systems were both critical to the "future of kinship studies" and configured "dispersed affinal alliance" structures proved influential.

Héritier's intensive study of marriages among the Samo of Burkina Faso showed how generational repetition of opposite-sex affinal alliances promotes dispersal of same-sex kin (Héritier 1981, 1999; see also Bowden 1983). Héritier presents Samo kinship as of Omaha type with patrilineal descent. Marriage rules prohibit repeating an alliance for three generations, ruling out for ego the patrilineages of his father (i.e., also his own), his mother, his father's mother, and his mother's mother, thus providing the most extensive lineal prohibitions of any of the semi-complex variants identified by Lévi-Strauss. Héritier finds that among the Samo, although the marriage rules are negative and marriage choices are not prescribed, in practice people marry among kin who are just beyond the limit of the prohibitions. She hypothesizes that all semi-complex systems, "although conceptualized locally in terms of negative rules and marriage prohibitions, might (at a more global level of analysis) be seen to accommodate a closed, regular alliance structure of a specific type" (Tjon Sie Fat 1998a:262). Héritier's trenchant and detailed ethnographic analysis launched a widespread comparison of semi-complex systems in African societies (Héritier-Augé and Copet-Rougier 1990–94).

Where Lévi-Strauss did not make kinship terminology the explanandum of his discussion of Crow-Omaha, Robert McKinley (1971a, 1971b), in a pair of articles, gives a highly original explanation that joins the marriage rules called semi-complex with the terminological skewing of Crow-Omaha. McKinley proposes that terminologies do active cultural work of some kind, and in Crow-Omaha the work they do is to resolve the internal contradiction of societies that wish to prolong the effects of marriage alliances while promoting *dispersed alliance* through the marriage rule prohibiting the repetition of previous marriages. Crow-Omaha does this cultural work by "freezing time," and thus perpetuating the memory of past alliances. If a man in the Omaha system is prohibited from finding a wife where his father did—in his mother's clan—the fact that his uncle's son is also an uncle creates an illusion of continuity where the marriage rule forbids it and this serves to keep the bond with his mother's clan alive. This is persuasive only if we first excise the Kachin and other skewed systems that practice asymmetrical cross-cousin marriage from the explanandum, for the Kachin also freeze time in the same way but, contrary to the Omaha, repeat marriage alliance each passing generation (Barnes [1976] is also skeptical). Meanwhile, skewing in general remains without an explanation, though in a sense, we know, as we have known all along, that it is connected with unilineal descent in some way.

Other important ventures into this field include Barnes's *Two Crows Denies It* (2005 [1984]), a rigorous inquiry into the facts of Omaha ethnography based on archival sources and reanalysis of the existing record. Barnes is frankly skeptical of "Crow-Omaha" as a category and of explanations, like McKinley's and Héritier's, that elide salient ethnographic differences among societies labeled with these terms. He addresses this particularly via an assessment of the (non)correspondence between "Omaha systems," as these have come to be imagined by anthropologists, and the historical actualities of Omaha (proper) kinship and marriage. David Kronenfeld (e.g., 2009, and see his chapter herein), focusing on the West African Fanti, has, since the 1970s produced a series of new formalist analyses of Crow skewing in Fanti kin terminology, based on his discovery that the Fanti have an unskewed terminology, Iroquois in crossness, Cheyenne in form, as well as a skewed system that he interprets as an overlay on the unskewed terminology. From the Fanti case Kronenfeld has developed the thesis that Crow-Omaha skewing always represents an overlay onto another terminological system that is concurrent in the same society, a view whose influence can be seen in various chapters of this volume. So a Fanti speaker may switch from one terminology to another depending on context, which further suggests that kinship terminologies may vary by social situation. If, as Kronenfeld suggests, this proves to be true across the board, "semi-complex alliance," representing marriage practices of those with Crow-Omaha terminologies, must become a moot category. This question of the relationship between Crow-Omaha terminologies and whether they may be defined by marriage practices reappears in several chapters of the present volume.

Kronenfeld's conclusions about Crow-Omaha terminologies have significantly influenced Maurice Godelier's thoughts in this regard in his recent book on kinship, *The Metamorphoses of Kinship* (2011; first published in 2004 as *Métamorphoses de la parenté*). This study represents a third major benchmark in kinship studies, after Morgan and Lévi-Strauss. It is also, like this book, a further fruit of the *Transformations* volume from the Maison Suger conference, which Godelier devised, and his book draws in many of the contributions in that volume. Prior to that conference, kinship studies had gone into abeyance in anthropology. A wave of critical analyses of the field by its own practitioners reached its apogee in David Schneider's *Critique of the Study of Kinship* (1984). Attacking the premises of kinship concepts, including terminology, descent, and alliance, claiming they are projections of European folk theories, Schneider sought to deconstruct the field and pretty effectively succeeded. Post-Schneiderian kinship studies have largely emphasized his culturalist perspective, and shifted the object of analysis to cultural models of relatedness and shared substance, away from biological models (e.g., Feinberg and Oppenheimer 2001; Franklin and McKinnon 2000). However, refuting the force of the Schneiderian critique, and building what amounts to a reconstruction of the entire field, Godelier treats the major components of the traditional study of kinship—including descent and filiation, terminology, exchange, alliance, and the incest taboo, social organization, and cultural conceptions of relatedness—to reposition the field of kinship studies, both the older formalist work and the newer "cultures of relatedness" work, within and against the context of contemporary Western practices and ideas of reproduction.

One of Godelier's arguments is that transformations among kinship systems should be interpreted in evolutionary terms. Even if the pace of evolutionary change for kinship systems is slow, he believes certain demonstrated historical transformations—like that from a Sudanese to an Eskimo pattern in Latin and its daughter languages in Roman Europe, or from Iroquois to Crow-Omaha in North America—are not only directional but also irreversible—without the possibility of return to previous systems (Godelier 2011:510). Also, following Kryukov (1998), Godelier suggest that all kinship systems evolved from a form closest to the Dravidian type. Concerning Crow-Omaha, Kryukov brought forward evidence that in different but closely related branches of the Yi, a Tibeto-Burman-speaking people of Yunnan, we find suggestive historical transformations. Among western Yi, a Dravidian kinship pattern with prescriptive cross-cousin marriage and no distinctive terms for affines lost the prescriptive marriage rule and developed into an Iroquois pattern. For the eastern Yi branch called Nasupo, the original Dravidian form gave way to a system with asymmetric prescriptive marriage, very similar to Jinghpaw terminology, though lacking the Omaha-type Jinghpaw lineal equations. Crow-Omaha terminologies represent a further step along the trajectory of both, Godelier argues. The special value of the evidence that Kryukov has developed is that it suggests the "fish" and "whales" of Lévi-Strauss can develop out of the same (Dravidian) initial conditions. Thus, Godelier believes that Crow-Omaha can develop either from Iroquois or from Nasupo, though he makes clear that he also supports Kronenfeld's sense that this is merely an overlay onto the underlying system. Moreover, Godelier argues that there is no necessary correspondence between terminology and other aspects of social structure, including descent and alliance. As we shall see, all of these questions are taken up in one way or another by contributors to the present volume.

Where do we stand now? How shall we make our way forward?

We have identified the central problem—that we have two different ways of defining Crow-Omaha—on one hand as terminologies containing skewing (associated with unilineal descent) and sometimes accompanied by asymmetrical prescriptive cross-cousin marriage, and on the other hand as semi-complex marriage structures (associated with skewed terminologies but not those accompanied by asymmetrical cross-cousin marriage). Our first task is to be sure that we do not talk past one another by failing to recognize the way the object of study is being delimited. Our second task is to decide which fork of the road to take and be clear about the consequences for interpretation. Our feeling for the situation is that the matter of semi-complex alliance or dispersed alliance has its own logic and inhabits its own universe. Because this approach by definition excludes skewed systems having asymmetrical cross-cousin marriage, it seems impossible to give a comprehensive explanation for skewing on such a basis. In addition, the proper horizon of this definition of Crow-Omaha includes (or should include) systems like those of north India mentioned by Nicholas Allen in his chapter in this book, in which the four patrilineal clans (*gotras*) of the mother, father, mother's mother, and father's mother (in other words, the clans of the four grandparents) of both the boy and the girl constitute an obstacle to marriage but have no skewing of the terminology. (This, it should be noted, is similar to the pattern of the Samo, according to Héritier.) That is, the proper terrain for analysis of semi-complex marriage structures ought to be all cases of semi-complex marriage prohibitions, whether or not they are accompanied by terminologies containing skewing. Such systems are numerous and should be part of a discussion of dispersed alliance or semi-complexity, and it is arbitrary to confine the horizon of view to societies whose terminologies have skewing. There are certainly many systems involving a dispersed alliance strategy. The boundaries of this ocean are indeterminate but large. Perhaps it will be found to include both whales and fish.

The historic starting point of the Crow-Omaha question was how it came to be that a certain man came to tell Morgan that his uncle's son was also his uncle, though a mere boy. Skewing is the originary question, and Crow-Omaha is most profitably used as a label for terminologies with skewing.

On this classic problem the chapters of this book offer a number of advances. Historically, progress on this topic has not been continuous, nor has it moved forward a step at a time; rather, what progress has been made has resulted from deepening and widening the horizon of discussion. Deepening has occurred through closer, more informed, and attentive ethnographies of individual cases and widening through mapping its locational attributes among other kinds of systems geographically, structurally, and historically. The chapters of this book result from and extend this deepening and widening in particular directions.

The Chapters of This Volume

We have grouped the chapters around four themes: "Crow-Omaha in Theory," which deals with the Crow-Omaha concept in relation to the big picture in space, time, and structure; followed by regional studies in sequence from North America, Africa, South America, and Australia. The regional studies comprise an array of differing theoretical approaches.

Crow-Omaha in Theory

Thomas R. Trautmann, writer of a book on Dravidian kinship, co-authored a regional study with R. H. Barnes in the *Transformations of Kinship* volume. In chapter 2, "Crossness and Crow-Omaha," he resumes the investigation of structural aspects of that study. Defining Crow-Omaha as forms of skewing (rather than tying it to semi-complex marriage rules), Trautmann shows that there are two distinct and indirect routes from Dravidian crossness to Crow-Omaha skewing, one via Iroquois crossness and the other via asymmetrical cross-cousin marriage—the latter represented particularly by classic cases, Jinghpaw and Karen, from northeast India and Myanmar. In showing these routes, he argues against Lévi-Strauss's claim that Crow-Omaha and asymmetric-prescriptive systems should be kept distinct as "fish" from "whales."

Tetradic theory, the brainchild of Nicholas J. Allen, is a model of kinship that combines egocentric and sociocentric structures in a unitary account. It offers a model of the simplest possible kinship system, with the smallest possible terminology—having only four terms, hence "tetradic"—and the successive steps of its expansion through the breaking apart of equations. (Thus, for example, FB = F is tetradic; FB ≠ F is post-tetradic). In chapter 3, "Tetradic Theory and Omaha Systems," Allen shows the "counter-tetradic" character of Crow-Omaha skewing and explores ways of accounting for its place in the evolution of kinship systems.

Regional Studies: North America

R. H. Barnes has written two books of central importance on Crow-Omaha, a translation of Kohler's pioneer treatment, and an examination of the Lévi-Straussian construction of Crow-Omaha as a semi-complex system against the ethnographic record of the Omaha people (*Two Crows Denies It*), as well as several articles. Out of this extensive experience he gives us, in chapter 4, "Omaha and 'Omaha,'" an analysis of the distance between the ethnography of the Omaha and Omaha kinship as a structural type. Barnes questions the ethnographic viability of the latter, challenging those who would use it uncritically. He nevertheless acknowledges the value of comparing actual Omaha with geographically proximate and linguistically related societies, which is to say, regional studies.

An ethnographer of the Hopi (a Pueblo society with Crow skewing) who has examined Hopi social structure historically, and ethnologist of Native North America generally, Peter M. Whiteley outlines Crow-Omaha types in regional context in chapter 5, "Crow-Omaha Kinship in North America: A Puebloan Perspective." Focusing on Hopi social processes as exemplary for Pueblo Crow types, he argues that diachronic marriage practices corroborate Héritier's view of Crow-Omaha alliance structures as semi-complex, confirming the analytical value of Lévi-Strauss's category, though not in its original form. The chapter also confirms and widens the geographical reach of relations among Dravidian and Iroquois crossness and Crow-Omaha skewing in North America posited by Trautmann and Barnes 1998, which had limited itself to the Great Lakes area.

Ward C. Wheeler, Peter M. Whiteley, and Theodore Powers formed a team to bring the biologist's rapidly advancing expertise in mapping phenomena through tree and network diagrams of relatedness or relative likeness to bear on the Crow-Omaha phenomenon. The result is chapter 6, "Phylogenetic Analysis of Sociocultural Data: Identifying Transformation Vectors for Kinship Systems." What is surprising about the method is that it applies a genealogical mapping on phenomena such as Crow-Omaha skewing and Dravidian and Iroquois crossness, which are not, or not always, genealogically related—a field of variation over likenesses we do not assume are the result of co-descent. In this study, which focuses on North American ethnological data, it is not just the variation of kin terminology structure but its association with numerous other social and economic variables characterizing the societies in question that is being mapped for likeness. The authors duly note that the application of phylogenetic models to sociocultural data "is in its infancy" but argue for its value in finding previously unseen patterns and testing existing hypotheses.

Regional Studies: Africa

Wendy James, whose field research among the Uduk of the Blue Nile and other peoples of Africa has been the foundation for anthropological publications in a wide array of topics, makes an important contribution to showing the existence of structures having Dravidian crossness in Africa. In chapter 7, "A Tetradic Starting Point for Skewing? Marriage as a Generational Contract: Reflections on Sister-Exchange in Africa," she brings sister-exchange to the fore, restoring to visibility and analytic purchase a practice that, she argues, Lévi-Strauss had cast into the shadows. Rejecting the Lévi-Straussian apparatus that locates Crow-Omaha, denominated semi-complex, as a halfway house between elementary and complex systems of marital exchange, she resorts instead to Allen's tetradic theory to speak of the crossing of gender and generation as operators that combine and are selectively suppressed in different ways to produce different patterns of social reproduction.

David B. Kronenfeld's studies of the Fanti of Ghana, who simultaneously hold and in certain contexts use different but related unskewed and (Crow) skewed kinship terminologies, has been of fundamental importance to the study of Crow-Omaha. This work is an important prior text for the *Transformations* volume (it was the provocation for Trautmann and Barnes 1998), and hence this volume as well. Kronenfeld's concept of Crow-Omaha skewing as an "overlay" has been very influential, and it is put to use with great effect in the interpretation of Australian materials by McConvell and Dousset in this volume, chapters 12 and 13. In chapter 8, "Crow- (and Omaha-) Type Kinship Terminology: The Fanti Case," Kronenfeld draws on this rich history of research to develop the implications of the Fanti case for the understanding of Crow-Omaha.

From the very beginning, in Morgan, the comparative analysis of kinship terminologies has had little direct connection with historical linguistics, being largely the study of kinship terminologies as logically integrated semantic sets, without regard for the phonetic attributes of the set. This volume has two chapters, by Ehret and McConvell, that show how historical linguistic methods can be used to give time depth to the study of kinship systems.

Christopher Ehret has written a number of studies of historical linguistics of African peoples and the deep history of kinship systems there, working at a depth of time, in the case of the Nilo-Saharan family, very much greater than the reach of most other language families. He explores the historical-linguistic record of shifts in kinship with economic shifts documented by archaeology. Chapter 9, "Deep-Time Historical Contexts of Crow and Omaha Systems: Perspectives from Africa" is the outcome of this research.

Regional Studies: South America

Lowland South America is an especially rich terrain for the study of Crow-Omaha kinship, especially among societies of the Gê language family in Amazonia, and Marcela Coelho de Souza is the leading expert on the topic, having written a major comparative study of it as her doctoral dissertation. Chapter 10, "The Making and Unmaking of 'Crow-Omaha' Kinship in Central Brazil(ian Ethnology)," is an elegant synthesis of her interpretation, growing out of the studies making up the Harvard-Central Brazil Project (HBCP) of David Maybury-Lewis and his associates, furthered by her own extensive, continuing ethnographic fieldwork. The approach involves showing the interplay between naming and kinship recognition, and treating kinship not as a steady-state system but as a series of transformations, strangers being transformed into affines, affines into consanguines, and consanguines into (marriageable) strangers. This chapter is a window, however small, into Coelho de Souza's important work (700 pages, in Portuguese) on Crow-Omaha and other variations among Gê societies.

Terence Turner, an original member of the HBCP, brings more than four decades of continuous engagement as ethnologist and activist with a single Gê people, the Kayapó, to bear in chapter 11, "Schemas of Kinship Relations and the Construction of Social Categories among the Mebêngôkrê Kayapó." Though it shares with the previous chapter a concern with transformations of kin and strangers, it affords a different lens through which to view kinship and Crow-Omaha skewing, namely, the concept of the *schema*. The interpretation of Kayapó kinship hinges on the mismatch between the life stages of males and females, as a mechanism that produces skewing, among other things.

Regional Studies: Australia

Crow-Omaha skewing is abundant in North America, South America, and Africa, as we have seen. But if one went by the older literature—George Peter Murdock's *Ethnographic Atlas* (1967), for example—Australia would seem to be a place of abundant crossness but no Crow-Omaha.

Patrick McConvell has decisively changed that and brought Australia into the Crow-Omaha discussion by tracing out what he calls the "Omaha trail" in Australia. Chapter 12, "Omaha Skewing in Australia: Overlays, Dynamism, and Change," continues the hunt, conducted through historical linguistic comparisons of Australian languages. He identifies "upstream" and "downstream" effects of language spread and specifies the relation of Omaha skewing to the opposite ends of a dynamic process. In this perspective, skewing is not a steady state but a potential of the process that is realized and lost under changing conditions.

Laurent Dousset, an ethnologist of Australian aboriginal societies, writes chapter 13, "'Horizontal' and 'Vertical' Skewing: Similar Objectives, Two Solutions?" He argues that the ethnographic record contains faults produced by rapid survey methods; only attentive, long-term ethnographic research reveals that kinship terminology varies by context. Thus, in certain contexts, kin of ego's generation are all brothers and sisters; in others, these same kin are partitioned into cross and parallel sets. Multiplicity of contexts is virtually the same thing as a multiplicity of kinship terminologies, simultaneously held but alternatively activated. The cross-parallel distinction persists, but it is suspended in certain contexts—a phenomenon Dousset names "horizontal skewing" (compare with the Cheyenne pattern in North America) to encourage us to think of Crow-Omaha "vertical" skewing in the same perspective. An implication of this argument is that we may have to give up the idea that we need to find *the* kinship terminology of a given people but rather identify the various kinship contexts and their specific kinship terminologies.

Afterword

In chapter 14, "Crow-Omaha, in Thickness and in Thin," Thomas R. Trautmann and Peter M. Whiteley summarize the volume's principal themes and suggest some ways forward. This chapter draws on some key moments of the Amerind seminar's discussions, including remarks contributed by Maurice Godelier. Themes of particular interest include (1) skewing as overlay and as "social technology" in the realization of kinship systems, with Dravidian crossness seen as lying in the "deep structure" of Crow-Omaha; (2) the correlation between Crow-Omaha terminologies and both semi-complex and asymmetric-prescriptive marriage rules, and how these "fish and whales" might be fruitfully conjoined; and (3) transformations among kinship system types and their potentially evolutionary elements.

Crow-Omaha in Theory

2

Crossness and Crow-Omaha

Thomas R. Trautmann

Crow-Omaha kinship—by which I mean kinship terminologies containing skewing—invariably also contains crossness. But there are many terminologies that have crossness without skewing. Skewing is something that is added to (some) systems that have crossness; it is not something that exists independently of crossness, nor can it combine with other dimensions that occupy the structural location of crossness. The fact that skewing presupposes crossness (the evidence for which I give in this chapter) is an important datum. Because of it, we can advance our understanding of Crow-Omaha by advancing our understanding of crossness, which in practice will mean locating it comparatively in space, in time, and in structure. Conversely, if we want to find cases of skewing, we will find them among terminologies that contain crossness.

Morgan's surprise that among the Iroquois the father's brother "is equally a father" and the mother's sister a mother was the impulse that led him from an ethnographic study of the Iroquois to a large-scale ethnological comparison of kinship systems. Crossness or the cross–parallel distinction contrasts with the principle in Morgan's American-English kinship terminology called lineality (following Lowie—see later discussion) or the contrast between lineals and collaterals, which occupies the same structural location. Because of the sameness of location, we can make a simulacrum of Iroquois terminology in English translation by turning lineality into crossness, such that father, mother, sister, brother, son, and daughter are now parallel kin, and uncle, aunt, cousin (f.), cousin (m.), nephew, and niece are now cross-kin (figure 1.1).

Mapping Crossness

Morgan's great comparative study of kinship, *Systems of Consanguinity and Affinity of the Human Family* (1871), was intended to locate the difference between Iroquois and English (crossness versus lineality) in a worldwide map of kinship systems. The two cases fall within the two large categories Morgan constructed called classificatory and descriptive systems, the classificatory so called because it *classified* or *merged* FB with F, MZ with M, and so forth.

Lowie (1928) and Kirchoff (1932) doubled Morgan's typology by taking into consideration the treatment of MB as well. This created a four-term field for the patterning of mergers or nonmergers of F, FB, and MB, as in table 2.1.

The four terms of the Lowie-Kirchoff typology correspond to the four ethnic names of the terminology types recognized by Murdock: Iroquois, Sudanese, Hawaiian, and Eskimo. The types refer not to whole terminologies but to a single dimension of terminologies. We do not have a general name for the dimension in question—should we call it laterality? I will use that name until a better one comes along. We need an agreed-on name so that we can immediately correct what has just been said. This is not a typology of *terminologies* as wholes but of *modes* of *laterality* in terminologies.

This fourfold set is a list. But we can take the analysis further, following Kryukov, who formed four modes in a ring (1998), and order the list as a two-by-two grid formed by the intersection of two distinctions, as in table 2.2.

In this analysis the four terms occupy four sectors of a space. The space is ordered such that it takes a structural "walk" of only one step (or one transformation) to get from any given type to the two neighbors with whom it shares a border, and two steps to reach the fourth, noncontiguous type. There is no beginning or end or overall directionality,

Table 2.1 Typology of kinship in Morgan, Lowie, and Murdock

Kintype mergers			Morgan	Lowie	Murdock
⎡F FB MB⎤			Classificatory	Generational	Hawaiian
⎡F FB⎤ ⎡MB⎤			Classificatory	Bifurcate merging	Iroquois
⎡F⎤ ⎡FB⎤ ⎡MB⎤			Descriptive	Bifurcate collateral	Sudanese
⎡F⎤ ⎡FB MB⎤			Descriptive	Lineal	Eskimo

Source: Trautmann 1981:84. © 1982 Cambridge University Press. Reprinted by permission.

Table 2.2 Kinship terminology types as a two-by-two set

		FB ≠ MB	FB = MB
(Classificatory)	FB = F	Iroquois	Hawaiian
(Descriptive)	FB ≠ F	Sudanese	Eskimo

Source: Trautmann 1981. © 1982 Cambridge University Press. Reprinted by permission.

all of which would be needed to turn it into a series of evolutionary stages or a pathway of development over time.

Bifurcate merging is another name for crossness; Iroquois and Crow-Omaha fall into this sector. English falls in the Eskimo sector, at a maximal structural distance from Iroquois. One can readily show that these two sectors are inversely distributed. Crossness is abundant in the Americas; South, Southeast, and East Asia; Oceania and Australia; and Africa, where Eskimo is marginal. The opposite is true of Europe and the Middle East.

Iroquois and Crow-Omaha

One of the attractions of Lounsbury's formal analysis is that it operates at the subatomic level, so to say, getting at the significant moving particles of a kinship system and not assuming that the types such as Iroquois and Crow-Omaha are well-bounded things, clearly separate from one another. These attributes are in full display in his classic article (Lounsbury 1964a) giving a formal account of Crow-Omaha systems (plural). In it he provided a clear and parsimonious analysis of leading variants of such systems, rather than boiling them all down into an essential principle. Yet there is a kind of unity in what he calls the *skewing rule*, which produces the generational skewing characteristic of Crow-Omaha systems. The skewing rule has several varieties, yielding four types each of Omaha and Crow systems, seven of them with real-world ethnographic examples. The varieties of the skewing rule all take the form FZ → Z for Omaha Type I, or MB → B for Crow Type I, but are limited by context in different ways that I need not go into for present purposes. Variation among the types has to do with variation in the content and context, but the variations form a set.

In his article, Lounsbury introduced rules for the formal analysis of Crow-Omaha, of which the most important are the *skewing rule* and the *merging rule*—which he later gives the more accurate name of *same-sex sibling merging rule*. Let us use this analysis to identify what Crow-Omaha does and does not have in common with Iroquois.

It is evident that Crow-Omaha shares the same-sex sibling merging rule with Iroquois; this is the general principle underlying the merger of FB with F and MZ with M. This shows clearly that there is crossness in Crow-Omaha, because what the same-sex sibling rule describes is crossness. Indeed, this must be so because skewing acts on the cross-kin— uncles, aunts, cousins, niblings (nephews and nieces) as redefined by the same-sex sibling rule—whereas it leaves the parallel kin untouched. We have seen that Lounsbury's skewing rule is directed to transformations of the cross-kin FZ and MB. This is a significant finding, because it is not at all obvious from inspection of Crow-Omaha systems that crossness is the underlying form of laterality. This is because the effect of generational skewing is to alter the generational level among subsets of cross-kin, promoting some of them to a higher generation, demoting others to a lower generation, and so breaking the unity of the set of cross-kin. In the extreme of skewing, Lounsbury's Type IV, Lounsbury says the FZ and MB class are eliminated, the former lowered to Z, the second raised a generation to grandfather, and indeed, the whole of the cross-kin terms (aunts, uncles, cousins, and niblings in figure 1.1) are replaced by parallel kin terms.

Paradoxically, we know that all Crow-Omaha systems in Lounsbury's analysis of them have crossness because the same-sex sibling rule is integral to them, but cross-kin categories are emptied of content—or rather, replaced by parallel kin terms–by the increasingly strong forms of the skewing rule. No crossness is visible on the surface in Type IV, but formal analysis shows that Crow-Omaha nevertheless has crossness in its deep structure, underneath the skewing that obscures it. This result tells us that terminologies with Crow-Omaha skewing have a feature in common with Iroquois that they do not share with systems lacking crossness and having other modes of laterality, namely, Eskimo, Sudanese, and Hawaiian. Because crossness is not evident from inspection of Crow-Omaha systems, it is a result we can reach only through Lounsbury's formal analysis.

Varieties of Crossness: Iroquois and Dravidian

I turn now to a matter central to the question of crossness and Crow-Omaha: the varieties of crossness that are lumped together in Murdock's Iroquois category, especially the difference between Iroquois and Dravidian crossness.

Since Murdock published the *Ethnographic Atlas*, crossness has been discovered to come in more than one variety, so his "Iroquois" contains other forms of crossness besides Iroquois. Lounsbury was the first to note the difference between Dravidian and Iroquois crossness (Lounsbury 1964b; Trautmann and Barnes 1998:27). Subsequently Pospisil found the Iroquois pattern among the Kapauku Papuans (Pospisil 1959–60) and Reay (in Scheffler 1972) found a new variety, Kuma. Viveiros de Castro (1998) recognized five varieties—Dravidian, Iroquois, Kuma, Yafar, and Ngawbe—and Tjon Sie Fat posited sixteen possible structurally different varieties of crossness, some of which, however, yield contradictory equations and are therefore unstable, which is probably why only some of them are ethnographically attested (Godelier, Trautmann, and Tjon Sie Fat 1998:10–11; Tjon Sie Fat 1998b). Far and away the most common in the real world are Dravidian and Iroquois,[1] and these are the two kinds I discuss in this chapter.

When surveying Dravidian kinship in South India and Sri Lanka, the difference between Iroquois and Dravidian crossness was on my mind, as well as the value of Lounsbury's formal analysis as a tool for exact description. Scheffler and Lounsbury (1971) had applied formal analysis to the Sirionò Indians of Bolivia, who have asymmetrical cross-cousin marriage, and I aspired to further develop formal analysis and apply it to Dravidian kinship so as to exactly and fully reproduce its classifications by formulating a parsimonious set of rules. I found that seven rules were needed, but only two of them do the heavy lifting of classifications for crossness. One of these is the same-sex sibling rule that we have seen at work in Iroquois crossness. So this is shared between Iroquois and Dravidian crossness.

Dravidian has an additional rule for the classification of relatives that Iroquois lacks: the rule of cross-cousin marriage, for which Dravidian kinship is famous. In Dravidian systems, if parallel kin of one generation are of opposite sex (i.e., are in a brother-sister relation), their children are cross; if those children are of opposite sex they should marry, whence their children are parallel, but if they are of the same sex, *their* children are cross. The Iroquois do not have a rule of cross-cousin marriage, and it does not structure their classifications. In the case just described, "siblings" or parallel kin of the same sex have children who are parallel to one another, and if of opposite sex have children who are cross, relative sex in one generation becomes crossness in the next. We may say that Iroquois and Dravidian are structurally very close, and we can transform the one into the other by the subtraction or addition of the rule of cross-cousin marriage. The difference in crossness can be seen in figure 2.1, giving the Dravidian pattern and the Iroquois differences from it among the children of cousins. This difference works its way through the system to the classification of remoter kin.

Dravidian and Iroquois differ in two ways. (1) Classifications for crossness of the children of first cousins and the crossness of second cousins and other kin at that range show exactly 50 percent of same and 50 percent of opposite classifications between the two. Tables 2.3 and 2.4 give second cousin classifications. Dravidian classifications are consistent with a rule of cross-cousin marriage, whereas Iroquois are not. (2) Terminologies of Dravidian crossness merge affinal terms with consanguineous ones, whereas terminologies of Iroquois crossness have a separate affinal terminology. Here again, the difference has to do with the presence and absence of a rule of cross-cousin marriage.

The exact form the rule takes in formal analysis is the *opposite-sex cross cousin-spouse equation rule* (for short, the *cross-cousin marriage rule*), and it reads ♂MBD/FZD = ♂W; ♀MBS/FZS = ♀H. That may seem formidable, but in plain English it provides that an opposite-sex cross-cousin is equivalent to a husband or wife as the case may be.

We need to be clear that the rule in question is one of kin classification, not a rule of marriage, nor again a pattern of actual marriages. Although the three are undoubtedly related, the relation among them may not be simple, and we must remember to keep them separate. In particular, actual Dravidian societies vary greatly in the form of the

Crossness and Crow-Omaha

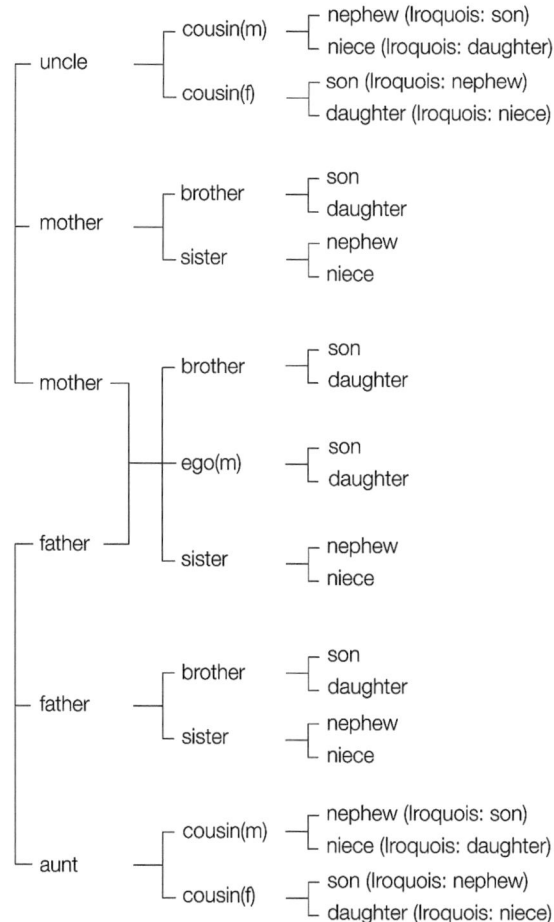

Figure 2.1 Dravidian crossness

marriage rule—some bilateral, some preferring the MBD or FZD, and so forth—but at the same time most all of them have a rule of bilateral cross-cousin marriage embedded in their kinship classifications, so there is some discrepancy between classifications and marriage rules. The Iroquois do not have a rule of cross-cousin marriage; the only limitation on marriage Morgan speaks of is clan exogamy. It appears that Iroquois crossness has little affinal content.

Thus, Iroquois and Dravidian, though different, are structurally very close, and we can readily imagine the one turning into the other

Table 2.3 Classifications of second cousins in Iroquois and Dravidian

		Iroquois	
		Cross	Parallel
D	Cross	MMZSCh	MMBDCh
r		FFBDCh	FFZSCh
a		MFBSCh	MFZDCh
v		FMZDCh	FMBSCh
i			
d	Parallel	MMBSCh	MMZDCh
i		FFZDCh	FFBSCh
a		MFZSCh	MFBDCh
n		FMBDCh	FMZSCh

Source: Trautmann 1981:87. © 1982 Cambridge University Press. Reprinted by permission.

by the addition or removal of the rule of cross-cousin marriage. We may render the relation thus:

$$\text{Dravidian} \leftrightarrow \text{Iroquois}$$

Or, at the "subatomic" level of formal analysis, we can show the Dravidian type is a composite of two rules whereas a single rule underlies Iroquois. We can represent the relation thus, where SSS stands for the same-sex sibling rule, and XCM stands for the cross-cousin marriage rule:

$$(\text{SSS} + \text{XCM}) \leftrightarrow (\text{SSS})$$

Does this structural closeness and ease of transformation have real-world instantiations? In the *Transformations of Kinship* volume we reported excellent ethnographic sources on the Ojibwa, showing the

Table 2.4 Classifications of second cousins, Iroquois, Dravidian and Kuma

		Iroquois	Dravidian
G^{+2}	If relative sex of two siblings or parallel cousins is	[irrelevant]	= = ≠ ≠
G^{+1}	and relative sex of their children is, to one another	= ≠	= ≠ = ≠
G^{0}	then the crossness of *their* children is, to one another	// X	// X X //

Source: Trautmann 1981:87. © 1982 Cambridge University Press. Reprinted by permission.

coexistence of Iroquois and Dravidian crossness in different sectors—Iroquois in the denser populations to the south, Dravidian in the thinner, more widely scattered populations to the north (Trautmann and Barnes 1998:34–39; see also Hallowell 1928, 1930, 1937).

In the case of the ethnic Iroquois, kinship relations, extended by the clans, may encompass an entire large group with a population in the nineteenth century on the order of 10,000 persons. Morgan says that four of the clans are brother-clans to one another and cousin-clans to the other four, who are brother-clans to one another. Although he does not say so, it would seem that this logic of clan relations—which are relations of cross (cousin-clans) and parallel (brother-clans)—can serve any given Iroquois individual to place any other Iroquois individual, no matter how distant, in a relation of kinship. The absence of the cross-cousin rule among the Iroquois, plus the strong system of matrilineal clans, appears to open the system out to more far-flung marriage connections and a more extensive field of relationships. In the *Transformations* volume, Barnes and I (1998) showed that in the Great Lakes and Mississippi Valley region of North America, Crow-Omaha systems were contiguous to Iroquois ones in the more populous, southerly regions, while Dravidian crossness dominated the north. Geographical patterning, then, converged with the structural pattern:

Dravidian ↔ Iroquois ↔ Crow-Omaha

The opening out of the field in which marriages may occur is the step that puts Iroquois crossness between Dravidian crossness and Crow-Omaha skewing, at least in North America.

Iroquois Crossness and the Cheyenne Type

The foregoing account is complete as far as it goes, but there is one other feature of Iroquois that distinguishes its crossness from the Dravidian variety. To capture it, we need to take a slight detour.

Among Plains Indian peoples, both Dakota-Siouan and Algonquian, there are several, including the Cheyenne and Arapaho, who have Iroquois crossness in the parents' and children's generations, but among whom all kin of ego's generation are brothers and sisters (Eggan 1937a, and Fig. 2-2 in Trautmann and Barnes 1998:35). This pattern, called Cheyenne, implies, as David Kronenfeld (this volume) shows, a rule of "cross-parallel neutralization" in that generation; the Fanti is an African example of this pattern. Cheyenne is unmistakably Iroquois in crossness, and the suspension of crossness in ego's generation does not change that. It is necessary to emphasize this point, because Murdock, in his cross-cultural comparisons, which use ego's generation as the criterion, regularly assigns the Cheyenne pattern to the Hawaiian sector of the fourfold typology. This is wrong and misleading, giving, for example, an impression that there are many terminologies of Hawaiian laterality in North America, among others of Iroquois type. True Hawaiian or generational terminologies are the negation of crossness.

Since the Cheyenne type is Iroquois in crossness, we may ask whether Iroquois crossness contains the distinctive element we find in the Cheyenne type, or is it something entirely foreign? That element, we have seen, is cross-parallel neutralization. Reverting to figure 2.1, we can see that in Iroquois crossness the children of cousins are classified just as the children of siblings, as if being cross-kin made no difference. It is exactly here that Iroquois and Dravidian crossness differ, and this difference works through the system to affect the second-cousin classifications in tables 2.3 and 2.4. Cross-parallel neutralization of cousins is operative in Iroquois and Cheyenne, but differently contextualized, so that it affects only linking kin in Iroquois and does not appear in the surface structure but applies to designated kin (the cousins' children) in Cheyenne, and does appear in the surface structure, the cousins themselves becoming siblings to ego. If this is acceptable, we may say that Iroquois and Cheyenne have the same underlying rules, but with slight differences in the contextualization of the cross-parallel neutralization rule. That being so, structurally they are only a fraction of a step apart. In any case, cross-parallel neutralization (CPN) is the something else that Iroquois has and Dravidian does not. Accordingly we revise the previous formula as follows:

$$\text{Dravidian} \leftrightarrow \text{Iroquois}$$
$$(\text{SSS} + \text{XCM}) \leftrightarrow (\text{SSS} + \text{CPN})$$

Crow-Omaha and Asymmetric Cross-Cousin Marriage

In the article previously mentioned, Barnes and I called for close-grained, comparative study of kinship systems within regions, as we had done for a part of North America. Chapters in this volume show that this kind of work is now being done. The new regional studies in this volume speak for themselves; I will only mention briefly a few regional patterns that bear on the relation of crossness and Crow-Omaha.

In Africa, Kronenfeld's publications on Fanti gave excellent direct evidence of part of this proposal, showing the coexistence of crossness (in Cheyenne form) and Crow-Omaha skewing in one and the same people. I take it from Kronenfeld that all people having Crow-Omaha skewing are able to translate their terms into an unskewed version of their system, and that unskewed version, *ex hypothesi*, would be Iroquois. As there are a great many "Iroquois" systems reported for Africa by Murdock, we want to know whether this group includes Dravidian as well as Iroquois crossness. Hage (2006) has directly and convincingly shown that Dravidian crossness is represented in Africa, James (2008) shows Dravidian crossness in process of formation, and Ehret (this volume) gives linguistic evidence for cross-cousin marriage classifications in the deep past. We can reasonably conclude, pending more detailed investigation, that Africa, like North America, shows the coexistence of Dravidian, Iroquois, and Crow-Omaha and gives direct evidence of the close link between Iroquois crossness and Crow-Omaha skewing. The pattern is similar to that of North America and adds support to the proposed relationship among the two types of crossness and Crow-Omaha.

In South India, however, the pattern is quite different. I have conducted an extensive study of the history and anthropology of the Dravidian kinship of South India (Trautmann 1981). Thus far, for South India only Dravidian crossness has been shown—not a single instance of Iroquois crossness and no skewing. This serves to confirm the proposed relationship negatively, for had Crow-Omaha been shown for South India but not Iroquois, that would be evidence against the hypothesis, drawn from the North American data, that Iroquois crossness mediates between Dravidian crossness and Crow-Omaha skewing. Taking it that there is no Iroquois crossness in South India, is there Iroquois elsewhere in the vicinity? Subsequent to my work on Dravidian kinship, Parkin elicited evidence for the first example known to me of Iroquois in South Asia, but it is in the far northwest, among a people speaking an isolated language: Burushaski (Parkin 1998:257–59). Thus, although in North America both types of crossness coexist and perhaps transform from the one to the other, South India seems to be an echo chamber in which Dravidian crossness alone gets endlessly replicated back and forth across the peninsula, though with many small diacritics of local difference.

Only in northeast India and the bordering region of Myanmar do we find skewing, and here it is associated with asymmetrical cross-cousin marriage, that is, marriage of the matrilateral cross-cousin (MBD marries FZS).

The kinship system of the Karen of Myanmar has played an exceptional role in kinship analysis. Granet, drawing on British colonial period ethnographies of the Karen (cited in chapter 1), connected this system with that of the Gilyak of Siberia and used them as tools by which to reconstruct the kinship of ancient China. Lévi-Strauss (1969 [1949]), refined this argument and made it the centerpiece of his book on kinship. Leach (1945) published an account of the Kachin, or rather, Jinghpaw terminology (the Kachin are a group of intermarrying clans of peoples speaking several different languages, Jinghpaw being one of them). Finally, Burling (1971) published newly elicited terminologies of the Jinghpaw (collected by Lounsbury) and the terminology of the Maru (collected by Burling), a group that intermarries with the Jinghpaw and has a terminology nearly identical in structure but different in vocabulary. Because Lounsbury corrects some errors in Leach's account of Jinghpaw, and because Burling's article is in a difficult-to-find publication, I present the data here. In the exceptionally clear light of Jinghpaw we are in a position to refine the original formulation regarding the relation among Dravidian, Iroquois, and Crow-Omaha. It should be understood that the Karen/Jinghpaw case stands for a large series of contiguous Tibeto-Burman tribes in the India-Myanmar borderland and probably also the Tibeto-Burman speakers of Nepal in Allen's chapter of this volume.

The Karen/Jinghpaw have a rule of cross-cousin marriage, both as a rule of actual marriage and as a principle of classification, whence we would have to say that they have Dravidian crossness. The rule, however, is unidirectional or asymmetrical (MBD) and not reciprocated, unlike the Dravidian rule, which is a rule of bilateral or symmetrical cross-cousin marriage. Both Leach and Burling make it clear that MBD marriage is embedded in the kinship terminology. From this we presume that the terminology contains a version of the Dravidian rule, but differently written, as MBD = W; FZS = H.

Here, then, is a second context in which we can find skewing. Only in this asymmetrical form, I think, can cross-cousin marriage as a rule of classification and generational skewing be compatible, for skewing of terminologies splits the set of cross-kin down the middle and treats the two halves in an asymmetrical way. The asymmetrical cross-cousin marriage rule in patrilineal groups entails a one-way circulation of brides, whence the cross-cousin category is partitioned into marriageable and nonmarriageable kin. Among the Jinghpaw the kinship terminology is notionally organized around five patrilineal groups: that of ego, that of his mother and mother's mother (wife-givers and wife-givers of wife-givers), and his father's sister and father's father's sister (wife-takers and wife-takers of wife-takers). Generational skewing follows lineage membership, but only partly. This is nicely shown by diagrams of Jinghpaw terminology by Lounsbury and of the neighboring Maru by Burling. The Jinghpaw and Maru intermarry in spite of having two quite different languages, and they have kinship terminologies whose semantic structure are nearly identical in spite of a completely different vocabulary of terms.[2] The two intermarrying people, then, have a word-for-word interchangeable vocabulary of kinship and share only one identical vocable: the word for male cross-cousins, which is self-reciprocal. In the diagrams (see figures 2.2 and 2.3), for example, with ego's patrilineage in the central column, a male Jinghpaw speaker calls his father and all the males of his lineage in his father's generation *wà*, his MB and WF *tsʔà*, his FZH and ZHF *kù*, and so forth, in accordance with the rule of marriage of daughters of the lineage to the sons of the lineage to the left. The generational skewing is evident.

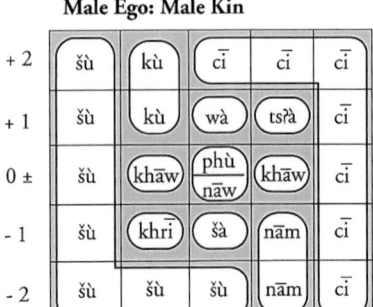

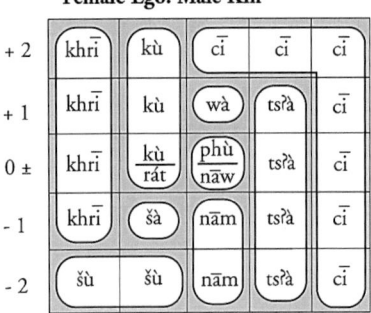
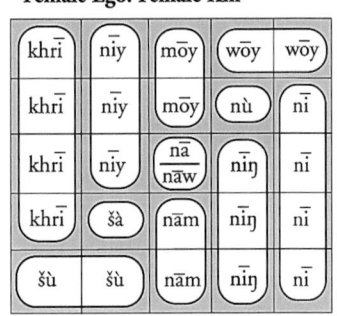

Figure 2.2 Jinghpaw kinship terms. The five columns represent kin of five patrilineages, of which ego's patrilineage is the middle one. Daughters marry out, into the patrilineage to the left. *Source:* From Lounsbury, in Burling 1971. Reprinted by permission.

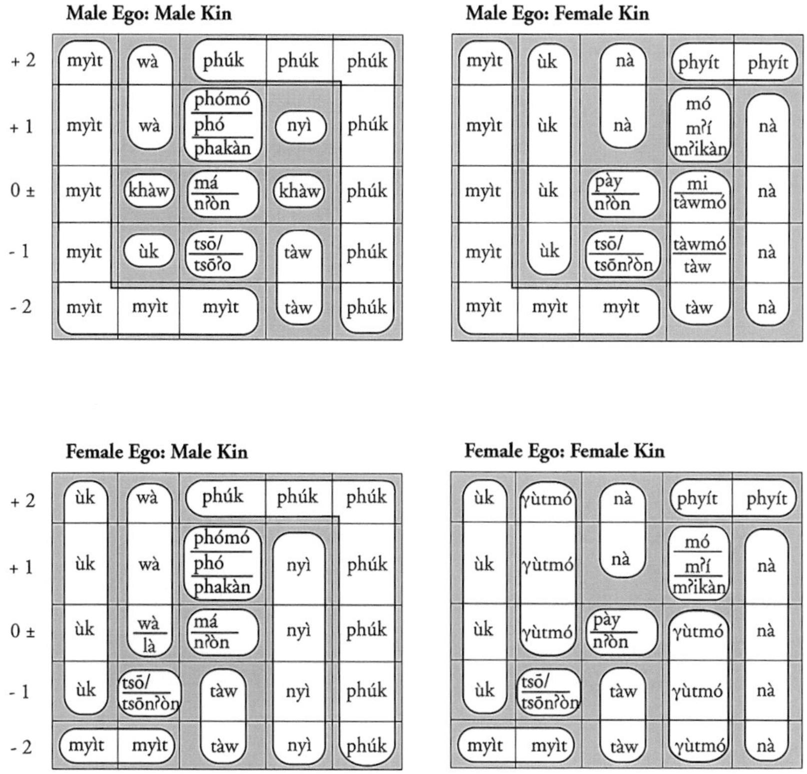

Figure 2.3 Maru kinship terms. As Jinghpaw, Fig. 2.2. *Source:* Burling 1971. Reprinted by permission.

The Jinghpaw and Maru cases show that skewing can combine with asymmetrical cross-cousin marriage as a norm and a principle of classification, in addition to the same-sex sibling rule of Iroquois and Dravidian. The crossness here is not Iroquois. But the full Dravidian pattern of crossness, which assumes bilateral or symmetrical cross-cousin marriage as a principle of classification, is not and cannot be present. Full Dravidian crossness is incompatible with skewing; its tight symmetries have to be broken open before generational skewing can be imposed, because there is no systematic "sidedness" essential for skewing in the Dravidian classification rule.

Two Routes to Crow-Omaha Skewing

We are now in a position to improve on our original analysis of the relation of the two types of crossness and Crow-Omaha skewing. At the subatomic level we see that the ethnic-name terminology types are composites of rules in different configurations, the same-sex sibling rule (SSS), the cross-cousin marriage rule (XCM), cross-parallel neutralization (CPN), and the skewing rule (Skewing):

$$\text{Dravidian} \leftrightarrow \text{Iroquois} \leftrightarrow \text{Crow-Omaha}$$
$$(\text{SSS} + \text{XCM}) \leftrightarrow (\text{SSS} + \text{CPN}) \leftrightarrow (\text{SSS} + \text{CPN} + \text{Skewing})$$

I make no assumptions about the overall directionality of evolutionary change. Thus, Crow-Omaha is one structural step from Iroquois, so that Iroquois becomes Crow-Omaha by the addition of skewing, and Crow-Omaha becomes Iroquois by the subtraction of skewing. Dravidian is two steps of structural distance from Iroquois, and three steps from Crow-Omaha.

The Karen–Jinghpaw case developed by Granet, Lévi-Strauss, Leach, Burling, and Lounsbury gives a second possible route from Dravidian to Omaha skewing. From Burling's article it seems that if a formal analysis were made (and this is my judgment, because neither author gave a Lounsbury-style formal account of either terminology) it would find that Jinghpaw and Maru have (1) the same-sex sibling rule, (2) the skewing rule, and (3) a modified, asymmetrical form of the Dravidian rule of cross-cousin marriage (AXCM). Here is how rule 3 would look in each case:

Dravidian: $\male$MBD/FZD = $\male$W; $\female$MBS/FZS = $\female$H
Jinghpaw: $\male$MBD = $\male$W; $\female$FZS = $\female$H

The Jinghpaw rule appears to be structurally close to Dravidian. We could propose a second possible path from Dravidian to the skewing rule:

$$\text{Dravidian} \leftrightarrow \text{Jinghpaw}$$

Is this justified? At the subatomic level it appears that Jinghpaw is *two* structural steps distant from Dravidian, not one:

$$(SSS + XCM) \leftrightarrow (SSS + AXCM + \text{Skewing})$$

Breaking this down further, the structurally necessary sequence would be

$$(SSS + XCM) \leftrightarrow (SSS + AXCM) \leftrightarrow (SSS + AXCM + \text{Skewing})$$

That is, there is an intermediate step in which symmetrical cross-cousin marriage is turned to asymmetrical cross-cousin marriage, before skewing is imposed. Whether this structurally possible scenario has real-world instantiations remains to be seen. And whether there is a matrilineal version of this pattern needs investigation.

Formal analysis of these cases leads us to conclude that Crow and Omaha skewing has two distinct paths leading to it. One of them, no doubt, corresponds to those North American cases of skewing that Morgan got by personal inquiry and announced with such amazement and incredulity for the first time in the pages of *Systems of Consanguinity and Affinity*. One may readily verify by inspecting the published terminologies of any of them, such as the excellent report on the terminology of the Meskwaki or Fox by Sol Tax (1937]), an "Omaha" group included in the Trautmann and Barnes study. The Fox have Iroquois crossness, cross-parallel neutralization plus skewing, and a separate affinal terminology unlike Dravidian. They have no cross-cousin marriage rule of any kind. Contrast this with the Jinghpaw:

Fox: SSS + CPN + Skewing
Jinghpaw: SSS + AXCM + Skewing

Because Crow-Omaha kinship systems of North America have *negative* marriage rules, forbidding marriage into the clan of the father and the mother, whereas Karen and similar systems of Eurasia have *prescriptive* marriage rules of asymmetrical type, Lévi-Strauss (1949) considered them as different as fish and whales; but that amounts to a refusal to account for skewing, which they have in common. It is not a solution but a refusal of the problem.

Do these fish and whales swim in the same ocean? Are they kin after all? In structural terms it seems they are two steps distant from each other. One can be transformed into the other by the addition or subtraction of asymmetrical cross-cousin marriage and cross-parallel neutralization. Kryukov (see chapter 1) offers Tibeto-Burman cases that tend in that direction. Both paths include crossness, and in both cases Crow-Omaha skewing excludes Dravidian crossness as a rule of classification.

Toward Deep History

We may hope that ultimately kinship analysis will join with archaeology and primatology to elucidate the deep history of kinship systems. A beginning has already been made (Allen et al. 2008; Chapais 2008; Trautmann, Feeley-Harnik, and Mitani 2012), but the process clearly has a long way to go. In the meantime, we make what advances we can with kinship analysis alone.

We have seen that skewing is something that is always imposed on crossness, and it is associated with dispersed alliance and asymmetrical cross-cousin marriage, quite different in themselves but sharing a quality of opening out the marriage scene, compared to symmetrical cross-cousin marriage. There is a modicum of directionality in these findings on which, perhaps, we can build.

The place of crossness in grand theory will be the locus of Crow-Omaha skewing as well, as skewing contains crossness. The dominant tendency of grand theory identifies crossness with the structurally elementary or the evolutionarily early, beginning, really, with Morgan, and continuing with Granet (1939), Lévi-Strauss (1969 [1949]), Allen (1982, 1986, 1989, 1998a, 2008, this volume), Kryukov (1998), and Godelier (2011 [2004]). For all of these the evolutionary starting point is something like Dravidian crossness, and, for all but Godelier's pluralism, the end point is something like English or Eskimo or lineal.

Although this is the dominant mode of grand theory, there is a subordinate tendency, in the opposite direction, positing a developmental sequence from something like lineality to something like crossness. Lounsbury is an example. He envisioned his equivalence rules as modeling the extension of meaning from proximate ("focal") kin types to more distant ones, a process moving outward from ego to his or her immediate family and thence to more distant kin. He mentioned Malinowski as a forerunner, but he might also have pointed to Morgan. In the unpublished draft of *Systems* that I found in the University of Rochester Library, Morgan considered the English-American system *natural* and crossness as *artificial*, a "stupendous invention" and a deliberate departure from the promptings of nature by which remote kin were kept from getting lost (Trautmann 2008), an insight that expresses very well the cultural work of crossness in North America, especially among far-flung, thinly distributed hunting populations of the north. This thesis survives in vestigial form in the published *Systems*, in which, however, Morgan adopted a schema of the evolution of marriage types that naturalized crossness and reversed the direction of the deep history of kinship. There are, in short, opposing tendencies in grand theory from the start, both at war with one another in Morgan's book. More recently, Barnard (2008) revives and modernizes the "stupendous invention" mode of argumentation. There is no clear way of submitting the two entirely opposed positions to a test that does not contain assumptions predetermining the outcome. But as we search for a way forward, it is essential to keep it in mind that there is an alternative to the now-dominant view and that the dominant view leaves lots of problems unsolved.

Detailed ethnography and regional survey, as this volume shows, will continue to be the surest ways to achieve durable gains. As regional studies have become more fine-grained and reliable, we increasingly find that the different regions have very different configurations, the meaning of which we need to figure out. Inter-regional comparison will become increasingly valuable as a way of working toward the deep history of kinship. To my mind, the most refractory problem is the difference between North America and South India. The North American pattern shows Dravidian crossness in the least populated hunting territories of the north, Iroquois crossness in the more densely populated southerly regions, and Crow-Omaha skewing in the most densely populated situations (Trautmann and Barnes 1998; Whiteley, this volume; Wheeler, Whiteley, and Powers, this volume). In this region, Crow-Omaha is a kind of "climax growth" and not a transition to something more complex. In South America, Africa, Australia, and the Tibeto-Burman region of northeast India, Myanmar, and Nepal, chapters of this volume show the coexistence of crossness and skewing. But in

South India, symmetrical cross-cousin marriage as a rule of classification reigns supreme and alone; Dravidian crossness, not Iroquois crossness and not Crow-Omaha skewing, is the pattern. The reasons of this contrast, I sense, have to do with the pattern of endogamous castes combined in larger economic and political structures in South India, emulating one another but also generating diacritics of difference.

Tetradic Theory and Omaha Systems
Nicholas J. Allen

Tetradic theory has been presented previously in several contexts and from various points of view (Allen 2004, 2008); here I briefly summarize some of its main features. At its base lies the notion of tetradic society. This type of society is hypothetical and has never been attested ethnographically or historically, but it consists of various well-attested kinship phenomena, assembled in their simplest forms. The focus of the theory is on social continuity—the relationships, rules, and categories governing the production of children and their placement within society.

The model is formal, covering only selected features, abstracting them from the rest; for instance, among much else, it ignores residence patterns. It rests on certain anthropologically reasonable assumptions about human kinship. The system involves marriage as distinct from casual mating; it prohibits marriage with primary relatives ("incest"); it allocates a child to some category or division of society, distinct from merely adding it to the total population. Moreover, a tetradic society is a bounded whole in which, as in many small-scale societies, all members are regarded as relatives.

In a tetradic model, the rules of marriage and recruitment divide the population into four categories (whence "tetradic"). The categories can be identified either absolutely (e.g., by means of a name), in which case they are sociocentric, or relative to an ego (by means of a kin term), which makes them egocentric. A whole family of tetradic models can be constructed, but in the model on which I focus the four sociocentric categories are "sections" (to follow standard Australianist usage). However, the kin terminology cannot be allotted to any of the standard types discussed by Trautmann (this volume) and can only be called tetradic. Its distinguishing feature is that its categories use the same dividing lines as the sociocentric division: for one ego, each kin term covers all and only members of one section. If males and females within a category are distinguished lexically, the simplest method is to mark one sex with an affix.

In a four-section society, each section is exogamous, but it is paired with one other to form an endogamous generation moiety. The marriages resulting from these two rules produce children who belong to the other generation moiety, and *its* children belong back in the moiety of their grandparents. So the moieties exchange children: A gives them to B, and B reciprocates. To translate from this sociocentric view to an egocentric one, we need a genealogical diagram showing the reciprocated child exchange and representing the sections by brother-sister symbol pairs (figure 3.1).

Figure 3.1 differs from the Dravidian-type diagram (figure 1.5) in showing only two levels. It is as if G^{-1}, instead of appearing below G^0, is superimposed on G^{+1}, and G^{+2} on G^0; in fact, all odd-numbered generations are superimposed (or "folded in") on each other, as are all even-numbered ones. Consequently, the term *generation* loses its normal sense: within the model, its nearest equivalent is the distinction between relatives of ego's level and those of the other level. Thus, ego's spouse is not exactly a "classificatory bilateral cross-cousin" (which connotes ego's generation). He or she comes from a larger category, *into which new members are constantly being born.*

More can be said about the properties of the model, for instance, about the implicit descent moieties (patri- or matri-; they need not be named) or about the prohibition of incest, but my main point is the model's logical simplicity. Why does this matter? First, those asking synchronic questions (e.g., typological ones) now have extra types

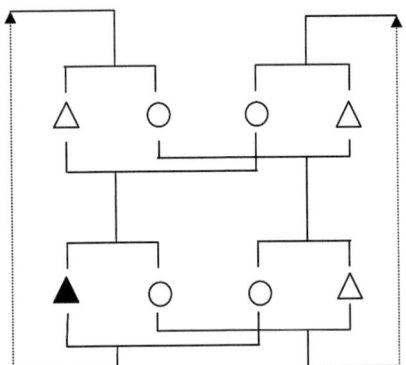

Figure 3.1 Focal tetradic diagram. In each level the brother-sister pairs represent intermarrying sections, and their children do the same. Whereas a Dravidian-type diagram would continue down the page in the same format, the tetradic diagram bends back on itself, as shown by the dotted outer lines.

whose very simplicity gives them an interest that may outweigh their absence from the ethnographic record. Second, those asking diachronic questions now have a reasonable starting point. If all attested human societies have something like a kinship system, why should our species have started off by inventing anything other than the simplest type? But if this is where we started, all attested systems must ultimately derive from it.

The problem now becomes: what processes led from tetradic societies to Omaha types?[1] More theoretically, how should we envision the transformations that bridge the gap between them? One sort of answer would confine itself to a level of abstraction at which empirical cases are replaced by models or ideal types, and the gradual, overlapping, "messy" processes of real-world history are replaced by crisp structural transformations. On the other hand, the notion of a definable Omaha type is debated and can be deconstructed (Barnes, this volume); and (following L. H. Morgan), we hope to ultimately understand real-world history. So I try to combine models and empirical material.

Once we leave the hypothetical realm of tetradic societies, socio- and egocentric categories begin a long process of divergence (Allen 1998a).[2] I start with the egocentric branch and discuss the topic of skewing (see chapter 1)—first abstractly (figure 3.2), then drawing on some Himalayan data. Moving to a Lévi-Straussian or alliance perspective, I explore one particular Omaha-type model, first abstractly (figures 3.3–3.4) and then in the light of facts and interpretations taken from Indo-European (IE) comparativism. I present some ideas for thinking about a complicated problem, but I do not pretend to exhaust it.

Terminology: From Tetradic Type to Omaha Type

To transform into an Omaha type, the tetradic model needs elaboration along both its axes. Vertically, it must be unfolded so as to introduce generations in the normal sense. Ascending generations now contrast with descending, by having (at least some) different kin terms. Horizontally, or laterally, it must be unfolded so that the two lines of figure 3.1 increase to at least three—the smallest number that can separate wife-giver and wife-taker lines. But this transformation is not obviously simpler than symmetrically splitting both original lines to give a total of four (distinguished again by at least some kin terms). The four lines can interrelate in various ways. Thus, to continue with our male bias, they can transfer women unilaterally, in a ring (as in the well-known MBD marriage pattern), or they can retain bilateral exchange, alternating their exchanges between two of the other lines (Aranda-style, involving marriage with certain second cross-cousins). Details are omitted because to approach classic Omaha systems, we must eliminate both these positive marriage rules. However, I mention the possibilities to make an important point: *tetradic theory does not offer a unilineal schema*. A given end point can be reached by paths that vary either in the stages traversed or in the ordering of the transitions. Both types of unfolding could even occur before socio- and egocentric categories lose their congruence.

Despite such flexibility, it is not true that "anything goes." The theory predicts that historical change has generally led *away* from tetradic structures, such change typically being irreversible.[3] Thus, a tetradic terminology allows ego to classify all members of society—past, present and future, however remote genealogically—under its four categories. In other words, it implies an infinite number of equations or, more meaningfully, indefinite reapplication of certain *types* of equation—alternate-generation, prescriptive, and classificatory. Tetradic theory predicts a world-historical trend toward rupturing these types of equation, which will not normally be re-created. But departure from the tetradic model can also consist of introducing new types of equation overruling the original discriminations. The three well-known types of countertetradic equations are generational (or Hawaiian), cognatic (exemplified by English *uncle*), and Crow-Omaha (though others can be found—see the "Siberian generational" terminologies of Dziebel 2007: 207).

The type of terminology into which Omaha equations are introduced is a difficult question, but can be left for now while we consider simply how to conceptualize them. The standard metaphor of skewing implies that cross cousins, instead of staying in ego's generation (where they "belong"), are "raised" on the matrilateral side and "lowered" on the patrilateral one. It is as if in figure 3.2 the MBS on the left and the FZS on the right have rotated clockwise around ego.

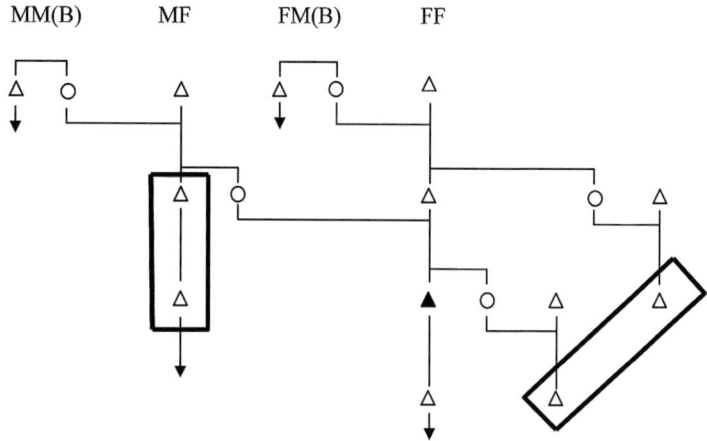

Figure 3.2 Minimal Omaha-type model, to illustrate skewing. The descent lines indicated at the top will be relevant to figure 3.3. Ego's marriage is not shown. The enclosures in bold represent the characteristic minimal equations.

The imagery is intelligible and suggests, reasonably, that the equations on the two sides constitute a single transformation. However, it needs two clarifications. First, the processes on the two sides differ, as the figure shows. MBS and MB are in the same line and are linked by filiation; if the lines represent clans, they are both in one clan. Neither form of closeness applies to FZS and ZS. This asymmetry between the two sides makes the former the natural starting point for thinking about Omaha terminologies. Second, the raising and lowering can be viewed in two ways: as applying to the cross-cousin kin type (MBS is raised) or as applying to the term (the term for MB descends). I favor the latter, with its anticlockwise rotation, and explain why by referring to two societies from the Tibeto-Burman area.

The Byansi, who live around the northwest corner of Nepal, had bilateral cross-cousin marriage and a Dravidian-type terminology (Allen 1975), whereas the Sherpas in the northeast of the country lacked a positive marriage rule. The Sherpa terminology, analyzed in Allen (1976), came largely from the brief appendix in Fürer-Haimendorf (1964), who did not discuss it or refer to the Omaha type. But consider the terms *ashang* or *ajang* MB and *ashang* or *shangbu* MBS. In languages related to

Sherpa the root *shang* is regularly confined to G^{+1}, but here it has extended its semantic field downward. This claim is not affected by the affixed *a-* and *-bu*, and the extension may reach further, to MBSS.

The reciprocals of a man's MB and MBS are, respectively, ZS and FZS, which are equated under *tsabyuk*; comparison confirmed that in this case a root had extended its field upward. The terminology thus exhibited the minimal Omaha equations, which, as usual, were accompanied by others involving females: *uru* MZ, MBD, and *tsabyung* ♂ZD, FZD. So the term for MB's sister extended downward to cover MBS's sister (i.e., MBD), and a reciprocal change affected the patrilateral side. Further vertical equations exist or have existed in the Sherpa terminology, involving $G^{\pm 2}$ and/or affines;[4] but I focus on the minimal Omaha equations.

Why did they develop? My answer was as follows: Byansi and Sherpa are cognate languages. If Sherpa terminology developed from one of Dravidian type, then, like Byansi, it once had terms for bilateral cross-cousin. When the Sherpas lost the rule prescribing marriage with this type of relative, they no longer had a clear reason for equating the two sides, and the terms became obsolete. The vertical equations developed to cover the kin types that were thereby vacated. However, innumerable societies must have lost the same marriage rule and the corresponding Xc terms without developing vertical equations, and other reactions to the loss are possible.

1. Despite the loss of a raison d'être, the old bilateral cross-cousin terms can simply remain, though often losing their affinal specifications, as in Iroquois-type terminologies.
2. The kin types in question can remain without a kin term. Terminologies are not obliged to classify all tertiary kin types as relatives. English lacks simple terms for children's in-laws (ChEP), and the Kangra terminology does not cover GEF or ZHZ (Parry 1979:299). However, most languages classify all types of first cousin, so this response is unlikely to be more than temporary (no doubt terminologies can have periods of stasis and periods of rapid change).
3. New terms can be devised for MBCh and FZCh. Invention of completely new terms may well be less common than adaptation of old ones, for instance, by affixes (an empirical issue that needs study).

4. New terms can be borrowed from other languages. In the Himalayas, Tibeto-Burman languages often borrow from Indo-European (IE) languages, though Sherpa has also borrowed from Tibetan.
5. The meanings of existing terms can be extended. The two obvious alternatives are to extend the G = //c terms (to "Hawaiianize ego's level") or, under patriliny, to adopt the Omaha solution.

How societies choose among such options is not obvious, and various factors could contribute. Moreover, the same choice could be made for different reasons, and the situation is complicated by the variety of contexts within which Omaha-type equations can appear. Despite the views of Lévi-Strauss (chapter 1, this volume), a Dravidian-type system that replaces its symmetrical prescription with a matrilateral one could separate the two sides, repattern affinal equations accordingly, lose its Xc terms, and substitute Omaha-type equations—all without instituting Omaha-type marriage prohibitions. The vertical equations would here appear before the loss of prescriptive equations.[5] Omaha equations occur in the much-studied terminology of Ambrym (Héran 2009:496–97), and can even develop within a Dravidian terminology: where marriage occurs with sister's daughter, or more precisely with y(eZD), an MB = FZH term can extend downward to take over e(MBS) = e(FZS), and an osGS term can extend upward to y(MBS) = y(FZS) (Good 1991:65–74).

Although it emphasizes the diachronic semantics of changing kinship systems and the need to empathize with language users, tetradic theory can only answer certain questions. To give up marrying bilateral cross-cousins does not automatically lead to loss of bilateral Xc terms, for speakers have to perceive the old terms as unsatisfactory and, if they wish, choose other ways to cover the relatives in question. I doubt if a world-historical theory can do much to explain the local choices.

Alliance: Toward a Simple Omaha-Type Model

Whether one likes it or not, the term *Omaha* has come to connote a society that not only has Xc vertical equations but also marriage prohibitions bearing on lines. For simplicity, let us assume that these lines correspond to exogamous patriclans. The number of prohibited lines

58   *Nicholas J. Allen*

can vary, but I initially chose four because this figure is prominent in Crow-Omaha literature. Thus our ego cannot marry into the line/clan of his father and FF, nor into that of any other grandparent. Omaha systems commonly also prohibit marriage with MZD (Héritier 1981: 104), but this simply leaves unchanged the tetradic prohibition on marriage with //c. (According to Héritier [1981:89], androcentrism in expressing the rules is a cultural universal, but I prefer to justify the male bias in my formulations on the grounds that patrilineal systems are most easily grasped by positing a male ego.)

If four clans are prohibited to ego, the society needs a minimum of five, the "extra" one providing ego's wife. Perhaps the potential patrimoieties of a tetradic society have each split in two and become recognized patriclans, and one patriclan has split again. This last step, from four clans to five, is crucial, because four lines are too few to approximate an Omaha-type alliance system; I do not attempt to model the transition and simply present the minimal system, assuming equal duration of generations for males and females (figure 3.3). Exactly how the model relates to any real Omaha-type society is debatable, as we shall see, but it turns out to possess interesting features.

The clans are labeled A–E. Because each gives away sisters and receives wives, the simplest arrangement is to form a ring: in G^{+2} A gives to B, B to C . . . and E back to A. Repeating this in G^{+1} would mean MBD prescription, and reversing the arrows would mean FZD prescription—both impossible in a model Omaha system. Instead, let X (meaning any patriline) give to the line next-but-one on its right. G^0 is best drawn by reversing the arrow so that X gives to its left-hand neighbor (arrows pointing to the next-but-three on the right mean the same but are harder to read). Any other pattern for G^0 would violate the prohibitions. Symmetry suggests that G^{-1} will give to neighbor-but-one on the left, and this is confirmed by the prohibitions. Line X has now given to and received from all other lines, so G^{-2} can and must revert to the pattern of G^{+2}.

The model is orderly in various ways. Consider ego's relatives in G^{+2}, and the lines they head. If a father is always closer to ego than a mother is, FF is closer to ego than his wife's FM is, and both are closer than MF (the father in FM carrying more weight than the grandfather in MF). MM is the remotest of the four. So, leftward horizontal movement

Tetradic Theory and Omaha Systems

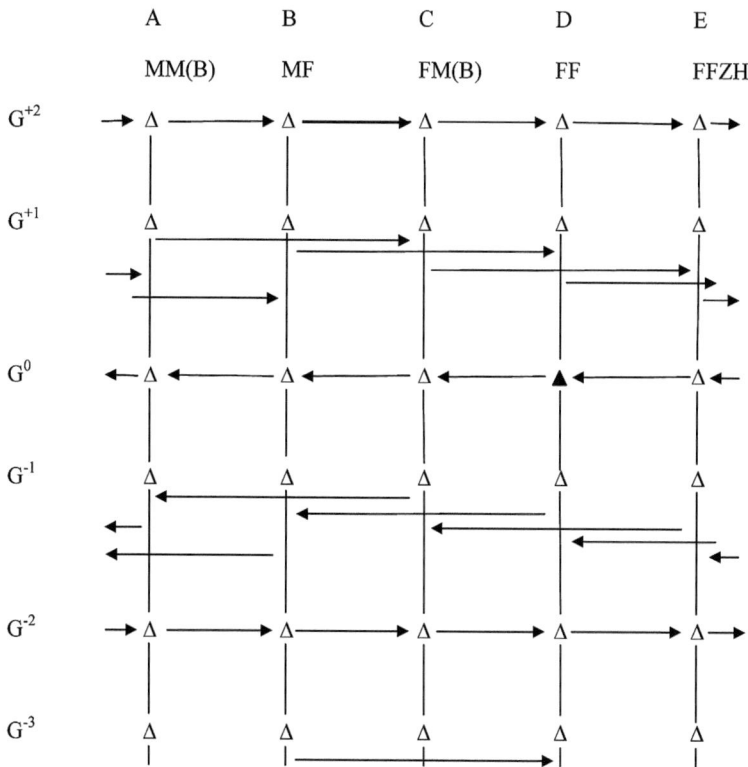

Figure 3.3 Four exogamous lines. Five-patriline model system in which a male may not take a wife from the line of any grandparent. Females are shown by arrows: the tail shows them as lineage sisters of their natal group, the head as wives joining a different group. Ego is in line D.

from D is movement toward lines that are increasingly remote; the next step moves to the nongrandparental line, that of FFZH, into which ego marries. But there is also a vertical pattern. Each generation situates its "mobile" G^{+2} relatives in different lines. For ego's son, FF of course remains in D, but FM is in B, MF in E, MM in C and FFZH in A. If these mobile kin types are followed down the diagram, one always finds the repeating cycle ACBE. For the position MM the cycle starts in G^{+2}, for FFZH in G^{+1}, and so on.

Let us turn to G^0. Ego's //c are of course in D, and of his first Xc, FZCh are in A, MBCh in B. The remaining two positions are ego's wife-givers and -takers. If we emphasize the patrilines, ego marries his

FFZSD and gives his sister to FMBSS (I deliberately minimize reference to second cousins).[6]

The model can be depicted in other ways, which bring out different features. In figure 3.4a the five clans are disposed symmetrically around an empty center (imagine a dancing area, sacrificial ground, village square). One sees clearly how, over the course of the four generations, each clan is both giver and taker for every other one. Each "gift" or transfer is reciprocated two generations later. Figure 3.4b takes an egocentric perspective. Starting in G^{+2}, ego's line gives successively to E, A, C, B before the cycle starts again, and it takes successively from C, B, E, A. Note again the ACBE cycle.

A society that operated the model would need an appropriate terminology, but we have to be realistic about appropriateness. Where tetradic society gave ego eight sorts of relatives to classify, he now has

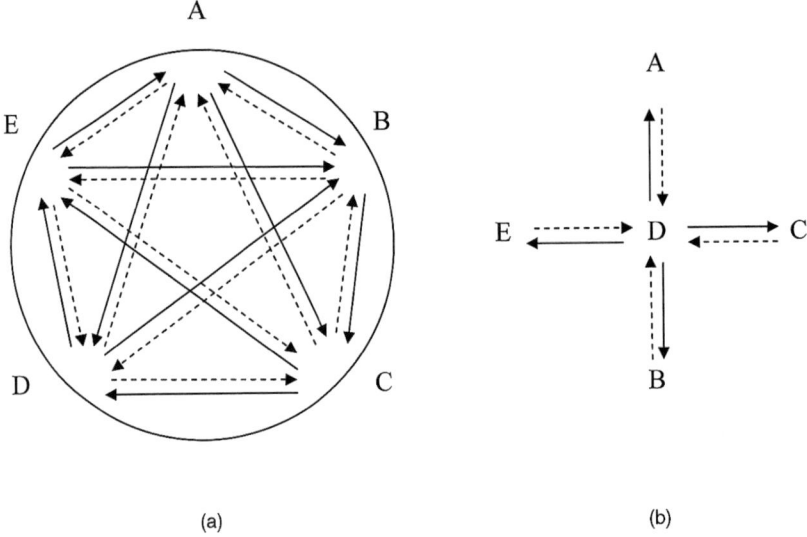

Figure 3.4 Circular diagrams. The lines of figure 3.3 are reduced to points indicated by A, B, C, D, E. Part a: Five clans in a circle. The interclan transfers are as in figure 3.3. If a solid arrow shows the transfer in one generation, the parallel broken arrow shows the reverse transfer in the next-but-one or previous-but-one generation. Part b: Center and cardinal points. Ego's group, in the center, exchanges with the four remaining groups, whose mutual dealings are not shown.

fifty (five lines, five generations, two sexes). As we noted, when society and its rules change, creation of new kin terms is far from being automatic, so the egocentric branch deriving from tetradic society is likely to lag behind the sociocentric branch: a fifty-term terminology exactly congruent with figure 3.3 is ethnographically implausible. We could be more precise if we knew how best to model the processes leading up to the model, but we can assume that of the fifty positions, some would be left uncovered by a kin term, and many others would be covered by equations. Equations could be horizontal (e.g., in the remote G^{-2}), and theoretically FZCh = MBCh could be among them. But the juxtaposition of Xc in lines A and B is irrelevant (ego's F and S find *their* Xc in C and E), and in a society where marriage rules are governed by so few lines, speakers would surely find it awkward and confusing to equate two of them within G^0. A more natural solution is provided by a vertical equation in the mother's patriline, covering minimally MB and MBS (and maybe others), together with its minimal reciprocal, ZS = FZS.

Figure 3.3 is interesting partly because it is typologically ambiguous. On one hand, it incorporates the two features often used to define Omaha systems—vertical equations and prohibitions on marrying into the lines of grandparents.[7] On the other hand, it is an elementary structure of kinship in that the pattern of alliances is repeated (after four generations, as in some Australian systems), and the spouse-giver category is predetermined. A typological decision might even turn on the lexicon. If FFZSCh are not covered by kin terms, ego marries a "non-relative" and the system is more Omaha-like. If they are equated with W and WG, they are classificatory affines, and the system is more elementary. The divide between elementary and semi-complex becomes blurred.

One use for the model could be as starting point for further development, leading toward more obviously Omaha-type models or toward attested societies that have received the label. For instance, one might segment each of the five clans into lineages and make some or all of the prohibitions apply to the smaller units, introduce different prohibitions bearing on ego's siblings, or simply increase the number of clans. I explore instead a different reason for an interest in the five-clan model.

The Model Alliance System and Indo-European Ideology

For two decades most of my research has been not on kinship but on IE cultural comparison. In the twentieth century this field was dominated by Georges Dumézil, who claimed that the early IE speakers organized their ideology into three hierarchically arranged categories ("functions"). But for reasons unrelated to kinship, I have argued that the ideology was not so much triadic as pentadic; roughly speaking, Dumézil's three categories formed the core of a more embracing hierarchy. The argument concerns not mere numbers but categories whose content can be defined quite precisely. Details are irrelevant here; one-word pointers toward the definitions are sufficient. The categories are as follows, in descending hierarchical order (adapted from Allen 2007a): transcendence, knowledge, force, plenty, devaluation.[8] Sets manifesting this schema turn up repeatedly in early IE contexts, such as the pantheon, myth and epic, ritual and law—and often in social structure, or rather in folk-theoretical accounts of it. India provides a classic instance: king, priest, warrior, producer, serf. The basic idea of a classificatory schema running through multiple cultural domains probably came ultimately from Durkheim and Mauss via Granet (Allen 2000:39–41). The French authors located the origin of the phenomenon in early tribal social structures: the patterning that applied first to human society was secondarily projected onto other domains.

Bringing together the two theories (pentadic and Durkheim-Mauss) suggests that early IE ideology arose in a society structured into five components. The materials used by comparativists mostly come from ancient societies that were either literate themselves or in contact with literate societies, but proto-IE society was of course non-literate, and in that sense tribal. Comparative philology cannot reconstruct its social structure in detail, but it must have been patrilineal and the components may well have been exogamous clans. Moreover, the ideology could have arisen before the protolanguage, and an earlier origin would make it even less likely that the components resembled the more or less endogamous strata in India. So I postulate that originally each of the ideological categories was correlated with one of five clans (it is irrelevant whether the correlations governed everyday life or were limited to special contexts such as myth or ritual), and that the correlations survived a change in mode of recruitment to the largest units of society.

One additional factor needs to be brought into the argument: philologists have often argued for Omaha-type equations in early IE kin terminology (Mallory and Adams 2006:202–18). The five-clan model of figures 3.3 and 3.4 was initially set up to explore Omaha alliance rules, but it begins to look as if the model may have applied at some period in the history of Indo-Europaea. Despite the many uncertainties, it is worth exploring relations between the kinship model and the ideology.

An obvious link is the number five, and also (less obviously) its square. In the model the five lines are cross-cut by five generations (or vice versa), giving twenty-five positions (or brother–sister pairs). Regarding ideology, an important branch of Hindu philosophy (called Sāṃkhya, literally "enumeration"), when it lists the contents of the universe, organizes them into sets of five, for example, five senses or five elements; it recognizes five such sets—a pentad of pentads—the twenty-five *tattvas*. Arguably, both levels of organization manifest the pentadic ideology (Allen 1998b, 2005). The virtual silence of the earliest texts has usually suggested a late Vedic or post-Vedic date for this philosophy, but such negative evidence is hardly conclusive.

The pentads are not just sets of five entities: the entities are ordered into meaningful sequences. In the kinship model, the vertical ordering or ranking is by generation, from senior to junior. We have already touched on the horizontal ordering of lines, in terms of closeness or distance of G^{+2} relatives from ego's FF in figure 3.3: each step leftward round the ring was a step toward a wife-giver, and conversely, in G^0, each step leftward is toward a wife-taker. In the ideology the categories are ranked in terms of status.

Apart from being ranked, the pentads may also be articulated into a central or core triad and a peripheral pair. The three central *generations* include all of ego's primary relatives (those composing his nuclear family, whether he is child or parent), as distinct from the grandparents. The latter are in fact quite often equated by self-reciprocal kin terms, as in Kariera (to cite a well-known terminology). The three central *lines* are those of ego and his direct affines (WB, ZH), and the remoter pair contain FZCh and MBCh. Ego is the core of the core, both vertically and horizontally.

In the ideology the core categories contrast with the others, which are in some sense other—outside or beyond it. For instance, empirically, their three representatives may have in common a feature that is not shared by the outsider pair. Thus, in the *Mahābhārata*, the five successive leaders of the Baddies fit the pentadic schema, but whereas the middle three all die on the battlefield, the first and last survive the Great War.

Three other Indian institutions deserve mention in connection with ordering and subgrouping. First, in the Sanskritic cult of the ancestors (*śrāddha*), five entities are involved—a male worshiper; three rice balls representing his F, FF, and FFF; and the nonindividualized Fathers. When the worshiper dies, his son takes over and drops his most distant forebear (F^4), merging him with the nameless ancestors (Allen 2007b: 244–45; Parry 1979:142). It is as if the worshiper stands to the Fathers as the devalued category to the transcendent, while the rice balls represent stages in a transition between them (though whether each ball represents a single core function is unclear).

Second, the horizontal ordering, already discussed in terms of distance from ego, can be reconceptualized in terms of hypergamy, that is, the theoretical or actual higher status enjoyed by the north Indian wife-taker. Suppose figure 3.3 applied to that region: the left-pointing arrows starting from ego would indicate ascending status (ZH, ZHZH, and so on, until the return to ego); the reverse direction (WB, WBWB . . .) would indicate a descent. Representatives of the ideological categories can likewise appear in either descending or ascending hierarchical order.

Third, the centrality of ego in our kinship models finds a parallel of sorts in the centrality of the Indian king. In rituals such as inauguration (for which figure 3.4b could easily be adapted), the king may literally be placed in the center, and, rather than transcending the four estates, he is sometimes ranked among the warriors—that is, positioned centrally within the pentad (Allen 1999:247–50).

The cyclicity of the kinship model is clear both horizontally and vertically (though only four generations differ in their transfers, the circle is complete only when the fifth generation returns it to its starting point). As for the ideology, though it was introduced as a linear hierarchy, it applies just as well to contexts that are intrinsically cyclical, provided the cycle contains some breakpoint. I can here provide only (hopefully suggestive) hints. Consider the year, the breakpoint being the passage from old year to new. The new is both welcomed (valued) and transcendent (it represents the *whole* year), and the seasons, three in Vedic heortology, lead on to the year's end, which is often ritually expelled (devalued). Space, too, can be conceived in circular or cyclical terms. The center-plus-cardinal point schema (see figure 3.4b) tends to represent all space, which is epitomized in the transcendent center, and can be traversed or claimed by circumambulation (from and to a breakpoint). Sociosymbolic space can share its structure with kinship space.

However, the various links between our kinship models and the IE ideology cannot hide a fundamental difference. A diagram with an ego is egocentric and relative. In figures 3.3 and 3.4 the alphabetic sociocentric labels were arbitrary: a clan had no enduring or absolute properties, and even its place in a hierarchy varied with the position of ego. But the ideology, whether as an abstract schema or embodied in a context, is not relativistic in this way. The difference must go back to the tetradic stage when, apart from their congruence with egocentric categories, the sections were no doubt accorded some absolute properties. One can envision a division of labor among IE ego's relatives, for instance, in ritual contexts, corresponding to the absolute division of labor in society, but each division will have its own long history.

Conclusion

Although this attempt to link tetradic theory and Omaha systems has left many issues unresolved or undiscussed, it has at least constructed and explored a model incorporating features of "Omaha" terminology and alliance. No claim is made that it is the best such model or even a necessary precursor to one. Possibly an ideal-type Omaha system is a mirage, though the point could only be decided by collecting and comparing a sufficient number of candidates—and also by including Crow systems, which might offer additional insights.

More generally, the male bias of this chapter, though deliberate and due partly to the patrilineality of the Sherpas and Indo-Europeans, risks being misleading. For instance, consider figure 3.1. Male and female egos use the same terms and use them to make the same divisions between categories, but the terms they each use for odd-level relatives can be combined in two ways (Allen 2008:112 n4). If both sexes use the same term for father, they use different terms for son, and if they use the same term for son, they use different ones for father (for *his* ssP, *her* osP). The former pattern makes sense if male and female egos are siblings still in their natal family, the latter if they are spouses in their family of procreation. The former seems preferable theoretically, but my point here is that neglect of female ego may oversimplify our model-building.

Similarly, when constructing paths leading away from tetradic patterns, we need to give full weight to the emic aspect: what changes in marriage and recruitment rules will members of a society find reasonable? The question applies equally to changes in the meaning of kin terms, where the viewpoint of the two sexes may differ and sociolinguistic perspectives are needed. Both Kronenfeld and Dousset (this volume) show that a single society can have more than one terminology at one time, even for reference, and the point can be generalized. Changes in kinship systems do not take place overnight, so old and new inevitably coexist for a time. Given the level of abstraction at which it works, tetradic theory is likely to downplay such intrasocietal variation.

Finally, a word on India, which has so often represented the IE speakers. This prominence reflects both my former teaching duties and Parry's discussion of "Crow-Omaha" marriage prohibitions in Kangra (1979:224–25, 290). As he notes, Kangra is typical of north India in that although Omaha-type equations are absent (G^0 is generational), it prohibits marriage into the clans of the four grandparents. In addition, however, comparative work on IE narratives and ideology has suggested that in these respects India is a particularly conservative part of the older IE-speaking world. Perhaps north Indian kinship is equally conservative. Obviously India in historical times is far removed from the culture of proto-IE speakers, but it offers much to fascinate the comparativist.

North America

4

Omaha and "Omaha"
R. H. Barnes

The manifold ways that "Omaha" has been used to indicate a class of societies on several continents provide endless opportunities for misunderstanding. Institutions and practices in, say, Africa or South America may be totally divergent from the features described by the existing ethnography for the Crow and the Omaha. Considerable agreement may be found on underlying issues in the comparative analysis of social structures and processes once we get away from limitations of the Crow-Omaha label. This chapter explores how the constitutive elements of "Omaha" as a typological category depart from the facts of Omaha (proper) ethnography.

Alliance and the Omaha

In 1984 I published a book (*Two Crows Denies It: A History of Controversy in Omaha Sociology*) surveying the ethnographic information available for the Omaha Indians of Nebraska. This information exists in published and unpublished form, including important genealogies and other materials on the Omaha that are held in the National Anthropological Archives in Washington, D.C. I had recently finished my doctoral dissertation on the Kédang of Lembata in eastern Indonesia, a society that practiced a form a marriage alliance with a "positive" marriage rule (Barnes 1974). During the same period, I also worked on translating (with Ruth Barnes) Josef Kohler's landmark study of Crow (which he called "Choctaw") and Omaha kinship terminologies, *Zur Urgeschichte der Ehe* (*On the Prehistory of Marriage,* Kohler 1975 [1897]). Using Morgan's data, Kohler developed the first systematic explanation of these terminologies as associated with social organization by unilineal descent; Durkheim's famous review of this work underscored the analytical point (Barnes 1975). Thus, my interests in the Omaha proper, and how their social system might or might not speak to any such thing as an "Omaha type," were converging from a variety of perspectives.

My supervisor, Rodney Needham, had introduced me to the early Dutch work on such societies and to Lévi-Strauss's classic study of kinship, *Les Structures Élémentaires de la Parenté* (1949), the English translation of which Needham had edited. The difficult relationship between these two men was accentuated by a preface to the new French edition of 1967, which originated in a lecture given at Oxford University on the occasion of Lévi-Strauss's honorary degree, an event organized by Needham. The same talk became his 1965 Huxley Memorial Lecture for the Royal Anthropological Institute (Lévi-Strauss 1966). That preface, retained in the English translation, included Lévi-Strauss's repudiation of Needham's interpretation of his theory in *Structure and Sentiment* (Needham 1962). Despite the fact that Needham continued to translate Lévi-Strauss's work, the relationship between the two men never recovered. The preface also contained the suggestion that Crow-Omaha marriage arrangements produced "semi-complex" structures of marriage alliance. This represented a development away from "elementary structures" or societies with positive marriage rules, in that Crow-Omaha involved extensive marriage prohibitions, which led in the end to *implicit* marriage prescriptions:

> [Crow-Omaha systems] only set up preventions to marriage, but apply them so widely through constraints inherent in their kinship nomenclature that, because of the relatively small population, consisting of no more than a few thousand persons, it might be possible to obtain the converse, viz., *a system of unconscious prescriptions* which would reproduce exactly and in full the contours of the mold formed by the system of conscious prohibitions. (Lévi-Strauss 1969 [1949]:xxxvi, emphasis added)

It seemed a natural step to move from my work on a society with a positive marriage rule to look at a society with only negative rules and investigate this intriguing suggestion. Furthermore, I had been interested in the classic monographs on the Omaha by the Rev. J. Owen Dorsey (1884) and by Alice Fletcher and Francis La Flesche (1911) since my undergraduate days, and I welcomed an opportunity to explore them in greater detail. Somewhere in the gestation of this project, Lévi-Strauss's student Françoise Héritier came to Oxford in an attempt to establish ties with Oxford anthropology, and as one result I went to

Paris for a few months in 1980 as Directeur d'Études Associé, École des Hautes Études en Sciences Sociales. Officially, Lévi-Strauss was my sponsor, but he was just leaving for a trip to Japan, and I ended up spending more time with Louis Dumont's *équipe* and with Southeast Asianists. Nevertheless, my work on the Omaha began to take shape.

The result of my Omaha inquiry did not bear out Lévi-Strauss's speculation about an implicit prescription. I would have been happy (perhaps even happier) if it did. I attempted to test it against the available genealogical information in every sympathetic way I could think up, but in no case did the genealogies bear out the notion that an Omaha person was constrained to marry either into a specific category or with a specific individual. Dorsey's unpublished genealogies in the National Anthropological Archives were extensive and extended back into the eighteenth century, but they concerned only some of the ten Omaha clans. I asked where the others might be and was told that that was all there were, but that there were genealogies of the closely related Ponca. At some point in prehistory the Ponca and the Omaha had formed a single tribe. Thinking that Ponca genealogies might be of some interest, I looked at them. I found that they contained the genealogy of the clan of Francis La Flesche's paternal uncle, Frank.

It needs to be explained that Francis' father, Joseph, and his brother were by birth half-French and half-Ponca. Joseph was adopted into the Omaha tribe and became a chief as well as a trader. More important for my purposes was the fact that most of the genealogies were not Ponca at all, but were the missing Omaha genealogies. So I had complete genealogies for all ten clans. This information could be supplemented with census data and personal letters written in Omaha by Dorsey at the request of individual Omaha and published by him. In fact, he was preparing the genealogies for publication, but he died in 1895 of typhoid fever before he could complete the project (McGee 1897:207).

Had he succeeded in publishing them, perhaps someone else would have exploited them for exploring Omaha marriage prohibitions much earlier. It must be said that at the time Lévi-Strauss wrote about them they were completely unanalyzed. Information about them comes from a few dense pages in *Omaha Sociology*. Dorsey was unable to say much about them, although he might have been able to do so later had he lived. I think that he recorded the genealogies (or most of them) subsequent to collecting the information on the prohibitions. In any case, the information in question was given to him by Two Crows and Joseph La Flesche during a visit to Dorsey in Washington. What Dorsey may not have known is that each of Two Crows's several brothers had broken one or the other of the prohibitions. What he may also not have known, at least at the time, is that one of Two Crows's brothers had stolen Francis La Flesche's wife, a circumstance that surely would have put a constraint on candor with Two Crows and Joseph La Flesche sitting in the same room.

Dorsey seems not to have explored the question of how constraining these prohibitions were or how extensive their application. It is also true that for no other Siouan group has there been any report of an extensive list of marriage prohibitions (Barnes 1984:160–62). There is at least the possibility that the marriages of many collateral relatives are of little concern in determining marriage choice and that what most matters is what the women in the relevant clan segment remember about other marriages that may be of importance (Barnes 1984:175). I concluded that Omaha were not particularly constrained in choice and that they did not practice "Omaha alliance" in anything like the form suggested by Lévi-Strauss. I was led to question the value of assigning "Crow-Omaha" societies to the transitional category of "semi-complex" on the basis of this form of alliance.

Comparison

This issue brings up the perplexing fact that there are societies in Africa that are described by their ethnographers as practicing Omaha alliance. In the case of the Samo, as studied by Héritier, we have been offered an exhaustive description of a very extensive set of marriage prohibitions, backed by genealogies and computer analyses of the consequence these prohibitions have on marriage choice (see, for example, Héritier 1974, 1975, 1976, 1981). This work goes far beyond anything that it is possible to provide today for the Omaha. Nevertheless, there is reason to doubt that these African arrangements have anything to do with the social structure of the Omaha.

What is at question here is the matter of comparison. Broadly, comparison can be undertaken within an ethnographically and historically related region, as exemplified by Whiteley's contribution to this volume, or it can be conducted across continents. An example of the latter is the studies by Lévi-Strauss (1949), Leach (1951), and Needham (1962) of marriage alliance that have successfully identified social structures operating on the same principles located at great distances from each other. Many of the contributions in this volume are of this global kind. It is definitely possible in principle that social structures very like that of the actual Omaha might be found on other continents than North America.

Comparison is about similarities and differences. Both need to be considered at the same time when undertaking comparison (Kroeber 1954:285; Evans-Pritchard 1965:25). As Evans-Pritchard said, "Comparison is, of course, one of the essential procedures of all sciences and one of the elementary processes of human thought" (1965:13). Furthermore, "there is no other method in social anthropology than observation, classification and comparison in one form or another" (1965:31). We compare all the time without asking ourselves academic questions about the process. Does the Omaha system exist? The system of the Omaha themselves, whatever that is, certainly does exist, as do those of other peoples whose systems are sufficiently similar. It seems reasonable to me to speak of Crow-Omaha systems in North America, where similarities are sometimes close and where there is reason to think there may be historical and ethnological connections between the societies of the relevant kinds. But what does "sufficiently similar" mean, and who is to decide?

The "Omaha system" has at least three meanings. The first is whatever the relevant institutions of the Omaha happen to be. This is the safest meaning. The second derives from Morgan's study of kinship terminologies and subsequent analytical developments, for example, by Kohler (1897), Rivers (1914), Lowie (1934), and Murdock (1949). The third meaning is Lévi-Strauss's definition of "Omaha alliance," which has taken on a life of its own. "Omaha alliance," it turns out, is what Lévi-Strauss said "Omaha alliance" is. Lévi-Strauss's meaning has attracted all the attention concerning alliance and, at least in some quarters, is referred to as though it actually existed in various places. I have tried to show that the third meaning has nothing to do with the first meaning, that is, Lévi-Strauss's "Omaha alliance" is foreign to the institutions of the actual Omaha.

Regarding the second meaning, for reasons that are entirely historical but not intrinsic to the Omaha or their circumstances, "Omaha" has come to mean a relationship terminology containing equations that might be termed "patrilineal" (e.g., MB = MBS = MBSS). The name "Crow" has acquired the same meaning, but in respect of terminologies that have "matrilineal" equations (e.g., F = FZS = FZDS). It is necessary to put quotation marks around "patrilineal" and "matrilineal" because some anthropologists, including Lewis Henry Morgan, denied that features of terminology had anything at all to do with descent. Kohler (1897) and Durkheim (1898) influentially argued that terminologies with these lineal equations flowed from social practices emphasizing unilineal descent. Kroeber (1909) argued forcefully against this inference. Anthropologists who want to maintain that there is any link between unilineal groupings and features of social classification face persistent counterexamples. The relationship system of the Algonquian Fox, so conveniently described by Tax (1937), is nearly identical in its pattern to that of the Siouan Omaha. It is also curious that while the Omaha have patrilineal descent groups—although not ones that fit well structural-functional preconceptions of British anthropology of the 1930s—the Fox have none at all. Even more curious is that Radcliffe-Brown (1941) had nothing to say about this fact when in an article on the Omaha system, he used Fox (rather than Omaha) data. In any case, anthropologists have named this discrepancy between classification and social groupings "the Crow-Omaha problem."

Characterizing societies by types is a risky business. In saying that a society practices a particular custom X—for example, prescriptive marriage alliance—you also assert that X exists. There are always those who will deny the premise, or at least that has been the fate of my example. Those who want to maintain in the face of skepticism that X really does exist run the risk of being accused of essentialism. As a matter of fact, the ethnographic record currently available to us shows many arrangements other than X, including perhaps some that are very close to X, but not completely so. Those who think that X is real might say that these examples are societies undergoing some sort of transition. Those who deny that X is real might say that the first lot are just shoring up their theory by special pleading in the face of contrary evidence. I chose prescriptive alliance as my example because this is more or less the position Needham, who has had the most to say about the topic and has been the center of the greatest amount of polemic on the subject, ended up in.

I am among those who, based on my research in two eastern Indonesian communities, Kédang and Lamalera, Lembata, think that prescriptive marriage alliance actually is real. The work of other researchers into the same area reinforces my confidence (e.g., Forth 1981; Renard-Clamagirand 1982). However, I am not so sure that I can claim, on the basis of my own research, that this institution is found in Witihama, Adonara, where I have also done research, even though it is a Lamaholot-speaking community like Lamalera.

Variation is a fact in the ethnographic record and poses problems for anthropology, with its very restricted view into the past, in respect to establishing the proper categories for comparison and deciding how to account for change, especially the direction of change. Anthropologists generally are good at guessing but not so good at convincing others that their guesses are right. We are not a natural science and do not have the means of establishing the certainty that some sciences can achieve.

Some Doubts

The identification of "Omaha systems" with the mere presence of "patrilineal" equations contains within it a large assumption, namely, that no matter how these equations are distributed they constitute the same thing and perhaps derive from the same cause. I disagree with this assumption, or, better, I would like to have it shown. As Godelier (2011:179–180) comments, there are anthropologists who do not accept that "Crow-Omaha" systems are a valid type. Needham (1971:14) said that nothing of any real elucidatory value has come out of the comparative attention to the "Omaha" type. "The reason is simply that a variety of terminologies all posses this supposedly definitive feature [the equation of mother's brother with mother's brother's son] but differ from each other in practically everything else." "Intensive analyses of individual 'Omaha terminologies' have repeatedly confirmed the invalidity of the type." The terminology of the Omaha of Nebraska differs in significant respects from the terminology of the Samo of Upper Volta, although the Samo are said to have an "Omaha" terminology. The differences between the Omaha and the Samo terminologies parallel the important differences in the marriage rules. Although there are some important similarities, I have also demonstrated that there are major differences (Barnes 1982:116; see Héritier 1981).

The Samo and the Omaha are similar in the first four rules, but otherwise differ in every one of the rules indicated in table 4.1. The Omaha have a further series of prohibitions for which there is no Samo counterpart, involving lines traced through ego's junior relatives and children. There is another respect in which there is an important differ-

Table 4.1 Samo and Omaha comparison

Samo	Omaha
1. F's lineage (prohibited)	F's clan (prohibited)
2. M's lineage (prohibited)	M's clan (prohibited)
3. FM's lineage (prohibited)	FM's subclan (prohibited)
4. MM's lineage (prohibited)	MM's subclan (prohibited)
5. Any lineage from which a classificatory F has taken a wife (prohibited)	Doubtful, but to judge by unpublished information **not practically true for the Omaha**
6. FMM's lineage (permitted)	FMM's subclan (**prohibited**)
7. MMM's lineage (permitted)	MMM's subclan (**prohibited**)
8. Any lineage from which a classificatory B has taken a wife (prohibited)	Any subclan from which a classificatory B has taken a wife (**permitted**)
9. W's lineage (prohibited)	W's subclan (**permitted and preferred**)
10. WM's lineage (prohibited)	WM's subclan (**permitted**)
11. WFM's lineage (prohibited)	WFM's subclan (**permitted**)
12. WMM's lineage (prohibited)	WMM's subclan (**permitted**)

ence between the Omaha and the Samo. According to Godelier (2011: 174, see also 169 and 506 n42), the Omaha and the Samo both practice sister exchange. In fact, the Omaha prohibit marriage with ZHZ, which precludes sister exchange, and in the Omaha genealogies recorded by Dorsey there are no examples of the exchange of sisters (Barnes 1982:117).

In a classic paper, Kroeber (1909) wanted to undermine Morgan's distinction between classificatory and descriptive terminologies and provided a list of features by which terminologies are ordered (Morgan 1871:12). Kroeber could be paraphrased by saying that all relationship terminologies are classificatory from someone's perspective and may also contain some descriptive terms; the principles ordering a given terminology are several and, given a limited number of terms, will therefore be in competition to some degree for expression in the terminology; European terminologies express a smaller number of his list of features than do those of American Indian languages; and sociological inferences from relationship terminologies must be subjected to extreme caution (Kroeber 1909:83–84). From Kroeber, Lowie (1928: 265) drew the conclusion that "kinship terminologies are not so many coherent 'systems' but are each founded on a variety of disparate principles, all of which must be enumerated for a complete definition" (see also Lowie 1917:122). "We shall . . . do well to amend our phraseology and to speak rather of kinship categories, features, or principles of classification than of types of kinship systems" (Lowie 1917:105, see also Needham 1971:17).

It is important to note here that neither meant that relationship systems cannot be analyzed but that the analysis consists in establishing the principles of order and the degree to which they are realized. This approach necessarily means that comparison can be done, without, however, prejudging issues of sameness and difference.

In *The Metamorphoses of Kinship*, Godelier (2011) classifies terminologies of asymmetric prescriptive marriage alliance, such as those of the Kachin of highland Burma, the Gilyak of Siberia, the Toba Batak of Sumatra, and others, as not only (1) asymmetric prescriptive, but also (2) Dravidian, (3) asymmetric Dravidian, (4) Kachin, and (5) Jinghpaw (a language of one of the Kachin groups). As merely ethnic or linguistic descriptions, the last two characterizations require no comment. The third implies that Dravidian terminologies prescribe marriage and come in two varieties, symmetric and asymmetric. The term "Dravidian" has been reserved historically for the symmetric prescriptive terminologies of South India, and it is most unusual to say that asymmetric prescriptive terminologies are Dravidian, as Dravidian speakers have no such terminology.

On the other hand, Kryukov (1998:308) says that Kachin terminology is normally considered to be of the Omaha type. However, in terminological features and marriage rules, the Kachin differ systematically in absolutely essential ways from the Omaha of Nebraska. Calling Kachin terminology "Omaha-type" derives from a practice, especially since Murdock (1949), of using the equations and distinctions of a single genealogical level or segment of the terminology for the classification of terminologies, instead of looking at the complete relationship terminologies and giving full consideration to the other social institutions that accompany them.

The major respect in which the Dravidian terminologies of south India differ from that of the Iroquois of North America is that the former have a marriage prescription into a specific category of relative and the latter do not (Trautmann 1981:85). Exactly the same distinction obtains in respect of the difference between the Kachin and other societies with asymmetric marriage alliance and the Omaha—a point made more generally already by Lévi-Strauss (1966:17), who said that they were as different "as fish and whales." It is wrong, therefore, to say that the Kachin have a terminology of the Omaha type because the Kachin terminology expresses this categorical prescription, which the Omaha certainly does not.

It is conceivable, but by no means proven, that a terminology of asymmetric prescriptive alliance could lose its prescription and begin to look something like that of the Omaha (as Kryukov [1998] and Godelier [2011] have suggested), but no one has ever shown that sort of thing happening. The reverse transformation is formally conceivable, but I do not see in what circumstances it would ever occur. Needham (1962:54–55, 1964) identified the Sirionó of Bolivia and the Miwok of California as having asymmetric marriage alliance on the basis of the form of their relationship terminologies. His interpretation of the Sirionó has been questioned (Scheffler and Lounsbury 1971), and Forth

(2008) has shown that the evidence available for the Miwok does not bear out Needham's interpretation of the relationship terminology. I do not know of any other indication that there might be asymmetric marriage alliance systems in the Americas, although given that they do exist in Siberia, I see no reason in principle why that should be. Nevertheless, there is no compelling reason at the moment to try to link the Omaha with any such arrangement in the past.

Descent

As noted already (and see chapter 1), so-called Crow and Omaha terminologies have long been associated with unilineal descent. This became especially true after Radcliffe-Brown (1941) entered the fray, seeing unilineal descent groups everywhere as comprising jural "corporations." The terms in which we specify our interest in kinship have been given many definitions. Whatever their intrinsic merits may be, the various definitions are incompatible among themselves, and, more important, any given definition defines its own field of relevance. The value of any particular definition depends on its purpose and the degree to which it helps achieve that purpose. Societies with descent groups are those societies which have groups which fit a specific definition of descent groups. Given the great variety that exists in approaches by societies to each of the topics commonly identified as pertaining to kinship, any definition also defines a large field of irrelevance. The question not often addressed that arises implicitly is, what is to be done with societies that lack the feature in question? The obvious and easy answer is to use methods other than those suited for the given topic. For societies that lack marriage alliance, do not use the methods appropriate for studying marriage alliance. But what do we do with examples of societies that have, say, descent groups by one definition but lack them by another? In general, why should we feel sure that societies that lack, say, descent groups are uninteresting for that reason?

That puzzle has always struck me when I have thought of the following comment by Radcliffe-Brown (1952:48): "Unilineal institutions in some form, are almost, if not entirely, a necessity in any ordered social system." This necessity derived from two sociological laws, which were, (1) "the need for a formulation of rights over persons and things sufficiently precise in their general recognition as to avoid as far as possible unresolved conflicts"; and (2) "the need for continuity of the social structure as a system of relations between persons, such relations being definable in terms of rights and duties." Furthermore, "if any society establishes a system of corporations on the basis of kinship—clans, joint-families, incorporated lineages—it must necessarily adopt a system of unilineal reckoning of succession" (Radcliffe-Brown 1952:46–47).

Using figures taken from Roger Keesing, Godelier (2011:100) estimated that 45 percent of societies had patrilineal groups, 12 percent matrilineal groups, 4 percent an arrangement of double unilineal descent, and 39 percent were cognatic in some way without unilineal groups. There are always difficulties about which units count as a society for comparative statistical purposes, but these results suggest that Radcliffe-Brown's generalization may not stand up. Of course, the question remains whether any of the examples in the 39 percent of the sample in the cognatic category form a system of nonunilineal corporations on the basis of kinship. In a well-known article Firth (1957) observed that in most Polynesian societies descent groups are not unilineal. In any case, if the figures are truly representative, they (as well as Firth's examples) demonstrate that unilineal institutions are not necessary.

Goody (1961:5) surveys a series of criteria that might be used to define corporate groups, namely, the presence of a leader (in a hierarchical system of authority), ownership and transmission of property, physical proximity, and periodic assembly. Goody chooses to regard unilineal descent groups as corporate if they are vested with rights in material property that is inherited. This criterion poses an immediate problem because it may well be that the only property such a group owns is rights over a specific ritual or myth. Or perhaps not even that: Turton (1980:73) states that Mursi descent groups only exist by virtue of claims on the distribution of bridewealth. Goody defines descent as concerning eligibility for membership in kin groups. He also requires that there be a general term in the language for such groups or that they be named. Whichever of these criteria is selected or whatever combination of them, each choice produces a different set of societies with and without corporate descent groups.

I tried to respond to Leach's suggestion that "we think again about the relationship between 'corporateness' and 'descent'" (Leach 1957:54, 1961:122) by examining the considerable variety of descent arrangements in a region of eastern Indonesia (Barnes 1980). I concluded, at least for my sample, that there was no clear comparative tie between functions and the principles that constituted groups and that it was not clear why descent groups needed to maintain exclusive corporate boundaries (1980:117). Perhaps we can echo a point Leach made about another institution and say that all universal definitions of descent groups are vain.

Scheffler (2001:x–xii) has introduced a new set of definitional criteria. He agrees with Fortes in regarding a rule of descent as not the relation of filiation between parent and child but a relation to antecedents prior to the parent in question. Furthermore, he accepts the tradition of which Fortes is a representative, which sees the term *descent group* as appropriately applied only to groups constituted by a unilineal rule, which of course has been controversial. He also distinguishes three forms of filiation, depending on whether the filiation is necessary and sufficient, necessary but not sufficient, or sufficient but not necessary. In addition there are three further possibilities depending on whether descent is without regard to sex of the parent, patrifiliation, or matrifiliation. Multiplying the two sets of possibilities reveals nine logical possibilities. Scheffler (2001:xi) makes the further reasonable observation that the different possibilities have systematically different implications for the groups they may constitute and that "any attempt to generalize across the board about such groups as equally patrilineal descent groups is bound to prove unproductive."

There is, after all, no "true" definition of descent. None of the empirical examples we know of is any less true or interesting than any other. Most definitions of descent that have been offered can be buttressed with known examples. The problem is not that anthropologists have not known about the variety. Most have taken it as a starting point in their deliberations. But many seem not to have accepted that the variety is in fact the message. My view here, of course, is closest to that of Leach (1961:4) and Needham (1971:8–13). We have no evidence to conclude that societies with corporate descent groups as defined by

Goody or anyone else represents either a stage toward which all other societies are tending or one from which they are changing. A century and a half of evolutionary speculation has produced no confidence in any evolutionary scheme for the development of systems of descent. It is true that evolutionary thought reappears in surprising places (Lévi-Strauss 1949:275–77; Needham 1967:44–48). Plausible arguments are not the same thing as certain ones.

Final Remarks

Given that anthropologists rarely agree on the definitions of even their most fundamental concepts, it is perhaps wrong to expect them to agree on what "Omaha systems" are. The Omaha of Nebraska have ten named patrilineal clans in two moieties subdivided in ways that vary from clan to clan, and these clans have various ritual properties. I do not think that we have a complete description of their sociology, despite the value of the two classic monographs. They appear to be corporate in some respects. There are also extensive equations in the Omaha terminology that appear to be compatible with their patrilineal institutions. They do not have any form of marriage alliance, and their relationship terminology lacks any features indicating a positive marriage rule. Their marriage prohibitions do not lead to an implicit marriage prescription. They do not practice sister exchange but prohibit it. My interpretation is that their marriage prohibitions are not especially constraining on marriage choice, at least not to the degree suggested by Lévi-Strauss.

What is Omaha depends on which of several different definitions of "Omaha" is used. The different definitions do not necessarily produce similar results. By at least one current definition, the Omaha themselves do not have an Omaha system. My preference is to let definitions adhere closely at least to the actual institutions of the Omaha. If we stopped talking about "Omaha systems" and instead talked about principles, we would no longer need to worry about defining them and could put comparison on a proper footing.

5

Crow-Omaha Kinship in North America
A Puebloan Perspective
Peter M. Whiteley

As the names imply, Crow and Omaha kinship systems were first described in Native North America, where they have also given rise to some major controversies (e.g., Barnes 1975, 1984; McKinley 1971a; Needham 1971). In what sense and to what degree widely dispersed societies—in different language families, with different economies and polities—may be said to share the same kinship system has long vexed anthropology. Whether kinship nomenclature entails any social corollaries at all, notably for descent and marriage, is still a point in argument (as Barnes, this volume, emphasizes). Lévi-Strauss (1969 [1949]:xxiii) announced the "basic purpose" of his magnum opus was to demonstrate that nomenclature, marriage rules, and descent principles "are indissociable aspects of one and the same reality." Others have declared this collocation analytically misleading (e.g., Barry 2008). Whether kinship systems correlate with political or economic features is seriously questioned (e.g., Trautmann 2001, Godelier 2011), not least because terminologies typically appear in a wide variety of settings.

To avoid sweeping and perhaps vacuous generalizations, comparative analysis of kinship systems should be grounded in regional concentrations (Trautmann and Barnes 1998). This chapter focuses on Pueblo, especially Hopi, kinship and marriage against the larger regional backdrop of Native North American Crow-Omaha systems.

What Is a Crow-Omaha System?

The classical "Crow-Omaha problem" concerns why these terminologies override the distinction of generations (e.g., White 1939). Seen thus, it is a problem of nomenclature. I argue that Crow-Omaha systems require explaining via marriage practices, at least among the Hopi. I am thus in sympathy with Lévi-Strauss's position against isolating nomenclatures from social contexts, because, linguistically speaking, kinship *terms* denote *relations*: they are not free-floating signs in some autonomous field. Nevertheless, the classic types, including Crow and Omaha, are first and foremost nomenclatures. Therefore, we begin with nomenclatures.

Lounsbury's (1964a) equivalence rules remain the most precise formal definition of Crow-Omaha terminologies. Underlying *structural* or *genealogical* equivalence—distinct from kin type equations per se (like MB = FB, in English "uncle")—refers to the logic by which kin terms are "extended" from primary to more distant relatives (Lounsbury 1965:151; for a critique of extensionism, see, e.g., Read 2007). For any given system, the definitive rules comprise "a minimal set of equivalences that will imply all the others" (Gould 2000:54). Lounsbury specifies three structural equivalence rules for Crow-Omaha: skewing, merging, and half-sibling. The first, skewing, is diagnostic of the type. Lounsbury's equivalence rules have been reduced to elegantly simple algorithms by Gould (2000; for a fuller representation of Gould's system, see Kronenfeld, this volume). Gould introduces a few unconventional symbols, notably for the primary kin types parent and child. Because P (parent) and Ch (child) elide gender distinctions, Gould substitutes two pairs of terms: F (father) and $\overline{F}$ (fatherling, or man's child); and M (mother) and $\overline{M}$ (motherling, or woman's child).

The *Crow skewing rule* (table 5.1) is defined by the equivalences $F\overline{M}$ ↔ F, and reciprocally $M\overline{F}$ ↔ $\overline{F}$ (where ↔ denotes structural equivalence). That is, as a linking term to other relatives, the kin type father's motherling (e.g., in practice, a FZCh) is structurally equivalent to a father. Reciprocally, a mother's fatherling (e.g., MBCh) is equivalent to a fatherling (e.g., ego male's own child, or ego of either sex's BCh). In actual nomenclatures, this equivalence rule produces the following exemplary equations or, in Gould's terms, "concurrences" (marked by the symbol ≈): FZS ≈ F, FZD ≈ FZ, MBS ≈ BS, MBD ≈ BD, and so on (Gould 2000:296–97).

The *Omaha skewing rule* entails opposite equivalences, again reciprocal: $M\overline{F}$ ↔ M, between mother's fatherling (e.g., MBCh) and mother; $F\overline{M}$ ↔ $\overline{M}$, between father's motherling (e.g., FZCh) and motherling (e.g., ego female's own child or ego of either sex's sister's child). In practice, Omaha kin term concurrences include MBS ≈ MB, MBD ≈ MZ,

Table 5.1 Diagnostic Crow-Omaha rules and concurrences

Omaha skewing rule	Crow skewing rule
MF̄ ↔ M reciprocal FM̄ ↔ M̄*	FM̄ ↔ F reciprocal MF̄ ↔ F̄
Exemplary concurrences:	
MBS ≈ MB, MBD ≈ MZ	FZS ≈ F, FZD ≈ FZ
FZCh ≈ ZCh, FZChCh ≈ ZChCh, etc.	MBS ≈ BS, MBD ≈ BD, etc.
Additional concurrences configuring subtypes:	
MF ≈ MB, ♂ZCh ≈ ♂DCh	FZ ≈ FM, ♀BCh ≈ ♀SCh
FZ ≈ eZ, ♀BCh ≈ ♀yB/yZ	MB ≈ eB, ♂ZCh ≈ ♂yB/yZ
	MMB ≈ MB, ♂ZDCh ≈ ♂ZCh
	FMB ≈ FB ≈ F, ♂ZSCh ≈ ♂BCh ≈ ♂Ch

Notations after Gould 2000, with adjustments (♂, ♀, Ch)
*F̄ = "fatherling," or man's child; M̄ = "motherling," or woman's child

FZS ≈ ZS, and FZD ≈ ZD, and so on. As the skewing equations of Crow and Omaha are mirror images (figure 5.1), the systems form a pair: for Crow the structurally "basal sex" of the linkages is female; for Omaha, it is male (Hammel 1965).

Crow-Omaha nomenclatures encompass eight subtypes (table 5.2),[1] each respectively characterized by additional concurrences to the core set (Gould 2000:310–34). Seven derive from Lounsbury's original typology (he shows another, but this is notional and never yet observed), and a (genuine) eighth, the Hopi subtype, Gould dubs "Crow V."

Hopi kin terms (e.g., Lowie 1929a:380–83) show the core Crow concurrences (terms are given as stems without reference or address modifiers):

na (glossed "father" in Hopi English): F ≈ FZS
kya ("aunt"): FZ ≈ FZD
ti ("child"): MBCh ≈ BCh

As Crow V, Hopi has the additional concurrences:

na (as above): FMB ≈ F ≈ FB
ti (as above): ZSCh ≈ Ch ≈ BCh

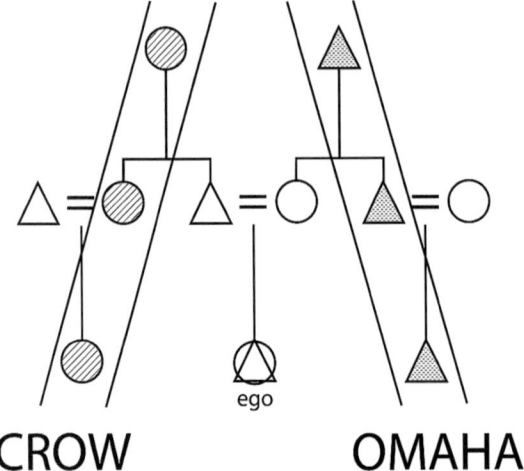

Figure 5.1 Exemplary lineal equations in Crow and Omaha kin terminologies.

taha ("uncle"): MB ≈ MMB
tiw'aya ("nephew/niece"): ZCh ≈ ZDCh

This terminological scheme provides the context within which Hopi social relations, including descent and marriage, play out. Before approaching these, I sketch the historical and theoretical backdrop.

Crow-Omaha Characteristics in North America

Morgan (1871:178–93) first noticed lineal equations in some terminologies of societies in the Plains, Prairies, and Southeast Woodlands (see chapter 1). Further cases were subsequently identified: Tlingit and Haida on the Northwest Coast had Crow skewing (Swanton 1908: 424–25). Some central California nomenclatures included both Omaha- and Crow-type equations (Gifford 1916). All the Western Pueblos (beyond Morgan's [1871:262] own listing of Laguna), were Crow-type, notably Hano, Zuni, and Hopi (Freire-Marreco 1914; Kroeber 1917; Lowie 1929a). With Seminole (Spoehr 1942), western Kaska (Honigmann 1954), and Tonkawa (Johnson 1994)—all Crow—the inven-

Table 5.2 Crow–Omaha subtypes

	MBS≈ MB	MBD≈ MZ	FZCh≈ ZCh	FZChCh≈ ZChCh	MF≈ MB	♂ZCh≈ ♂DCh	FZ≈eZ	♀BCh≈ ♀yB/yZ
						Omaha		
I	x	x	x	x	o	o	o	o
II	x	x	x	x	o	o	x	x
III	x	x	x	x	x	x	o	o
IV	x	x	x	x	x	x	x	x

Examples I Omaha, Miwok
         II Tzotzil
        III Latin, Old English
         IV Wintu

(continued)

Table 5.2 Continued

						Crow						
	FZS≈F	FZD≈ FZ	MBS≈ BS	MBD≈ BD	FZ≈ FM	♀BCh≈ ♀SCh	MB≈eB	♂ZCh≈ ♂yB/yZ	MMB≈ MB	♂ZDCh≈ ♂ZCh	FMB≈ FB≈F	♂ZSCh≈ ♂BCh≈ ♂Ch
I	x	x	x	x	o	o	o	o	o	o	o	o
II	x	x	x	x	o	o	x	x	o	o	o	o
III	x	x	x	x	x	x	o	o	o	o	o	o
IV	x	x	x	x	x	x	x	x	o	o	o	o
V	x	x	x	x	o	o	o	o	x	x	x	x

Examples I Republican Pawnee, Fanti (skewed)
         II Crow
        III Seminole, Trobriand
         IV no examples yet found
          V Hopi

After Gould 2000

tory of Crow and Omaha cases in North America was effectively completed.

Continental distribution is uneven (figure 5.2, table 5.3). Clusters tend to follow linguistic and culture-historical associations and correlate with geographical regions. Omaha systems occur in the southern Great Lakes, Prairie-Plains, and central California. With marginal exceptions (Crow proper, Tonkawa, Kaska), Crow systems occur only in the Southeast Woodlands, Prairie-Plains, Pueblo Southwest, central California, and the northern Northwest Coast. Both systems generally coincide with higher population densities (see Ubelaker 2006) associated with sedentism and/or horticultural adaptation. With a High Plains adaptation to bison-nomadism, the Crow proper exception is explicable on historical grounds (e.g., Lowie 1912): acquisition of horses in the eighteenth century promoted nomadism and demoted horticulture, a transition that accompanied Crow migration from the upper Missouri Valley. Significantly, Crow-Omaha clusters in the Eastern Woodlands and Puebloan Southwest also correlate with regions of greatest late pre-Columbian sociopolitical complexity (see Ensor 2002).

Central Valley California and the northern Northwest Coast, although lacking horticultural adaptation, coincide with high precolonial population density and abundant resources. Haida and Tlingit typify the intensive Northwest Coast adaptation to anadromous fish (salmon, etc.), associated with sedentism and sociopolitical stratification. They are also immediate neighbors to and past competitors with societies (Kwakwa̱ka'wakw, Tsimshian, Coast Salish) foundational to Lévi-Strauss's (e.g., 1982) conception of *sociétés à maison*, "house societies." Just like Crow-Omaha kinship systems (see later discussion), house societies fall midway between elementary and complex structures: "they constitute a hybrid, transitional form between kin-based and class-based social orders" (Carsten and Hugh-Jones 1995:10).

From these broad associations—more intensive adaptation, sedentism, higher population density, incipient or developed social hierarchy, and house societies—North American Crow-Omaha systems occupy the middle range on a continuum of societal complexity (of the band-tribe-chiefdom-state sort). Consonant with the importance of circumscription (social, geographic, or both) for the origin of the state (Carneiro 1970), it is striking that North American Crow-Omaha systems

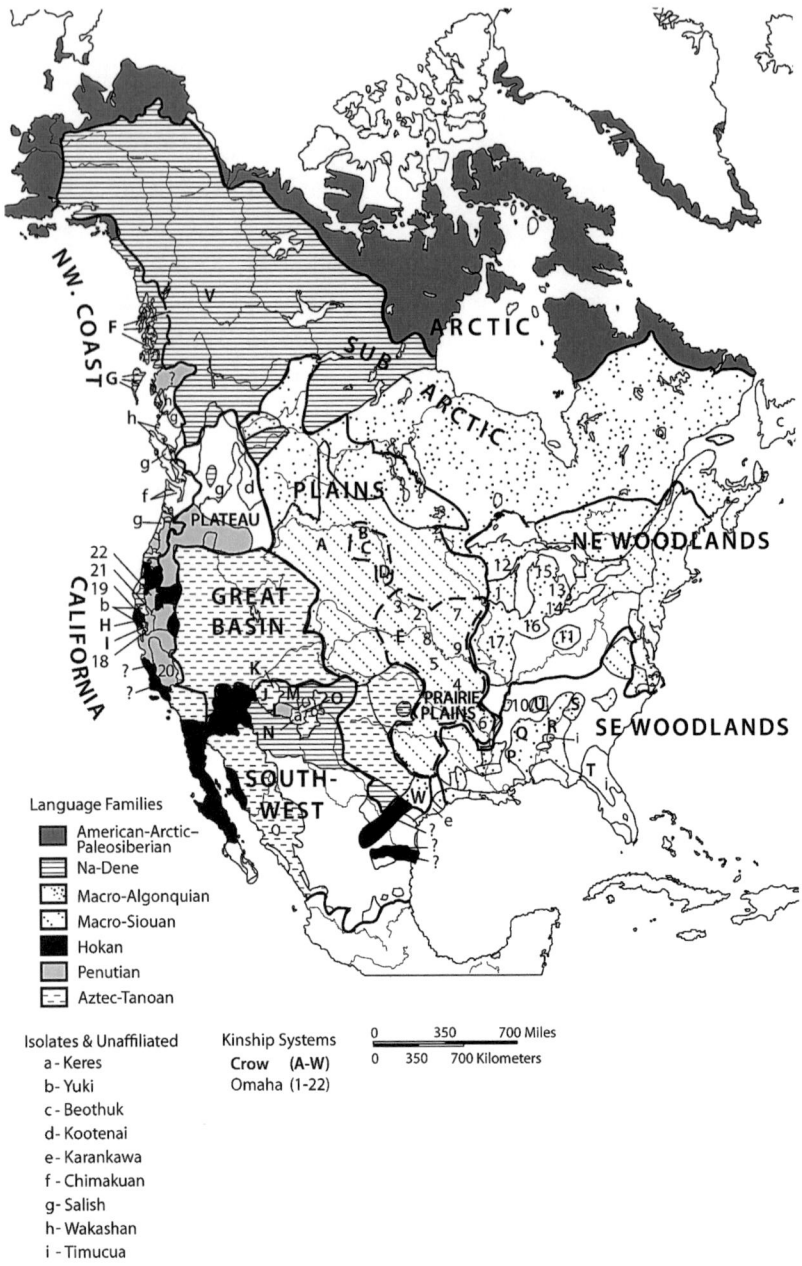

Figure 5.2 Societies with Crow and Omaha terminologies in Native North America (base map represents the "Consensus Classification" of languages, 1964 [Foster 1997:69]; for subsequent changes, see Goddard [1997]). *Source for basemap:* Ives Goddard, ed., *Handbook of North American Indians,* vol. 17, *Languages* (Washington, DC: Smithsonian Institution, 1997). Reprinted by permission of the National Museum of Natural History.

Table 5.3 Societies with Crow and Omaha terminologies in Native North America

	Omaha					Crow		
	Society	Language	Language Family		Society	Language	Language Family
1	Winnebago	Winnebago	Siouan-Catawba	A	Crow	Crow	Siouan-Catawba
2	Omaha Thegiha	Omaha	Siouan-Catawba	B	Hidatsa	Hidatsa	Siouan-Catawba
3	Ponca	Ponca	Siouan-Catawba	C	Mandan	Mandan	Siouan-Catawba
4	Osage	Osage	Siouan-Catawba	D	Arikara	Arikara	Caddoan
5	Kansa	Kansa	Siouan-Catawba	E	Pawnee	Pawnee	Caddoan
6	Quapaw	Quapaw	Siouan-Catawba	F	Tlingit	Tlingit	Nadene
7	Iowa Tciwere	Iowa	Siouan-Catawba	G	Haida	Haida	isolate
8	Oto	Oto	Siouan-Catawba	H	S Pomo	S Pomo	Pomoan
9	Missouri	Missouri	Siouan-Catawba	I	Wappo	Wappo	Yukian
10	Yuchi*	Yuchi	isolate	J	Hopi	Hopi	Uto-Aztecan
11	Shawnee	Shawnee	C. Algonquian	K	Hano	Tewa	Kiowa-Tanoan
12	Menominee	Menominee	C. Algonquian	L	Zuni	Zuni	isolate
13	Sauk and Fox	Sauk/Fox	C. Algonquian	M	Laguna	W Keresan	Keresan
14	Kickapoo	Kickapoo	C. Algonquian	N	Acoma	W Keresan	Keresan
15	Potawotamie	Potawotamie	C. Algonquian	O	Zia	E Keresan	Keresan

(*continued*)

Table 5.3 Continued

	Omaha				Crow	
Society	Language	Language Family		Society	Language	Language Family
16 Miami Miami	Miami	C. Algonquian	P	Choctaw	Choctaw	Muskogean
17 Peoria	Illinois	C. Algonquian	Q	Chickasaw	Chickasaw	Muskogean
17 Kaskaskia	Illinois	C. Algonquian	R	Creek	Creek	Muskogean
16 Piankashaw	Miami	C. Algonquian	S	Cherokee	Cherokee	Iroquoian
16 Wea	Miami	C. Algonquian	T	Timucua	Timucua	Timucuan
18 Miwok	Miwokan	Utian	U	Yuchi*	Yuchi	isolate
19 N Pomo	NE Pomo	Pomoan	V	Kaska	Kaska	Nadene
19 E Pomo	E Pomo	Pomoan	W	Tonkawa	Tonkawa	isolate
20 S Valley Yokuts	Valley Yokuts	Yokutsan				
21 Wintu-Nomlaki	Wintu-Nomlaki	Wintuan				
21 Patwin	Patwin	Wintuan				
22 Wintu	Wintu-Nomlaki	Wintuan				

After Lesser 1929, Murdock 1967

*Yuchi is represented as having shifted from a Crow to an Omaha type, under the influence of Algonquian-speaking neighbors with Omaha kin terms (e.g., Eggan 1937) typically occur proximate to major linguistic and/or physiographic boundaries.

Geographically, there are additional features of interest. Trautmann and Barnes (1998) observed that among Central Algonquians in eastern North America, terminological types follow a vector from north to south across the Sub-Arctic/Woodlands boundary. Dravidian systems (their "Type A") occur among the northernmost groups (e.g., Naskapi, Swampy Cree); adjacent to the south, Iroquois systems (their "Type B") take over (e.g., Eastern Ojibwa, Ottawa); and farther south these are replaced by Omaha systems (e.g., Fox, Illinois). The differentiation reflects patterns of demographic increase and intensification of production. Trautmann and Barnes (1998:55) argue that the progressive transformation of crossness—Dravidian → Iroquois → Crow-Omaha—accompanies an "opening out" of affinal ties, that is, expanding networks of potential alliances. This view accords with Lévi-Strauss's important thesis (1966, 1969) that Crow-Omaha systems *disperse affinal alliances*, a theme taken up especially by McKinley (1971a, 1971b) and Héritier (e.g., 1981).

Crossness in terminologies, Viveiros de Castro (1998:354) suggests, is invariably associated with marriage exchange. In the transformation of crossness Dravidian → Iroquois → Crow-Omaha, there is a progressive movement away from structural dualism toward pluralism in marriage rules. However, geographic proximity of Crow-Omaha to Iroquois systems in North America is striking, and, as the present volume shows, similar patterns occur in Africa, Amazonia, and Australia (see chapters 9, 10, and 12, and for West Africa, see Fardon 1993). Although somewhat submerged, this same juxtaposition has been shown to occur among Pueblo Indian societies, some of which also include Omaha-patrilineal elements (Fox 1967, 1972). I return to this issue later.

Semi-Complex Alliance

By insisting that they correlate with distinctive marriage practices, Lévi-Strauss (e.g., 1966, 1969) resituated Crow-Omaha kinship systems as "semi-complex" alliance structures. Semi-complex alliance combines elementary and complex rules, prohibiting marriage (as in a complex system) with a segment of society (much more substantially than for complex systems) but "prescribing" it (as in an elementary system) from among the remaining segments. In devising the semi-complex category, Lévi-Strauss (1966:18, 1969:xl) was expressly influenced by Hopi ethnology. Hopi society, long the exemplar of Western Pueblo systems, comprises multiple named matrilineal descent groups, including "clans" grouped into clan-sets or "phratries." At Third Mesa there are approximately twenty-eight clans in nine clan-sets (table 5.4). According to

Table 5.4 Orayvi clans and clan-sets, ca. 1900

Set	*ngyam* ("clan")	Trans.	Set	*ngyam* ("clan")	Trans.
I	*Tap-*	Rabbit	VI	*Mas-*	Maasaw
	Katsin-	Katsina		*Kookop-*	"Fire"
	Kyar-	Parrot		*Hoo-*	Cedar
	Angwus-	Crow/Raven		*Lee-*	Millet
				Is-	Coyote
II	*Hon-*	Bear		*Paa'is-*	Desert Fox
	Kookyangw-	Spider			
			VII	*Honan-*	Badger
III	*Tuwa-*	Sand		*Polii-*	Butterfly
	Tsu'-	Snake			
	Kuukuts-	Lizard	VIII	*Piikyas-*	Young Corn
				Patki-	"Water"
IV	*Tawa-*	Sun		*Siva'p-*	Rabbitbrush
	Kwaa-	Eagle			
			IX	*Kyel-*	Sparrowhawk
V	*Tep-*	Greasewood		*Atok-*	Crane
	Paaqap-	Reed		*Pat-*	Squash
	Awat-	Bow			

(Modified from Titiev 1944: 52)

Eggan (1950:121), "marriage is not permitted, in Hopi theory, within one's own, one's father's, or one's mother's father's phratry," a position that Lévi-Strauss explicitly followed. One third of society (approximately nine clans in three sets) is thus off-limits, leaving two-thirds (eighteen clans in six sets) among whom to seek marriage partners. Moreover, Eggan (1964:176) reported, "the choice of a marriage partner is apparently left to chance, beyond the restrictions of clan and phratry exogamy." Eggan's two statements provide the blueprint for Lévi-Strauss's notion of semi-complex alliance as an elementary/complex hybrid.

In contrast to elementary systems, semi-complex marriage proscriptions and prescriptions are constantly shifting. Each new marriage produces a new configuration of kin and affines, creating new prohibitions for the next generation. For example, according to Eggan's reported Hopi rules, if ego male is Bear clan (set II), his father is Snake (set III), and mother's father is Sun (set IV), all three sets are off-limits to him. If he marries, say, a woman of the Badger clan (set VII) whose father is Parrot (set I), marriage prohibitions for their children shift: sets IV and III (the children's FMF's and FF's sets, respectively) drop out of the prohibitions, but sets VII and I join set II to form a newly prohibited class. Moreover, if the first ego's brother marries a woman of the Bow clan (set V) whose father is Sparrowhawk (set IX), *their* children have a different class of prohibitions accordingly. In other words, prohibitions affecting siblings identically metamorphose differentially depending on whom each sibling marries. This is what Lévi-Strauss means by the "aleatory" aspect of alliances in semi-complex systems and why he concluded that their marriage permutations were intractable to structural analysis. With Hopi marriage possibilities approaching 300 million variants, semi-complex marriage patterns were only calculable mathematically and were probabilistic rather than predictable (Lévi-Strauss 1969:xl).

Semi-complex/Crow-Omaha systems were further defined by Lévi-Strauss (1966:18) by opposing them to asymmetric-prescriptive systems, his "fish vs. whales" contrast. Asymmetric-prescriptive systems produce regular, repeating cycles of exchange (A → B → C → A), representing a simple expansion of binary symmetrical exchange. Semi-complex systems, on the other hand, are *polynomial*, with "many more dimensions" (Lévi-Strauss 1966:18–20). An important additional feature of this distinction is highlighted by Héritier (1981:126). In asymmetric-prescriptive systems, spouses of one gender (for simplicity, let's say wives) always marry in the same direction (a woman from group A must marry a man from group B, a woman from group B must marry a man from group C, etc.): the "wife-giver/wife-receiver" relationship between two adjacent groups in the series cannot be reversed. In contrast, semi-complex systems allow *both* sexes to be transacted among giver and receiver groups (Héritier 1981:127). Crow-Omaha marriage patterns thus operate in "a state of permanent turbulence which is quite the reverse of that regularity of functioning and periodicity of returns which conform with the ideal model of an asymmetric marriage system" (Lévi-Strauss 1966:19).

The challenge of semi-complex alliance structures was taken up by Héritier, especially vis-à-vis the Samo of Burkina Faso. Within nomenclature of Omaha-type (though see chapter 4), Samo marriage rules prohibit reproduction of alliances from one generation to the next but ensure their resumption after four generations (Héritier 1981). Samo marriage is locally endogamous and tends to occur among the nearest nonprohibited cognatic relatives, producing a closed exchange structure similar in this regard to elementary systems (Tjon Sie Fat 1998a: 262). Within a descent system that is patrilineal or "agnatic," cognatic relatives (i.e., kin on both sides) are *prohibited* from marrying within a certain genealogical distance; beyond that, however, nonagnates (among these cognatic relatives) are *preferred* partners. Samo filiation progressively extrudes peripheral nonagnates (i.e., matrilineal or matrilateral relatives) from status as "kin," whereas marriage prescriptions channel them toward a status as preferred spouses. This corroborates Lévi-Strauss's (1969:xxxix) conception that Crow-Omaha systems seek to turn "kin into affines," and echoes McKinley (1971a, 1971b) that Crow-Omaha terminologies embody contradictory imperatives to retain existing alliances but also to establish new ones. The cause of Crow-Omaha terminology, Héritier (1981:127) concludes, lies in a particular conjuncture of descent and marriage customs that include "a closed, regular alliance structure of a specific type" (Tjon Sie Fat 1998a: 262). Héritier (1981:128) proposes that this hypothesis be tested against other Crow-Omaha cases. Barnes (chapter 4) argues against the similarity of Samo and Omaha proper marriage patterns. What may we learn from the case of the Pueblos?

Duality and Plurality in Pueblo Social Structures

Pueblo social structures range from the plural matriclan system of the Hopis in the west to the dual (agamous) patrimoieties (Winter and Summer) of the Tewas in the east. Eastern dual organization takes various forms, both kin-based and non–kin-based (Fox 1972:74–76). Nomenclatures vary from "classical Crow" in the west to bilateral—with Iroquois, Omaha, and Cheyenne elements—in the east (Eggan 1950; Fox 1967, 1972; Murdock 1949). There are Crow features in the eastern Pueblos also, but matrilineal descent groups decrease in strength from west to east. Among the Rio Grande Keresans (e.g., Cochiti), matrilineal clans are crosscut by patrilineal moieties (Turquoise and Squash). Matriliny fades out altogether among the Tewas, although Tewa personal names are similar to those associated with matriclans in other Pueblos. Eggan (1950) argued that the underlying system among all the Pueblos (figure 5.3) was Crow-matrilineal, a system least changed in modern times among the Hopi. Eastern Pueblo societies, Eggan maintained, had progressively acculturated to European kinship norms from the stronger effects of Spanish hegemony.

Fox (1967) contested this view and suggested Keresan social structure represented a double-descent form growing out of an Iroquois system and even a Dravidian proto-form of two-line prescriptive cross-cousin marriage. Fox showed Keresan kin term usage included both Crow and Cheyenne (Generational) forms in alternative contexts. In this regard, his argument supports Kronenfeld's position (chapter 8) that Crow-Omaha terminology is an optative overlay (I do not think the same is true, however, for the Hopi—see later discussion). Instead of *declining* historically from a Crow type, Fox posited that Keresan social organization was *incipiently* Crow-matrilineal, crosscut by patrimoieties that were once exogamous. Moreover, Fox suggested this pattern of intersecting descent lines and a symmetric rule of exchange could be generalized for all Crow systems: "Many so-called Crow systems show up with patrilineal features that are hard to explain away by acculturation, and also they often feature preferential marriage of an

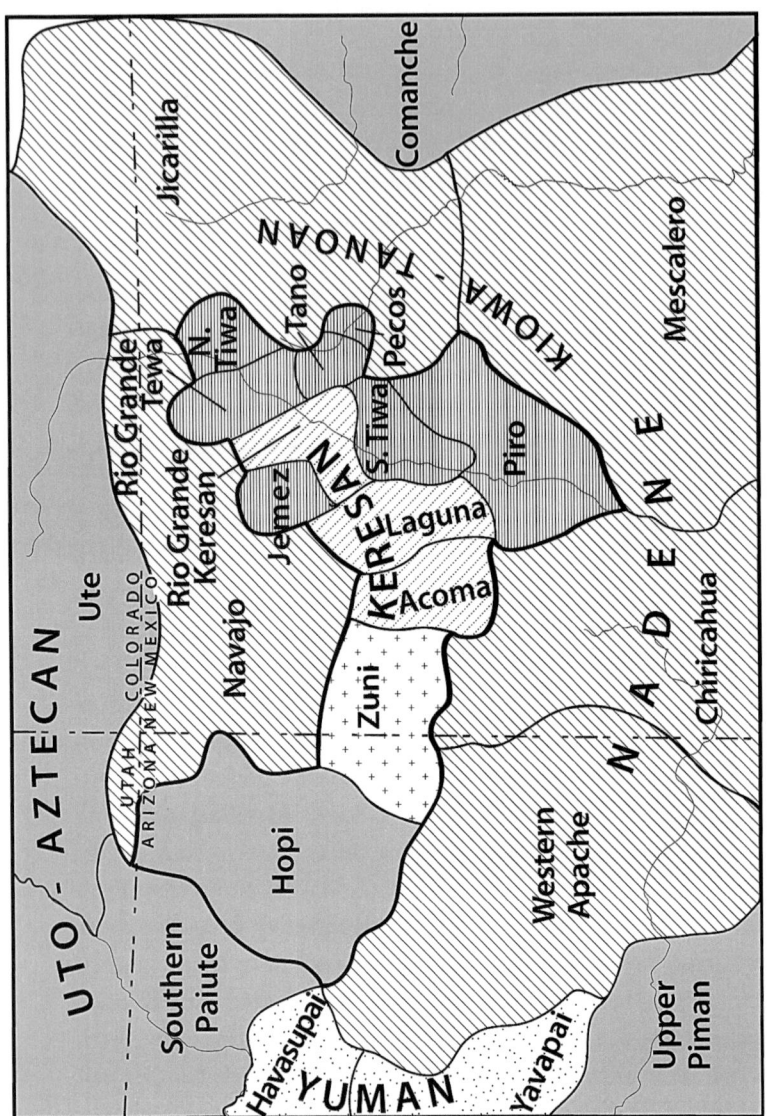

Figure 5.3 Pueblo societies and languages. Based on section of map, "Native Languages and Language Families of North America compiled by Ives Goddard" (Goddard 1997: in pocket). Used by permission of the National Museum of Natural History.

elementary type, such as marriage with a woman of the mother's father's clan (MFZDD), the father's father's clan (FFZDD) or both. . . . The Cochiti, for example, favor MFZDD" (Fox 1972:74).

Fox's view thus converges with Héritier's that Crow-Omaha rules progressively exclude more distant cognatic relatives from kin group membership, turning them into preferred affines. Fox (1972, 1994) suggests Pueblo social structures are not so mutually divergent after all, with alternately incipient or more developed Crow features on an underlying Iroquois/Dravidian base and intersecting Crow-matrilineal and Omaha-patrilineal elements. This perspective also resonates with variations among the Amazonian Gê (chapter 10). But just like Lévi-Strauss, Fox (1967, 1972) follows Eggan in representing Hopi as the extreme Crow archetype for the Pueblos, characterized by prohibitions on marriage within three ascendant lines (M, F, and MF).

Hopi Descent and Alliance

Hopi kinship thus figures prominently in several theoretical contexts: (1) the comparative conception of Crow terminologies (e.g., Lowie 1929a); (2) the origins of "semi-complex alliance"; (3) as one end of a west–east continuum among Pueblo social systems, which represents (4) either a Crow-matrilineal Pueblo prototype, departures from which owe to historical erosion (Eggan 1950), or the developmental transformation of an underlying Dravidian system still putatively discernible among Rio Grande Keresans (Fox 1967). Alliance features are actively or passively present in all of these notions, none of which, however, has ever been examined in the light of actual Hopi marriage *practices*.

Like the other Pueblos, Hopis deemphasize genealogy beyond two or three generations (see Titiev 1944), marking an obvious difference with the Samo and diminishing the value of the genealogical grid for modeling Hopi alliance. Although Hopis recognize "blood kin" based on primary household ties (Lowie 1929a), their kin term usages are calculated via clan relationships. A Third Mesa Hopi visiting First Mesa, for example, learns the appropriate kin terms for her hosts by inquiring into their clans (not identical but similar to those at Third Mesa) and mapping these onto her own framework of matrilineal and patrilateral relationship terms. One's matriclan provides the core set of relatives for property ownership (especially of a ritual nature), inheritance, and resource rights. But patrilateral ties in the cognatic household transect matrilineal allegiances and are graphically instantiated on ceremonial occasions. The most prominent is the *kya-mööyi* tie between a male and his father's female line, and between a female and her (clan) brothers' sons. A life-long sexual-joking relationship, the "aunt"–"nephew" tie is especially manifest in birth and marriage rites and both "social" and religious ceremonies. In naming practices, the skewed "aunt" (*kya*) is important for both male and female niblings ("nephews" and "nieces"). Names are conferred by patrilateral (or fictive-patrilateral) relatives, never by one's own clan. Names are poetic compositions by the name-giver: for example, Kyarwisiwma (a male name), referring to a line of scarlet macaws, or Masayesnöm (a female name), referring to an eagle alighting. Names reflect an event or image belonging to the totemic sphere of the name-giver (Whiteley 1992). Thus, although matriliny confers one's primary social identity, patrilateral ties are inscribed onto the subject via the names he or she bears.

Reciprocal exchange structures align female clan relatives vis-à-vis women of clans linked to them affinally via their clan brothers' marriages. Marriage rituals feature a mock attack on the groom's house by his female patrikin (his *kya'am*), who protest the bride's usurpation of their *mööyi* ("nephew") and mark this with a mud fight. Hopi reflexive consciousness of such structural principles was foregrounded in a clown ceremony I witnessed at Hotvela's main plaza in the early 1980s. The clowns, metacultural commentators par excellence, decided to stage a wedding (with mixed Hopi and Anglo elements) between a young boy and his much older aunt. While the couple made their way up a purported "aisle" escorted by (male) clown "bridesmaids," the plaza was suddenly invaded by the groom's many other clan-aunts wielding huge pails of wet mud. In carnivalesque bedlam, they cast the mud liberally on the groom's clanswomen (and anyone else within range), who responded in kind. The parody revealed affinity as structurally both potent and dangerous: an unstable agent that dissolves and crystallizes social bonds at the same time.

Insofar as ego's primary kin are matrilineal, a father and his matrikin (i.e., the very relatives subjected to terminological skewing) in a sense *remain affines*, especially in the core *kya-mööyi* dialectic. Neither in my own experience at Hopi, nor in that reported by Lowie (1929a) or Titiev (1944), does this kinship dialectic appear as optative. The hinge on which Hopi social structure articulates, the *kya-mööyi* pair, is an entrenched (Crow) feature of Hopi roles and relationships. Indeed, Crow skewing is highlighted and extended in the creation of fictive-patrilateral ties, via ritual initiations by a ceremonial "godfather" and his clanswomen—more *kya'am*—who are chosen from a different clan than one's own or one's father's. These ties add an extra dimension of "affinity" that interplays with marriage alliances: *ritual* affines/patrikin serve as one ground from which *marital* affines may be generated.

Even today Hopi remains a predominantly endogamous society and continues to practice matriclan and clan-set exogamy. Marriage is monogamous, but unions are often brittle and easily broken by either partner. There are only two affine terms proper, both generic, transgenerational, and used by speakers of both sexes: *mö'wi* ("woman married into my clan set") and *mö'önangw* ("man married into my clan set"). But whom do Hopis marry in practice?

Hopi-Tewas on First Mesa informed Barbara Freire-Marreco (1914) that cross-cousin marriage (which they did not practice themselves) was widespread among their Hopi neighbors. From fieldwork at First and Second Mesas, Lowie (1929a) confirmed this, but noted it occurred between more distant classificatory rather than close cross-cousins. My own fieldwork agrees: skewed cross-relatives (*kya-mööyi* and *ti-na*) form a prohibited class of unions ideologically, but in reality only actual FZD-MBS or MFZDD-MMBDS unions are proscribed. In other words, those truly prohibited (beyond my own clan-set) are just relatives attached by birth to my father's natal household and my mother's father's natal household. Conventional genealogical amnesia underwrites the status of more distant cross-kin as marriageable, echoing the transition from proscribed to preferred, as one moves outward from the cognatic house, noted by Héritier for the Samo. Yet these perspectives are clearly at odds with the standard view of Hopi marriage proscriptions.

Titiev (1938) hypothesized that the joking relationship of skewed cross-kin (*kya-mööyi*) was a survival from an older condition of *prescriptive* patrilateral cross-cousin marriage, which somehow evolved into its opposite, proscribed form. Eggan (1950:121) agreed and dismissed Freire-Marreco's report of contemporary conditions as simply "erroneous." Yet this seems peculiar: how or why would Hopi-Tewas, who had by this point lived cheek by jowl with First Mesa Hopis for 200 years and married not just a few of them, be so ethnogaphically mistaken?

Marriage Alliance at Orayvi: Dispersal and Restriction

Hopi marriages at Orayvi on Third Mesa up to 1906 (see Whiteley 2008) show alliances interweaving among the nine exogamous clan-sets. Simultaneously, however, there is disproportionate serial repetition of marriages between pairs of clan-sets. As an example, consider marriages between set II (comprising two clans, Bear and Spider) and set VI (comprising six clans, *Maasaw*, *Kookop*, Coyote, Desert Fox, Cedar, and Millet).

Figure 5.4 shows four generations of Orayvi Bear clan marriages. The total range includes all clan-sets except set IX, the smallest demographically. But alliances with set VI are prominent and persistent. In some instances where marriages per se are not known, an alliance is suggested by the names borne by its offspring, in keeping with the patrilateral naming conventions already discussed. Although men's names usually change on initiation, women often retain names conferred at birth (which thus index their paternal clan relatives).

In *Generation 1*, Tawanömqa (born ca. 1800) and her (unnamed) sister are the origin for all others recorded for this clan:

- Tawanömqa was married to Kuyngwu (Desert Fox, set VI).
- Tawanömqa's unnamed sister's marriage was not remembered, but she too may have been married to set VI, based on a daughter's name, Tuvewunqa (approximately, "pinyon pine standing woman"). *Tuve*, pinyon pine, belongs totemically to set VI; unless she received this name later in life, it likely points to her father's clan-set.

In *Generation 2*, two of Tawanömqa's four children married set VI:

- Loololma (Orayvi's Kikmongwi, village chief) married his *kya* ("FZ"), Nakwavenqa (*Maasaw* clan).
- Humiwunsi married her *na* ("F"), Tangaqnömtiwa (*Maasaw* clan, Nakwavenqa's MZS).

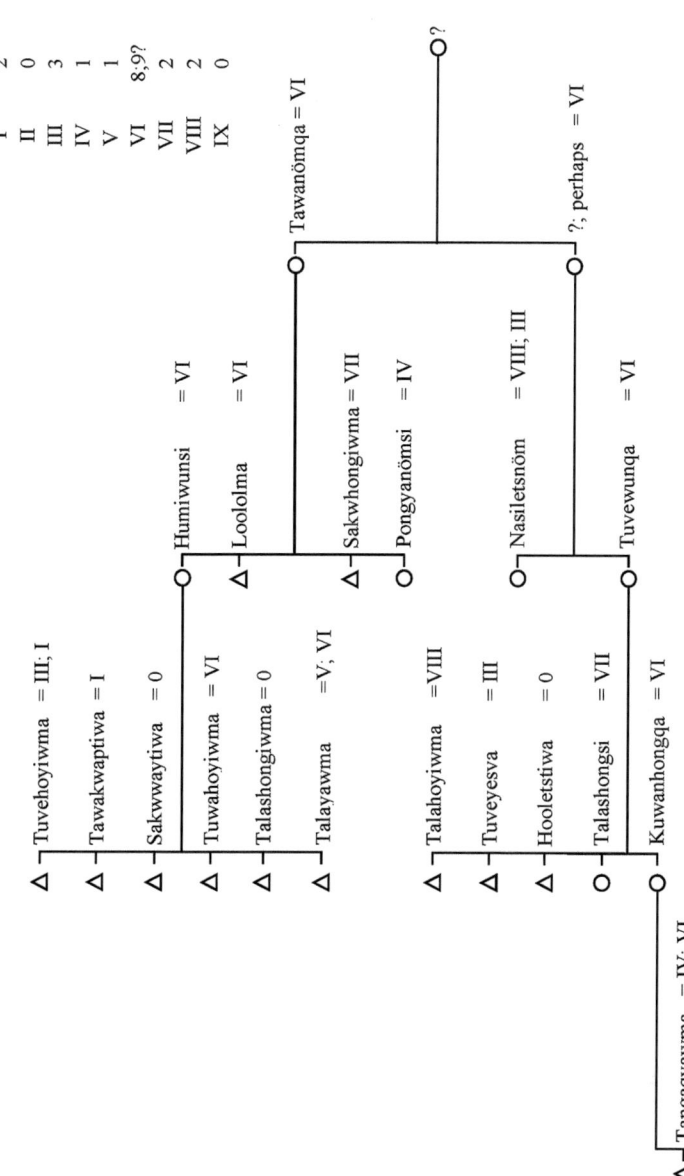

Figure 5.4 Orayvi Bear clan marriages, ca. 1830–1900

Within set VI, Desert Fox and *Maasaw* are not especially close clans (unlike *Maasaw* and *Kookop*, or Coyote and Desert Fox), so although alliance was reproduced down consecutive generations, in the shift from Desert Fox to *Maasaw* it was neither with the same "lineage" nor with a close clan within the total set. Tawanömqa's other two children, Sakwhongiwma and Pongyanömsi, married into sets VII (Badger) and IV (Sun), respectively. Thus, two of her four children married classificatory patrilateral (skewed) cross-cousins, the other two did not.

In this same generation, Tawanömqa's unnamed sister had two children (both female), Nasiletsnöm and Tuvewunqa. Nasiletsnöm married twice, first to a *Patki* man (set VIII), and then to a Snake man (set III). However:

- Tuvewunqa married a *Maasaw* man.

If Tuvewunqa's father was in fact set VI, as suggested, her own marriage reproduced the alliance.

Of Generation 2's four women, only Humiwunsi and Tuvewunqa had children. In *Generation 3*, two of Humiwunsi's six children (all male) never married, two married other sets, but two indeed married into set VI:

- Tuwahoyiwma married a Coyote woman.
- Talayawma, after a first marriage to set V, remarried to Masahongsi (*Maasaw*).

The latter marriage was thus into Talayawma's own father's clan, although the genealogical tie (known in this case) was not that close: Masahongsi was Talayawma's FMMZDDD. Thus, of the four children of Humiwunsi who ever married, two renewed the alliance with set VI via *kya-mööyi* ("FZ" = "BS") marriages, marking a third consecutive generation of quasi-restricted exchange.

Generation 2's Tuvewunqa had three sons and two daughters: one son never married, the other two married women of other sets. As to her daughters, however:

- Kuwanhongqa married a Coyote man.
- Talashongsi married a Badger man (set VII), whose father was Desert Fox.

The II–VI alliance was thus renewed by Tuvewunqa's first daughter and, if considered from the perspective of the "house" (including cognatic relatives lying outside the formal prohibitions—see Whiteley 2008), for her second as well.

In *Generation 4*, one marriage shortly after Orayvi fissioned in 1906 is notable:

- Tangaqyawma first married Sand (set IV), but shortly (before 1912) remarried to a woman of the Desert Fox clan.

With the latter marriage—for a man and woman who, as members of the "hostile" faction, never attended school, probably spoke no English, and had minimal involvement in the external economy—the Bear clan's serial alliances with set VI continued into every consecutive generation known in nineteenth- and early twentieth-century Orayvi.

For Bear's clan-set mate, Spider, the pattern is similar (figure 5.5). The total range of Spider marriages is again with all clan-sets but one (as for Bear, set IX). But marriages with set VI are disproportionate, occurring over at least three generations and possibly four (names of all three children of Qömangaynöm [Generation 1] derive from set VI, suggesting their father was of this set).

These actual Hopi marriage practices show both restriction and dispersion of alliances at the same time, according well with McKinley's (1971a) explanation of Crow-Omaha systems as motivated by contradictory imperatives to both retain existing alliances and add new ones. Some children in each generation reproduce their parents' alliance, though almost always with more distant classificatory patrikin. Others marry outside their father's sets. The conclusion seems indefeasible: there is an unstated preference to marry with an ideologically prohibited class—that marked by the skewed "cross-cousin" term—although only its more distant representatives. Héritier's thesis that Crow-Omaha marriages recycle more peripheral cognatic kin into affines is thus confirmed, albeit within a quite different cultural frame. Hopi cross-cousin marriage submerges genealogy and instead of distance in time (the Samo's four generations) operates via distance in social space (nonproximate members of the same paternal clan or of another clan within the set). I have focused here on patrilateral alliances, but the Orayvi data (Whiteley 2008) indicate that marriages with MF's sets were equally

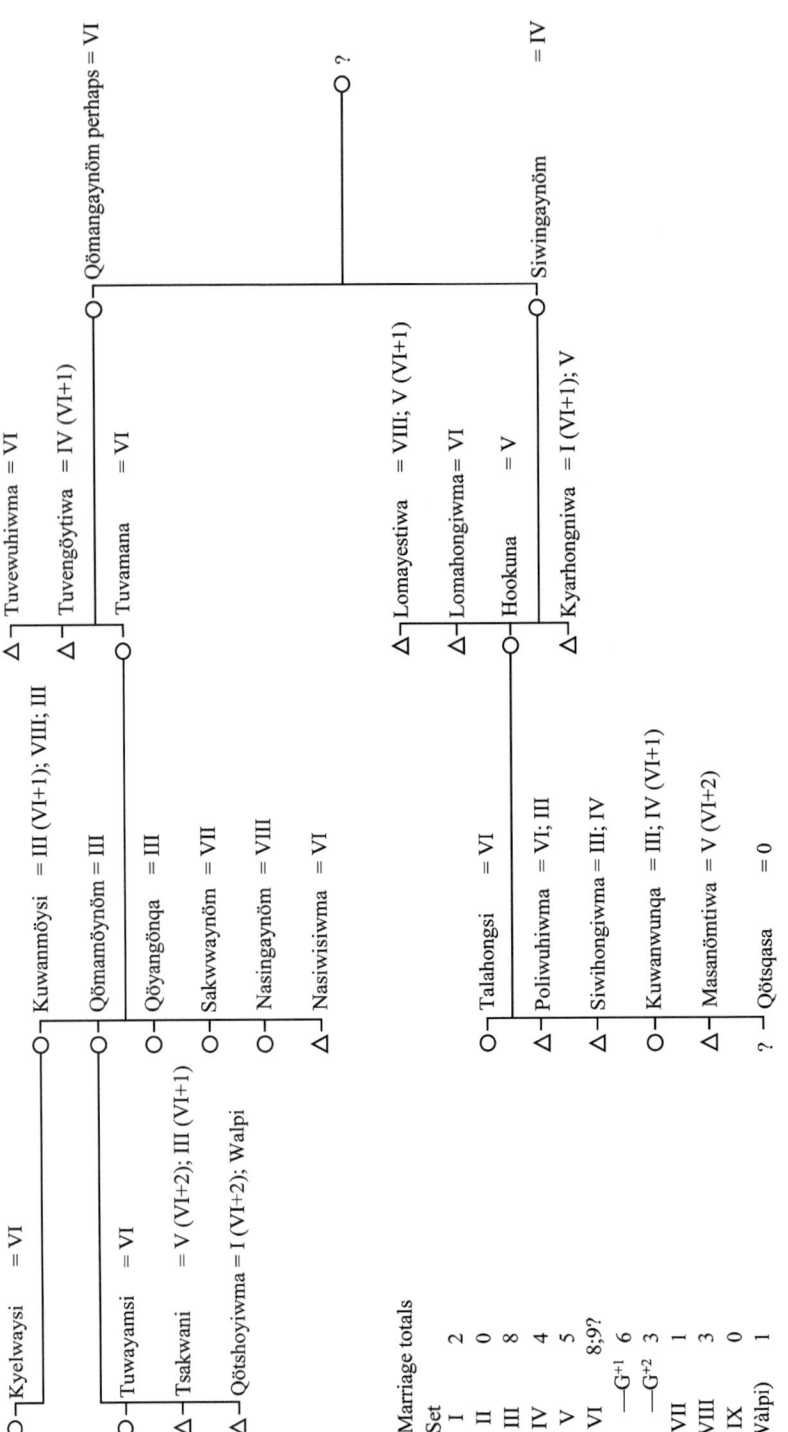

Figure 5.5 Orayvi Spider clan marriages, ca. 1830–1930

common, in this regard echoing Fox's (1972, 1994) demonstration of Cochiti marriage preferences with MF's line. Such marriage preferences suggest that the ostensible differences between western and eastern Pueblo social structures, as respectively plural and dual, if seen through the prism of alliance (*pace* Eggan 1964), are less than imagined. Semi-complex alliance at Hopi includes a form of regular restricted (dual) exchange as well as polynomial alliances dispersed in more generalized exchange.

Conclusion

Crow-Omaha systems in North America coincide with forms of environmental adaptation, ethnolinguistic distribution and/or spread, and increased population density. These patterns in turn appear to correlate both inter- and intraregionally with increased sociocultural complexity over systems with Dravidian or Iroquois crossness. Insofar as Crow-Omaha systems disperse affinal alliances, this may have direct implications for sociopolitical formations as well. But the conjoint tendency to preserve and disperse alliances argued for semi-complex structures elsewhere is clearly present in the Hopi case also. In this Crow instance at least, the nomenclature appears "indissociable" (in Lévi-Strauss's terms) from marriage alliance. Lévi-Strauss's notion of semi-complex alliance, as mediated by McKinley and modified by Héritier, is confirmed as analytically valuable (*pace* Parkin 1997:109–17).

Regarding fishes and whales, the distinction semi-complex versus asymmetric-prescriptive, it is surely not insignificant that in North America there are no known instances of the latter, with the arguable exception of the Miwok (Forth 2008; Needham 1962). Crow-Omaha systems are typically close by Iroquois systems, which in turn are the nearest neighbors to Dravidian cases (e.g., for central Algonquians). In North America, the most obvious place to look for systemic transformations is between Iroquois and Crow-Omaha and between Dravidian and Iroquois, as suggested by Trautmann and Barnes (1998; see also Godelier 2011:507). Conversely, asymmetric-prescriptive systems in South Asia are found in proximity to Dravidian, whereas systems with Iroquois crossness are virtually absent. Such regional patterns may give an important clue to structural relationships among the four types and alternative transformation trajectories: Dravidian → Iroquois and Iroquois → Crow-Omaha in North America (the Trautmann-Barnes hypothesis), and Dravidian → asymmetric-prescriptive in South Asia (see also chapter 2, and Kryukov 1998). In North America, the loosening of a two-line exchange system (with a shift from Type A to Type B crossness) seems a precondition for the emergence of Crow-Omaha/semi-complex alliance, but the Hopi case shows that some "prescriptive" exchange persists in Crow-Omaha formations.

Pueblo social structures emerge as more similar to each other than is generally allowed, as exemplars of "a closed, regular alliance structure of a specific type" (Tjon Sie Fat 1998a:262). Marriage prohibitions for key descent lines fade out beyond a close range of cognatic kin, and more distant relatives of supposedly prohibited classes make a preferred category of spouses. In the Hopi case, one's father and his clan-set remain, as it were, affines, a condition marked by the skewed crossness terms. These terms also express affinity as a renewable value in the evident marriage preferences they connote. Crow skewing appears as the key articulating principle of Hopi social structure, proceeding from the conjuncture of matrilineal descent with patrilateral alliance. I find no evidence of an alternative unskewed system for Hopi (as Kronenfeld [e.g., chapter 8] argues for other Crow-Omaha cases), nor, therefore, that Crow skewing is an optative overlay. Hopi Crow nomenclature and semi-complex alliance reflect the co-presence of restricted and generalized exchange principles. On this combination may rest the principal structural advantage of Crow-Omaha systems: the simultaneous maintenance and flexible enhancement, under certain conditions of circumscription and adaptation, of alliance networks, those engines of emergent polity.

6

Phylogenetic Analysis of Sociocultural Data

Identifying Transformation Vectors for Kinship Systems

Ward C. Wheeler, Peter M. Whiteley, and Theodore Powers

The use of trees as metaphor to describe the historical kinship of creatures has a long history in biology. Today, we tend to look to the "I think" illustration of Darwin (1859) and the explicit phylogenetic tree of Haeckel (1866) as origins, but implicit tree thinking extends back at least an additional 2,000 years to natural philosophers such as Theophrastus (Nelson and Platnick 1981). The basic idea of the tree representation is to both model the evolutionary process of diversification from root to tip and represent sets of related taxa as branches of the tree. The narrative was that some ur-creature or overall common ancestor was at the root of the tree, which grew and subsequently split into branches and sub-branches as time progressed. Any one time would be a horizontal slice through the tree, with current time at the tips and current taxa the leaves. The goal of systematic biology is to reconstruct the entirety of the tree when only given the leaves.[1]

When we abstract this notion, trees are a form of graph with two sorts of components: vertices and edges (figure 6.1). Vertices are points connected to each other by edges. In the biological tree metaphor, edges are branches that connect splitting points (crotches) to other splitting points or leaves. A tree must not have any "cycles" or paths from vertex to vertex via edges that return to their starting point. For analytical convenience, we usually treat trees as dichotomous, where each vertex is connected to a single other vertex if it is a leaf, or three others if it is not a leaf. If the tree is "directed," a root is present, which is a special vertex along an existing edge that connects to two other vertices. Less abstractly, the leaves are observed entities, whereas internal (i.e., nonleaf) vertices are hypothetical ancestral taxa.[2]

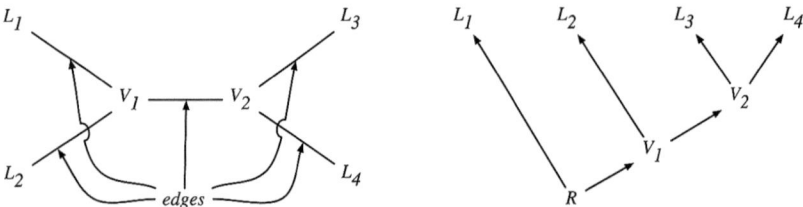

Figure 6.1 Trees, undirected and directed. Left, an undirected tree with leaf vertices $L_1 \ldots L_4$, internal vertices V_1 and V_2, and edges labeled. Right, a directed (rooted) representation of the left tree with root R along edge $L_1 V_1$.

One of the strengths of such a tree representation is that we can infer the sequence of events (at least from edge to edge) that have occurred among the observed taxa and localize them on the tree. Such changes would occur between ancestor and descendent vertices on a directed (rooted) tree. Those entities that descended from a common ancestor share unique features that are evidence both of their relationship and of the transformations that occurred in the past. Transformations along adjacent edges form a chain of events describing the history of diversification in the features of the taxa.

There are an enormous number of trees, more than particles in the known universe, for relatively small sets of taxa (table 6.1).[3] So many, in fact, that identifying the "best" one is impossible to guarantee for non-

Table 6.1 Number of binary trees for n taxa

n	Unrooted	Rooted
3	1	3
4	3	15
5	15	105
10	2,027,025	34,459,425
20	8.20×10^{21}	3.03×10^{23}
50	2.84×10^{74}	2.75×10^{76}
100	1.70×10^{182}	3.35×10^{184}

trivial problems,[4] and we are forced to rely on heuristic computational techniques when analyzing real data.

The challenge and promise of phylogenetic tree analysis of sociocultural data is to identify trees that best represent the historical branching patterns among cultures and/or their component elements; then, based on this tree, identify those elements that are shared due to common history and those due to multiple origin or exchange; and finally determine whether there are general, even directional, patterns of cultural transformation between human behavioral systems. The value of this approach to human societies and their histories, so far realized only in limited fashion, was predicted by Lévi-Strauss almost three decades ago:

> It is striking that this new systematics of living or extinct species, called cladistics, may be interpreted, alternatively and sometimes simultaneously, as a method for determining a temporal order of succession among more or less related species, *or* as a classification indifferent to the search for [parent] stocks. In the latter case, the formulation of rigorous procedures for defining groups, establishing a hierarchical order among them, and their embedded and inclusive relationships, may offer heuristic value not only in biology but in every field of study where we observe relationships comparable to homologies. (1983:1227, our translation)

Trees as Explanations

Trees are explanations of data in that they present scenarios of change that require the smallest amount of "extra" change over the minimum possible given observed variation (Farris 1982). The amount of extra change can be measured in a variety of ways, such as parsimony steps, likelihood units, or posterior probability (see later discussion), but in each case a "best" tree description represents the ensemble minimum over all the data. It may be that the favored tree is not minimal for any of the observed features individually (table 6.2, figure 6.2) but is optimal for their combination.

A rooted tree offers historical explanation in that some aspects of features temporally precede others. In this sense, they are "primitive" with respect to the "derived" condition. Given the nonminimal changes in nearly all features (i.e., homoplasy), taxa are mosaics of primitive and

Table 6.2 Binary data of nineteen characters for twenty taxa

Taxon	Characters																		
t0	0	0	0	0	0	0	0	0	0	0	0	0	0	0	0	0	0	0	0
t1	1	0	0	0	0	0	0	0	0	1	0	0	0	0	0	0	0	0	1
t2	1	1	0	0	0	0	0	0	0	1	0	0	0	0	0	0	0	1	0
t3	1	1	1	0	0	0	0	0	0	0	0	0	0	0	0	0	1	0	0
t4	1	1	1	1	0	0	0	0	0	0	0	0	0	0	0	1	0	0	0
t5	1	1	1	1	1	0	0	0	0	0	0	0	0	1	0	0	0	0	0
t6	1	1	1	1	1	1	0	0	0	0	0	0	1	0	0	0	0	0	0
t7	1	1	1	1	1	1	1	0	0	0	0	1	0	0	0	0	0	0	0
t8	1	1	1	1	1	1	1	1	0	0	0	1	0	0	0	0	0	0	0
t9	1	1	1	1	1	1	1	1	1	0	0	0	0	0	0	0	0	0	0
t10	1	1	1	1	1	1	1	1	1	1	0	0	0	0	0	0	0	0	0
t11	1	1	1	1	1	1	1	0	1	1	0	0	0	0	0	0	0	0	0
t12	1	1	1	1	1	1	0	1	1	1	1	0	0	0	0	0	0	0	0
t13	1	1	1	1	1	1	0	1	1	1	1	1	0	0	0	0	0	0	0
t14	1	1	1	1	1	0	1	1	1	1	1	1	1	0	0	0	0	0	0
t15	1	1	1	1	0	1	1	1	1	1	1	1	1	1	0	0	0	0	0
t16	1	1	1	0	1	1	1	1	1	1	1	1	1	1	1	0	0	0	0
t17	1	1	0	1	1	1	1	1	1	1	1	1	1	1	1	1	0	0	0
t18	1	0	1	1	1	1	1	1	1	1	1	1	1	1	1	1	1	1	0
t19	0	1	1	1	1	1	1	1	1	1	1	1	1	1	1	1	1	1	1

derived aspects. Mammals, for instance, possess external hair, which is derived with respect to other vertebrates, yet they are also characterized by the primitive feature of lungs (with respect to the swim bladder of teleost fishes).

Historical explanation is "vertical" in that transformations occur between ancestors and descendants. Those features that do not fit this mode of change require secondary (ad hoc) explanation as either convergence or perhaps nonvertical transmission. Convergence refers to the

Identifying Transformation Vectors for Kinship Systems

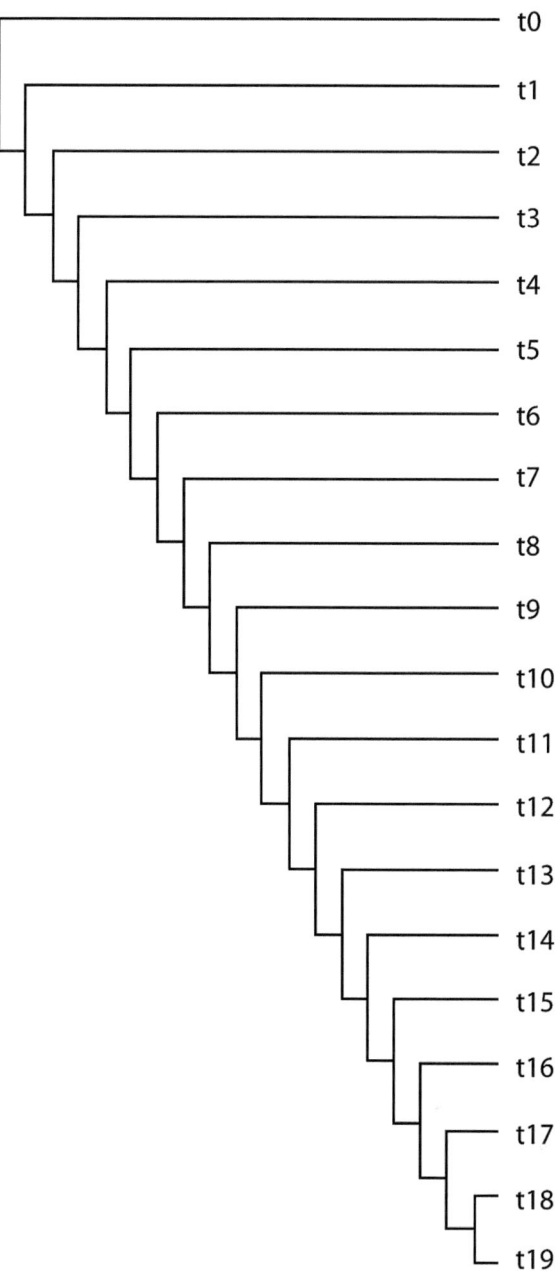

Figure 6.2 Tree for the data of table 6.2. Assuming the minimum number of character changes, two for each of the nineteen characters for a length of thirty-eight steps.

nonunique acquisition of derived features, such as wings in bats, pterosaurs, and some dinosaurs (birds). The identity of these features does not necessarily indicate errors in any way but signifies actual multiple origins, which then continue to change in a vertical fashion. A second explanation of homoplasy is "horizontal" inheritance. In this non–tree-like form of transformation, descendants may have multiple ancestors resulting in a phylogenetic network. For trees to be a reasonable explanatory framework, vertical change should be more prevalent than horizontal change. For most biological variation, this is clearly true and has been shown to be the case as well for a variety of human cultural features (Collard et al. 2006).

Networks and Multiple Explanations

A network is a tree with edges added to signify multiple ancestry for some vertices (figure 6.3). To avoid cycles, networks must be directed, hence rooted. Given that there are many extra edges that can be added to a tree to form a network,[5] the number of networks is considerably

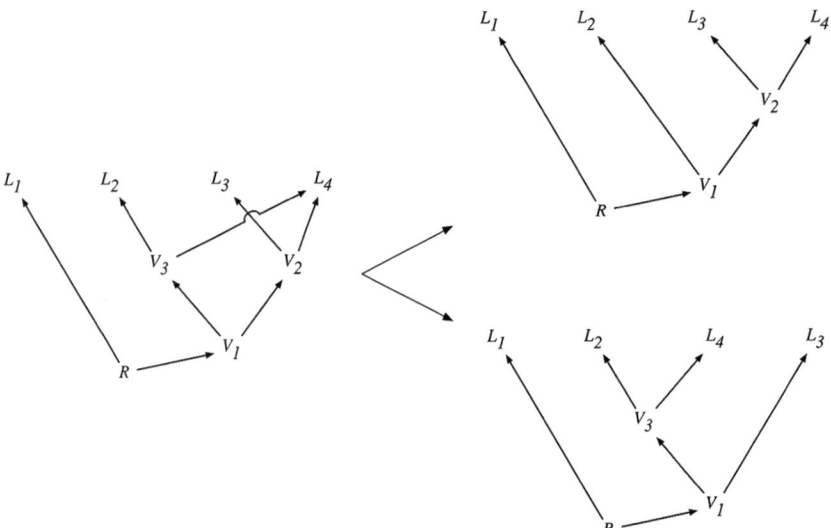

Figure 6.3 A network of four taxa (as in figure 6.1). Shows a network edge ($V_3 \rightarrow L_4$) on the left and the two trees derivable from alternate resolution of the ancestors of L_4.

larger than that of trees. Networks are usually treated as sets of largely similar trees (e.g., Jin et al. 2006; Nakhleh et al. 2005) based on alternate resolution of ancestral edges (choosing each in turn to generate an alternate tree). This allows for networks to be employed as multiple tree explanations, each tree yielding alternate explanations of homoplastic data. The network-derived trees can then be ordered based on optimality (see later discussion), offering quantitative levels of explanatory power. Such a ranking of explanations allows the assessment of the relative importance of alternate historical scenarios. For many aspects of human behavior, networks have demonstrated explanatory value (e.g., Borgerhoff-Mulder et al. 2006; Hage and Harary 1998; Hamberger et al. 2009; White and Johansen 2005).

Hypothesis Testing, Optimality Criteria, and Models

A tree (or network) is a hypothesis of the phylogenetic relationships of a set of taxa. This includes not only the groups described by the tree (subtrees or "clades"), but the transformations required by the tree as well. Each tree implies an optimal set of transformations (which need not be unique), allowing the calculation of a numerical value that lets the hypotheses be compared. The search for the best or optimal hypothesis consists of evaluating candidate trees in pairwise fashion, in each case retaining the tree with better optimality value. As long as the optimality value is transitive (if a > b and b > c, then a > c), such a search guarantees the optimal result (or results, if multiple equally optimal trees are identified). In practice, there are usually such a large number of trees that only a heuristic subset is actually considered.

Of the diversity of possible optimality criteria, three are in common empirical use. They are the simplicity-based parsimony and the statistical approaches of likelihood and posterior probability (Bayesian). These methods differ in whether they employ stochastic models of change and how they incorporate such models (Farris 1982; Felsenstein 1973; Rannala and Yang 1996). All these methods are optimality based; they simply differ in the entity being optimized.

Regarding sociocultural data, parsimony has been used by Rexová et al. (2003) for Indo-European languages and by Tehrani and Collard (2009) in their study of Iranian weaving practices.[6] Bayesian statistical approaches have used both likelihood (e.g., Fortunato et al. 2006; Holden and Mace 2005) and posterior probability (e.g., Fortunato et al. 2006; Fortunato and Mace 2009; Holden et al. 2005; Pagel 2009; Pagel and Meade 2005). Yet problems result from models of biological processes lacking clear analogues for human sociocultural data. For example, Fortunato et al. (2006) employ the HKY model (Hasegawa et al. 1985) to construct their likelihood tree based on human speech variation. The HKY model is based on specific molecular structural and empirical properties of nucleic acid sequence data (transitions, transversions, and stationary frequency of nucleotide types). These aspects are without obvious correspondence in sociocultural practices.

In posterior probability approaches, specific problems occur owing to the need for priors that affect the calculations. There are two flavors of Bayesian analysis in current use that are quite different in approach. In the first, the hypothesis that maximizes the product of its prior probability and its integrated likelihood is referred to as the maximum a posteriori tree or MAP (Rannala and Yang 1996), which is the optimal tree based on posterior probability. In the second, a tree is constructed from subtrees with greater than 50 percent posterior probability (Larget and Simon 1999; called "clade-posteriors" by Wheeler and Pickett 2008), irrespective of the trees within which they are nested. This is returned as the Bayesian tree. There are many problems with this second approach, foremost that this sort of tree does not attempt to optimize anything in particular, and hence cannot participate in hypothesis testing as defined here. Furthermore, this flavor of tree may conflict with the MAP tree (Wheeler and Pickett 2008). For clade-posterior analyses, see, for example, Fortunato et al. (2006), Fortunato and Mace (2009), Pagel and Meade (2005), and Pagel et al. (2007).

No-Common-Mechanism and the Unity of Methods

Each of the three phylogenetic methods discussed here has strengths and weaknesses, mainly centering around the lack, or specific assumptions of, a stochastic model of character change. Much blood has been spilled on this battlefield. There are, however, analytical circumstances in which these three methods converge, or at least intersect. In these situations, parsimony and likelihood estimators converge, and MAP results can, too, with appropriate priors. The situation of greatest interest here concerns the stochastic model. Usually, a single time parameter is applied to all characters through the stochastic model. This time parameter (μt) is the product of the time between tree splitting events, t, and the rate of change, μ. In essence, all characters share the same overall rate (even if modified by gamma classes). This may or may not be appropriate for nucleic acid sequences (there is even argument there), but it seems inappropriately restrictive for sociocultural features. Is it reasonable to assume that aspects of language, textiles, ceramics, and marriage practices evolve at the same rate?

A generalization of the Neyman (1971) r-state model (r signifying the number of states for each character) that relaxes this condition, allowing each feature to have a unique time parameter over each edge of a tree, has been described by Tuffley and Steel (1997) and Steel and Penny (2005). This no-common-mechanism (NCM) model allows each feature to change such that the overall tree likelihood (lik_T) is maximized with all state-to-state transformations equally likely. This likelihood occurs precisely on the most parsimonious tree when each feature is weighted by the negative logarithm of its states (r_i states and l_i parsimony changes in character i on tree T):

$$lik_T = \prod_i^{characters} r_i^{-(l_i+1)}$$

Not only are the best likelihood and parsimony trees identical, but the ordering of each tree from best to worst is preserved. If the priors are set to be suitably uninformative, the MAP solution will be this same tree. NCM offers a robust, agnostic transformation model, with unique time parameter flexibility. For these reasons and the confluence of methods, NCM appears to be uniquely well suited to sociocultural phylogenetics.

Example Analyses

Kinship Systems

Sixteen kinship systems were chosen as an initial data set (data were drawn from literature sources): eight Crow (Hopi, Hano, Zuni, Cherokee, Tlingit, Sirionó, Trukese, and Senufo Fodonon), three Omaha

(Fox, Menominee, and Omaha), two Iroquois (Seneca and North-Central Ojibwa), one Dravidian (Northern Ojibwa), one Hawaiian (Southern Paiute), and one Eskimo (Taos). Eighty-five features of each culture were scored, including aspects of kin nomenclature, social organization, marriage patterns, linguistic features, demography, economy, and polity (see http://anthro.amnh.org/CrowOmaha6). Sample societies were chosen with various associations in mind: (1) to represent contrasting culture areas (Southwest Pueblos, Southeast, Northwest Coast); (2), culture types in regional clades with contrasting languages (Pueblos, with Crow systems, but three unrelated languages); (3) culture types within regions with contrasting kinship systems (Pueblos with Crow versus Eskimo type); (4) language groups (Uto-Aztekan among proximate Crow and non-Crow systems on the Southwest–Great Basin divide; Central Algonquian societies reflecting adjacent Dravidian, Iroquois, and Omaha systems); (5) some deliberate Crow outliers from outside North America (Trukese, Sirionó, and Senufo Fodonon).

Most coded variables were binary, marked as either present or absent. Features include diagnostic kin term equations, descent emphasis, type of kin groups, other associative groups, marriage rules, residence; language relationships, ritual emphases; population size and density, settlement pattern, community distribution, house form, economic type, domesticated species dependencies, and production emphases; and polity, including general levels of sociocultural integration. As well as features identified by prior analysts of Crow-Omaha systems, these features were inductively developed from a partial rereading of the ethnographic record. Some variables were drawn from the *Ethnographic Atlas* (Murdock 1967, 1970; see also Gray 1999), and were informed by some in the Standard Cross-Cultural Sample (Murdock and White 1970; Standard Cross Cultural Sample 2006; Fischer, n.d.). Specific variables chosen and grouped mostly reflect our own designations.

Figure 6.4 is derived from an analysis using POY4 (Varón et al. 2008, 2010) adapted to sociocultural data. It includes both tree and network hypotheses. The underlying tree (straight, solid black lines) represents a strict majority consensus tree (unrooted) for the sixteen kinship systems. This depicts an analysis (100 Wagner builds + TBR branch-swapping) resulting in 8 equally optimal (parsimonious) trees at length 244; strict consensus (total agreement among all 8) is shown

Identifying Transformation Vectors for Kinship Systems 119

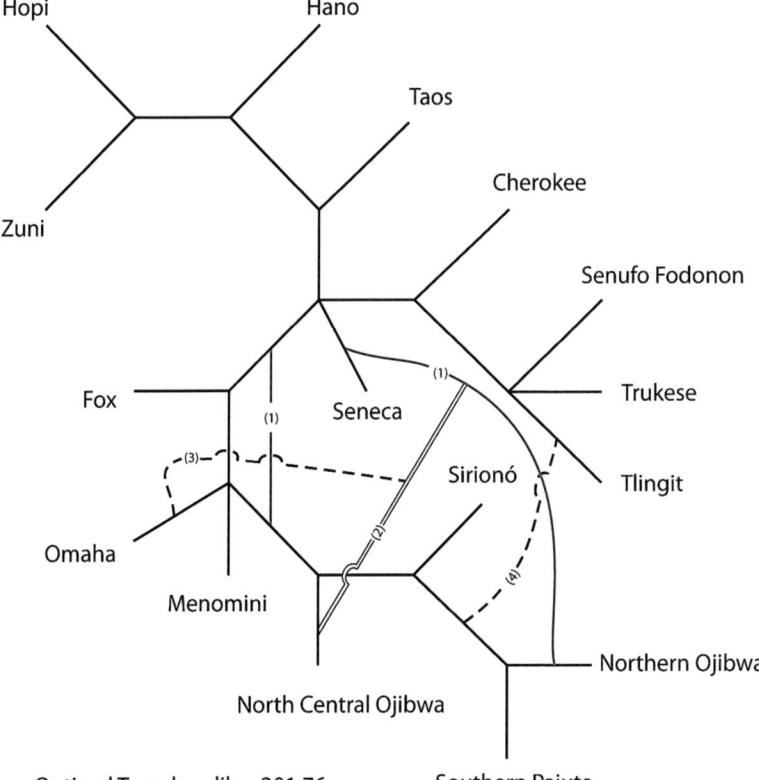

Optimal Tree -$\log_e$ lik = 201.76
(1) Unique origins -$\log_e$ lik = 214.12
(2) Dravidian to Iroquois -$\log_e$ lik = 220.33
(3) Omaha to Dravidian to Iroquois -$\log_e$ lik = 214.58
(4) Single Foraging Origin -$\log_e$ lik = 220.10

Figure 6.4 Tree/network for sixteen social systems (thirteen North American, three outliers). Most likely scenario of cultural relationships (straight, solid black lines) at log –lik 201.76. Alternate modes of transfer based on hypotheses in text: (1) log –lik 214.12; (2) log –lik 220.33; (3) log –lik 214.58; (4) log –lik 220.10.

unrooted. A ten-minute timed search resulted in the same consensus after 1,549 hits at the shortest length.

Propinquities are suggestive of correlations: for example, among Puebloan Crow systems (Hopi, Hano, Zuni) and among Omaha systems (Fox, Omaha, and Menominee)—in both cases, transecting linguistic boundaries. The leaf cluster of Sirionó (Crow), Southern Paiute (Hawaiian), and Northern Ojibwa (Dravidian) reflects similar economic adaptations (foraging) and low population densities. The Senufo Fodonon-Cherokee-Tlingit-Trukese (all Crow) proximity suggests the influence of social complexity (i.e., all are chiefdoms). The leaf clusters thus promote the identification and testing of hypotheses concerning linguistic, cultural, demographic, and other correlations.

If we examine alternate scenarios, four hypotheses (depicted on figure 6.4 with dashed, gray, or parallel reticular lines, respectively) merit immediate examination: (1) all kinship systems have a unique origin; (2) Iroquois systems are uniquely derived from Dravidian; (3) Iroquois are derived from Omaha and then from Dravidian; and (4) the kinship systems of foraging-based societies (here Tlingit, Northern Ojibwa, and Southern Paiute) share a single origin. We can (using NCM) assign likelihoods to these hypotheses and their overall contribution to an ensemble network hypothesis. The best hypothesis (straight, solid black lines of figure 6.4) contains over 99 percent of the overall likelihood.

Analysis of Characters from the *Ethnographic Atlas*

The revised *Ethnographic Atlas* (Gray 1999) represents cumulative additions to the comparative societal database begun by G. P. Murdock in the 1930s and published in abbreviated form in the 1960s (Murdock 1967). It has been the target of both blame and praise ever since its publication (e.g., Callan 2008), and some of its variables remain in question, but it remains the most comprehensive coded database of human social systems available. While acknowledging its shortcomings, we believe the data are adequate to disclose broad patterns of the type shown in the present demonstration (for the features and their codings see http://anthro.amnh.org/CrowOmaha6).

In treating cultures as taxa and their behavioral aspects as characters, we have limited ourselves to those aspects of societies that are intrinsic. By this, we mean features of the cultures themselves as opposed to their environments. Environmental mean rainfall or temperature are external to cultures, and hence are not included as phylogenetic data. Responses to such conditions, through technology or custom, would be included because they are determined by the cultures themselves.

Our two subsets of data, "Algonquian systems" and "Eastern North American systems," are both selected from the revised *Ethnographic Atlas* (EA). Ninety sociocultural features from the EA total (115: see Gray 1999) were selected for analysis (EA variables 1–88, 90, and 94).[7] Extrinsic features (climate, environment, region) were excluded, as well as inconsistent column entries, and those based on EA name and date identifiers. Given that the analysis includes high ratios of cultures (30, 55) to variant features (90), complete resolution of resultant trees is not expected.

Analytical Methods

For all analyses, the program POY version 4.1.2 was used (Varón et al. 2008, 2010). In all cases, the searches were accomplished by six parallel executions of the "search (max time:0:2:0)" command for two hours, three times for a net processor time of thirty-six hours on an eight-core Mac Pro (3.2 Ghz). This procedure employs a mixture of random addition sequences + TBR, tree fusing, and ratcheting. The set of optimal trees was selected, and strict consensus cladograms were produced.

In the parsimony analyses, all characters were treated as unordered and equally weighted. The likelihood searches were performed with a Jukes-Cantor model (Jukes and Cantor 1969) under NCM (Steel and Penny 2005; Tuffley and Steel 1997). Characters were weighted as the natural logarithm of the number of states.

Algonquian Systems

This subset comprises all those representatives (thirty) in the *Ethnographic Atlas* of the Algonquian language family encompassing environments from the Plains, Woodlands, and Subarctic and showing variant kinship terminologies. The goal here is to compare social system distributions within a single ethnolinguistic clade. The resultant trees (figures 6.5, 6.6) rooted (arbitrarily) on Naskapi suggest clusters correlative to variant aspects of economy, polity, kinship, and social organization.

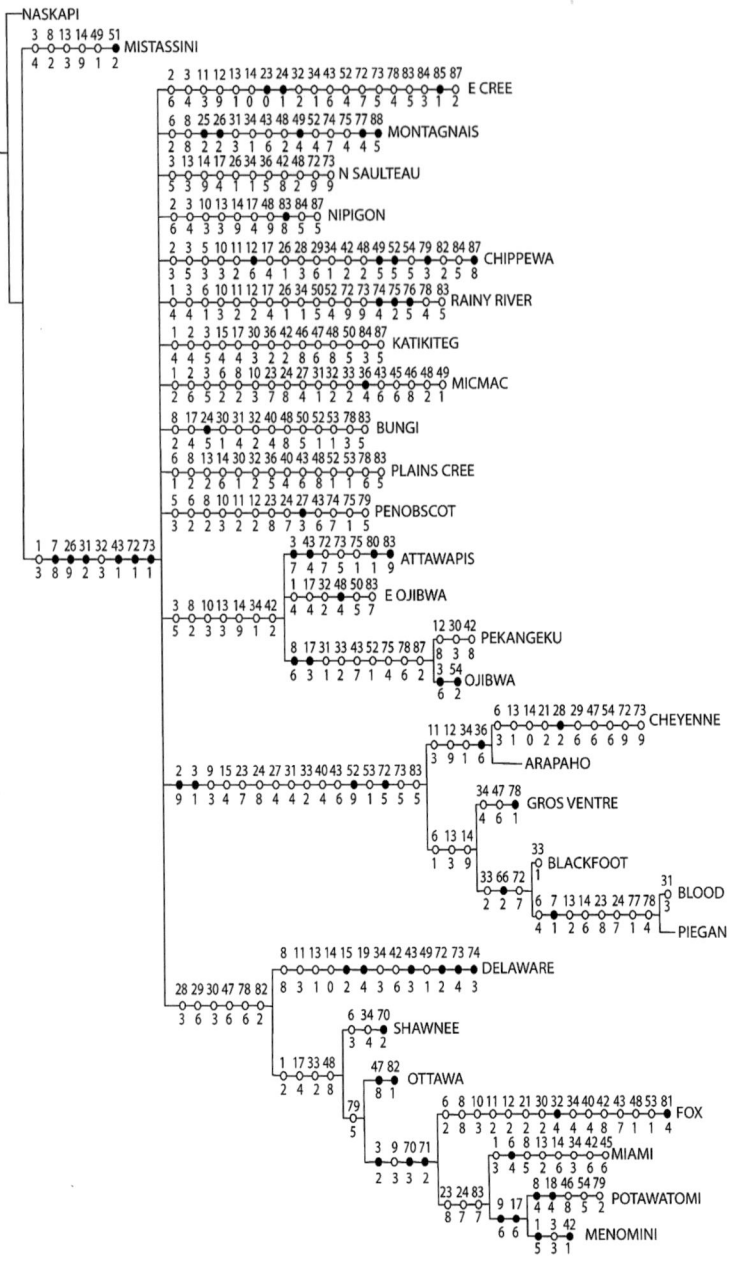

Figure 6.5 Tree for social systems of the Algonquian language family (Parsimony). Analysis of thirty lineages and ninety characters under parsimony. Five equally parsimonious trees were found at length 362. This strict consensus is arbitrarily rooted on Naskapi. This cladogram and those in Figures 6.6–6.8 are visualized with CLADOS (Nixon 1993).

Identifying Transformation Vectors for Kinship Systems

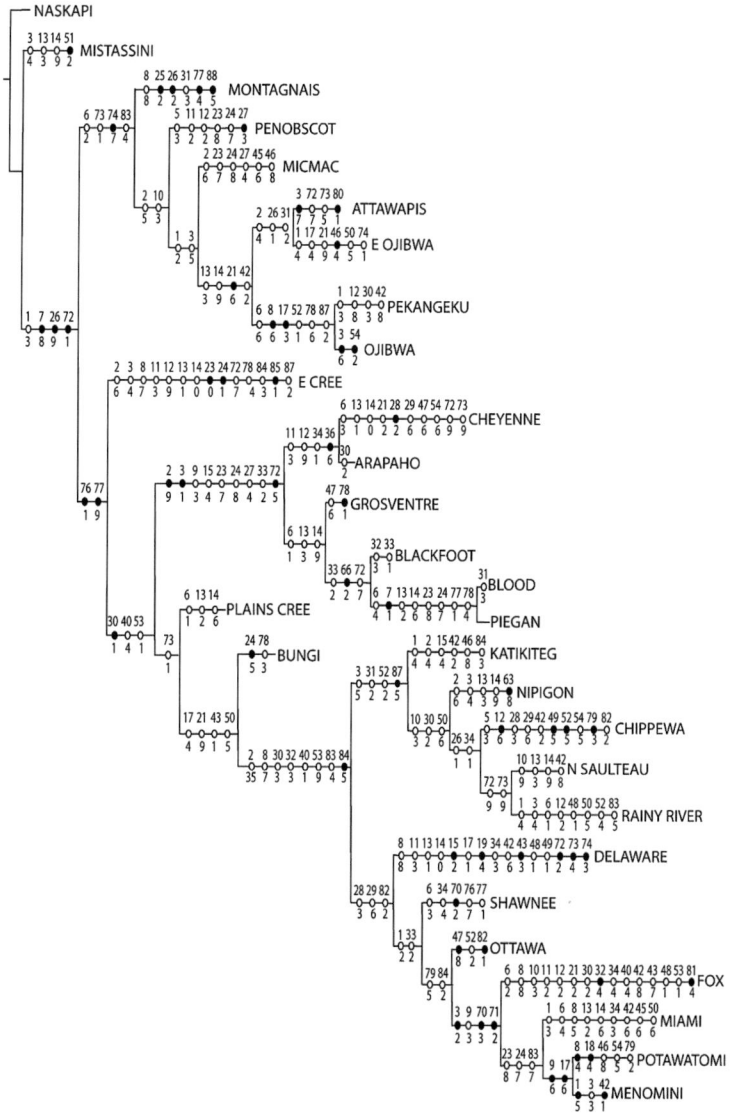

Figure 6.6 Tree for social systems of the Algonquian language family (No-Common-Mechanism). Analysis of thirty lineages and ninety characters under likelihood –NCM. A single tree was found at cost –log lik 772.127. Tree is arbitrarily rooted on Naskapi.

Figures 6.5 and 6.6 offer a condensed description of features producing branching patterns under parsimony and NCM, respectively. EA character numbers are shown above the edges and character states (the EA coded entry for a particular society) below. Only unambiguous character changes are shown—thus, optimizations on polytomous clades represent the most conservative set of changes for each clade. Each character-state pair embraces an open or solid circle, representing changes that occur in more than one place on the tree (open) or only once (solid). In figure 6.5 there is no weighting of changes, with the assumption (implausible) that all changes occur at a similar rate (e.g., hunting dependency [v. 2], postmarital residence [v. 10–14], and games [v. 35]). In contrast, NCM allows differential weighting for changes, resulting in a more resolved tree. Note, for example, in figure 6.6, the Montagnais-Ojibwa clade, whose primary node forms partly on patrilineal inheritance of land (v. 74, state 7). The comparable grouping in figure 6.5 (Eastern Cree to Penobscot) is far less resolved. Where patterns are similar on both trees (e.g., the Cheyenne-Piegan clade), clades gain in robustness, resulting from different methodologies. In most instances, kinship and marriage characters (notably, v. 17–27, 43) are not obviously major causes of branching patterns, although, to take one example, v. 27 state 4 (Generational cousin-terms) is one among several branching causes for the Cheyenne–Piegan clade in both figures. However, branching and clusters, especially under NCM, are often highly indicative for societies with similar kinship structures, notably Crow and Omaha—suggesting these do indeed correlate with economic, political, and other sociocultural features that cause branching at specific nodes (see later discussion).

In figure 6.6, branches generally follow a north–south trajectory from top to bottom, with a westward Plains grouping in the center of the tree. Northern foraging "bands" branch into more sedentary, more complexly structured agricultural "tribes," with the western cluster representing an equestrian, nomadic, bison-hunting adaptation. The main branch of systems with Generational cousin terms correlates neatly with this High Plains adaptation—Cheyenne, Arapaho, Gros Ventre, Blackfoot, Blood, Piegan—thus corroborating the inference of Eggan (1937a) that Prairie societies moving onto the High Plains after acquiring horses adopted the more "flexible" social systems associated with Generational terminologies. Only two other cases here have Generational cousin terms: Micmac and Delaware, both originally along the northeastern seaboard. Delaware's propinquity to Shawnee on the tree may well reflect historical change: in the eighteenth century (the "ethnographic present" for the EA Delaware entry) Delawares moved west to Ohio nearby the Shawnee. Penobscot, adjacent to Micmac, represents the only Algonquian case with Eskimo cousin-terms (v. 27, state 3), probably reflecting assimilation to colonial society (EA ethnographic present: 1900).

Societies with Omaha cousin-terms (v. 27, state 6)—Shawnee, Fox, Miami, Potawatomi, Menominee—all cluster tightly on the tree, corresponding with southernmost Algonquian presence in the Eastern Woodlands and greater agricultural adaptation. The only intervener here is Ottawa (Iroquois cousin-terms). EA ethnographic present for Ottawa is 1650, but this is retrojected: in the eighteenth century, Ottawa were proximate geographically to Potawatomi and Fox but had migrated earlier from the Ottawa River, their terminology thus perhaps reflecting closer proximity to a Sub-Arctic adaptation and geographical proximity to Huron and Iroquois.

All remaining societies have Iroquois cousin terms (v. 27, state 5; Mistassini and Eastern Cree are EA unknown [state 0] in this regard). Figure 6.6's subtrees, again more definitive, cluster in two clades: (1) Naskapi through Ojibwa, and (2) Plains Cree through Rainy River. Societies with both Iroquois cousin-terms and preferential symmetrical cross-cousin marriage (v. 25, state 1) are found *only* in the Sub-Arctic (identifiable within the EA's "Arctic America" class): Naskapi, Eastern Ojibwa, Attawapis, Chippewa, Rainy River, and Northern Saulteau. Following Trautmann and Barnes (1998), we hypothesize that all these in fact had kinship systems with Type A (Dravidian, rather than Iroquois) crossness. Moreover, even though Mistassini cousin-terms are marked unknown, preferential cross-cousin marriage (v. 25, state 1) together with geographical proximity to Iroquois systems with the same marriage type predict Type A terminology. Systems where cross-cousin marriage was permitted (v. 23, state 1) but not preferred (v. 25, state 15) cluster in two groups: (1) Ojibwa and Pekangeku, and (2) Plains Cree, Bungi, Katikiteg, and Nipigon, where again subtrees are better resolved under NCM. All live within the same area along the Sub-Arctic/Plains border, and their closest Plains neighbors all have (Dakota-) Iroquois kin terminologies, with no cross-cousin marriage. This would corroborate the Trautmann-Barnes hypothesis: that is, that greater opening out of affinal ties from Sub-Arctic to Woodlands, north to south, progressively transforms cross-cousin marriage from prescription (where cross-cousin terms = same-generation affines)—or at least preference—to possibility, and finally to proscription (where cross-cousin ≠ affine).

Systems of Eastern North America

This subset represents all fifty-five EA representatives of the major language families from the Plains eastward throughout the Woodlands and eastern Sub-Arctic: thirty Algonquian (as before), five Muskhogean (Choctaw, Creek, Seminole, Timucua, Natchez), twelve Siouan (Crow, Hidatsa, Mandan, Winnebago, Omaha, Ponca, Oto, Iowa, Santee, Teton, Assiniboine, Catawba), five Caddoan (Caddo, Pawnee, Arikara, Wichita, Hasinai), and three Iroquoian (Cherokee, Huron, Iroquois).[8] Included are the classical Crow and Omaha cases first described by Morgan (1871) and all their linguistic relatives throughout these three (Murdockian) culture areas. The aim is to see what light may be shed on kin terminology distributions across major linguistic boundaries. Again, nonintrinsic variables—notably including the language group identifiers themselves (v. 98, 99)—were excluded.

The major pattern of Algonquian distribution (figures 6.7, 6.8) remains similar to figures 6.5 and 6.6, with a few shifts, and some interesting intrusions. Some of the latter are evident under both parsimony (figure 6.7) and NCM (figure 6.8), others are noticeably clearer under NCM. In figure 6.8, all cases with Omaha cousin-terms (Winnebago through Iowa) group in a tight subtree (transecting the Algonquian–Siouan language boundary and the Plain-Woodlands culture area boundary), with only Ottawa (Type B terminology) intruding by the Winnebago edge. Moreover, with only Penobscot (oddly) intervening, Plains Omaha systems group adjacent to Plains Crow societies (Arikara through Pawnee), which all group tightly, except for the Crow proper. Moreover, the Plains Crow clade branches proximately into Southeastern Crow systems. Except for Delaware (the non-Crow Algonquian intruder), figure 6.8 shows a more discrete clade of Southeastern Crow societies (with Cherokee and Choctaw edges) than figure 6.7, where

Huron and Iroquois (Iroquoian speakers with Type B terminology) intrude into the subtree edged by Timucua and Creek. Moreover, in figure 6.7, Natchez, Hasinai, and Caddo—all geographically near the Southeast–Plains boundary—appear remote from this Southeastern Crow cluster, with no ostensible reason to look for associations. In figure 6.8, however, both their independent subtree clustering and their propinquity to the Southeast Crow subtree are striking. None of the three is EA Crow (v. 27, state 1), yet the broader ethnographic record indicates that Caddo (and implicitly Hasinai, a subgroup) formerly had Crow terms (Rogers and Sabo 2004:625). Although Natchez cousin-terms are unknown, Urban (1994:179), who does not infer Crow terms, suggests Natchez and Muskhogean proper (Choctaw et al.) social structures are "transformations of one another."

Crow proper is the stark outlier among Crow systems, intruding among Plains Algonquians—Gros Ventre, Blackfoot, Cheyenne, Arapaho, Blood, and Piegan—all with Generational (Cheyenne) terminology, but all are immediate geographic neighbors to the Crow. Eggan (1937a) suggested the Crow—recent arrivals on the High Plains from the Missouri River in the early nineteenth century, and the only High Plains society recorded with Crow kin terminology—were in a process of transition toward Generational terminology at the time of American annexation. The hypothesis represented by the subtree (Gros Ventre through Piegan) would favor Eggan's prediction, that is, if we assume Crow society's adaptive and reproductive conditions were most similar to its immediate neighbors on the tree.

In short, the tree propinquity under likelihood NCM of most Omaha and Crow systems (by Murdock's cousin-term classification, at least)—both to each other, and within each type—across major language families and culture area boundaries is quite striking. A hypothesis represented by this clustering should target similarities of social structural, economic, and political forms, including alliance mechanisms, among near neighbors of the Prairie Plains and Woodlands.

Discussion

As Popper (1959) enduringly demonstrated, a methodological procedure is valuable insofar as it operates to disclose meaningful patterns

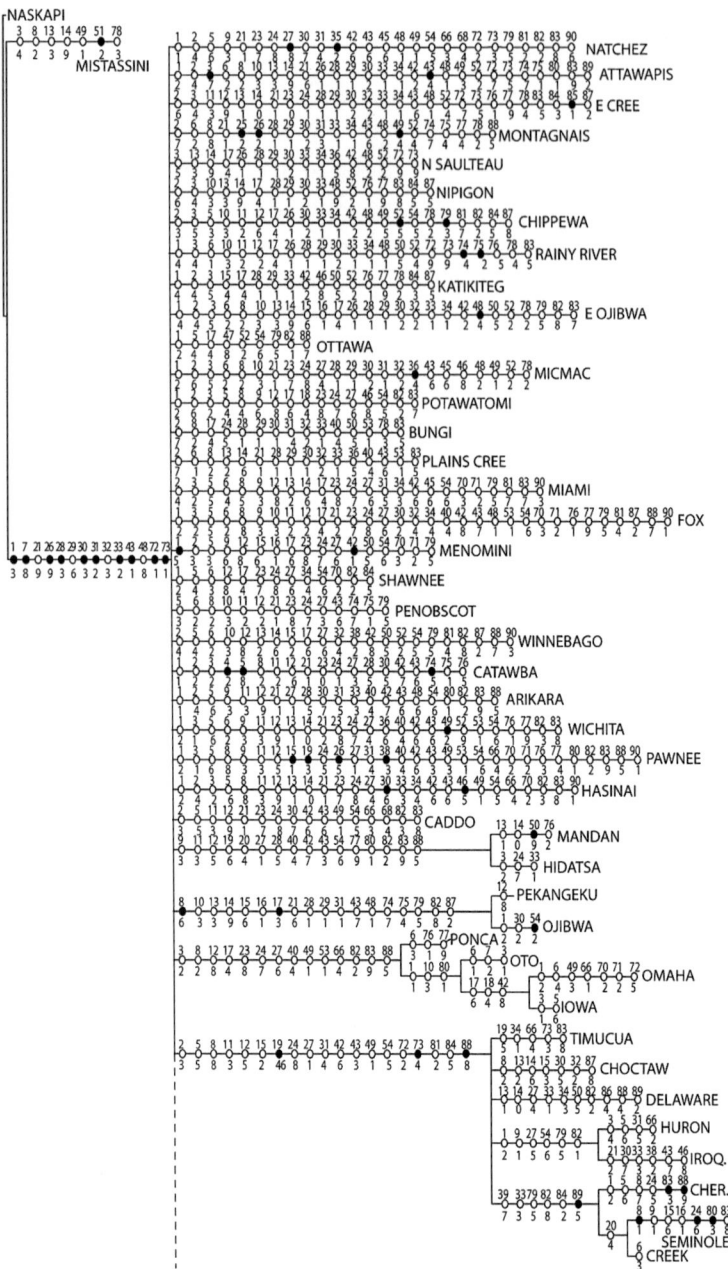

Figure 6.7 Tree for social systems of eastern North America (Parsimony). Analysis of fifty-five lineages and ninety characters under Parsimony. Seven equally parsimonious trees were found at length 667. Tree is arbitrarily rooted on Naskapi.

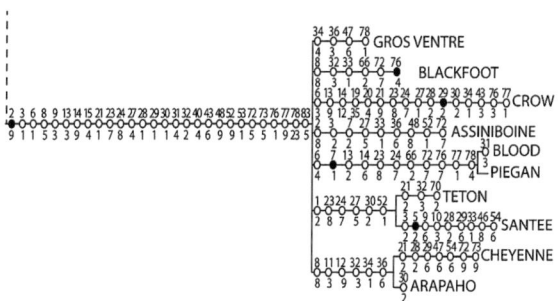

Figure 6.7 Continued

among empirical phenomena, patterns from which testable hypotheses may be generated to explain the phenomena with maximum parsimony and adequacy. Application of phylogenetic models to sociocultural data is in its infancy and has encountered some substantive obstacles (e.g., Borgerhoff-Mulder 2001). Overcoming these is no simple issue. We believe that existing approaches that depend on restricted applications of parsimony, likelihood, and posterior probability, do not provide effective solutions, primarily because they borrow biological models that are inadequate for the explanation of sociocultural phenomena. In contrast, NCM approaches, which permit testing of multiple scenarios, offer more promising possibilities. We hope to have shown here that tree analysis with POY4 can provide a powerful and salient method for discovering patterns in social system distributions that (1) are susceptible to the generation of meaningful testable hypotheses, and (2) speak directly to existing hypotheses about the emergence and spread of kinship systems. In particular, the clusters of Omaha systems in the Woodlands and Plains generated from the EA data seem ripe for testing against the McConvell and Alpher (2002) model of ethnolinguistic expansionism near language family boundaries and against the hypothesis that Crow-Omaha systems disperse marriage alliances (e.g., Héritier 1981; Lévi-Strauss 1966; McKinley 1971b; Trautmann and Barnes 1998), associated with broader extension of sociopolitical alliances. Alliance structures in Crow-Omaha systems are in turn evidently correlated with forms of economic adaptation and, although we have excluded these from direct analysis, with patterns of ecological and/or

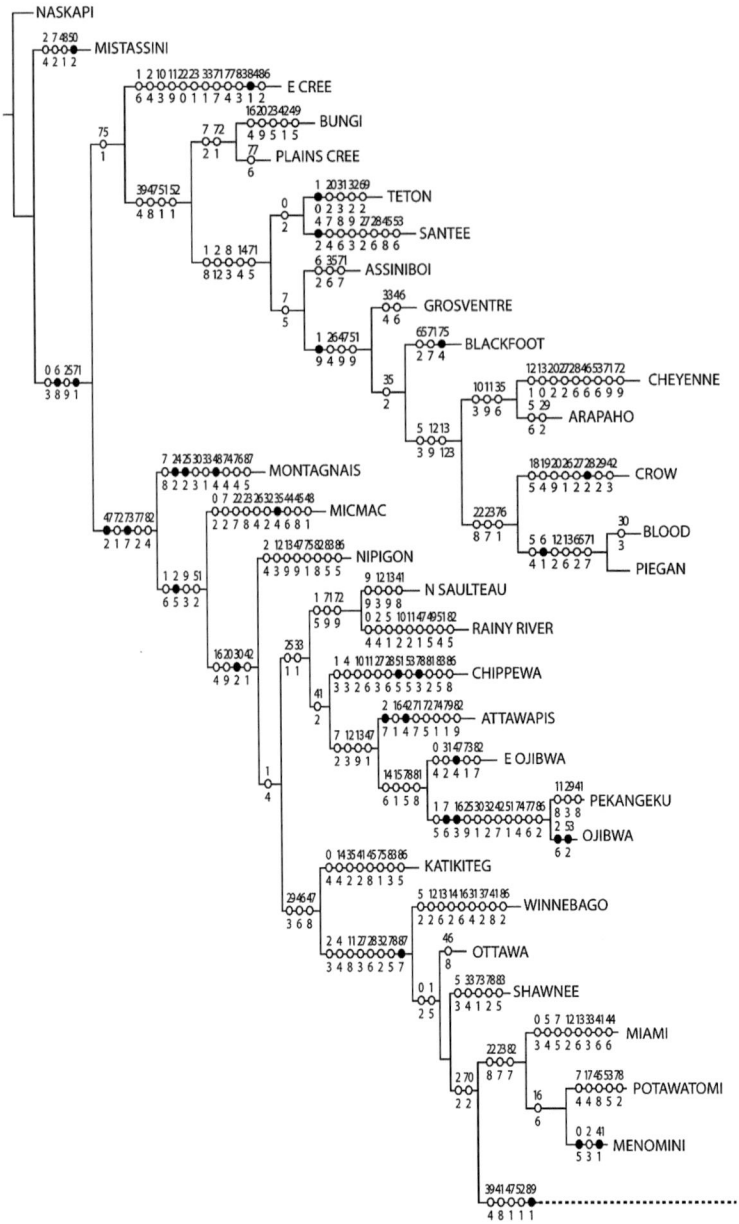

Figure 6.8 Tree for social systems of eastern North America (No-Common-Mechanism). Analysis of fifty-five lineages and ninety characters under likelihood –NCM. A single tree was found at cost –log lik 1268.686. Tree is arbitrarily rooted on Naskapi.

Identifying Transformation Vectors for Kinship Systems 131

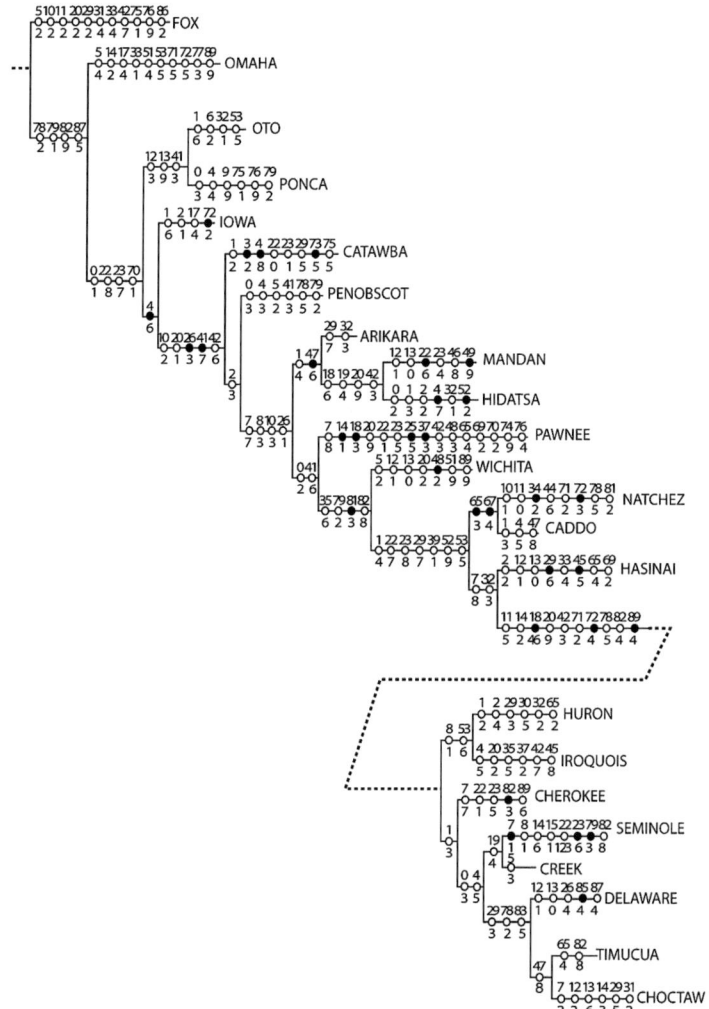

Figure 6.8 Continued

sociodemographic circumscription (after Carneiro 1970). Exceptions clearly require explanation, but hypotheses focusing on particular forms of historical influence (e.g., for Crow, Delaware, Micmac), of the type most prominently associated in North American ethnology with Eggan (1937a, 1937b, 1950), should be investigated.

Africa

7

A Tetradic Starting Point for Skewing?

Marriage as a Generational Contract: Reflections on Sister-Exchange in Africa

Wendy James

Embarking on fieldwork decades ago, I was puzzled that African exchange marriage was so little discussed; it was intriguing to me, but I found little guidance in the anthropological kinship theories of the day. These were dominated on the one hand by pragmatic Africanist models of the corporate lineage, and on the other hand by Lévi-Straussian models of "elementary structure"—holistic kin terminologies within which recurring marriage links between categories maintained a harmonious social system. Lévi-Strauss dismissed direct sister-exchange (along with *patrilateral* cross-cousin marriage) as a "short-cycle" pattern of reciprocity that could have no overall coherence or historical stability. However, the evidence illustrates that sister-exchange, as with barter versus large-scale economic systems, does persist in practice, despite—or possibly in response to—considerable historical disturbance (James 1975, 1986).

Unlike larger scale marriage patterns, whether elementary or complex, the direct forms of sister-exchange are between small groups of people. The reciprocal marriages conducted between these parties should be balanced in every way: implicit in the bond being created is the expectation that each side will be fruitful and bear children. The "short cycle" of this reciprocity extends beyond the wedding celebrations to the successful arrival of offspring; establishing new life completes the closure of the cycle, which we could therefore fairly represent as a "generational contract." But demography may make things awkward. Individuals on either side of a proposed exchange may have to be reclassified to make the exchanges work, including not only the lateral merging of kin (with which we are very familiar) but also a kind of "vertical" merging in which an individual may be recruited to stand in the place of someone of a generation above (or occasionally below).

Because of the relevance of "generations" to the Crow-Omaha discussion, my argument takes as its starting point Nicholas Allen's tetradic model (as outlined in his chapter here; see discussion in James 2003:159ff, and Allen 2008). Being purely abstract in the logical or cognitive sense (its evolutionary relevance an open question), it offers principles that, as a full set, do not match any one empirical case but individually resonate with practices found widely in the ethnographic record. The model is one of social reproduction through symmetrical give-and-take in two dimensions, analytically of equal importance. First, with respect to "crossness," is the gender complementarity between male and female siblings whose reproductive pathways diverge in the making of exchanges. Second is the field of give-and-take produced by the birth of children, providing a temporal rhythm in reproductive life of a kind rarely found in structuralist discussions. In the tetradic model, the initial asymmetry between parents and offspring is complemented with the birth of grandchildren. In Allen's terms, a "gift of life" is transferred from one generation to the next, and then returned, creating a solidarity between "grandkin."

Anthropologists have often tended to treat marriage separately from the arrival of offspring. Our present efforts to review the phenomenon of Crow-Omaha skewing in kin terminology remind us that it turns on the situational bracketing of a parent with a same-sex child. The logic of such "fictional" labels, or what Godelier has called "social technologies" (see chapter 14) is relatively easy to grasp if we adopt a perspective on marriage as a "generational contract"—a concept not limited at all to cases where sister-exchange is practiced, but one that can take a very explicit form in that context. The concept also works very well in contexts where people understand the male and female contributions to reproduction as rather different and may embody these ideas in forms of unilineal social organization—as typically found in kinship systems marked by crossness.

My own primary research has been in various parts of northeast Africa, and my argument about the relevance of the tetradic approach to African ethnography goes beyond generational marriage contracts and skewing as such. It enables us to see analogies between practices conventionally seen as quite different.

For example, initially we might point to the prevalence of generation moieties—what I call "alternating birth classes"—in various parts of eastern Africa (James 2008). This evidence recalls the Dravidian or Type A variant of crossness, associated as it often is with the potential marriage of (classificatory) bilateral cross-cousins (see chapter 1; see Hage 2006). This is currently distinguished from the Iroquois or Type B variant, where the gendered pathways of reproduction go on diverging over several generations and are banned from recombining at an early stage—that is, there is a ban on the marriage of bilateral cross-cousins (Trautmann and Barnes 1998:30–31). But if we take the tetradic model as a starting point, the Dravidian-looking features of social organization in eastern Africa do not look so very different from those Iroquois cases where sister-exchange is practiced. Both seek to maintain the distinct identity of generations in respect of sexuality/marriage/birth: in the first case, through socially abstract but ritually celebrated generation moieties or birth classes extending over wide regions; in the second, at the pragmatic level where the making of one-off reciprocal marriages is part of cooperation, conflict, and peace-making within local population clusters.

Crossing Siblings, Exchanging Sisters, and Marking Generations in Africa

Some time after I had first been puzzled by the anthropological neglect of exchange marriage in Africa, new high-quality ethnography (e.g., Gell 1975, Godelier 1986, on the Umeda and Baruya of New Guinea, respectively) and theoretical speculation on direct sister-exchange (Muller 1980) opened up a fresh debate. In West Africa, French anthropologists were breathing new life into exchange-based notions of kinship. Françoise Héritier (1981) and her colleagues set a new agenda, initially with their studies of the Samo and related peoples of Burkina Faso, for whom they recorded "Omaha" kin terms and what were taken to be associated marriage patterns of a kind dubbed semi-complex by Lévi-Strauss. These included, crucially for my argument, prohibitions on the repetition of marriages between the same parties for the succeeding three generations, with increasingly narrow definitions of the lineal composition of these parties.

Elisabeth Copet-Rougier offered a particularly clear analysis of the theories held by the Mkako people of Cameroon about the exchange of classificatory sisters in marriage, and their ideas about reproduction, which helped explain their prohibitions on the early repetition of these same exchanges. For them, blood is the basis of life, even in the making of bone. It originates in the brain, and when it mixes with the "water of the body" in the testicles, it forms sperm, "the pathway of the male" (*le chemin de l'homme*). This carries the man's blood to the woman, where it joins with her own blood to form the beginnings of the fetus. The new life comes equally from the male and female parents, drawing together gendered lines of "descent" from each of the four grandparents. There was a fundamental equivalence between the two gendered pathways of reproduction, but a dominance of the male element would result in the birth of a boy, and conversely a dominance of the female element would produce a girl. Although women's marriage options were restricted in the traditional Mkako system of alliance and kin terminology, which echoed the classic Omaha pattern, modern conditions were providing more freedom of choice and eroding these constraints (Copet-Rougier 1987, esp. 80–84).

The insights of Héritier and her colleagues were immediately welcomed by British anthropologists, for example Adam Kuper (1982), and woven into Richard Fardon's analytic overview of the transformations of sister-exchange in Nigerian-Cameroon regional history (1984–85), where the rise of chiefly power was distorting such egalitarian practices. Fardon's later survey (1993) traces how matriliny and dual descent systems have persisted among the core peoples of the Adamawa region, along with Crow equations in their kin terminology, while these have been replaced among emigrant diaspora groups by patriclans.

A regional perspective also provides a way of seeing marriage patterns in northeast Africa as variations on an interplay of fundamental principles that people are trying hard to implement—rather than a patchwork of fixed kinship systems, as Barnes (2005 [1984]) argued for the original Crow-Omaha populations themselves. The minority groups whose current or recent practices I have selected here, with one exception, speak languages from "ancient" branches of the Nilo-Saharan family (see Christopher Ehret's chapter in this volume). They all live either in the borderlands of the western Ethiopian escarpment, overlooking the Sudanese plains, or in the western uplands of Uganda, overlooking the Congo basin (see map 7.1).

The traditional subsistence of these peoples includes hunting and gathering along with hoe cultivation and small stock. Unlike the fa-

A Tetradic Starting Point for Skewing?

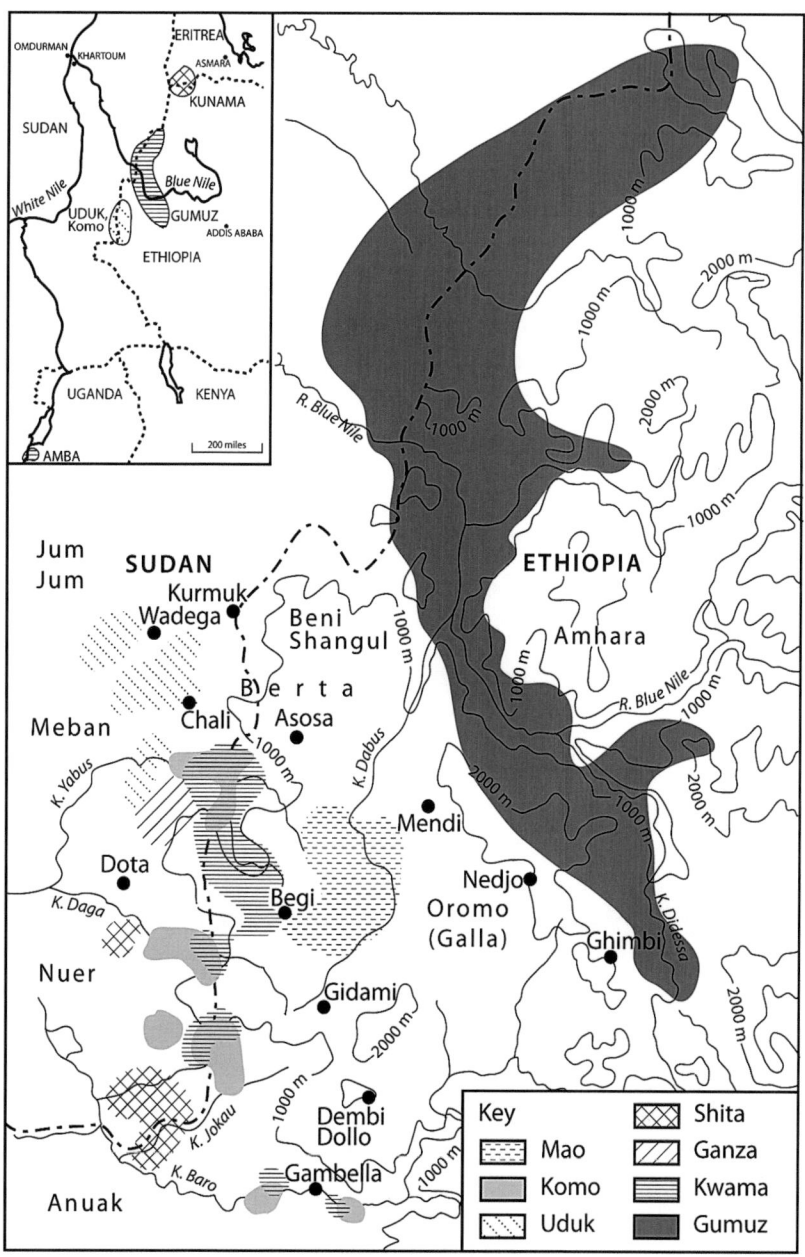

Map 7.1 The Koman speakers and other minorities of the Blue Nile borderlands (after James 1979:6, Fig. 1). Inset: The Greater Nile Basin, locating the Kunama and Amba peoples. By permission of Oxford University Press.

mous pastoral peoples of the Nile Valley or the Ethiopian highlands, none possess large herds of cattle (if any at all), and even where bridewealth is paid today it is not very substantial, nor fundamental to the local economy. However, all these groups present in their own way the logic of a straight exchange of a woman for another woman in marriage, and all practice or have practiced this, whether as a thoroughgoing system (as among the Gumuz), "for fun" among the southern Uduk, or just as an occasional experiment (as among the Kunama). In their shared tendency to formulate Crow-style patterns of thinking, these largely isolated and defensive groups have something in common with Fardon's core peoples of northern Nigeria/Cameroon. On the other hand, the western border regions of Uganda have seen a relatively peaceful long-term history of assimilation between larger and more stable neighbor populations. There, specifically among the Amba, we can identify a system of Omaha kin equations along with former exchange-marriage practices remarkably similar to those described for the Samo.

Gumuz: Thoroughgoing Sister-Exchange

The Gumuz people, whose homeland extends across a wide area both north and south of the Blue Nile, mainly within Ethiopia, are by far the largest group in the whole region known to operate sister-exchange as their primary form of marriage. They represent their social organization and history in terms of loosely defined, dispersed patriclans. Localized descent groups I call "patrigroups" are associated on the ground in mixed clusters. Patrilineal descent is sometimes represented as a continuing line of bone. However, they also recognize a female pathway in the process of social reproduction (see Ehret 2010), speaking of a blood connection on the mother's side. This is not understood as a continuing matriline but as a sequence of separate links from mothers to daughters. In the context of exchange marriage, there are various situations in which a young woman might be substituted for an older sister or even her own mother, and her position in the kin terminology is adjusted accordingly, as described later. These adjustments are purely ad hoc, not amounting to Crow-Omaha-style equations, but all arise from the Gumuz view of marriage as a generational contract. The system as a whole is run by the elders who attempt to preserve (at least in theory) equal outcomes for the parties to a marriage/life-giving exchange, and hence the closure of that generation. Repetition of an exchange between the offspring of the same parties is banned; that is, bilateral cross-cousins are not marriageable.

At one time, there were relatively peaceful relations between the different groups of western Ethiopia. On the fringes of the grassy uplands, peoples like the Gumuz, all known by the derogatory term "Shangalla," used to trade with highland neighbors such as the Agaw (exchanging ivory, rhino horn, gold, and some cotton for highland goods). In the early 1770s, traveler James Bruce described how the trade was secured despite dangers of slave raiding: "The way this trade . . . is established, is by two nations sending their children mutually to each other; there is then peace between these two families which have such hostages; these children often intermarry; after which that family is understood to be protected, and at peace, perhaps for a generation" (Bruce 1804, 5:401). This vignette throws sharp light on the general regional practice of sister-exchange, for which we have an early account provided to Henry Salt by Oma-zéna, a Gumuz slave whom he met in 1810. In his home country of Dabanja: "When a young man is desirous of marrying, it is customary for him to give his sister to another man, and to take his in return; or, if he have no sister, he will go to war for the purpose of taking a female prisoner, who is immediately adopted as his sister, and formally exchanged" (Salt 1814:379). Since my own limited fieldwork among the Gumuz south of the Blue Nile in the 1970s (James 1986), others, including Ethiopian scholars, have provided further accounts, confirming the continuing centrality of sister-exchange—most notably, Berihun Mebratie Mekonnen (2004) for the Gumuz of Metekkel, north of the Blue Nile.

The Gumuz language has special terms for talking about marriage: the root *anj* crops up in various ways. For example, *biyanjigu* means "they marry by exchange"; *anjia* are the two girls exchanged for each other; and the brother and sister paired in an exchange are *fanjela*. When a young man wishes to marry, he has to secure a *fanjela*—a real sister or other substitute exchange partner, or he has to abduct a woman and elope with her, which can lead to fighting. The Gumuz speak of key descent clusters as "houses," naming a male ancestor a few generations back as the "center pole" of the whole cluster. These clusters are variable in size, some including many patrigroups of different origin, who may have intermarried. Within the patrigroups, male elders are continuously engaged in pursuing exchange marriage links with similar units, seeking to allocate any marriageable girl from within their group as an exchange partner for one of their juniors. The theory is that a young man is entitled to use his younger sister as an exchange partner in making his marriage. In practice there are nearly always problems, while the elders try to sort them out, helping the young man without a sister extend the search so he can deploy a FBD, FBSD, and so on for purposes of making a regular exchange marriage. Girls are thus "borrowed" quite often from within the patrigroup or even the larger association known as "house" so a young man can use them in a marriage exchange. These "borrowed" girls then have to be replaced in some way, sometimes with a daughter of the marriage itself (this is not an exchange but a substitution).

Of course, it is very rare for all to go well, even with a suitable direct exchange of two younger sisters between men of different patrigroups. Problems of maintaining the balance frequently spill over into the next generation. Will each new bride have a brood of healthy children so that both parties feel they have had a good deal? All kinds of ad hoc adjustments may have to be made to equalize the relationship. If a wife on one side dies, her group will have to find a replacement (called *hirba*). Children may have to be transferred from one side to another, especially girls, who can then be used in further exchange marriages. If an in-married wife does not give birth (especially to daughters), her husband may demand that his out-married sister return a daughter, "in place of herself," to be deployed in a later exchange, probably on behalf of a younger brother or a son. From the point of view of the young man in this scenario, he is being allocated a ZD or FZD as an exchange partner so he can marry; from the girl's point of view, she is to be exchanged not in the usual way by her brother or another male of her patrigroup but by an MB or MBS. Other possibilities for a young man seeking an exchange partner would be among women who have been returned to the patrigroup because of earlier failed exchanges, in settlement of a debt, or in the making of a peace compact. There are no genealogical limitations, as such, to the recruiting of exchange partners; the possibilities and limitations have to do with the logic of the exchange system itself.

We conventionally assume that the basic and objective language for kinship must rest on a description of individual links of descent within a genealogical matrix and that folk systems of "kin terminology" can be reduced to this framework. But it is difficult to pin down the Gumuz system this way, because relationships and marriageability are not represented in terms of an individual's place in a matrix of personal descent. They are represented by the place he or she occupies, or comes to occupy, in the scheme and practices of exchange marriage. A striking example is that of the term *mama*, which an ethnographer will be told means FZ. In practice this is applied (with all its behavioral connotations) to any female used by one's father as a *fanjela*, an exchange partner, in making his own marriage. Ego's F could have borrowed not merely a BD, FBD, or FBSD to use as a *fanjela* but even a ZD, FZD, or FFZD (etc.) for reasons already described, resulting in ego applying the term *mama* (FZ) to a woman originally born as the father's ZD, that is, a cross-cousin. The latter, and analogous usages, show how members of a "hidden" matriline may be merged in a kind of skewing reminiscent of the Crow pattern, though without being generalized throughout the terminology. In the situation of widow inheritance, a woman may find herself transmitted on to her late husband's son (by a different wife). From her point of view especially, the equation *in practice* of a man with his own son resonates with what we call the Omaha pattern. Evidence in several hundred cases shows how varied are the actual kin positions of women exchanged in Gumuz marriages (James 1975:89).

We know that most Gumuz kin terms are "descriptive"—for example, we find distinct terms for parents and their siblings (F, *baba*; M, *yaya*; FB, *chamba*; FZ, *mama*; MB, *miya*; MZ, *ciya*). Children of parents' siblings can be described individually, for example, as "child of my FB" (*du chamba*) or "child of my MB" (*du miya*). Sibling terms (always inclusive of parallel cousins) strongly distinguish elder and younger, and all four types of cousins can be put in the plural, along with siblings, as *yideba*. It is true, intriguingly, that there is a special Gumuz term, *gatoja*, which translates as "bilateral cross-cousin." But this self-reciprocal term applies only between the children of an actual specific exchange; any other "classificatory" FZCh or MBCh is assimilated to the collectivity of *yideba*. This process used to be called "Hawaiianization of G^0" but is more comfortably called "cross-parallel neutralization" by Kronenfeld and Dousset in their chapters in this volume. People who are specifically *gatoja*, born on either side of an exchange, cannot marry each other (even if they are not genealogical first cousins). That is, the exchange in G^1 cannot be replicated, Dravidian style, in G^0.

The prohibitions on repeating a marital exchange between patrigroups extend over three generations, with narrowing lineal specification of the prohibited degrees. These rules about marriageability are the idiom in which clans, subclans, and patrigroups describe their inter-relations. Having cooperated, intermarried, and even fought together, different groups can become one player in the exchange game, borrowing and replacing girls as *fanjela* among themselves. Members of affiliated groups within the larger "houses" would explain to me that they could not marry each other's actual members but *could* perhaps marry their *gepokwa*, their respective "sister's children." Yet others, who had avoided each other's sisters' children and their offspring for some time, could now perhaps marry each other once again. There were so many overlapping marriage histories that my effort to map relationships for just one local cluster in these terms must remain very tentative (figure 7.1).

I did not have a chance to return to my research among the Gumuz, but Mekonnen (2004) has shed further light on all these matters. In this paragraph I have reworded his account and spellings slightly but retained his use of "clan" and "subclan." He notes that a male ego seeking a wife has to go outside the whole of his own clan in the first place. Beyond this, he may not marry into the A1 subclan of his MF, but can marry into other subclans, such as A2 or A3. Ego's S is, by contrast, allowed to marry into the subclan A1, that of his own MMF. In the next generation, ego's SS may marry not only into A1 but into the actual family line of his MMMF (ibid.:80ff). That is, an exchange cannot be exactly repeated between close patrigroups until the fourth generation, the range of prohibition being eased across the subclans and immediate family lines of the relevant clan in each succeeding generation. Mekonnen's informants represented the prohibitions in terms of marriageability from the point of view of the *gepokwa*, the "sister's children" (ZCh) of a clan, the *dugepokwa* (ZDCh), and the *bugepokwa* (ZDDCh)—the latter being able to replicate the exchange of their great-grandparents. As each marriage link is ideally an exchange, a line of "sister's children,"

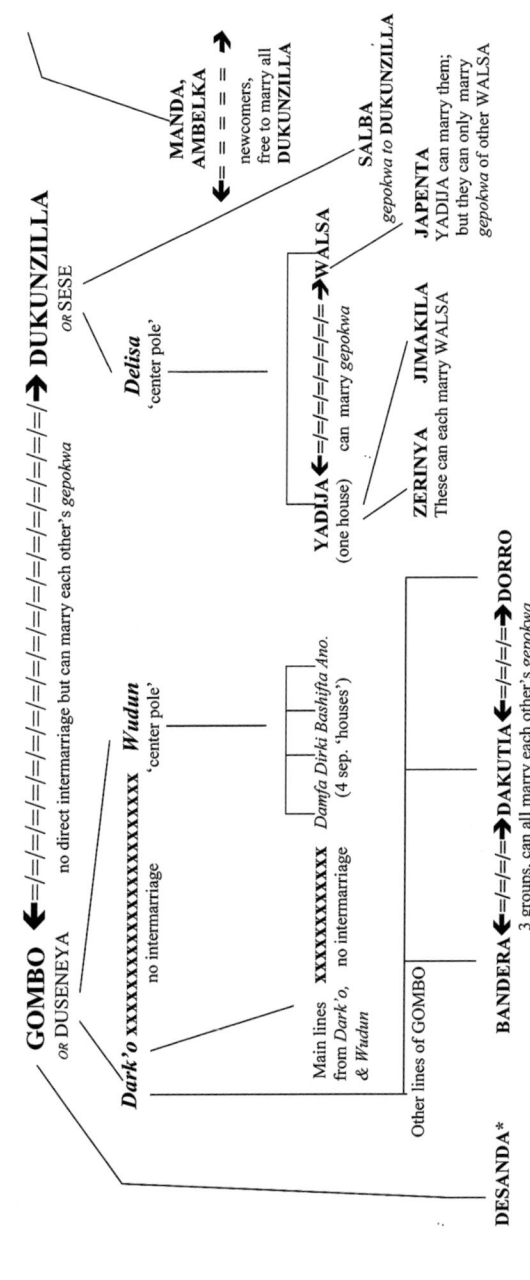

Figure 7.1 Marriageability within Gumuz paired clans of Gombo and Dukunzilla. Wallega Province, Ethiopia, 1975.

their offspring, and their grandoffspring, is produced on each side, as the prohibited degrees on repeating the original link are narrowed with each generation.

Whatever the analytic terminology, this pattern is surely reminiscent of the marriage prohibitions of the Samo, Mkako, and other West African cases. All are governed, I believe, by rules of give-and-take that help define generations as conceptual wholes, as well as the controlled crossing of male and female pathways. A diagram of this system offered by Tjon Sie Fat (1998a:274), incorporating one of Héritier's, and repeated here (figure 7.2), emphasizes the changing relationship of specific lines within a patrilineal descent group as the marital prohibitions between them are narrowed over time. But the pattern can also be read as a succession of sociocentrically defined generations, their distinct identities defined by these very prohibitions. This diagram cannot possibly describe real life with its demographic and other irregularities. It is a model, "fictitious" perhaps as all models are, but it reflects the principles by which people may try to live (or at least those that authoritative elders may try to impose). It certainly echoes the principles of the Gumuz case, contrasting with the messy realities I sketched in figure 7.1.

Uduk and Komo: Giving up Sister-Exchange, Formalizing Matriliny

In my first fieldwork in the 1960s, I noted how sister-exchange was practiced occasionally by the southern Uduk, almost as a prank—a sort of revenge elopement. The northern Uduk scorned the idea and strongly denied that they had ever done such a thing. The circumstantial evidence, however, indicates they probably had done it a few generations back, but in the course of northward migration, I believe they abandoned sister-exchange, probably along with generational marriage contracts, embracing matriliny as an alternative mode of recruitment to local groups (James 1979). But unlike the Gumuz, they retained a systematic cross/parallel distinction in cousin terminology. Cross-cousins (*'kwaskam*) on both sides are potentially marriageable, though a first cousin marriage would be unusual and the man would be laughed at, people told me, for only going courting as far as his father's village. There are also several self-reciprocals, such as FB/BCh (*iya*), a usage

A Tetradic Starting Point for Skewing?

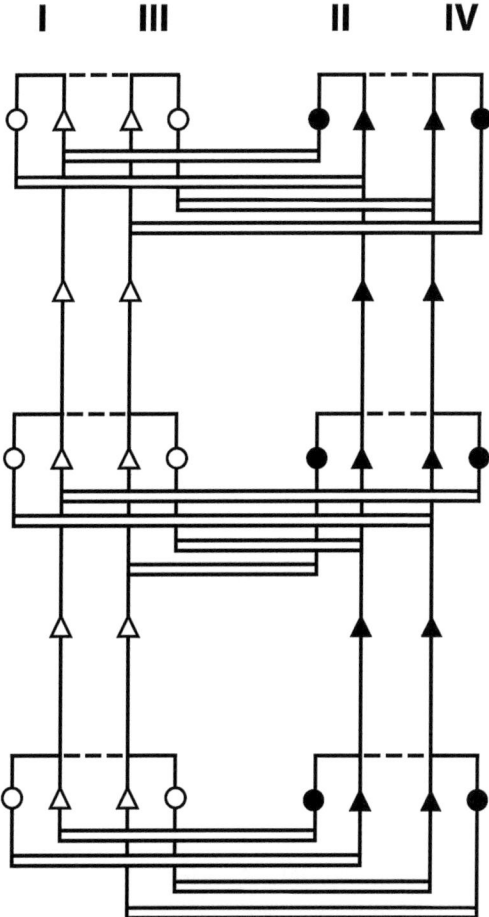

Figure 7.2 Schematic marriage patterns of the Samo and others of West Africa, giving equal weight to generational as to lineal distance in the making of alliances. *Source:* Tjon Sie Fat 1998a, in Schweizer and White, *Kinship, Networks, and Exchange.* © 1998 Cambridge University Press. Reprinted by permission.

that Nicholas Allen has pointed out to me connects *alternate generations* from a speaker's point of view. These terms are extended in clearly patterned ways. In G^{-1}, for a male speaker the children of all male *'kwaskam* are *iya*, that is, the same as "brother's children," whereas those of all female *'kwaskam* are *nam*, "sister's children." Thus, although cross-cousin marriage is an option (as in Dravidian systems), the terminology falls into the Iroquois or Type B category of crossness.

Despite the fact that *'kwaskam* is a self-reciprocal term for bilateral cross-cousin, the *social relation* between oneself and one's two kinds of cross-cousin was not symmetrical at all. A person's FZCh was one of those collectively called "father's people," and reciprocally a MBCh was one of those "fathered by us." This is clearly a Crow-style asymmetry in the relation between a specific person and their father's matriline. The Uduk explained very clearly to me that a *debt of life* was owed to one's father's people that could never be repaid. This is why, the people told me, a man should fight alongside his father's people on the battlefield, laying down his life if necessary. Also sharpening up the idiom of the matriline, the self-reciprocal of southern Uduk terminology, MB/ZCh (*shwakam*) came to be split in fairly recent times, as the main body of the people moved north—the northern dialect of Uduk has two different terms (MB: *shwakam*; ZCh: *nam*). At the same time, matrilines themselves acquired a new label—*wak*, otherwise meaning "animal species."

Later, I was able to confirm the continuing practice of sister-exchange—at least in part—among other Koman language speakers such as Komo, Shyita, and Kwama groups, as well as Ganza and "Mao" (covering at least two Omotic languages), all based in western Ethiopia. Among the Komo in particular, a good number of marriages were in principle "by exchange," but this was on a fairly casual basis. People spoke of overarching groups called *mos*, perhaps translatable as "patrilineal clans," but local communities were very "mixed." These were called *is*: that is, the term for "body." A man's sisters' children would easily become part of his "body" through co-residence and perhaps contract an exchange marriage in due course. Bridewealth was already becoming an alternative. I sensed there was a gradual erosion of the exchange system (James 1975) and a shift toward matrifocality in practice.

Amba: Sister-Exchange as it Was, with Omaha Skewing

The Amba people of western Uganda offer an interesting comparison with the examples already given. Although speaking one of a cluster of Bantu family languages, their practices were once very like those of the Koman group, especially the Gumuz. Sister-exchange was the main mode of marriage until its abolition by the colonial government in 1947 (Winter 1956). Over the Congolese border were several loosely organized peoples, small groups of whom became attached to Amba communities—particularly the Mbuti hunter-gatherers, who are still known for sister-exchange (Turnbull 1965). Amba society was organized around patrilineages, conceptualized on the basis of biological paternity (rather than the social fatherhood conferred in systems with heavy bridewealth).

Significantly, Winter (1956:256–60) records details of Omaha skewing in Amba kinship terminology, starting with the key equation of MB with MBS. Omaha cousin terminology is also found in Bunyoro to the east, linked by Beattie to the asymmetrical relation between inter-marrying, though not in this case exchanging, patrilineages (Beattie 1957, 1958). The Amba also had a very Omaha-looking—we might now prefer to say "Samo-" or "Gumuz-looking"—set of marriage prohibitions, persisting up to the time of Winter's fieldwork. In addition to being forbidden to have sexual relations with women of their own lineage, "a man is prohibited from having sexual relations with members of lineages linked to his own, any one descended from women of his own lineage within three generations, and any one of a lineage from which he is descended within three generations" (Winter 1956:45, n1).

A significant detail is the Amba rule that a man has a duty to assist his MB's lineage in warfare, and in turn they should lead the mourning at his death. The Omaha equation of MB = MBS as the naming of a position, rather than a person, makes obvious sense here in the context of "real" social events, such as a man joining both his MB and MBS on the battlefield. Reversing the Uduk prescription, these are the people who gave his mother in marriage to his father, and hence made his own life possible. He can expect to call for support on those who count as ZS and FZS to himself. These equations may look lopsided when considered from the point of view of "ego" in a line diagram of kin terms, where one set of cross-cousins are "raised" a generation and the other are "lowered": but in the Amba exchange marriage context, each man's debt to his mother's people transforms the asymmetry into a mutual bond—nicely illustrating the essence of the "generational contract."

Kunama: Matriliny Elaborated

The Kunama of western Eritrea frequently appear in travelers' tales. Only recently was a modern ethnographic study undertaken by Dominique Lussier (2000). From this work and from talking to his Kunama wife, Macca Teclehaimanot, I have come to see the Kunama case as a distinctive contribution to my main argument about the relevance of the tetradic model to African ethnography. Kunama society is known to be organized matrilineally; beyond this, there are concepts and practices based on images of large-scale symmetry that recall Dravidian analogues, including the symbolic marking of alternate generations.

Across all Kunama are four "natural kinds," *koshera*, associated with various animals and other markers, including distinctive ritual practices. There are two main territorial groupings of Kunama. In the case of Barka, seen as the more traditional, the four kinds are paired as two sets of what I take to be exogamous moieties: Shuwa/Karawa and Serma/Gurma. There is a formal relationship called *kosamata* between each pair, involving specific roles at rites of passage for the other moiety and institutionalized joking. In the case of the other territorial grouping of Marda, the four kinds have fragmented into a number of independent matrilineages. The substance of the matrilineage is represented as "bone"—an interesting contrast to the Gumuz idea of the patriline as bone. For the Kunama, the bones of the fetus are created from the blood of the mother and the "blood of the body" of the father (sperm). Among Marda people, the symmetrical intermoiety relationship of *kosamata* as found in the Barka section is replaced by the relationship between each matrilineage and its own "offspring of the menfolk," *kishkishe*. This category takes on similar ritual obligations to those who are *kosamata* in the Barka context. A given speaker will talk of "my *kishkishe*," including any individual MBCh, as "one of our children." Reciprocally, a person will speak of his or her own specific father's matrilineal kin as "my father's people"—including any particular FZCh. Perhaps at one time cross-cousinhood would have been embedded in the *kosamata* relationship still found in Barka; but the Marda grouping do not have any specific kin term for cross-cousins (whether matri-, patri-, or bilateral). Like the Uduk, however, the logic of relations between a person and his or her father's matriline follows a Crow-style asymmetry.

Given the historical disturbances the Kunama have experienced, it is not surprising that some of the overarching symmetries have been eroded. They still maintain a practice of pairing, *kedella*, between a brother and a sister, today explained in terms of their respective inheritance claims. Up to now, personal names are never repeated in *adjacent* generations (unless by chance), but there are sets of names formally bestowed according to the principle of *alternating* generations.

Are there projects to reestablish balance at local levels? At least among the Marda grouping, in fairly recent times elders have attempted to set up sister-exchange arrangements. From her home in Oxford, my friend Macca helpfully called up her mother in Eritrea to check on some of my questions. She learned, to her great surprise, that her own mother had originally been exchanged, only to run away on her wedding day! Macca's mother explained that such occasional exchanges did take place, to "strengthen the friendship between men." Although there is no Kunama label for "exchange" marriage, in negotiating any marriage the elders of two respective matrilines might say, "Let's bring our children together." These days the father is expected to take a greater role than was previously the case, especially in raising bridewealth (no doubt with the backing of market forces and the missions). In this case, although Macca's mother abandoned her allocated husband, her own MB welcomed the incoming exchange bride, and she remained with him. However, the abandoned groom demanded his bridewealth back and a tremendous row involving several parties ensued. Bridewealth—with all its entanglements in larger scale productive systems, does not sit well in the exchange marriage contexts I described here; it was regularly contested even among the Amba after the official abolition of exchange.

Conclusion

The tetradic scheme presented in Allen's chapter may indeed constitute merely a cognitive model. Regardless of its possible salience for long-term human history, it is good to find traces of its symmetries and complementarities in unexpected places. It contains logical and perhaps chronological starting points for two basic "recipes" for making human kinship. First there is obviously the possibility for developing extended lineality out of the crossness built in to the model, as the continuity of gendered pathways comes to be emphasized over their particular moments of combination and recombination. At the same time, the generational side of kinship, everywhere embodied in the birth of new people, has received less attention. However, where marriage is regarded as only the beginnings of a relationship between the parties, to be fulfilled in the birth of offspring, we should recognize that the contract spans a generation. That is how it is regarded by many of the peoples whose practices we study; from this point of view, Crow-Omaha skewing of the kind that merges a parent and his or her same-sex offspring is easily understandable. It is not helpful to see cases like the Samo (or those I have introduced here) as halfway between elementary and complex. In bracketing a child with its same-sex parent, even for rather pragmatic reasons, their practices of skewing are possibly quite basic to the theory, history, and perhaps origins of human kinship.

8

Crow- (and Omaha-) Type Kinship Terminology

The Fanti Case

David B. Kronenfeld

As techniques used in the formal semantic analysis of kinship terminologies have become more complex and esoteric, there has been an increasing tendency for formalists to ignore the social facts that give rise to the kinship terms. Conversely, those anthropologists who are interested in the social bases of kinship terminologies tend to eschew any formal precise accounting for the denotation of the terms. I suggest, however, that a proper goal of a formal analysis is the understanding of the social bases of a terminology and that a correct detailed understanding of such social bases can only be made on the basis of a precise formal analysis of the semantic relations among the terms.

I address formal analyses of the Fanti kin terminology to several theoretical concerns. One is the relationship of kinship terminologies to more broadly considered kinship systems. Implicated are questions concerning the "meaning" of kinship terms and the systems they make up. Linked to this issue I offer a substantive hypothesis—that Crow- and Omaha-type (i.e., skewed) terminologies always represent an overlay on top of an unskewed base. The second major concern is a methodological suggestion regarding the usefulness of formalisms, in particular, Sydney H. Gould's system.

I have no theory of the cause of Crow- and Omaha-type kinship terminologies, or whether there is such a thing as a Crow or Omaha kinship system. What I do have is one quite well-studied specific case, various kinds of comparative study, and a lot of questions. The basic question, of course, is "What is Crow/Omaha?" This breaks down into:

1. How encompassing an entity is it?
    a. Only a terminological rule, with no (or only few and minimal) general associations;

b. A complex of associations—terminological rule plus lineage type and some sort of cultural focus;
   c. An integrated system—terminological rule, lineage type, and relations among lineages as an organizing device for the wider social system.
2. Is it one thing everywhere or different things, perhaps in different culture areas?

Kinship Terminologies as Semantic Systems

Kinship terms are easier to understand than many other kinds of vocabulary for several reasons. First, they have a genealogical aspect that makes at least part of their definition very straightforward, easy, and available. This genealogical aspect does not necessarily imply that these terms are basically, primarily, emotionally, or intuitively genealogical. But they always have at least some referents for which genealogical information is crucial. These genealogical senses always provide a kind of fulcrum from which we can work on the other aspects of the terms' meanings—whatever they may be. We always have this genealogical aspect because people everywhere have mothers and (almost everywhere) fathers, who in turn have siblings. The genealogy flows from these connections and the adaptation of some set of terms to the genealogy flows from the importance of mothers, fathers, and siblings—that is, from people's immediate families of orientation and procreation.

Second, kinship terms are simple because they typically form a fairly clearly defined contrast set. The Fanti terms certainly do. That is, they clearly contrast with one another and do not contrast directly with other "role terms"—even though there may be slightly hazy borders represented by terms such as "friend" and "stranger." Third, kinship terms are particularly nonesoteric: everyone in the society learns them and learns them when young. This universality necessitates that their definition and correct use be reasonably straightforward and uncomplicated. In such a situation, complicated concepts are too likely to be bungled or mislearned in transmission, so the defining features and the operations performed on them must be simple enough for a child to grasp. This simplicity implies conjunctively (mutually) defined units or operations wherever possible and implies relatively few features or operations. Conjunctivity is essential for accuracy of transmission (from one generation to the next).

The Fanti Context

The Fanti are an Akan tribal grouping of somewhere over 1 million people in the central part of southern Ghana and are closely related to the Ashanti (e.g., Christensen 1954; for Ashanti, see, e.g., Fortes 1950; Rattray 1923). Prior to the colonial period, the Fanti comprised a number of independent political units; these units retain their "stools" (i.e., thrones) and chiefs and are now spoken of as traditional states (see Christensen 1954:7–18). The town where my study concentrated is "Egyaa No. 1" in the Anomabu Traditional State. Fanti coastal towns have had more than 500 years of continuous European contact and thus would seem to be in at least a stable contact situation.

The Fanti have matrilineages (*ebusuas*) that are grouped together into a small set of named clans. Fanti clans do not play a role in marriage or any other aspect of social organization. Matrilineages are corporate groups, whereas clans are social categories that provide a common sociocentric framework across the entire Akan area, fostering a sense of pan-Akan unity. This framework enables people who are away from their home lineage to create temporary pseudo-kinship ties in that removed locality, as needed, for social, political, and religious purposes. Additionally, when a lineage dies out, its property will be taken over by a nearby lineage of the same clan. The same term, *ebusua* ("family" by their translation) is used for both clan and lineage, and a lineage shares the same proper name (one out of a set of seven or so) with the clan to which it belongs. The matrilineage controls inheritance. When a man dies, the lineage elders meet and decide on the disposition of his property. The lineage is the residual owner of any property that the deceased inherited and in effect passes on to another of its members' lifetime use rights over that property. The major part of property that the deceased earned or created himself also passes to his lineage heirs, but a portion of it may be left to his wives and children (i.e., alienated from his matrilineage). The lineage elders may give use rights for the man's property to any person they choose (male or female, old or young, lineage member or not). However, there is a hierarchy of succession among the potential heirs that is expected to be followed unless the next in line is deemed inappropriate. Such a judgment could be based on incompetence, youth, nonlocal residence, or any other factor that could prevent him or her from effectively utilizing the inheritance. Ideally, property would only go to other lineage members if the person who created it had no eligible matrilineal descendants. Women's property descends similarly, but children are in-lineage and the spousal issue seems not to arise.

Two facts are important: (1) inheritance ideally should always go from senior to junior, and (2) inheritance goes first by generation and only by age within a given generation. A nephew can inherit from his uncle, but the uncle cannot normally inherit from his nephew. It is necessary for a man to distinguish members of his own generation from senior and junior generations because of the effect of generation on whether he can inherit from them or they from him. Inheritance is important to the Fanti in the sense that they talk about it a lot, are concerned with who will inherit from whom, and ascribe a basic feature of their kinship terminology (the terminological classing of mother's brother's child with own child) to it.

Fanti Kin Terminology

The Fanti kinship terminological system consists of at least three alternative subsystems, using the same set of lexemes in reference to the same set of kernel kin types. The subsystems differ in their rules and range of extension from the kernels. My informants recognized the existence of the separate subsystems; their use of one or the other at any given time was internally consistent. One subsystem is Crow-type. For reasons explained by Lounsbury (1964a, 1965), the nature of the terminological categories in Crow-type systems necessitates an extensionist analysis. This analysis assumes a process of *semantic* extension in the definition of kin term categories; it does not necessarily assume any extension-of-sentiment cause or any extension-of-behavior effect. An extensionist analysis shows the three Fanti patterns to be part of a single system.

Kernel kin types are the focal or primary kinfolk in the different terminological classes. The set of consanguineal kernel kin types consists of one kin term for each generation of the nuclear family and a separate kin term for the nearest matrilineal member of that generation if that kinsman is not in the nuclear family. The three subsystems represent three patterns of extension from these kernels. The central pattern, which I refer to as the unskewed pattern, is based on generational extension from the kernels but preserves the kernel distinction between mother's and father's side of the family for male relatives in G^{+1} and its reciprocal G^{-1} distinction (there is no G^0 distinction to be preserved). In this pattern, every consanguineal kinsperson of Ego is called by the same term as Ego's kernel relative of the kinsperson's generation on the correct side of the family. This pattern is the one most commonly used in speaking of actual kinfolk.

The next pattern, the skewed one, is less commonly used than the unskewed one, but it was described by all informants as the more "correct" pattern. It adds one self-consciously held specific terminological equation to the generational base of the unskewed system: one's mother's brother's child (*wɔfa n'ba*) is equated with one's own child (*ba*), moving him or her down a generation. Father's sister's child (*egya n'awɔfasi*) is reciprocally equated with father or mother (*egya* or *na*), rising a generation. Relatives derivative from these connections move up or down accordingly, producing a Crow Type 1 pattern (see Lounsbury 1964a). Informants feel that this equation places together otherwise dissimilar kinsfolk, a feeling that they do not have about the equations implicit in the unskewed pattern. This equation appears to be counterintuitive to them, apparently because it breaks up the generational pattern of their terminology, so they feel a need to explain it. The explanation they give is very specific: a sister's son (ZS) inherits from his mother's brother (MB); among other things, formal kinship obligations are inherited; and thus ZS may become "father" (F) to his mother's brother's child (MBCh). No such explanation was offered for any part of the unskewed pattern. This equation represents the only basic difference between the two patterns; all the other differences in terminological labels of kinsmen follow logically from this one.

This equation produces an asymmetrical equivalence: ZS calls MB's child "child," but MB calls ZS's child "grandrelative." Taken simply as a terminological fact, this asymmetry seems quite strange, but it becomes less so when one realizes that according to Fanti inheritance norms, ZS can inherit from MB but MB cannot inherit from ZS. Inheritance is the only important behavior in Fanti culture that shows this particular asymmetric pattern for this pair of kinsmen, and thus I think one must accept the Fanti folk theory as the correct explanation of the skewed pattern, at least insofar as it differs from the unskewed one.

The third pattern is the courtesy use of kin terms to nonkinsmen. Villagers most frequently use kin terms in this manner. In this pattern of extension, the nuclear family terms (and the grandrelative term but not the lineal terms) are extended to everyone in town according to approximate relative age (biased a little by wealth and social importance).

Formalist Approaches to Kin Terminologies: Gould's System

Comparison necessarily requires a metalanguage that best lends itself to recognition of similarities and differences across a range of systems, and thus necessarily loses some of the detail of particular systems. At the same time, the idiosyncratic detail of each individual system makes its categories and operations bad bets for the representation of other systems—the very reason that English kinship does not provide a good vehicle for describing Fanti kinship.

Various formalist systems have been devised to represent kin terminologies, and all have virtues, disclosing different structural aspects (e.g., Gould 2000; Keen 1985; Lounsbury 1964a, 1964b; Read 2001; Romney 1965). Fundamentally, a formalist model aims to reveal the "grammar" of a kin terminology beneath the surface expression of kin terms, its essential logical properties, and principles. In Lounsbury's (1964a, 1965) approach, a set of terms is analyzed into a set of kernel kin types, each representing a terminological category, and a set of equivalence (or expansion-reduction) rules that account for the assignment of other kin types into the given classes. The goal of the analysis is to find the minimal set of kernels and rules that logically entail all and only the terminological assignments. These kernels and rules may be considered the axioms of the terminological system. It will then be the case that a sociological explanation of these axioms necessarily constitutes a sociological explanation of the entire terminology. Lounsbury's approach has particular value for analyzing the contrasts between

Fanti unskewed and skewed terminologies, and I return to this later. First I want to introduce another formalist system (see also chapter 5).

Sydney Gould created an algebraic system for representing the relations among kin term categories and thus the relationship of kin types to kin term categories (the full system is explained in Gould 2000; see also Kronenfeld 2001). Gould's algebraic approach has two aims: (1) as clean and simple an analysis as possible, and (2) an analysis that accounts most parsimoniously for classes of systems even at the expense of ignoring idiosyncratic features of particular systems. Gould uses his own system of notation that requires some preliminary explanation. First, to resolve gender ambiguity in links to collateral relatives, he introduced the symbols $\overline{F}$ ("fatherling") and $\overline{M}$ ("motherling") to refer to a "man's child" and a "woman's child," respectively. These express the true reciprocals of F (father) and M (mother) in the underlying generative grammar of a terminology. Thus, a paternal cross-cousin, rendered in standard notation as FZD (i.e., FFDCh or FMDCh), in Gould's system becomes $FF\overline{F}\overline{M}$ ("father's father's fatherling's motherling") or $FM\overline{M}\overline{M}$ ("father's mother's motherling's motherling"). Second, he specifies an identity element as I (the "empty kin type," i.e., a kin type without a kin term) for the position we commonly speak of as ego. Third, to simplify longer expressions, he introduces J for sibling (equivalent to G in the present standard notation), and X for cross-cousin (Xc in our standard notation).

Gould's symbols allow the description of a system based on F and M (with $\overline{F}$ and $\overline{M}$) to be as logically simple as one based on P ("parent") and Ch ("child") but with the inclusion of gender. Strings of descendants can thus be represented in directly parallel form to ascendant strings. This innovation allows Gould to define the formal equivalences that characterize different types of kin terminologies neatly and succinctly. In Gould's system ↔ represents a structural equivalence of kin types, that is, one that is characteristic of the underlying logical relations linking kin terms to each other. Equivalence contrasts with "concurrence," or ≈ in Gould's notation, which refers to two kin types (e.g., a father's sister and a mother's sister) represented in a particular system by the same kin term (see Fanti *na*). The = in Gould's notation is used for definitional equivalences—basically relating similar expressions cast in different notational form.

Another noteworthy innovation was the creation of a simple graphic representation of his algebraic system. Gould's kin graph boxes are important because they directly embody the equivalence classes that generate the system. Everything within a given box is equivalent to all else in that box for purposes of calculation in the system. The graphic representation enables one to quickly and easily calculate kin term assignments and see the backbone structure of the different types of system (see Gould 2000:32).

The basic graph is made up of boxes connected via lines. Dashed lines connect a child's box with its mother's box; solid lines connect a child's box with its father's box. A line ending in an arrow only applies in the indicated direction; a line without an arrow works in both directions—that is, the direction in which a kintype string can be traced. Normally parent boxes are above child boxes, and ego's box (the I box) is in the center. The boxes contain structurally equivalent kin types; each is labeled on its outside in bold by its focus or foci (i.e., its shortest kin type or kin types). The interior of the box is split into structurally equivalent kin term categories—normally with a horizontal line dividing by relative age (older above) and a vertical line dividing by sex (male on left), and with further divisions as needed. If a kin term category includes parts that are not structurally equivalent, the parts appear in different boxes; an example in Fanti is *na* ("mother," see later discussion).

Fanti Terminology According to Gould's System

Some Fanti examples illustrate Gould's system in operation. The equivalence rules for the Fanti subsystems are in two parts.

1. The equivalence rules that characterize all of what Morgan spoke of as classificatory systems—including our Iroquois- and Dravidian-type systems (Morgan's Seneca and Tamil types), as well as our Cheyenne, Crow, and Omaha types. These rules indicate the structural equivalence of kin types to ego: that is, any of these particular kin types have the same value as links in a chain to other relatives (for the purpose of identifying the applicable kin terms for those relatives) as does ego directly. Thus, ego is structurally equivalent to a sibling, to a "man's child's father," and to a "woman's child's mother." In stan-

dard notation the structural equivalence is Ego = G = ChP (ego is equivalent to a sibling and to a child's parent). In Gould's notation, the structural equivalence rule is more distinctly expressed as I ↔ J ↔ $\overline{FF}$ ↔ $\overline{MM}$.

2. The rules specific to the particular type of system.

An equivalence rule of Cheyenne type (a variant of Generational terminology). This rule states that: FF ↔ FM, and MM ↔ MF, and reciprocally that a fatherling's fatherling (a man's male child's child, or ♂SCh in standard notation) is equivalent to a fatherling's motherling (or a man's female child's child, ♂DCh in standard notation). In Gould's system, the reciprocals for the Cheyenne structural equivalence rule are: $\overline{FF}$ ↔ $\overline{MF}$, and $\overline{MM}$ ↔ $\overline{FM}$ and X ↔ J.

The kin graph for the unskewed Fanti subsystem is shown in figure 8.1.

The equivalence rule for the skewed Fanti subsystem is the classic Crow structural equivalence rule: in Gould's notation, $\overline{FM}$ ↔ F (with reciprocal as $\overline{MF}$ ↔ $\overline{F}$). An example of this rule in practice, in standard notation, is FZS = F with reciprocal MBS = BS.

The kin graph for the skewed Fanti subsystem is shown in figure 8.2. Note that the lines connect to the box, not to delineated parts of the box, and thus sex of a line (dashed or straight) going up into a box need not match the sex of the terminological category in the part of the box that it touches. *Na*, again, is in two boxes, as is *ba*.

Gould's analytic system importantly gives us the axioms of each of the subsystems, and a comparison of those axioms allows us to see the key changes from one subsystem to the other. This comparison in turn enables us to focus on the likely social issues involved in the contrast: what does the one subsystem address that the other does not?

In comparing the equivalence rules of the two Fanti subsystems, we note that skewing keeps the two sides of G^{+1} distinct, as well as the two sides of each G^{+2} pair. These distinctions eliminate the condition that led to the equivalence of mother's side grandparents on one hand and of father's side on the other hand in the unskewed subsystem. The other difference concerns cross-cousins. In the unskewed subsystem, X ↔ J (Xc = G in standard notation) makes them equivalent to parallel cousins, whereas in the skewed subsystem the Crow rule skews cross-cousins

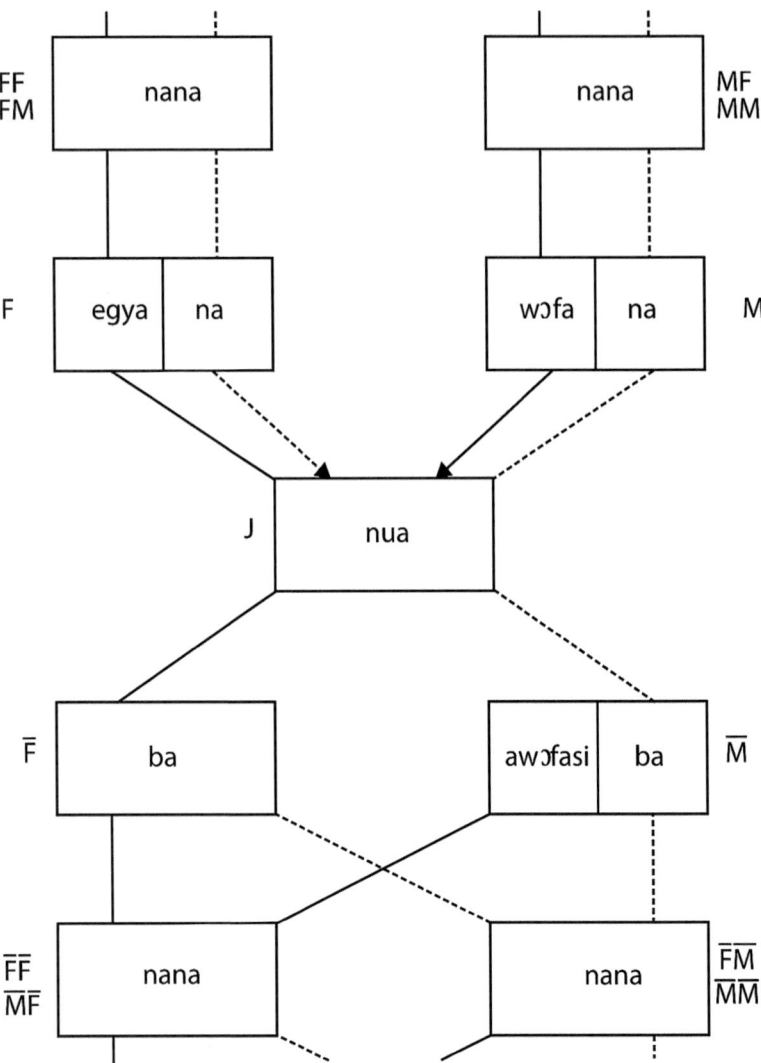

Figure 8.1 Fanti (unskewed) kin graph. *Source:* Gould 2000:287. Reprinted by permission of the University Press of America, a member of The Rowman & Littlefield Publishing Group. Equivalences: Specific Cheyenne type: X ↔ J. General Classificatory: I ↔ J ↔ $\overline{\mathrm{MM}}$ ↔ $\overline{\mathrm{FF}}$.

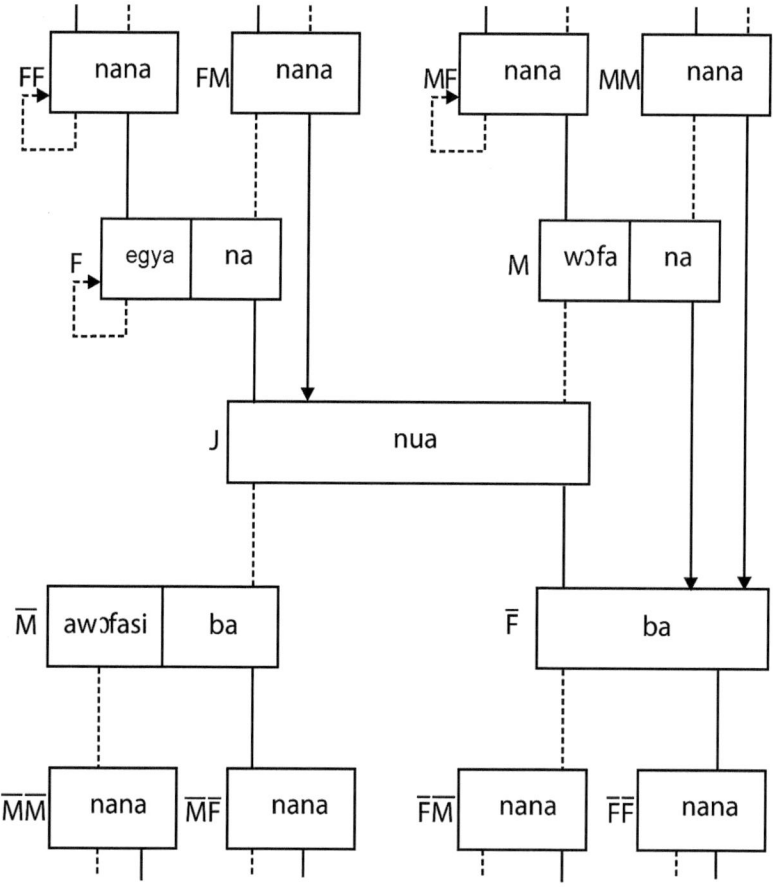

Figure 8.2 Fanti (skewed) kin graph. *Note:* FZ≈M. *Source:* Gould 2000:325. Reprinted by permission of the University Press of America, a member of The Rowman & Littlefield Publishing Group. Equivalences: Specific Crow type: MF̄ ↔ F̄ (and reciprocally FM̄ ↔ F). General Classificatory: I ↔ J ↔ MM ↔ F̄F̄.

while leaving parallel cousins unaffected. In sum, the *egya-wofa* contrast in G^{+1} and the reciprocal *ba-awofasi* contrast in G^{-1} represent a kind of cross-parallel (or side of the family) contrast that is absent in G^0 and does not carry over into G^2. In the unskewed subsystem, nothing much is done with this cross-parallel contrast, but in the skewed subsystem it provides the basis for skewing. Were it not for the needs of the skewed subsystem, the cross-parallel distinction might not be there: the possibility arises that a similar argument might apply to other Cheyenne-type systems as well.

Skewing as an Overlay

Regarding the relationship between the unskewed and skewed Fanti variants, I have elsewhere suggested that skewing, and thus the Crow-type variant it produces, can best be seen as an overlay on the unskewed variant. I now want to turn to some of my reasons for this suggestion. These reasons are both analytic and ethnographic. The analytic approach that best illustrates my overlay point, and was most instrumental in driving it home to me, was that of Lounsbury's classic rewrite rules. I am aware of the mathematical weaknesses of his rules and also of the sense in which they do not/cannot directly represent native operations—a point I have treated elsewhere and to which I return later. At the same time I assert that his approach is very consistent with a general approach to the semantics of word meaning, where algebraic treatments, in turn, are consistent with a general approach to pragmatic meaning.

Elsewhere (Kronenfeld 2009:43) I have used Romney's formal notation to represent Lounsbury's rewrite rules, and I refer the reader to that account for further details in this regard. For the present chapter, it is simpler to use standard notation (notwithstanding its formal limitations) to illustrate these diagnostic rules. Both unskewed and skewed systems share four of Lounsbury's structural equivalence rules: merging, half-sibling, step-kin, and generations-extension (see table 8.1).

The rules for the two subsystems are identical except for the presence or absence of the skewing rule. The cross-parallel neutralization (CPN) rule simply serves to eliminate the cross-parallel distinction for any kin type that has not been skewed.

Fanti Calculations

Fanti calculations (F Analysis in Kronenfeld 2009:53–62) show how they themselves actually operate within the system, including how they distinguish the one subsystem from the other. It is useful to group Fanti kin terms into three sets.

Table 8.1 Fanti equivalence rules

Rules common to skewed and unskewed variants

---

1. Merging rule: ego is equivalent to his or her same-sex sibling, i.e., ego = ssG

2. Half-sibling rule: a parent's child is equivalent to a sibling, i.e., PCh = G

3. Step-kin rule: a parent's spouse is equivalent to a parent, i.e., PE = P (with the terminological effect that a parent's spouse's kin = one's own kin)

4. Generations-extension rule: a great-grandparent is equivalent to a grandparent, i.e., PPP = PP

Rules that differentiate the two variants

---

5. Crow Skewing Rule
    skewed subsystem: Variant A: MGS = GS
    : Variant B: MB (kin) = B (kin), i.e., mother's brother's relatives = brother's relatives
    unskewed subsystem: nil

6. Cross-parallel-neutralization (CPN) rule
    skewed subsystem (general part): PosG(E) = PssG(E) (i.e., parent's opposite-sex sibling or sibling's spouse = parent's same-sex sibling or sibling's spouse).
        Variant A: limited to consanguines
        Variant B: including uncle's wife
    unskewed subsystem (general part): as with the skewed subsystem
        (special part): PosGCh = PssGCh (i.e., parent's opposite-sex sibling's child = parent's same-sex sibling's child)

The primary direct kin terms are defined by information outside the terminological system—by reference to procreation or marriage. This set includes real mother, real father, own child, real wife, and real husband[1]—which are the focal members of the sets of referents labeled by the relevant Fanti lexemes. The derivative direct kin terms are defined by relative products (in a mathematical sense) of the primary direct ones, as, for example, *mother's child* is *sibling*. This set includes Fanti lexemes for sibling, man's sister, mother's brother, and man's sororal nibling (nephew or niece).

The derivative indirect kin terms are defined by relative products of the direct ones. They are not normally used themselves in the calculation of terminological assignments. Figure 8.3 presents the basis of the Fanti's own calculation regarding kin term assignments, and figure 8.4 presents the remaining logically possible calculations that are not normally used because they are redundant. In general the calculations are 2:1 mappings of the form "one's X's Y is one's Z" (as one's mother's brother is one's uncle), where the tables are a symmetric matrix in which the rows are the X's, the columns are the Y's, and the interior of the tables contain the Z's. The X's, Y's, and Z's are all Fanti kinship lexemes. The system makes no distinction among the calculation of nonfocal exemplars of the primary kin term categories, focal exemplars of the various derivative kin term categories, and nonfocal exemplars of the derivative categories.

	NA MOTHER ♀	EGYA FATHER ♂	WƆFA UNCLE ♂	NUA SIBLING	AKYEREBA ♂SISTER♀	AWƆFASI ♂NIBLING	BA CHILD	YER ♂WIFE♀	KUN ♀HUSBAND♂
NA	NANA	NANA GRAND-RELATIVE	NANA	NA (♀) WƆFA (♂) UNCLE			NUA or ♂AKYEREBA♀		EGYA FATHER
EGYA	NANA	NANA	NANA	MOTHER NA (♀) EGYA(♂) FATHER	NA	MOTHER NA (♀) EGYA(♂) FATHER	SISTER NUA or AKYEREBA ♂ SISTER ♀	NA MOTHER	
WƆFA							BA	NA or MOTHER YER ♂WIFE	
NUA							BA	♀EKUMA +SISTER-IN-LAW YER ♂WIFE	♀KUN HUSBAND ♂AKONTA BROTHER-IN-LAW
AKYEREBA							AWƆFASI NIBLING		AKONTA BROTHER-IN-LAW
AWƆFASI							NANA GRAND-RELATIVE	ASEW	ASEW IN-LAW
BA							NANA	ASEW	ASEW
YER	ASEW	ASEW	ASEW	YER (♀) AKONTA(♂)			BA		MANGOW CO-HUSBAND
KUN	ASEW	ASEW	ASEW	KUN (♀) EKUMA(♂)	EKUMA	BA or KUN♂	BA	EKORA CO-WIFE	

Figure 8.3 Fanti equation matrix. *Source:* Kronenfeld 1980:154. Reprinted by permission.

Crow- (and Omaha-) Type Kinship Terminology: The Fanti Case 167

	NA	EGYA	WƆFA	NUA	AKYEREBA	AWƆFASI	BA	YER	KUN
NA									
EGYA									
WƆFA	NANA	NANA GRANDRELATIVE	NANA	NA (♀) WƆFA (♂)	NA	NUA			
NUA	NA MOTHER	EGYA FATHER	WƆFA	NA	NUA or SIBLING AKYEREBA(♂)	AWƆFASI SIBLING or BA CHILD			
AKYEREBA	NA	EGYA	WƆFA	NA					
AWƆFASI	NUA or SIBLING AKYEREBA(♂)	AKONTA BROTHER-IN-LAW	NUA	AWƆFASI	AWƆFASI SIBLING	NANA GRANDRELATIVE			
BA	(♂) YER (♀) NUA	(♂) KUN (♀) NUA	(♂) AKONTA (♀) NUA	BA CHILD	BA	NANA			
YER									
KUN									

Figure 8.4 Fanti redundant equation matrix. *Source:* Kronenfeld 1980:155. Reprinted by permission.

Longer expressions, such as mother's father's brother, require some traffic rules to guarantee correct assignments: (1) always calculate all possible pairs for which X, Y, and Z are all direct terms before calculating any others. Then calculate ones for which X and Y are direct before others. (2) Eliminate redundancies (see figure 8.4) before doing other calculations; that is, get strings reduced to a normal parent-sibling-child-spouse-parent type of order before doing other calculations. (3) Step-parents are reduced to parents before normal consanguineal reductions are calculated.

The difference between the skewed and unskewed subsystems depends on how mother's brother's child and father's sister's child are bracketed.[2] Mother's brother's child: [*mother's* male *sibling*]'s child reduces to *uncle's child*,[3] which in turn reduces to (own) *child*—while *mother's* [*brother's child*] is represented as *mother's* [*sibling's child*], which reduces to *mother's child*, which in turn reduces to *sibling*. Father's sister's child: [*father's* (female) *sibling*]'s *child* becomes [*father's sister*]'s[4] *child*, which reduces to *father's nibling*, which reduces in turn to *father* or *mother*, depending on sex—whereas *father's* [*sibling's child*] reduces to *father's child*, which in turn reduces to *sibling*.

Note that the Fanti terminology has no parent term, and the system of calculation explicitly recognizes none. Yet my behavioral data, many of the conversational patterns I observed, and much of their terminological patterning suggest that Fanti are well aware of the similarity of mothers and fathers versus uncles (and nonterminologically recognized) aunts. My sense is that because of the importance that they ascribe to their matrilineages, any explicit recognition of mother's similarity to father would be felt to undermine the centrality of the lineage. Consistent with this, their translation of the English word *family* clearly applies to the matrilineage and not the nuclear family. At the same time, for all behaviors that I could get data on—except for "inherit from"—mother's brother was much more similar to father's brother than to father or mother, and father and mother were similar to each other.

The Fanti system of calculations shows the cognitive efficiency of the relationship of their categories to their calculations. At the same time, for what seem to be sociopolitical reasons, Fanti leave out of their terminology conjunctivities that componential approaches (i.e., those based on features—as in Lounsbury 1964b) pick up on and that other ethnographic evidence suggests the Fanti are aware of.

Marking

On the basis of the observation that the skewed subsystem has the same analytic operations as the unskewed one plus one additional analytic operation, I have described this as representing a "marking" contrast (see Greenberg 1966), wherein the skewed system is the *marked variant* and the unskewed system the *unmarked variant*. My overlay point emerges from this marking relationship, which, although not clear from Gould's algebraic approach (or any other algebraic approach I am aware of), is clearly highlighted by Lounsbury's (1964a) semantic approach.

Once the marking relationship has been identified among the subsystems, I have ethnographic observations that support it. I have already noted that the Fanti have corporate matrilineages that control the allocation of property—especially in inheritance/succession situations. There is a default adelphic order (within the set of matrilineal heirs of the creator of the property or position, exhaust one generation before moving down to the next; circulate among all branches of heirs, and go from relatively senior to relatively junior within the generation [see Kronenfeld 2009:309–13]). Many informants independently gave me an explanation of skewing—the same explanation—to the effect that one's mother's brother's child was equivalent to one's own child because one inherits from one's mother's brother. I collected data on the actual incidence of various inheritance relations that made clear the potentiality of inheritance (including succession) was what mattered, rather than any particular actuality. This explanation came often unbidden, while I was unable to elicit any explanation for any other part of the kin term system. This presence versus absence of a folk explanation implies that the cross-generation extension of kin terms that is involved in skewing (such as a mature adult having a "father" who is a small baby) struck my Fanti informants as strange or counterintuitive—and thus requiring some explanation.

Comparison and Typology

We now come to the theoretical issue concerning the relationship of Crow- and Omaha-type kinship terminologies to more broadly considered kinship systems. One question concerns what these terminologies specifically reflect. I have suggested that one basic factor concerns relations of succession and inheritance. But clearly such a factor—if perhaps a necessary condition—is insufficient to account for the presence of such terminology. Presumably something has to foreground the succession issue to give us a skewed terminology. In the Fanti case, several factors pertaining to inheritance seem relevant, notably: (1) the potentiality of succession to some sort of ritually important relationship to a man's heir; and (2) the important role that the "children of [men of] the lineage" (*mba mbanyinfu*) play in public lineage events.

Other scholars working in other ethnographic areas have proposed some variety or system of marriage alliances among lineages as a cause for Crow-Omaha terminologies. From my own ethnographic work, I am certain that such alliances are not the case for the Fanti and thus cannot represent any universally necessary condition for skewed terminologies. In other words, I looked hard for such alliances and could not find them. The Fanti allow cross-cousin marriage on both sides, but informants strenuously denied that there was any preference for it, on the grounds that it gives affines too much authority in the case of disputes with one's spouse. Of the two close types possible, matrilateral cross-cousin (MBD) marriage is preferred over patrilateral (FZD)—as for the Ashanti (Fortes 1950:279). In practice, however, the extremely few cases of cross-cousin marriage I recorded (five in total) involved a higher incidence (three cases) of FZD marriage. Marriage with close consanguines within one's clan and with any consanguines within one's own lineage is prohibited. Because of past adoption of "slaves," lineages may contain nonconsanguines, and apparently these can be married. No marriage restrictions appeared to carry out to members of the wider clan. For the Fanti, marriage creates a link between the husband and his wife's lineage and a link between the wife and her husband's lineage, but it creates no link that I could find between the two lineages. In other words, marriage does not create an "alliance" between the lineages themselves.

A related question concerns to what degree—how often and where—there exists the kind of marking hierarchy I described for the Fanti wherein there exist variant terminological forms and the skewed variant is a "marked" variant of the unskewed. Elsewhere I have posed the possibility that this situation might be general. It is based on the notion that children always have to learn generational distinctions and how to figure these to understand the paradigm of focal kernel referents for kin term categories (no such foci that I am aware of cross generational lines). I would relate this terminological situation to the behavioral and juridical importance of the parent–child relationship within the immediate family. The combination of learning and importance makes gen-

9

Deep-Time Historical Contexts of Crow and Omaha Systems

Perspectives from Africa

Christopher Ehret

Historical Background

Crow systems of kin reckoning exist far back in time. Omaha systems are historically recent and not part of our ancient human cultural heritage. That, at least, is what the linguistic reconstruction of kin histories among the vastly spread Nilo-Saharan peoples of Africa indicates.

The Nilo-Saharan family captures our attention for a particular reason: the availability of a relatively detailed reconstruction of the history of its kinship terminologies (Ehret 2010). Reconstruction of early kin terms and terminologies offers direct and indirect testimony of early structuring of kinship across the family and reveals many particular changes in kin relations that occurred anciently along various lines of linguistic descent from the ancestral language and society, proto-Nilo-Saharan, to modern-day languages and peoples. The changes encompass numerous instances of shift from one kind of kin reckoning to another, including Crow and Omaha terminologies. Because of their quantity and variety, the Nilo-Saharan findings offer much new evidence for modeling normative directionalities of change in kin terminology and kin relations and suggest answers about the historical timing and social and economic contexts of different directions of shift. Moreover, because Nilo-Saharan is a very deep-time language family (twice as deep as Indo-European), reconstructing the history of its kin terminologies allows hypothesis testing over previously unmatched time spans.

Nilo-Saharan is also attractive for this kind of investigation because of the robust correlations between sequences of archaeological horizons and periods of linguistic history (Ehret 1993, 2006). From 8500 to 6000 BCE a three-stage transition took place in the eastern Sahara—

then a region of steppe rather than desert—from foraging to full-scale pastoralism. From 8500 BCE onward, deliberate tending of indigenous cattle began, along with one of the three earliest ceramic technologies in world history. Larger, more permanent settlements with significant cattle raising, and possibly rudimentary cultivation, emerged by 7200 BCE. Finally, sheep and goats were added 6500–6000 BCE. From 5500 to 4000 BCE, this economy and culture spread westward across most of the southern half of the Sahara.

Nilo-Saharan linguistic evidence reveals the same four-stage succession (figure 9.1). At the proto–Northern Sudanic stage, the first ceramic and cattle-raising terms came into use. In the next stage, proto-Saharo-Sahelian, a further body of new lexicon gained currency, including words descriptive of larger settlements, additional cattle terms, and the first words indicative of cultivation. At the third stage, during the contemporaneous proto-Saharan and proto-Sahelian periods (figure 9.1), another major new set of words, relating to goats and sheep, came into use. In the fourth stage, after the adoption of goat and sheep lexicons, a far-flung expansion of the descendant societies of the proto-Sahelians and proto-Saharans occurred. The linguistic geography of these descendant societies in later eras closely matches archaeological evidence for the spread of pastoral, ceramic-using peoples across the Sahel and southern Sahara (Ehret 1993, 2006).

The proto-Nilo-Saharan period lies at an undetermined time earlier than the proposed beginning of the proto–Northern Sudanic stage around 8500 BCE. A plausible conjecture is that earlier Nilo-Saharan expansion (see map 9.1) may have been a response to improved environmental conditions toward the end of the last Ice Age, ca. 12,700–10,800 BCE (Ehret 2008).

Reconstructing Ancient Kin Lexicon

How does lexical evidence reveal social and cultural history? A crucial characteristic is that each word in a language has a history, and each feature of the history of that word—why it came into use in the first place, for example, and the ways it has preserved or changed its meaning over time—reflects some aspect of the history of the peoples who used it. To possess a word for a particular thing or activity reveals, at

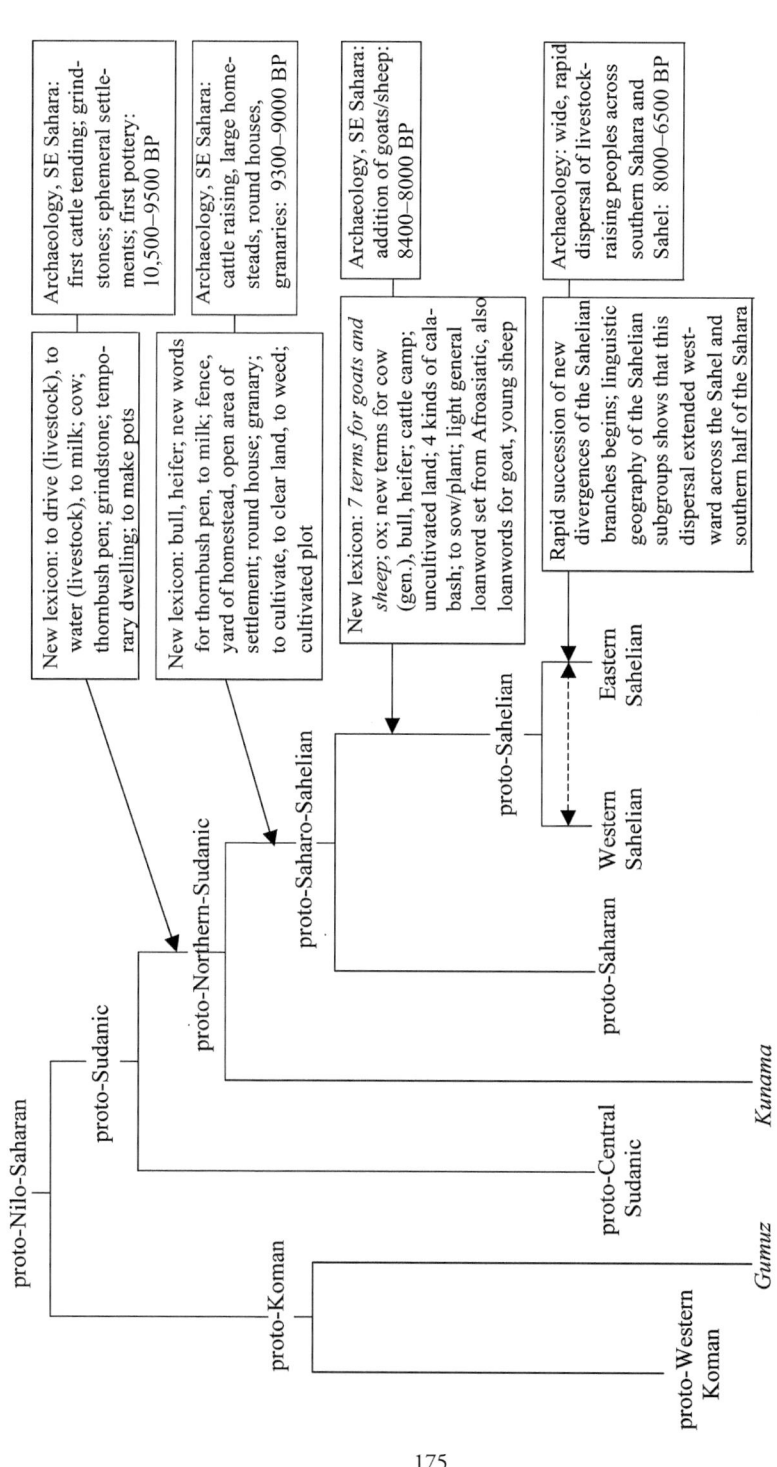

Figure 9.1 Nilo-Saharan family tree. New developments in lexicon from proto-Sudanic to proto-Sahelian with parallel archaeological sequence.

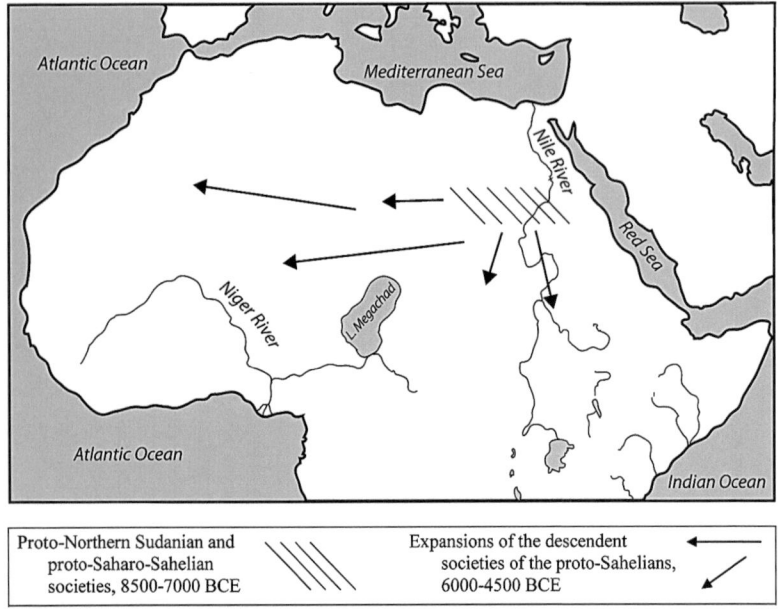

Map 9.1 Expansion of Nilo-Saharan speakers

minimum, that the people who used it were familiar with the thing or activity. If a word changed meaning at some earlier point in time, the meaning change came about because of historical changes, either in the uses or the form of the item named by the word, or in how people carried out the named activity, or in the views people held about the item or activity. The proto-Nilo-Saharan verb for "to squeeze or wring," for example, took on a new meaning, "to milk," in the proto–Northern Sudanic language. This meaning shift is one of several lexical indicators of the economic shift to cattle raising under way during the proto–Northern Sudanic era.

How do we trace the histories of words far back in time? Two criteria must be met.

First and most crucial, a characteristic feature of all language history is that sound change proceeds according to regular rules. If a consonant p, for example, changes to f in a particular phonological environment, such as at the end of words, it will do so in all words in the language in which the final consonant was previously p, and not just in a few such words. To be reconstructed as an ancient root word in a language family, the modern-day versions, or *reflexes*, of the root word in different languages of the family must show regular sound correspondences throughout the stem portions of the word (*stem* designates the original root word minus any prefixes or suffixes the daughter languages may have added to it).

The second criterion is distributional. To reconstruct a root word back to any particular earlier stage in the history of a language family, the reflexes of the root—besides showing regular sound correspondences—must occur in languages belonging to at least two of the linguistic descent lines that diverged out of the common ancestor language, or protolanguage, spoken at that stage in history. The preservation of reflexes of a particular root word, *with regular sound correspondences*, along the two separate lines of descent shows that the term was already in use in the protolanguage.

The early Nilo-Saharan root, *ap'o "grandmother" (Ehret 2010, Appendix 2, Proto–Northern Sudanic [PNoS] root 5), illustrates both criteria. With respect to sound change rules, Kunama *afa,* For *abo,* Nubian Midob *awa* and Dongolawi *aw,* Majangir *apo,* and Kwegu *apa,* all meaning "grandmother," show regular sound correspondences with each other. The initial vowel, short *a, is the regularly expected outcome in each of these languages of an original proto-Nilo-Saharan (PNS) *a located at the beginning of a word. (The asterisk preceding a root or individual consonant or vowel denotes a *reconstructed* pronunciation.) The consonant correspondence set following *a—Kunama *f* = For *b* = Nubian *w* = Majangir *p* = Kwegu *p*—is the regular product in each language of the PNS consonant, *p', when that consonant *follows* a vowel. (Note that the phonological environment matters: when *p' is at the beginning of a root, it has a different correspondence pattern: Kunama *f* = For *p* = Nubian *b* = Majangir *p* = Kwegu *p*.) The pattern of the final vowels fits the expected regular outcomes of PNS *o in word-final position, except for Midob and Kwegu, where an added noun suffix *-a* has replaced the original final vowel.

How does the root *ap'o "grandmother" fare with respect to the second essential criterion, distribution? The distribution of the root *ap'o in present-day Nilo-Saharan languages allows us to reconstruct it back to the proto–Northern Sudanic node in Nilo-Saharan stratigraphy (figure 9.1), but not earlier. Its reflexes occur, with regular sound correspondence, in languages belonging to both primary lines of linguistic descent leading from proto–Northern Sudanic. They occur in the sole remaining language, Kunama, of the Kunama branch, and in languages belonging to several of the sub-branches of Kunama's sister branch, Saharo-Sahelian. Regular reflexes of the root have been preserved, in other words, in languages whose lines of descent connect at the proto–Northern Sudanic node (figure 9.1). The root is entirely unknown, however, in the two branches of the family, Central Sudanic and Koman, that diverged from the Nilo-Saharan tree still earlier in time. Therefore, the word cannot yet be traced to periods earlier than proto–Northern Sudanic.

What if a particular language has what appears to be a reflex of a particular root, but its reflex does not show regular sound correspondences? In some cases the word may just be a chance resemblance and unrelated. But in most such cases this outcome indicates that the word was borrowed from another language. Loanwords bring to light different historical effects, including close interactions between societies in earlier periods. They often reveal the spread of particular knowledge, ideas, and items of material culture from one society to another. Consider the old Nilo-Saharan root word *ap'o: The word *afo* "grandmother" in the Nara language of the Astaboran subgroup of Nilo-Saharan (see figure 9.4 later) is also a reflex of this root. But Nara *afo* does *not* show regular sound correspondences throughout. Proto-Nilo-Saharan *p' regularly becomes *b* instead of *f* after a vowel in Nara. The presence of the *f* demonstrates that the Nara word was borrowed from the neighboring Kunama language, in which the change *p' > f *is* regular. Whereas regularity of sound change identifies common inheritance, irregular sound change allows one to identify the spread of terms from one language to another. In this case *afo* belongs to a much larger set of loanwords demonstrating that Kunama people had a major influence on the Nara.

One additional regularly corresponding reflex of PNoS *ap'o, the term *aba* in Sungor of the Tama group (see figure 9.4 later), exemplifies a second key element in the interpretation of word histories, namely, deciphering the historical significance of particular semantic changes. Intriguingly, Sungor *aba* today means not "grandmother" (PM) but "father's sister" (FZ). How and why did this meaning shift take place?

Two principles guide the deciphering. First, meaning shifts in words are motivated; they do not occur out of the blue. Second, meaning shifts also tend to proceed component by component. New components of meaning are added to words, and old components lost, because of the cultural associations of words and the social contexts in which people use them. The shift PM > FZ in the Sungor reflex requires three steps. The meaning "grandmother" has four components: second ascending generation (G^{+2}), female, paternal, and maternal. The first step in the shift particularizes the grandmother meaning to the paternal grandmother—in other words, it drops the component "maternal" but retains the component "paternal." The second step adds a new component, "first ascending generation" (G^{+1}). In this manner, *aba* comes to encompass two paternal relationships, the father's mother (FM) and her daughter, the father's sister. Finally, Sungor dropped the component "second ascending generation," leaving *aba* with only its present-day female, first ascending generation, paternal meaning, FZ.

In the Sungor case we can also retrieve the probable earlier historical context that motivated the meaning shift. One specific kind of kin relationships normally drives the sequence seen in Sungor. FM = FZ is an ascending-generation Crow equation. It indicates the former existence of Crow kin reckoning—and thus probably also matrilineal descent, which commonly accompanies Crow systems—in the historical past of the Tama group. The derivational history of the term for father's sister in Sungor enables us to infer a past kin organization strongly contrasting with the pervasive patrilineality of the Sungor and the rest of the Tama peoples today.

In general, three normative directionalities guide the course of kin semantic shift.

First, in cases involving the first ascending (G^{+1}), zero (G^0), and first descending (G^{-1}) generations, meaning shift proceeds normally from older generation to younger. The history of the Songay term for cross cousin (PosGCh), *baasa*, which derives from the proto-Saharo-Sahelian root *bɛɛs- "father's sister" (FZ) exemplifies this axiom as it applies to G^{+1} and G^0. A three-step shift in semantic components most parsimoniously explains the Songay outcome. First, the original meaning FZ added the component "zero generation," that is, it extended its meaning to include FZCh as well as FZ. Then the component "first ascending generation" dropped out, removing the meaning FZ. Finally, FZCh was generalized to all cross-cousins in modern-day Songay. (In formulaic notation, FZ > FZ *and* FZCh > just FZCh > PosGCh in general.)

The For language (see figure 9.4, later) offers a pertinent example of this axiom in the zero and first-descending generations (G^0 and G^{-1}) in Nilo-Saharan. The For reflex *dalang* (stem *dal-* plus a singular suffix *-ang*) of the early Nilo-Saharan root *Dal "sister (male speaking)" (♂Z) (see figure 9.3 later) today means "sister's child (male speaking)" (♂ZCh). The componential criteria imply the following sequence of semantic changes: first, the addition of the component "descending generation," thus extending the meaning of the term to include both ♂Z and ♂ZCh, and then, subsequently, the deletion of the zero-generation application to ♂Z, leaving just For ♂ZCh as the modern-day result.

Note that both the Songay and For semantic histories, like the Sungor instance already considered, imply the former existence of a particular motivating social context: FZ = FZCh and ♂Z = ♂ZCh are, respectively, zero- and descending-generation Crow equations. In other words, both languages passed through earlier historical periods in which their speakers maintained Crow kin systems.

The directionality, higher to lower, does not necessarily apply, however, in kin semantic shifts involving earlier or later generations than G^{+1}, G^0, and G^{-1}. The Sungor term *aba* FZ followed a downward meaning extension from second to first ascending generation. The root *ap'o clearly originally meant "grandmother" because that is its meaning everywhere except for Sungor. In contrast, in Baka and Kresh (see figure 9.4 later) of the West branch of the Central Sudanic languages, the proto-Nilo-Saharan root word for father's sister, *tayt^{h}a, shifted upward, taking on the meaning "grandmother." The most probable componential sequence in the Baka and Kresh meaning shifts was, first, FZ (female/paternal/first ascending generation) > FZ *and* FM, by addition of the component "second ascending generation"; then FZ *and* FM > FM, by deletion of the component "first ascending generation"; and finally FM > both parent's mothers by adding the component "maternal."

The second principle is that semantic shift in kin terms proceeds from primary to secondary relations. If an old root word has reflexes with the meaning "father" (F) in some languages and "father's brother" (FB) in others, "father" must be considered the original application, with the extension to FB arising secondarily. The same holds for applying one term to both M and MZ. Mother is the primary relationship, and calling the mother's sister "mother" is an extension to the mother's closest parallel kin. A third category illustrative of this axiom is siblings and cousins. An Iroquois system, for example, extends the primary category of B and Z to the parallel cousins. A Hawaiian system extends primary terms even further to include cross- as well as parallel cousins. Universally in Nilo-Saharan these directions of meaning extension—F to FB, M to MZ, and sibling to cousin—prevailed.

Third, semantic shift proceeds from consanguineal to affinal relations. The root *mbɛ, "spouse's father" in proto–East Central Sudanic—the ancestral language of the eastern sub-branch of the Central Sudanic branch of Nilo-Saharan (figure 9.4)—provides an especially instructive example. The direction of shift, affinal to consanguineal, is evident from the fact that *mbɛ is a phonologically regular East Central Sudanic reflex of proto-Nilo-Saharan *yɛmb "mother's brother."

The meaning shift, MB to EF, also has specific implications for early social history. For one thing, just one kind of motivating social context, preferential cross-cousin marriage, drives this particular meaning shift. In a society with cross-cousin marriage, the mother's brother, because he is the father of one's maternal cross-cousins, fills the role of an actual, potential, or classificatory father-in-law. The meaning change in proto–East Central Sudanic from MB to EF is a sure indicator of preferential cross-cousin marriage in the society or earlier along the line of social and linguistic descent leading down to that society. The applicability of the term to the fathers of both wives and husbands is indicative of bilateral cross-cousin marriage, with mother's brothers as givers of either wives or husbands. In addition, *mbɛ expanded its semantic scope in the East Central Sudanic languages to include the spouse's brother (EB) as well as spouse's father. This meaning extension evokes the previously stated principle—that semantic change in the generations G^{+1}, G^0, and G^{-1} follows an older-to-younger directionality.

A common pattern in Nilo-Saharan is to overtly mark the directionality, consanguineal to affinal, in the morphology of the word. Kunama *aiba* "husband's father" (HF), for example, derives from the same root as East Central Sudanic *mbɛ, but via the addition of a derivative prefix. The stem, *-ib-*, is the phonologically regular reflex in Kunama of *yɛmb "mother's brother." To this stem Kunama has attached the Nilo-Saharan *a- attributive noun prefix, explicitly encoding the husband's father as a kin role with attributes of or associated with the role of mother's brother. As for East Central Sudanic, the equating of HF with MB implies the existence earlier in Kunama history of a particular motivating social context, cross-cousin marriage.

Figures 9.2a and 9.2b identify the suites of kin terms, consanguineal and affinal, currently traceable to the various major nodes in Nilo-Saharan history, from proto-Nilo-Saharan down through the succession of descendant societies that were involved in the divergences and expansions of the overall period 8500–4000 BC (10,500–6000 BP). Figures 9.3–9.5 summarize and diagram changing kin relations and systems over the whole span of Nilo-Saharan language history, with particular attention to cross-cousin marriage, first-cousin terminology, matrilineal descent, and sibling's children's terminology (dates without question marks identify periods with robust archaeological correlations; dates with question marks are reasonable interpolations of time spans intermediate between those eras). (For detailed presentations of Nilo-Saharan kin reconstruction, see Ehret 2008, 2010, especially Appendix 2; and http://www.sscnet.ucla.edu/history/ehret/kinship/african_kinship_data.htm)

Identifying and Sequencing Kin Terminology Histories

Several features long prevailed in kin reckonings and relations among Nilo-Saharan peoples. A large number of lexical histories reveal cross-cousin marriage at every early node of the Nilo-Saharan linguistic stratigraphy, and along every early line of linguistic descent, not just those associated with early pastoralism (figure 9.3). Semantic derivations of affinal terms indicate that this custom usually involved symmetrical (bilateral) recruitment of spouses, with both FZCh and MBCh in the category of suitable spouses (Ehret 2010, Appendix 1).

Along with the general early presence of cross-cousin marriage, cousin terminology most probably of Iroquois type appears likely to

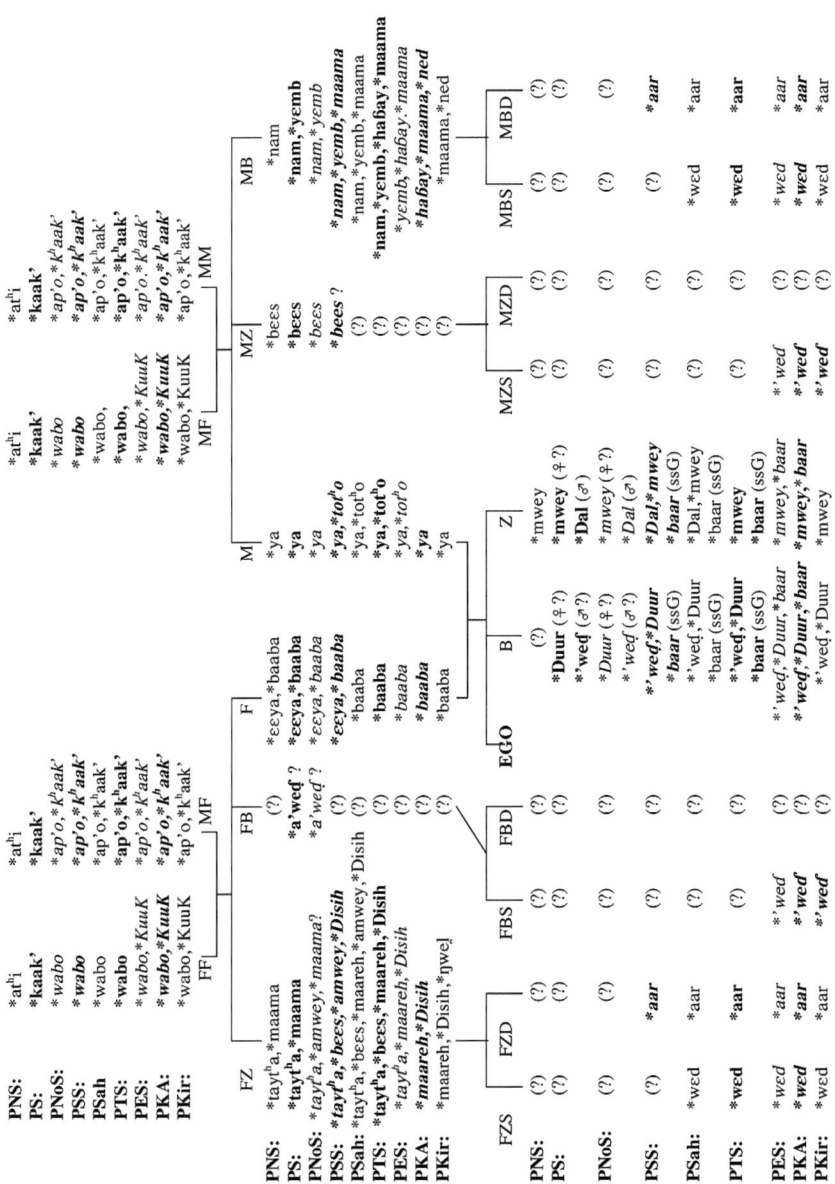

Figure 9.2a Kin terms at nine proto-language nodes of the Nilo-Saharan language family

183

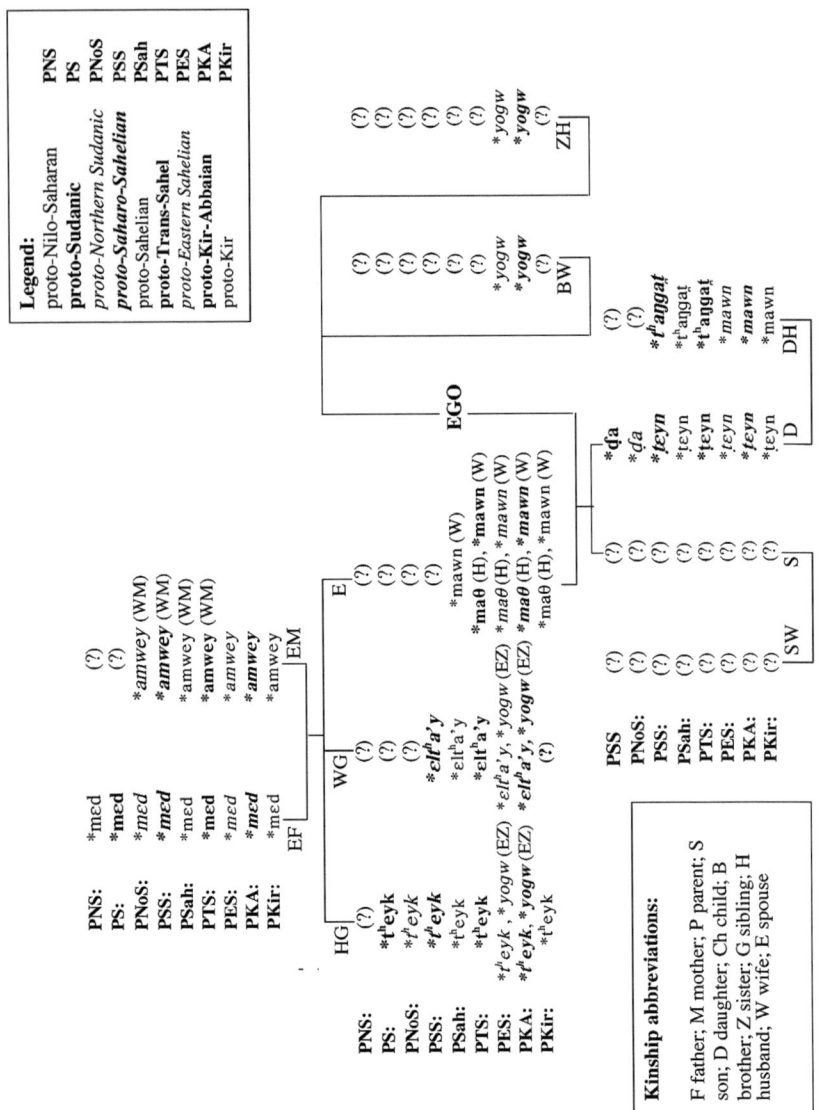

Figure 9.2b Affinal kin terms at nine proto-language nodes of the Nilo-Saharan language family

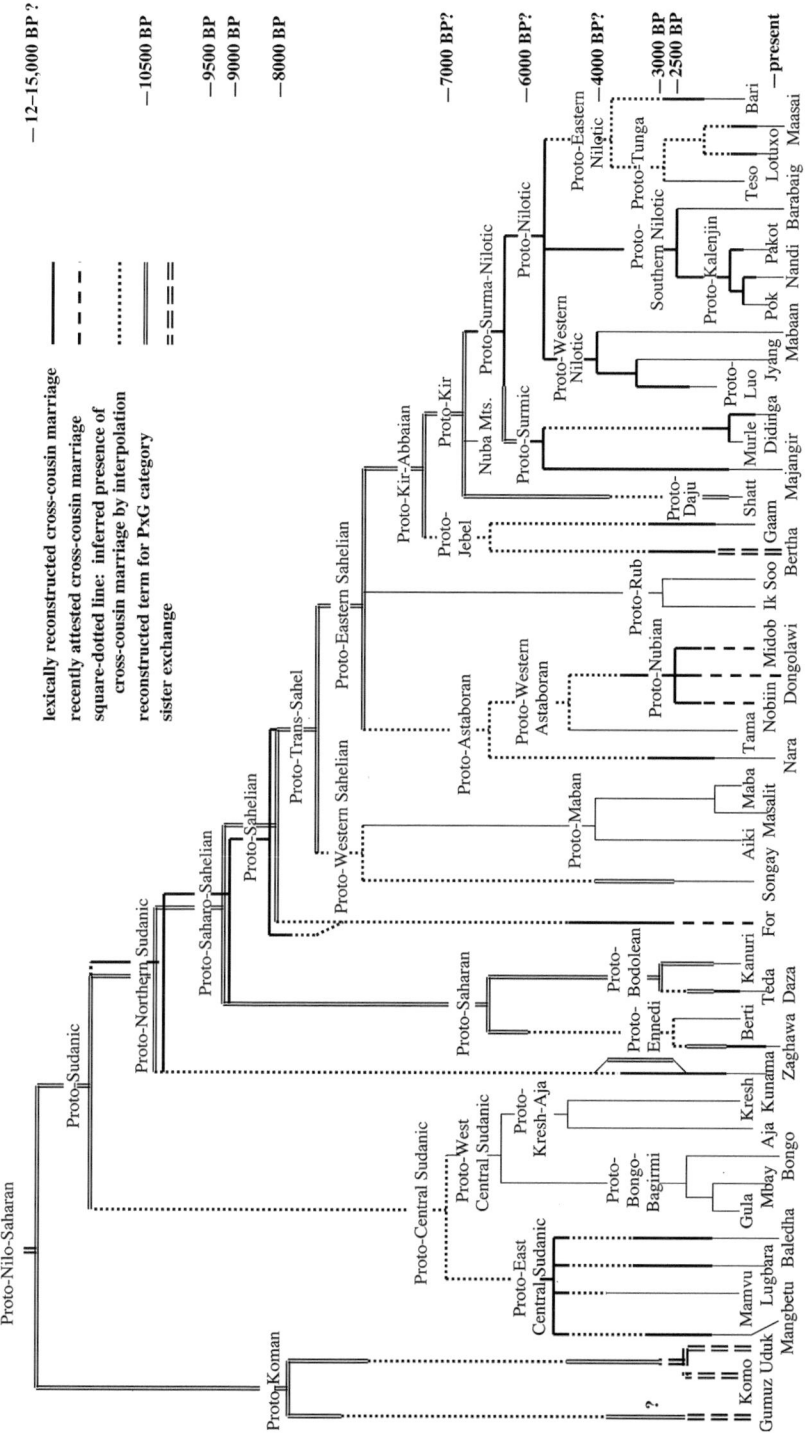

Figure 9.3 Cross-cousin marriage in Nilo-Saharan history

have existed among Nilo-Saharan peoples well before, and certainly predominated among most Nilo-Saharans for millennia after, the economic transition of the ninth through seventh millennia BCE (figure 9.4; see also figure 9.4b at http://www.sscnet.ucla.edu/history/ehret/kinship/african_kinship_data.htm). Consistent with this historical pattern, bifurcate-merging crossness can be reconstructed as characterizing the descending generation (G^{-1}) probably at all early periods (see figures 9.6a, 9.6b at http://www.sscnet.ucla.edu/history/ehret/kinship/african_kinship_data.htm). Interestingly, however, the ascending generation (G^{+1}) terms may have been partially bifurcate collateral at a number of the early nodes (figure 9.2a). Recurrent indications of symmetrical cross-cousin marriage over the same periods immediately raise the suspicion of early Dravidian rather than Iroquois reckoning. Because detailed information on second-cousin terminology and cousin terminology for generations other than ego's is currently lacking for most Nilo-Saharan cultures that have maintained crossness-marked systems, it is indeed possible that future investigation will uncover Dravidianate features.

Affine terms, as far as can be reconstructed for early Nilo-Saharan eras (figure 9.2b), are not specifically Dravidianate, and the Nilo-Saharan linguistic historical evidence overall does not entail reconstructing the former presence of canonical Dravidian systems. In no known contemporary Nilo-Saharan case and for no earlier node in the Nilo-Saharan tree does the evidence reveal the consistent assimilation of consanguineal to affinal terminology. Derivations of affinal terms from cousin and parents' siblings terminology have taken place on numerous occasions over the very long course of Nilo-Saharan linguistic history. But at every earlier historical node and in every known case from the ethnographic present, they appear to have been individual developments and not elements in a systemically Dravidian pattern. For these reasons I have chosen to stay with *Iroquois* as the cover term for the phenomenon of crossness in early Nilo-Saharan history.

Crow Terminologies

The striking feature in Nilo-Saharan cousin terminology is how relatively recent in historical time the adoption of alternative cousin systems has been among Nilo-Saharans. The one exception is Crow termi-

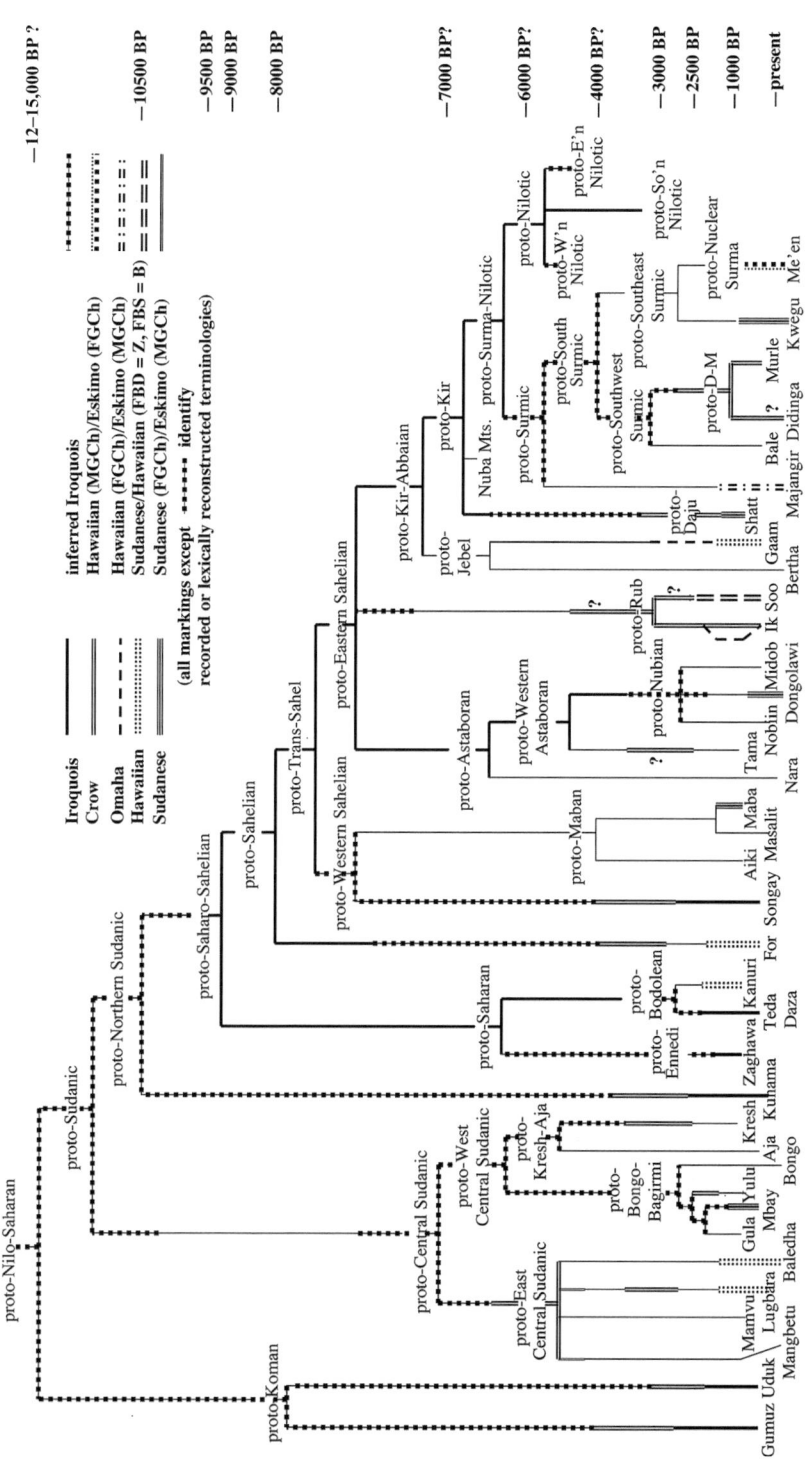

Figure 9.4 Nilo-Saharan first-cousin terminology

nology. Just two societies—the Murle and possibly the closely related Didinga—possess Crow cousin systems today, whereas one society, Ik (located in the same region as Murle and Didinga) has a mixed Crow-Omaha reckoning. Kin lexeme histories, however, identify the former presence of Crow patterns or elements of Crow terms at many earlier points in time:

1. at undetermined times along four different deep Nilo-Saharan lines of descent, represented by the Gumuz, Kunama, For, and Songay languages (figure 9.4);
2. at the proto–East Central node and separately along one line of descent within the East Central Sudanic branch and along two descent lines of the West-Central Sudanic branch (figure 9.4);
3. in the Rub, Daju, and Surmic subgroups of the Eastern Sahelian branch (figure 9.4);
4. in two different branches of the Nilotic subgroup of Eastern Sahelian (figure 9.4b at http://www.sscnet.ucla.edu/history/ehret/kinship/african_kinship_data.htm).

Different languages have preserved rather different relict signatures of earlier Crow reckonings. In the Gumuz and Songay languages, former Crow first-cousin terms arose in the usual fashion, via extension of terms for FZ to FZCh. Speakers of both languages then shifted back in subsequent times to Iroquois reckoning—in each instance via the generalization of their FZCh term to both sets of cross-cousins, that is, FZ > FZCh, and then FZCh > FZCh *and* MBCh with an attendant loss of the term's original application to FZ (Ehret 2010, Appendix 2, PNS roots 10, 12).

The Nilotic proto-Luo language and the Lugbara language of the Central Sudanic branch attest another relict pattern indicative of former Crow systems. In each of these lines of linguistic descent, a term originally for FZ came to apply to HZ (Ehret 2010, Appendix 1). Given the normative directionalities of semantic shift in kin terms, this outcome requires an intermediate meaning extension, FZ > FZD, followed by a further extension of meaning, FZD > HZ. This inferred history implies two features: Crow kinship and cross-cousin marriage. The first shift in this sequence, FZ > FZD, is the defining marker of Crow terminology. The second shift, FZD > HZ, reveals customary cross-cousin marriage, in which a husband's sister is typically a daughter of a parent's opposite-sex sibling.

In other Nilo-Saharan cases, adoption of Sudanese or Hawaiian terminologies in recent centuries has removed all potential evidence of Crow terminology at G^0. The determinative evidence in these instances comes from reconstructed former ascending- and descending-generation Crow equations. Among these are the shifts of FZCh > ♂ZCh, as in Bari and Lotuxo (Ehret 2010, Appendix 2, proto-Kir root 2) and ♂Z > ♂ZCh in the For language (Ehret 2010, Appendix 2, proto-Sudanic [PS] root 3). A recurrent marker of Crow is the linkage FZ = FM, as in Uduk (proto-Saharo-Sahelian [PSS] root 5) and as reconstructed for earlier proto-Daju and proto–East Central Sudanic and separately for Yulu and for Baka and Kresh (Ehret 2010, Appendix 2, PNS roots 10 and 17, PS root 3, and PSS root 4).

For the most part, the reconstructed Nilo-Saharan occurrences of Crow systems are not at all recent. The proto–East Central Sudanic language was spoken most likely somewhere in the time range of the third millennium BCE (Ehret et al. 1974), and the proto–Eastern Nilotic language was of similar antiquity (Ehret 1983). The proto-Daju period probably dates to around the first millennium BCE (Thelwall 1981). The only instance in which Crow terminology certainly dates since 1000 CE is that of the Murle and probably the Didinga, which have this kind of cousin reckoning today. Recurrent indications of very early Crow terminologies along so many lines of descent fit well with recurrent evidence of an ancient and, at one time, pervasive presence of matriliny among Nilo-Saharans (figure 9.5).

Omaha Terminologies in Nilo-Saharan History

The occurrences of Omaha nomenclature in Nilo-Saharan societies, in contrast, are historically recent and geographically restricted developments. All six recorded instances of Omaha systems are from Nilotic societies, and they occur in just two contiguous groups of peoples.

Three adjoining societies of far southern Sudan and far northern Kenya, the Acholi and Lang'o (Western Nilotic) and the Bari (Eastern Nilotic), have Omaha reckoning. In the emerging proto-Acholi-Lang'o dialect spoken around the seventeenth century (Atkinson 1994), an

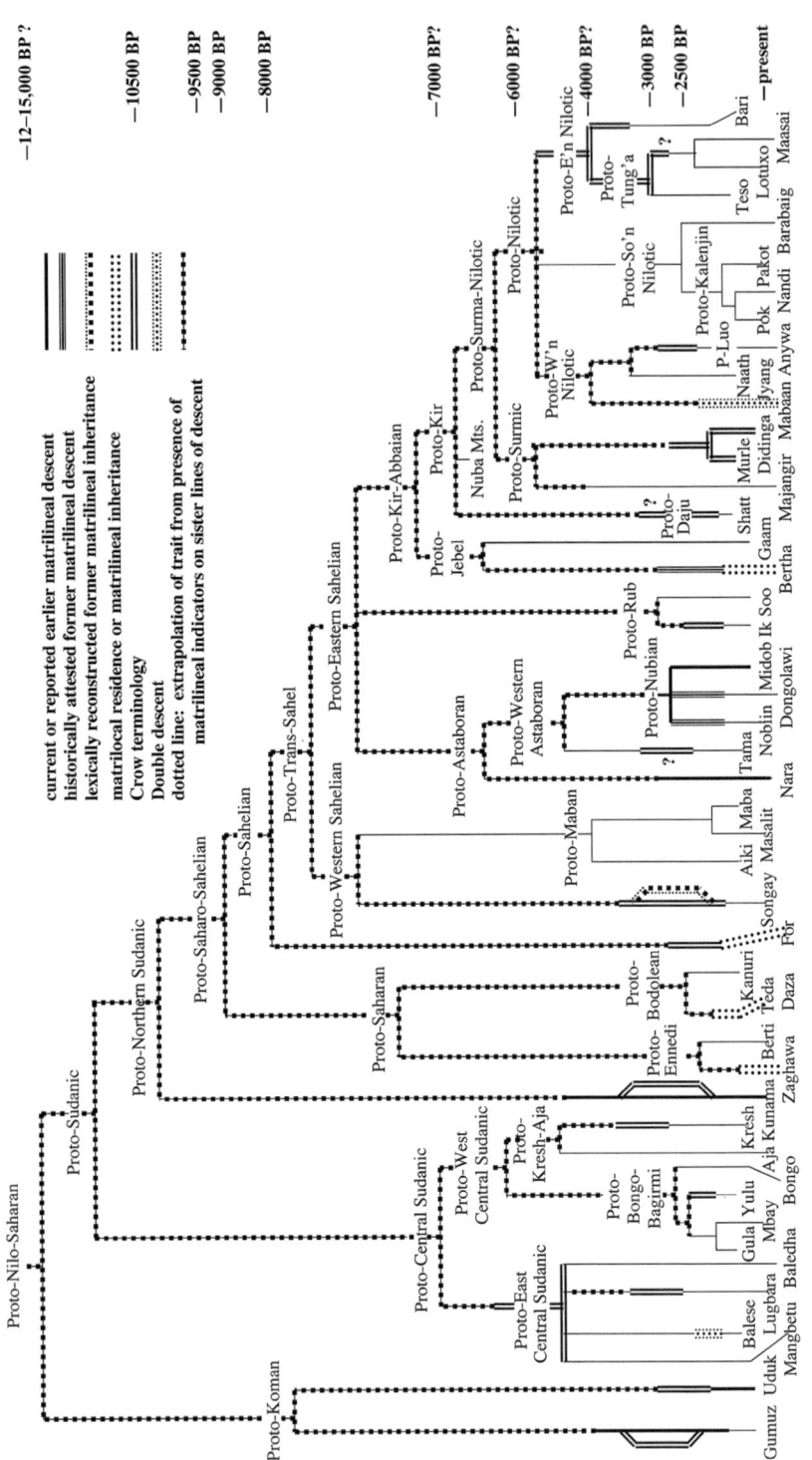

Figure 9.5 Matrilineal descent in Nilo-Saharan history

Omaha system directly superseded the reconstructed proto-Luo Iroquois system. Omaha was possibly older in the Bari language group, but that remains to be fully determined.

The speakers of two near-neighbor Kalenjin dialects in western Kenya, Endo (Marakwet) and Nandi, also have Omaha systems. In these dialects the development of Omaha terminology dates to the period following the separate divergences of Nandi and Endo out of proto–Central Kalenjin, which had an Iroquois system. The divergence of proto–Central Kalenjin began no earlier than around the fourteenth or fifteenth century (Distefano 1985; see figure 9.4b at http://www.sscnet.ucla.edu/ history/ehret/kinship/african_kinship_data.htm), so the separate emergences of Omaha reckoning in these cases date after that time. The speakers of a sixth language with elements of an Omaha system, the Maasai, surely contributed to this regional development in kin terminology. Maasai-speaking communities dominated the Rift Valley areas of Kenya west of the Endo and Nandi since 1500 CE and, more important, controlled the Uasingishu plains of western Kenya, between Endo and Nandi lands, from about 1650 to 1850, making this a plausible time span for the wider spread of this kind of cousin terms.

A possible former, seventh instance involves Gaam, an Eastern Sahelian language spoken near the Abbai (Blue Nile) River 800 km north of the Bari and Acholi. It has been tentatively proposed that an earlier Omaha system in this language gave way to Hawaiian terminology in modern-day Gaam (Ehret 2010, Appendix 2).

The Southern Nilotic Barabaig (Datooga) of Tanzania, uniquely, have a nomeclature that is simultaneously Omaha and Crow. On the maternal side it is Omaha, that is, MBS = MB (although the MBD is called Z). On the paternal side it is canonically Crow, that is, FZD = FZ and FZS = F. Because the Barabaig nowadays are strongly patrilineal, this mixed terminology looks like a lagging indicator of an earlier transition from matriliny to patriliny.

Cousin Terminology Shifts as Concomitants of Descent Shifts

Omaha systems, in other words, have been relatively rare and usually very recent outcomes in Nilo-Saharan societies, limited (with the possible exception of Gaam) to three independent developments of the past several centuries involving seven societies of the Nilotic subgroup of the family. In each instance the evidence either positively indicates, or is consistent with, a history of the shift passing from Iroquois to Omaha or, as currently for Barabaig and possibly earlier for Bari, from Crow to Omaha. I argue, however, that these shifts were one expression of a much more widespread historical trend among Nilo-Saharan-speaking peoples during the past three millennia, particularly the past several hundred years. Elsewhere this trend manifested itself in shifts from Iroquois to Sudanese or Hawaiian systems.

The linking feature of Sudanese and Hawaiian cousin nomenclatures is their particular association, like Omaha, with patrilineal descent. Sudanese systems universally seem to co-occur with patrilineal descent, and Hawaiian with either patrilineal or bilateral rules but not with matriliny. The Nilo-Saharan outcomes, I propose, are rooted in the separate histories (figure 9.5) of recurrent shift from matriliny to patriliny. All present-day Nilo-Saharan-speaking matrilineal or recently matrilineal societies for which the first-cousin terminologies are well recorded—Uduk, Gumuz, Kunama, and Nara—have Iroquois systems (table 9.1).

Sudanese systems now characterize a majority of the Western Nilotic societies, and Sudanese or Hawaiian naming of first cousins occurs commonly in Eastern and Southern Nilotic cultures. But here is the important point: each language has separately developed its Sudanese or Hawaiian nomenclature. The same point holds true for the developments of Omaha systems in several Nilotic societies. None of the Sudanese systems of Western Nilotic can be traced to an earlier node in the descent tree of the Western Nilotic group.

In some instances, the next node back in time is relatively far back. The Jyang (Dinka) and Naath (Nuer) languages, closest relatives to each other, have a common ancestry, a shared node on the descent tree, dating to around 1500–2000 BP (figure 9.4b at http://www.sscnet.ucla.edu/history/ehret/kinship/african_kinship_data.htm), so it is conceivable that each society separately developed this Sudanese terminology more than 1,000 years ago. In the instance of the Ateker subgroup of Eastern Nilotic, the proto-Ateker split dates to a bit over 1000 years ago (Ehret 1983), so in this instance, too, the adoption of Hawaiian and

Table 9.1 Crow in Nilo-Saharan

Society	Cousin system	Descent	Politics, society in nineteenth century	Economy in recent centuries
Gumuz	Iroquois > Crow > Iroquois at undetermined points in the past	Patrilineal; but possibly matrilineal in early twentieth century	Clan, village, elders	Subsistence farming
Uduk	Iroquois > Crow > Iroquois	Matrilineal	Clans, villages, elders	Subsistence farming, herding, and hunting
Kunama	Iroquois > Crow > Iroquois at undetermined points in the past	matrilineal	Clan, village, elders	Subsistence farming
Songay	Iroquois > Crow > Iroquois at undetermined points in the past	Patrilineal at present; transparent derivation of PxGCh from verb "inherit" indicates historically relatively recent matriliny	Highly stratified society (nobility, merchants, clerics, artisans, peasantry), centralized monarchical rule over the past 1800 years	Long-distance commerce, manufacturing (ceramics, iron, textiles, carnelian beads, etc.); farm production for the market
For	(Iroquois >) Crow (> Iroquois?) at undetermined points in the past > Hawaiian	Patrilineal, but matrilocal	Highly stratified society (nobility, peasantry), centralized bureaucratic monarchical rule 1600s–1915, and probably before	Long-distance commerce (slaves, imports, etc.)

(continued)

Table 9.1 Continued

Society	Cousin system	Descent	Politics, society in nineteenth century	Economy in recent centuries
Proto-Daju	Iroquois > Crow at undetermined time plus-2000 years ago	Matrilineal?		
Proto-Didinga-Murle	(Iroquois >) Crow before 1000 CE	Matrilineal?		
Didinga	Crow or Iroquois	Patrilineal	Clan, village, elders	Subsistence farming and herding
Murle	Crow	Patrilineal?	Clan, village, elders	Subsistence farming and herding
Proto-E'n Nilotic	Iroquois > Crow, ca. 3–2000 BCE	Matrilineal?		Iroquois > Crow, ca. 3–2000 BCE
Pre-proto-Luo	Iroquois > Crow, at undetermined point, probably well before 1200 CE > Iroquois before 1200 CE	Pre-proto-Luo		Pre-proto-Luo
Proto-Rub	Crow or Iroquois, at ca. 1000 BCE	Matrilineal?		
Soo	Crow or Iroquois > Sudanese/Hawaiian	Patrilineal	Clan, village, elders	Subsistence farming and herding

Sudanese in different descendant societies may have taken place almost that long ago, although the retention of crossness in G^{-1} is in keeping with more recent change (see figures 9.4b and 9.6b at http://www.sscnet.ucla.edu/history/ehret/kinship/african_kinship_data.htm).

To sum up, the shifts to Sudanese, Hawaiian, and Omaha systems in Nilo-Saharan took place independently in the different languages, and in most cases they probably took place in recent historical time. Where the most recent nodes of relationship between particular languages lie well back in time—such as 1500–2000 BP in the case of Naath and Jyang, more than 2,000 years ago for Kanuri and Tibu and for the Nile Nubian languages, and as much as 4,000 years ago in East Central Sudanic—the shifts to Sudanese or Hawaiian systems could conceivably date back to any intermediate point along the relevant lines of descent. But whenever the linguistic divergence points are more recent, we find that the shifts from Iroquois to Sudanese and Hawaiian, as well as to Omaha, first-cousin nomenclatures date to the past 600 years, whether in the eastern or central Sudan belt.

Directionalities of Kin System Shift

The overall evidence of the various courses of change in Nilo-Saharan kin terminologies supports postulating several normative directions of system shift involving Crow and Omaha terminologies, some already familiar. A search down the numerous Nilo-Saharan linguistic descent lines diagrammed in figure 9.4 (and also figure 9.4b at http://www.sscnet.ucla.edu/history/ehret/kinship/african_kinship_data.htm) reveals a variety of such historical sequences:

1. Iroquois > Crow (Gumuz, Uduk, proto–East Central Sudanic, pre-Yulu, pre-Kresh, pre-Kunama, pre-For, pre-Songay, proto-Didinga-Murle [proto-D-M], Barabaig)
2. Crow > Iroquois (Gumuz, Uduk, Songay, Acholi, Lotuxo, and possibly Kunama)
3. Iroquois > Sudanese (Mbay, Dongolawi, Ocolo, Turkana, Sapiny)
4. Iroquois > Hawaiian (Kanuri, Teso, Barabaig, Pok)
5. Iroquois > Omaha (Acholi-Lang'o, Nandi, Endo);
6. Crow > Sudanese (Ik, Soo, Shatt)

7. Crow > Hawaiian (For, with an intermediate Iroquois stage?)
8. Crow > Omaha (Barabaig; Bari, with an intermediate Iroquois stage?)
9. Omaha > Hawaiian (Bari, underway; earlier in Gaam?)

The most arresting feature is that Iroquois succeeds only Crow systems. One particular order of change, Iroquois to Crow and back to Iroquois, is attested along a number of different deep and not-so-deep lines of Nilo-Saharan linguistic descent. At least in some cases, the semantic steps in this process, with respect to first cousins, proceeded as follows: FZ > FZ *and* FZCh, yielding a Crow system, and then, later, FZCh > PosGCh in general, re-creating Iroquois reckoning.

Otherwise, the progression appears consistently unidirectional—from Iroquois to Crow or Omaha, or from Crow to Omaha, or from Iroquois, Crow, or Omaha to Hawaiian or Sudanese. Iroquois is a starting point, but not a final destination. Crow and Omaha are neither starting points nor destinations but interludes along the way. In most Nilo-Saharan cases, the Hawaiian and Sudanese nomenclatures, whether full or limited to G^0, appear to have directly replaced earlier Iroquois systems, although in some cases the immediately preceding stage may have been Crow or Omaha.

Two questions follow from these data. First, are there other normative directions of change still to be discovered between Omaha and Sudanese and between Sudanese and Hawaiian systems? The available Nilo-Saharan evidence does not offer answers.

Second, where does Eskimo cousin terminology belong in this scheme? No outright Eskimo systems exist anywhere in Nilo-Saharan. Several present-day Nilo-Saharan languages do attest mixed Sudanese-Eskimo or Hawaiian-Eskimo terminologies, in which either MGCh or FGCh is expressed by a distinct cousin term, but the remaining part of the cousin pattern in a Sudanese or a Hawaiian fashion (see figure 9.4 and table 9.3 for examples). In these cases, the elements of Eskimo reckoning fit at the end of the chain of system shifts, in that they combine with Sudanese or Hawaiian in replacing earlier Iroquois or Crow terminologies.

Eskimo as an outcome rather than a starting point is separately attested in the evolution of southern African Khoesan hunter-gatherer kin terminologies: the Zhu (Ju) branch of southern African Khoesan today has an Eskimo reckoning, but the comparative ethnographic and linguistic evidence convincingly establishes Iroquois systems as original in Khoesan (Ehret 2008). That finding in turn has a potentially major implication for our ideas about the connections of Eskimo terminology with other aspects of society and culture and with the ultimate beginning and ending points in the directionality of kin system shifts. It suggests the hypothesis that, in foraging as much as in modern industrial societies, Eskimo systems are secondary, and Iroquois-like systems with pervasive crossness (even if not outright tetradic systems, as Allen [e.g., 2008] proposes) were indeed the founding systematic formulations of human kinship.

By combining these considerations with the evidence of Nilo-Saharan kin histories, one can propose a global scheme of normative directionality of kin-system shift for testing against the wider evidence of kinship around the world. "Iroquois" functions in this scheme as a cover term for systems with nonskewed crossness, including Dravidianate. Parentheses identify permitted but nonobligatory intermediate steps:

Iroquois (> Crow) (> Iroquois) (> Omaha) > Hawaiian or Sudanese or Eskimo

Historical Cause in Kin Terminology Shifts

Not a single event, nor a single history of diffusion, can account for the multiple historically recent shifts to Omaha and other patriliny-associated cousin systems among Nilo-Saharan peoples. Instead, there seem to be recent and restricted regional diffusions of particular directions of shift. Among the East Central Sudanic peoples of the Congo-Nile watershed regions in northeastern Congo and southwestern Sudan, the change tended to be to Hawaiian systems, for example; among the Nilotes of the Middle Nile Basin, the shift was more often to Sudanese terminologies.

Why should these kinds of developments in cousin terminology have emerged relatively recently across such a wide expanse? One possibility is that they reflect lagging responses to change in the basis of unilineal descent, from matriliny to patriliny. If we understand the shifts to Sudanese, Hawaiian, and Omaha systems as developments enabled by shifts to patrilineal descent reckoning, we can, of course, expect there to be lag times between the logically prior and the logically secondary, nonobligatory shifts. The existence of lags helps explain why, in a few cases, Crow systems, despite their tight association with matriliny, might persist for some time past the transition to patriliny (table 9.1). Anthropologists have long used such relict preservations of Crow terminology to infer former matriliny (see figure 9.5). In contrast, the long and resilient persistence of Iroquois descent in a number of patrilineal Nilo-Saharan societies, often down to the present, should not be unexpected, in view of the worldwide evidence that Iroquois systems occur with either matrilineal or patrilineal descent.

The histories of Nilo-Saharan kin terminologies raise further questions, including why the past 3,000 years produced so many separate shifts to patriliny, creating conditions amenable to the appearance of Sudanese, Hawaiian, and Omaha equations still more recently. The proposal that adoption of cattle raising, postulated for some Bantu societies (Holden and Mace 2003), impelled this shift does not hold here, because Nilo-Saharans of the Northern Sudanic branch have been cattle raisers, often on a relatively large scale, since ca. 8000 BCE and yet apparently often remained matrilineal into the past 3,000 years. This explanation for Bantu is doubtful in any case, considering the numerous historical shifts from matriliny to patriliny in Bantu societies that have never kept cattle (Ehret 2010).

As for the Nilo-Saharans, it is not at all evident from the comparative data on society and economy (tables 9.1–9.4) what new causative factors might have come into play in the past few thousand years. The ancientness and longevity of matrilineal allegiances in Nilo-Saharan history, persisting over many thousands of years, highlights just how little we know about the governing conditions and the varieties of history that lie behind the ways people have structured and experienced kinship over the very long term.

Table 9.2 Omaha in Nilo-Saharan

Society	Cousin system	Descent	Politics, society in nineteenth century	Economy in recent centuries
Gaam	Omaha > Sudanese (tentative)	Bilateral	Clan, villages, elders	Subsistence farming
Acholi, Lang'o	Iroquois > Omaha between 1500 and 1750	Patrilineal	Acholi: chiefdoms, small kingdoms; Lang'o: clans, elders	Subsistence farming and herding
Bari	Crow (> Iroquois?) > Omaha at uncertain point in time	Patrilineal	Clans, age sets, elders	Subsistence farming
Maasai	Crow (> Iroquois?) > Omaha at uncertain point in time	Patrilineal	Age grades, age sets	Subsistence herding and farming
Nandi	Iroquois > Omaha since 1500	Patrilineal	Age grades, age sets	Subsistence farming and herding
Endo	Iroquois > Omaha since 1500	Patrilineal	Age grades, age sets	Subsistence farming with terraced irrigation agriculture
Barabaig (Datooga)	Iroquois > Omaha > Hawaiian; since 2500 BP	Patrilineal	Age grades, age sets	Subsistence farming and herding
Ik	Crow or Iroquois > Crow-Omaha	Patrilineal	Clan, village, elders	Subsistence farming

Table 9.3 Selected Sudanese and Hawaiian in Nilo-Saharan

Society	Cousin system	Descent	Politics, society in nineteenth century	Economy in recent centuries
Lugbara	Crow (> Iroquois?) > Hawaiian	Patrilineal	Segmentary clan system	Subsistence farming and herding
Baledha	Hawaiian	Patrilineal	Clans, villages; chiefs	Subsistence farming
Mbay	Iroquois > Hawaiian			Subsistence farming and herding
Kanuri	Iroquois > Hawaiian at uncertain period	Patrilineal	Highly stratified society (nobility, merchants, clerics, artisans, peasantry), centralized monarchical rule over the past 1100 years	Long-distance commerce (slaves, salt), manufacturing (ceramics, iron, textiles, etc.); farm production for the market
Dongolawi	Iroquois > Sudanese at uncertain period	Patrilineal; indications of matriliny in early historical records	States; stratified society (landed aristocracy; merchants; peasant farmers in some areas; enserfed farmers in other areas)	Commercial sector; subsistence farming
Shatt	Crow (> Iroquois?) > Sudanese/ Eskimo	Matrilineal?	Clans, chiefs	Subsistence farming
Majangir	Hawaiian/ Eskimo	Patrilineal	Clans, elders	Subsistence farming
Kwegu	Sudanese	?	Bands	Foragers
Me'en	Hawaiian/ Eskimo	Patrilineal	Clans, elders	Subsistence farming and herding

(*continued*)

Table 9.3 Continued

Society	Cousin system	Descent	Politics, society in nineteenth century	Economy in recent centuries
Jyang	Sudanese	Patrilineal	Clans, elders, spear "chiefs"	Subsistence farming, herding, and fishing
Naath	Sudanese	Patrilineal	Clans, elders	Subsistence farming, herding, and fishing
Ocolo	Iroquois > Sudanese since ca. 1300	Patrilineal	Sacral kingdom	Subsistence farming, herding, and fishing
Anywa	Iroquois > Sudanese since ca. 1500	Patrilineal	Chiefdoms	Subsistence farming, herding, and fishing
Teso	Iroquois or Crow > Hawaiian, since 800–1000	Patrilineal	Clans, elders	Subsistence farming and herding
Turkana	Iroquois or Crow > Sudanese, since 800–1000	Patrilineal	Age grades, age sets	Subsistence herding and farming
Pok	Iroquois > Hawaiian since ca. 1600	Patrilineal	Age grades, age sets	Subsistence farming and herding
Sapiny	Iroquois > Sudanese since ca. 1600	Patrilineal	Age grades, age sets	Subsistence farming and herding

Table 9.4 Persistent Iroquois in Nilo-Saharan

Society	Cousin system	Descent	Politics, society in nineteenth century	Economy in recent centuries
Zaghawa	Iroquois	Patrilineal	Stratified society; segmentary clan system; chiefs	Herding for subsistence and trade
Teda, Daza	Iroquois	Patrilineal, but with matrilocal residence early in marriage	Stratified society; segmentary clan system; chiefs	Herding for subsistence and trade
Kenya Luo	Iroquois	Patrilineal	Clans, hereditary chiefdoms	Farming and fishing for subsistence and trade, iron trade, regular markets
Kipsigis	Iroquois	Patrilineal	Age grades, age sets	Subsistence farming and herding
Pakot	Iroquois	Patrilineal	Age grades, age sets	Subsistence farming and herding

South America

10

The Making and Unmaking of "Crow-Omaha" Kinship in Central Brazil(ian Ethnology)

Marcela Coelho de Souza

This contribution is intended as an overview of the ethnography of so-called Crow-Omaha kinship systems prevalent in central Brazil. The groups I discuss here are all Gê-speakers, the different languages of this family having spread along the savannas of the central Brazilian plateau over perhaps the last 3,000 years.

Flourishing in an environment considered harsh compared to the rich forests of the Amazon, Gê societies exhibit intricate institutional arrangements that bewildered observers prone to see them as examples of "marginal" cultures at the bottom of the social complexity ladder. Their cross-cutting moieties and apparently anomalous kinship systems puzzled and fascinated Lévi-Strauss, among others, but very little ethnography was available until the 1970s, when the results of the Harvard-Central Brazil Project (HCBP), directed by David Maybury-Lewis,[1] started to appear.

Gê languages are classified into three groups: Northern Gê, subdivided into an eastern branch (the Timbira groups, including the Canela, the Krahô, and the Krinkati, among others, who live in the states of Maranhão and Tocantins) and a western branch (Apinajé, Kayapó, Xikrin, Kĩsêdjê, and Panará, spread across Pará and Mato Grosso); Central Gê (Xavante, Xerente, and Xakriabá in Tocantins and Mato Grosso); and Southern Gê (Kaingang and Xokleng in Paraná, Santa Catarina, and Rio Grande do Sul) (see map 10.1).

Gê terminologies offer a broad spectrum of variation from the Crow-Omaha systems of the Northern Gê to the Kariera and Hawaiian patterns of the Kaingang and Xokleng in the extreme south, passing through more Dravidianate types (with perhaps some Omaha interference) among the Central Gê. This makes for an array of mixed, unstable, and interesting arrangements, whose variations correlate (in a com-

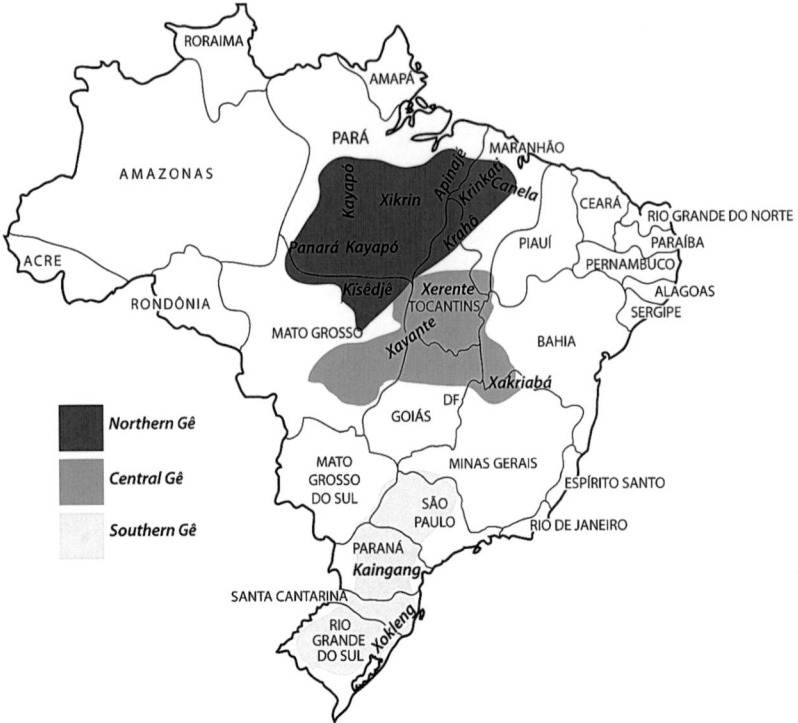

Map 10.1 Distribution of Gê-speaking peoples

plex way) with an equally wide range of group structures. The Northern Gê live in circular villages of uxorilocal houses with a men's house or ceremonial patio at the center and an elaborate ceremonial organization, featuring nonexogamous moieties and groups based on names, age classes, age categories, and voluntary societies. Uxorilocality generates multihouse units that are exogamous and, some argue, could be conceptualized as Lévi-Straussian (matri-) "Houses"; apart from this, there are not descent units, while the bilateral kindred is recognized as a category in all groups.[2]

Central Gê peoples live in semicircular villages formed by uxorilocal extended family households; their marriage practices and ritual and political life are based on a system of nonlocalized patrilineal lineages and a moiety dichotomy. Southern Gê take this patri-orientation further, abandoning uxorilocality and breaking the circular spatial structuring of village life: the Kaingang retain a system of patrilineal, exogamic moieties, whereas the small Xokleng group seems to have "lost" the dualistic scheme once seen as the common denominator of all Gê societies—hence the epithet "dialectical societies" (Maybury-Lewis 1979).

I focus on the Northern Gê, among whom we find the Crow-Omaha patterns of most interest here; however, we must not forget the continuity—linguistic, historical, and cultural—between these patterns and those found among related and/or neighboring peoples. Besides other Gê peoples, there are Amazonian (forest) groups that exhibit terminologies evocative of Northern Gê and/or Crow-Omaha patterns, combined in some cases with oblique ZD marriage and in others with matrilateral (MBD) preferences. There is much to be done before we can understand the transitions that link these various configurations.

Northern Gê Kinship: An Overview

Northern Gê societies are very similar in basic traits: an economy that strongly emphasizes hunting and gathering, combined with slash-and-burn horticulture based on manioc; circular villages of uxorilocal houses with a men's house or ceremonial patio at the center, varying from a few score to more than 1,000 people; and an elaborate ceremonial organization. Villages tend to be endogamous, although this varies with size, stage of development, (contact) history, and political circumstances. Although everyone in a village may consider everyone else "kin" in certain situations and for some purposes, Northern Gê peoples do not ordinarily marry *relatives*—that is, persons they address using kinship terms. Other interpersonal relationships—notably naming relations and formal friendship—involve different terminologies and are connected in specific ways to marriage and kinship. Any analysis of Gê kinship terminologies not taking these relationships into account neglects crucial processes and meanings that generate those terminologies.

Basic (address and reference) terms for cognatic kin are homogeneous among all Northern Gê (except the Panará) and mostly are applied to the same kin types—the crucial exception being cross-cousins and their descendants. Unusual features include the assimilation of cross-kin of $G^{\pm 1}$ to $G^{\pm 2}$ relatives, that is, maternal uncles, paternal aunts, nephews, and nieces, who are generally classified as "grandmother," "grandfather," and "grandchild." Northern Gê classification of cross-cousins follows an east–west axis from a Crow to an Omaha pattern, with some variations. Among most Eastern Timbira, patrilateral cross-cousins are classified in Crow fashion as F and FZ; matrilateral cross-cousins are "grandchild" for a woman and Ch for a man. The Omaha pattern (with the equivalences MB = MBS = MBSS, M = MBD = MBSD, MBDCh = G, and FZCh = ♂ZCh/♀Ch) is found to the west, among the Kayapó, Xikrin, and Kïsêdjê. The Apinajé, linguistically closer to the Kayapó but neighbors to the Timbira, present a more unstable picture: cross-cousins are classified sometimes in Crow, sometimes in Omaha fashion, and are sometimes called "siblings," in Hawaiian fashion. Such instability is also typical of the Krinkati and affects other Eastern Timbira, as we will see.

Affinal relations are everywhere referred to through a complete set of terms (sometimes with contextually alternative designations). But consanguineal and affinal sets are not the only relationship terms among the Gê. Crocker (1990:235), for instance, lists nine different relationship terminologies for the Canela,[3] of which, naming, formal friendship, and teknonymy are the most important. Beyond this, additional "indirect reference" or "triadic" terms (alternatively) refer to two or three relationships simultaneously, for example, "your mother, who is my sister" (see Lea 2004; Seeger 1981; Turner 1966; Vidal 1977). These additional terminological sets are difficult to elicit in interviews and impossible to understand outside their natural contexts of use.

Name transmission among the Northern Gê is fairly homogeneous. Each individual has a set of semantically independent names (usually five to twelve, sometimes more). In some groups (Timbira, Apinajé, Kïsêdjê), these name sets are transmitted in a closed block, shared by many persons related as namesakes: such name groups are ceremonially important units. In other cases (Kayapó), individuals may receive names from different relatives, thus combining names from two or more different sets. In general, individuals are known by one of their names, with each person called by a different name, thus avoiding homonymy. This individuating function, as well as the composite nature of the sets, makes the distinction title versus name difficult to apply here. Names pass from "grandfather/uncle" to "grandson/nephew" and from "grandmother/aunt" to "granddaughter/niece." In all cases, name-givers are preferably persons in grandparent categories classified as opposite-sex siblings (not as "mother" or "father") by the child's parent. In this sense, name transmission follows a cross-transmission rule, from MB to ZS and from FZ to BD, but with differing emphases. Among the Timbira, the name-giver chooses and transmits his or her name to the child. Among the Apinajé, this role is performed by a "name-arranger," someone in the category of F or M, who plays the role of "substitute" or adoptive "father/mother." Among the Kayapó, the person who announces the name is ideally (but not necessarily) its bearer (a MB or FZ).

HCBP researchers seized on the connection between naming and kinship as an alternative to descent and alliance theories, tying kinship classification to the cultural construction of the person, via the complementary transmission of substance and onomastic identity. Melatti analyzed Krahô terminology in two sets, one defined by the actual or potential implication in procreation (parallel relatives), the other by actual or potential involvement in naming (cross). Given the basic homogeneity of name transmission, an additional hypothesis is necessary to account for the transition from the Crow outline of Timbira terminologies to the Omaha pattern for Kayapó or Kïsêdjê. HCBP anthropologists put forward explanations that linked terminology to the public/domestic, male/female opposition they believed central to the workings of Gê society. Separation and mediation between these spheres or domains was the crucial point. From this perspective, male statuses, because they carried more decisive ceremonial/public implications, would always be more critical than female ones. Whereas the Timbira emphasized names as criteria for membership in ceremonial groups—and hence, the name-giver/receiver relationship (MB/ZS)—the Kayapó stressed substitute father/son relationships (for introducing boys to men's societies and moieties). This contrast could be construed as between "matrilineal" and "patrilineal" transmission of *male* ceremonial statuses: patrilineal/Omaha for the Kayapó and matrilineal/Crow for Timbira. The Apinajé, with their split of functions between name-giver (an "MB") and adoptive father (an "F"), would naturally sit halfway, oscillating between the two patterns (see Da Matta 1979:123ff; Maybury-Lewis 1979:239).

The Kïsêdjê, however, appear to offer a counterexample to this new explanation, combining Omaha terminology, onomastic recruitment to ceremonial groups, absence of "substitute father" roles, and even possibly named "matri-houses"—with, to top it off, an alleged preference for (distant) MBD marriage (Seeger 1981). In any case, as Viveiros de Castro (1990:18) noted, the new explanation failed to specify how ceremonial patrifiliation could generate Omaha equivalences (appealing to a simplistic association between patri-orientation and Omaha skewing) and neglected critical associations (e.g., between the Apinajé oscillation and similar patterns among the Krinkati, who had no "adoptive parent" figure).

An obvious alternative explanation is to relate Crow and Omaha patterns to male and female names, respectively. Cross-transmission of names is easily seen as when generating a Crow outline when male names are the reference point and Omaha when female names are used. In the first case, identification of male ego with his name-giver turns the latter's children into "children" for the former, generating the equation ♂MBCh = Ch (and, for his sister, ♀MBCh = BCh); classification of patrilateral cousins as "F" and "FZ" can be deduced by reciprocity. As ego's F will give his names to ego's FZS, we have again FZS = F, FZD = FZ. In the second case, a woman's identification with her FZ transforms the latter's children into "Ch" for ego ("ZCh" to her brother); the equations MBD = M and MBS = B follow from reciprocity, reinforced by the fact that M may pass her name to MBD. These contradictory alternatives seem to be differentially exploited by Northern Gê societies (generating the Crow-Omaha variations among them), and by individuals within a single society according to context and circumstance (figure 10.1).

Onomastic identity is essentially ceremonial in nature but with clear influence on kinship terms' everyday use. In general, individuals tend to employ the same kinship terms used by their name-givers to refer to the same persons, although the limits of this reclassification vary: a Krahô refrains from "changing" the terms for his or her real children, siblings, and parents (Melatti 1976:144), whereas a Krinkati man may call his own sister "grandmother" if she was named by their FZ (Lave 1979:23). Even among the Krahô, where Crow skewing is dominant, *actual* naming relations produce Omaha equivalences: a woman named by a particular FZ will call the latter's children "children" in Omaha fashion, but will continue to call the children of her other aunts "father" and "aunt/grandmother" (Melatti 1979:72–73). In some cases, even nonre-

"Crow-Omaha" Kinship in Central Brazil(ian Ethnology) 211

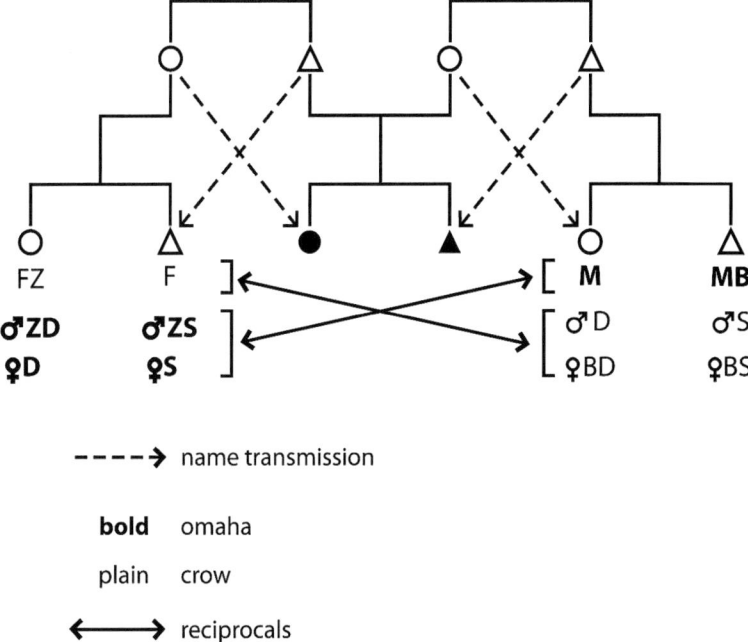

Figure 10.1 Crow-Omaha skewing and name transmission among the Northern Gê

alized, potential naming seems to affect terminological usage (apparently more for affines than cognates). That naming motivates kin classification is especially clear among the Krinkati (see similarly, the Apinajé [Da Matta 1979:120ff]): "Egos of each sex use the [Crow or Omaha] rules which most accurately reflect the name-transmission relations in which they are involved. . . . Where the rules generate alternative usages, the Krinkati express indifference as to which pair of reciprocals is chosen, and they occur in free variation" (Lave 1979:22).

There is, then, abundant evidence that the "anomalous" combination of Crow and Omaha features and the oscillations in the classification of cross-cousins are linked to the naming rule and the different alternatives it affords. The possibility of interpreting Omaha equivalences as a reflection of female name transmission was envisaged by Da Matta, but he rejects it based on the argument that "the male side always takes precedence. . . . As a result, female names do not acquire the power to influence the terminological system *qua* system" (Da Matta 1979:122–

23). The unshakeable preeminence of the male sex and ruling out female naming identity as a possible reference point for kin classification are, however, questionable for societies in which a significant part of social life and group organization—the so-called domestic domain—is structured by uxorilocality, and thus relationships between and/or through women are obviously of some importance. There are no compelling reasons to dismiss female naming as a factor.

The explanation of Omaha equations as reflecting female name identity is defended by Lea (1986:183–86), who sees Kayapó names as the property of matri-Houses as corporate units, and female names as the system's critical point. According to Lea, while male names never leave the House, passing from MB to ZS, female names do, given to a woman's BD until they are ideally returned (to her DD). From a woman's point of view, her MBD is the holder but not the owner of her own mother's name, a name she expects to get back to pass to her own daughter. This difference in the circulation of male and female names would account for the preeminence of the latter among the Kayapó. We do not have to agree with Lea that the Kayapó have corporate descent units to consider this a possible explanation, particularly if we take into account the role of women in negotiations regarding the circulation of names and persons among Northern Gê domestic units (Ladeira 1982; Lea 1986). Given the generally common Northern Gê patterns in onomastics and kinship and the indications regarding their concomitant variation, this might represent the beginnings of a potentially economic and elegant hypothesis.

Succession, Substitution, and Transformation

In his seminal article on Crow-Omaha kinship, Lounsbury hypothesized that his transformational rules expressed laws of succession to social statuses (1964a:383). The interpretations of Melatti, Da Matta, and other HCBP researchers "culturalized" the ethnosemantic approach of Lounsbury and others, taking the identity between name-giver and name-receiver as representing a distinctive mode of social continuity. Da Matta contrasts the continuity in unilineal systems, ordered in linear temporal terms, to that obtained through *substitution*: in Gê societies, "a person assumes a social mask from another and substitutes for him jurally and ritually. There is no obvious idea of *continuum*, but there is a clear notion of duality, even when substitutions over a long period are involved" (Da Matta 1979:127).

A Krahô man said to Melatti (1979) that when he died his name-receiver would "stay in his place forever"; Crocker (1990) reports that the Canela state that a man "takes the place" of his father-in-law and also of his maternal uncle or name-giver. They also admit a man may take his father's place. But to them, the most important form of substitution is the second, which is coordinated with female substitutions: "A man, however, takes his mother's brother's place principally when his sister takes their mother's place. He takes it in tandem with her, as the most important male succession of all, they say" (Crocker 1990:238). If the most important female succession here is that of the daughter who substitutes her mother (not the female name-receiver in relation to her name-giver), this is in perfect coherence with the Crow bias of Canela terminology and its focus on male names (we should not expect the Kayapó to say the same).

Here is the crucial point: this substitution of persons is more than a matter of an individual taking another's role, the recycling of persons through a fixed social structure. As the sister's son substitutes for his mother's brother, what is being substituted is not just a person for another in the same role, signified by the name. The continuity of the "role"—the name as a title—is, rather, the symbolic means by which substitution or transformation *of relations* is achieved. As my son takes the role and name/title of my brother, *it is my relation to my brother (among other relations) that is transformed*. This may be why onomastic identity produces reclassification and skewing.

The special behavior and terminology among siblings naming each other's children express and effect the *substitution* of new relationships created through (prospective and/or actual) naming for the ordinary kinship relations between siblings. The transformation of this relationship is crucial in Turner's (1979a, 1979b) analysis, where cross-transmission of names (linking "marginal" relatives like MB/ZCh and FZ/BCh) appears as a compensation of sorts for the dissolution of intrafamilial ties. Turner's approach has the inestimable value of calling attention to the fact that we are dealing with the production and reproduction (what I call transformation) of relations, not merely acting roles or putting things in categories. What Amerindians are trying to produce or create, most of the time, is *people*, that is, *persons* of a particular kind: fully social, *human* persons—*relatives*—as opposed to other types of persons that inhabit their cosmos (animals, spirits, enemies, strangers . . .). What I suggest is that an understanding of the way Northern Gê employ certain symbolic devices in the constitution of their relationships for the making of human beings or relatives is the key to understanding what we call their "kinship systems"—to its dynamic (or "dialectical") structuring, too often lost in our segregation of terminology/behavior, synchrony/diachrony, classification/action, and so forth.

Naming may be seen as a specific transformative route in the making of persons correlated with another route: marriage. My argument is that both are directed to the making of kinship. If kinship has to be made, it is because it is not given; even when it is already there, as a product of the kinship making of previous generations, it has to be sustained, for otherwise it lapses. Naming may be viewed as a way of blocking such lapsing and marriage as a means to reverse it. I will try to spell out these sequences.

Making Kin

One important way kinship connection is expressed among the Gê is through the notion of "substance." Identity of "substance" is culturally conceptualized mainly in terms of "blood" (an indigenous idiom); it is created through the fluids shared through commensality and procreation and expressed in dietary and other restrictions people "of the same blood" observe for one another's sake. This "community of substance" or "corporal group" is the reference point for a kinship identity manifest in relationships of sharing that obtain among more distant kin and is a dynamic, flexible, and gradable condition not established exclusively by birth (Da Matta 1979; Seeger 1975). The focus on bodies and bodily connections as socially constructed through everyday and ritual practices has provided anthropologists working with Lowland South American societies an alternative vocabulary to the corporate group and social person more in line with native conceptualizations of social relationships (Seeger, Da Matta, and Viveiros de Castro 1979).

Kinship relationships must then be actively produced; their production shows in people being born and growing as proper human beings. The fabrication of children affects the fabricators (who include not only the parents of the children but also the parents' relatives). It creates identity among them. This is sometimes expressed as husband and wife having "equivalent" "blood," to the point that they should observe restrictions for each other during sickness. Even when it is not, they tend to be classified as "true" or "close" kin. This points to a more general process of *consanguinization of affinal relations* also expressed in terminology and behavior.

Northern Gê marry people they consider nonrelatives and treat by personal names; in some groups, the terms for "husband" and "wife" may be applied in "classificatory" fashion to others besides an actual spouse, and they are frequently used to indicate sexual interest. Public acknowledgment of conjugal relations triggers a series of transformations in the relationships between the partners, who should replace the "husband" and "wife" terms with teknonyms formed from the name of the their future child (the basis for the construction of a new set of relations). Because sex and procreation also alter the relations of each of the spouses with the kin of the other, the latter, now distinguished by a complete series of affinal terms, become the object of a specific behavioral etiquette, marked by sexual prohibition, interactional restrictions, name interdiction, and special discourse markers, sometimes amounting to total avoidance. This stands in stark contrast with the behavior between spouses that is closer to the usually mild respect prevalent among kin.

Affinal relationships are also marked by obligations and prestations ("payments," in native parlance) conceptualized as different from the sharing and solidarity expected among kin. But not every contribution by an "affine" is an affinal payment; the "services" exchanged by spouses, notably, seem difficult to label as payments. As the marriage progresses, moreover, the respective contributions of husband and wife to the extended family economy and, especially, to the growing and caring of their common offspring (grandchildren to the wife's parents) tend to look more and more like sharing than exchange. As this happens, it seems that even those relationships that were the very paradigm of affinal distance and separation convert, to a certain (and variable) extent, into kinship (sharing) relations. A sign of this conversion is the progressive relaxation of avoidance as the marriage stabilizes and children are born. This evolution is explicitly interpreted by Da Matta (1982:107), reflecting direct Apinajé usage, as a conversion of affines into consanguines. Affinity consists, then, in an eminently transitory condition, "a phase through which relationships pass on their way from original unrelatedness to full kinship" (Turner 1979b:197). This "transitional category" (ibid.) is a critical link in the chain of transformations constituting the kinship process. Marriage makes kin, creating not only new persons but also kinship between affines connected by these new persons. Differentiated through the contrasting relationships they have to a third party—a daughter or sister (son or brother) for one, a wife (husband) for the other—affines will be made "similar" by their common kinship to the offspring produced by their alliance.

Concomitantly, a reverse process takes place among siblings, whose blood (the idiom is indigenous) becomes progressively differentiated as it mixes with that of their respective spouses and partners. So although the universe of kinship may be described as a network in which any two kinspeople are connected to each other by, in Canela parlance, one or more "bridges" (pairs of primary consubstantial relations),[4] it must be stressed that the B/Z and H/W relations amount to one-way bridges. They are inversely oriented pairs: spouses are gradually mixing together and becoming kin, that is, becoming similar, whereas siblings are gradually differentiating apart and becoming dissimilar. These two movements do not have the same status. The first is the one the Canela keep their eyes on: it forms the focus of their action. The second emerges as a nonintentional effect of the construction of kinship—and indeed, many of the obligations between "siblings" seem to be directed toward curbing this second movement, toward keeping kinship "alive" between those whom maturity and consequent engagement in new relations will inevitably separate to some degree.

Name exchange between opposite-sex (distant) siblings seems to be related to the need to counteract the lapsing of kinship as people marry and invest their efforts in new relationships with spouses, affines, and offspring. The ethnographers of the Timbira and Apinajé are explicit: "one declared purpose of a name-exchange agreement is to maintain and even increase the number of a person's significant relatives, and therefore, to broaden the person's social support base" (Crocker 1990: 252). Name exchange is consistently presented as a procedure to *create* close or "true" kinship, or to *prevent it from lapsing*, by fulfilling the reciprocity obligations—particularly those regarding each other's offspring —that link "true" and "close" opposite-sex siblings (Da Matta 1982; Ladeira 1982; Lea 1986:204).

Operating in the same "region" of the kinship field, viz. "distant" relatives, naming and marriage appear as alternative procedures for making true kin, for tightening ties that tend to fade with residential dispersal and genealogical distancing. The subsequent transformation of relations is, in the case of marriage, terminologically effected through affinal or indirect reference (or "ternary") terms and teknonymy. In the case of naming, through naming terminology (comprising the name-giver/name-receiver terms and the accompanying teknonymy employed concerning their relatives). The procedures are mutually exclusive, but the transformational sequences they trigger are connected. Skewing registers the connection.

Skewing

Let us pause to consider how skewing enters this picture. One thing skewing (in Northern Gê fashion) does is turn cross-cousins—who elsewhere in Lowland South America, given the Dravidianate landscape, tend to be equated with spouses/in-laws or called by terms carrying the possibility of marriage/alliance—into "mothers," "fathers," "children," "grandparents," and "grandchildren." This means, of course, blocking the possibility of cousin marriage, in a context where, accordingly, marriage is supposed to take place between nonkin (that is, kin distant enough for the kinship to be "forgotten" or disregarded). But such possibility is blocked *differentially* for the various sorts of cousins (and children of cousins). If skewing options in their Crow or Omaha versions are present here, as equally available to actors through the alternative male or female naming identifications produced by the onomastic system, we may infer something important about the way marriage and naming interact.

This was first shown by Ladeira (1982) for the Timbira. Taking into account the possibilities in the classification of cross-cousins afforded by name identity, she lists the alternatives (for male ego/female alter) shown in table 10.1.

Skewing thus (as an effect of name transmission) transforms cross-cousins into kin—but not of the same sort or to the same extent. From a man's point of view, female matrilateral cousins become D (Crow) or M (Omaha); from a woman's, male patrilateral cousins become F and S. These are respected relatives with whom (or with whose children) ego (or his or her children) can exchange names. From a man's point of view, female patrilateral cousins become FZ (Crow) and ZD (Omaha); from a woman's, male matrilateral cousins become ZS (Crow) or MB (Omaha), relatives with whom joking is permitted and name exchange precluded (for their respective offspring are not in a B/Z relation to fe-

Table 10.1 Alternative classification of female cross-cousins (Timbira)

Alter	Name/ transmission identity	Equation	Term	Goal
MBD	M → MBD (Omaha)	MBD=M	"mother"	Ego may exchange names with MBDD (his "sister")
	MB → Ego (Crow)	MBD=D	"daughter"	Ego's children may exchange names with their FMBD (their "sister")
FZD	F → FZS (Crow)	FZD=FZ[GM]	"aunt"	Neither Ego nor his children (for whom she is a "grandmother") can exchange names with her or her children (his "F/FZ")
	FZ → Z (Omaha)	FZD=ZD	"niece"	Neither Ego nor his children (for whom she is a "grand-daughter") can exchange names with her or her children (his "grandchildren")

male/male ego). In either case, a man's patrilateral (a woman's matrilateral) cross-cousins of opposite sex are more distant kin than cousins of the other side. "More distant" means they are equated to cross-relatives: no name exchange here, which means that the only way of making these relatives "close" again, of making true kin out of them, is through marriage.

There is a proximity axis on which we can arrange all (female) cousins (relative to male ego): the closest ones are matrilateral parallel cousins (MZD) who not only are "sisters" to him but also tend to live in the same house or village sector; "shame" prevents sexual or marital advances here. Next, matrilateral cross-cousins, considered as mothers or daughters (depending on naming strategies, as described in table 10.1), are also too close, and sex with them is considered too shameful. Her daughters are "sister" to him (and so he may exchange names with them), or she herself may be a "sister" to his children (and exchange names with them), so there are other ways of strengthening the tie. The same applies to patrilateral parallel cousins, "sisters" to ego, who are dispersed in different houses and village sectors and the ideal name-givers to his daughters. Marrying a FBD (or a MBD) is not impossible, but besides the shame attached to it (these are relationships marked by respect), it is a waste of human resources, so to speak, for this woman might be made kin (or recruited to help in making other kin) through naming. But patrilateral cross-cousins are not "consanguines": they are neither "mothers" nor "sisters" but the most distant of all cousins. They are equated to relatives with whom the respect that applies to all kinship relationships is less marked; they may be the focus of joking. Consequently, *classificatory* FZD marriage appears as a theoretical possibility. The model provides a scale of differential "distance" regarding cross-cousins oriented by the alternatives provided by the naming system, a scale that conditions ego's options in his (her) search for "sisters" ("brothers") and for "wives" ("husbands") with whom to make children, through sex in the latter case, through name exchange in the former.

How would this "model" fare with the non-Timbira groups, like the Kayapó or Kïsêdjê? In the spirit of opening this and other questions for further ethnographic research, I conclude by introducing one more transformation in Gê kinship for consideration.

The Northern Gê and the Unmaking of Crow-Omaha Kinship

The Northern Gê do not marry relatives—that is, persons to whom ego refers or addresses by a kinship term. The opposition between determinate and particular relations, labeled by kinship terms, and indeterminate relations, marked by the use of names, provides one of the idioms in which "incest" laws are expressed. The other is, in characteristically Gê fashion, spatial: "to marry on the other side [of the village]" is an ideal expressed by the Kayapó, Apinajé, Kïsêdjê, Krahô, and Ramkokamekra. Given ideal village endogamy, this may pose a problem, because everyone in a village is also, ideally, conceived of as related. The Gê cope with the problem through reclassification: all one has to do is to call the person by name and behave toward him or her as one behaves toward a spouse. But reclassification depends on the crucial axis of "distance" (it is dangerous to marry a close relative). We have seen how skewing, as an effect of naming, turns distant relatives (potentially marriageable) into closer ones; "cross-cousins" become terminological consanguines. We may ask whether there are not ways of doing the opposite: converting close relationships into distant ones.

This is exactly what formal friendship seems to do. This important ceremonial relationship involves a high degree of solidarity and many obligations among partners; it is marked by extreme *avoidance*. Formal friends appear then as hyperaffines with whom actual marriage is impossible. They are categorized ostensibly as "nonkin" and, like affines, recruited outside the kindred. But formal friendship and affinity are connected by more than analogy (avoidance, distance) and their incidence on the same area of the social field (nonkin). There are various references to an ideal of marrying the daughter of a formal friend among the Kayapó, the Apinajé, and also certain Timbira groups (see Lea 1995a). From this, based on the Kayapó statement that it is good for a man to marry the daughter of his female formal friend (and for a woman to marry her mother's formal friend), Lea (1995a) proposed a "simulated model" of marriage alliance, in which formal friendship emerges as a way of canceling or negating residual kinship to pave the way for marriage. This would make formal friendship a way of *unmaking* kin, not in the negative and uncontrolled way the lapsing of kinship does but in a manner that positively prepares the field for new, repeated, determined alliances: a positive marriage "rule" of sorts.

Viveiros de Castro (1998) has suggested that the transition between certain Amazonian transformations of the Dravidianate pattern and Crow-Omaha systems could be shorter than once thought, evoking the Crow equivalences of the Sirionó and other Tupian and Karib groups. Skewing, as a trace of semi-complex alliance structure on one hand, and as a feature of other marriage preferences (avuncular, asymmetrical MBD marriage) on the other, "whales" and "fishes," could be thought of as different realizations of a "*terminologically* underspecified Dravidianate, in which the position of cross-kin in G^0 is a sort of 'empty case'" (Viveiros de Castro 1998:374). Such a hypothesis depends on a redefinition of complexity, elementarity, or semi-complexity not as characterizing types of systems or societies, but as specifying regimes or conditions under which an ever-changing alliance structure could be seen to unfold its many versions. Pursuing this line of inquiry requires an understanding of kinship (and "systems") less hindered by overly restrictive definitions of "types" and "structure."

Restrictive definitions of types and structures are tied to a mode of anthropological description that operates by distinguishing levels and domains (e.g., concept/rule/behavior, categorical/jural/behavioral, terminology/group structure/marriage rules) and privileging one of them as the locus of primary order, structure, or meaning. This mode is built into the descriptive devices we use—the genealogical grid and the disjunction between classification and behavior it allows—by providing categories of relationship with a *reference* independent from the *content* of those relationships (Wagner 1977). But suppose there is no external referent to relationship categories other than the relationships themselves: ascription of kin or any other relationship category cannot then map social roles onto genealogy: it can only *transform* previous *social* relationships. To classify—to choose among the various alternative systems—is a form of social action, a transformative one, and this applies as much to consanguinity terms as to any other set. There is no primary, natural category a person should apply to someone else that does not imply the *making* of a specific relation where before there was another, different relation (perhaps an indeterminate one). In this sense, classification is always *reclassification*, and thus always involves transformation.

In this sense, all systems are "contextually variable," all are "overlays," for actors are always "adding meaning" when employing them. Of course some systems are more stable than others and this relative stability needs to be accounted for. That Crow-Omaha terminologies appear more contextual and unstable than others (see Kronenfeld; McConvell; Dousset, all in this volume) is an important result that opens new vistas for comparative research on the topic, but this should not lead us to believe those other patterns can be analyzed independently of contexts and uses.

Paying attention to the interface between alternative systems, we may see how those "types" and "levels" are related, temporally and dynamically, in social reproduction *and change*. Diachronic, historical change only happens because change is happening all the time. We need to understand kinship systems as intrinsically dynamic systems if we want to understand their long-term dynamics. We need a (*micro*) *history* of kinship, if we are to have a theory of its evolution.

Amerindians see kinship as the result of the positive relational transformations that produce human beings. Kinship is a way of making people, of creating the relationships that constitute proper human persons. From this standpoint, there is also the *unmaking* of kinship to be considered here, in a double sense: the way kinship ("consanguinity") is culturally undone, so that marriage is made possible where humanity and kinship are viewed as coextensive, and the way kinship as an anthropological object must be placed in a more encompassing scheme of the transformation of social relations.

11

Schemas of Kinship Relations and the Construction of Social Categories among the Mebêngôkrê Kayapó

Terence Turner

This chapter deals with kinship and social organization among the Kayapó, or as they call themselves, the Mebêngôkrê, a Gê-speaking people of central Brazil. I attempt to demonstrate how the social activities that produce families, domestic groups, kindreds, communal social groups, and social persons become the ontological forms and epistemological categories of kinship relations. The schema or form of these social activities not only constructs objectified forms of social relations, kinship relations among them, but when applied as an epistemological category to the classification of these objectified relations by a subject positioned within the system, the same schema can be shown to generate categories of kinship relations corresponding to Kayapó lexical categories of kin, including the classification of cross-cousins, which is of the "Omaha" type. I conclude with some general implications for the understanding of Omaha and other "generation-skewing" types of cousin classification.

My basic analytical concept is the schema, defined as the form of an activity or process of interaction. The schematic form of an activity is an integral part of that activity considered as an objective (material) reality but is also integral to the cognitive (ideal) conception of that form by the actor(s). The schema thus serves as a subjective epistemological category by which actors orient their actions and categorize aspects and components of the situation of action. Schemas thus figure both as objective social and subjective cognitive constituents of material activities. As such, they serve as subjective epistemological categories that guide their own objectification, both in consciousness and in material reality.

Kayapó Social Organization

The Kayapó, like the other Northern Gê peoples, live in large villages consisting of numerous matri-uxorilocal extended family households built around the periphery of a circular plaza. In the plaza stands a men's house, which serves as the focus of the ceremonial and political life of the village, including the men's and women's age sets and their activities (figure 11.1). Village populations may exceed 1,000, normally contain unrelated men and women of marriageable age, and tend to be endogamous. Marriage is monogamous. The extended family household constitutes the basic segmentary unit of the structure of society as a whole. Its internal structure consists of elementary families linked by ties of matrifiliation (mother-daughter and sister-sister) between the women who act as mothers and wives in each elementary family. I use the term "unit" for a set of relations or group that contains within itself the structural properties of the social whole of which it forms a part. The term "element" (as in "elementary family") is used for a relation or set of relations that forms a component of a segmentary unit.

Marriage (*aben wòrò mõ* or "coming together with one another") is only considered to be consummated by the pregnancy of the wife, and the birth of children is what definitively establishes an elementary family. Birth within a family established by a marriage or linkage by filiation to such an elementary family establishes "true" (*kumren*) or full kinship. Kinship is symmetrically bilateral and with one minor exception (a form of ceremonial companionship is patrilineally inherited) there is no rule of descent. The term *õ bi-kwa*, literally "one's surrounding curved space," denotes both kinship and the personal kindred, defined as a bilateral field of relations radiating from an elementary family at its center. Marriage is prohibited within the known range of genealogical relations. The affinal relations established by marriage are defined as a sort of incipient kinship, *aben wòrò mõrõ kam õ bi-kwa*, or "kinship by marriage," a step in the transition to full kinship, which is fully realized by the birth of the next generation. The offspring of affines are considered full kin, which reflexively consolidates the kinship relation of the spouse-parents with each other's kin.

Postmarital residence is uniformly matri-uxorilocal. Although some ethnographers have taken this to imply that the Kayapó possess some

Figure 11.1 Kayapó village of Pykanu. Matri-uxorilocal extended family houses, central men's house, and plaza for ceremonial activities.
Source: Apoio AER de Colider (MT) e Coordenação de Educação 2007.

form of matrilineal descent that serves as the basis of the matri-uxorilocal household structure, such is not the case (see Lea 1995b; Lowie with Nimuendajú 1943). The point is important for reasons that extend well beyond the Kayapó. Matri-uxorilocal extended family households constitute the basic segmentary units of all the Gê-speaking societies, as well as a number of other central Brazilian societies that speak unrelated languages. Some of these societies do have forms of matrilineal descent and possess ethnographically well-attested matrilineal descent groups at the communal level of organization, but others are patrilineal, and many are cognatic or bilateral. It is thus evident that the widespread matri-uxorilocal residential pattern cannot be explained as the product of matrilineal descent.

In the Kayapó case, at any rate, not only does descent (as distinct from filiation) not exist, but where we might expect to find it, as the principle of organization of communal groupings and their relations with household segments, there is instead an apparently bizarre system of symbolic antidescent. Both men and women are formally adopted before their marriages by "substitute" parents of their respective genders who must be unrelated to them by kinship, whose function is to formally sever the continuity of relations with the same-sex parent for purposes of recruitment to adult status in segmentary and communal-level groups. Nor does this set of parallel "antidescent" relations have either an antiunilineal form or a matrilateral bias. On the contrary, as a system of antiparallel descent, it has a pronounced patrilateral bias, for reasons we shall see later. This turns out to be a critical point for understanding why the matri-uxorilocal and bilateral Kayapó should have an Omaha cousin terminology.

Kayapó Social Structure as Schema

The pattern of Kayapó kinship and domestic group relations can be described as a schema for the reproduction of the segmentary unit of Kayapó social organization, the matri-uxorilocal extended family household, specifically consisting of its relations of formation and dispersion, which comprise inputs from and outputs to other segmentary household units of identical structure. The total system of relations comprising these relations of formation and dispersion constitutes the field of personal kinship relations recognized by all Kayapó of either sex. This field constitutes a bilateral personal kindred, for which, as noted, the Kayapó use the term *ō-bikwa*. The schema consists of the relations of production and dispersion of a linked pair of elementary families connected by the relation of filiation between their respective female spouse-parents, who are related as mother and daughter. Such linked pairs of families form the core of the localized extended families that constitute the units of Kayapó social organization. The core of the segmentary unit thus comprises two consecutive revolutions of the developmental cycle of the elementary family, consisting of the relations of formation, expansion, and dispersion of the elementary families of procreation of filially linked mothers and daughters, which may extend to include the elementary families formed by sisters and matrilateral female parallel cousins to form relatively large extended family households.

The bifamilial core is linked to units beyond the household through its various adult male members, who marry into and out of the extended family household in question. The manner and degree of attachment of these in-marrying male affines to their wives' families and households mirrors the displacement of out-marrying male offspring of the women of the household and their attachments to their own wives and affinal households. These male-linked relations with other households thus constitute integral elements of the schema of production and dispersion of the segmentary unit.

The bilateral kindred encompasses the relations of the household core, the linked natal families of its male affinal members, and the families of procreation and affinal relatives of its male offspring who are not coresidents of the matri-uxorilocal domestic group. The kindred is internally divided, like the household core itself, into two contrasting levels of relative structural distance. The lowest level consists of the internal relations of a single elementary family: the spouse-parents and offspring of a single monogamous marriage. This cluster of relations is functionally distinct within the household for purposes of the production and processing of food and utensils and minding children, but it is not recognized or valued as a fully social unit. It is, rather, conceived as a relatively "natural" set of relations, based on essentially animal-like biological relations of sexual intercourse, reproduction, and primary nurturance.

The relations between the members of this elementary group and those constituting the other linked families comprising the segmentary core and its male-linked families in other households comprise a higher level of fully social relations. Only these higher level, purely social relatives are able to transmit to the immature members of the family unit the basic elements of social identity and value. These include personal names, where possible, the "great" ceremonial names bestowed in great communal ceremonies, and a variety of "valuables" (*nêkrêtch*), items of social value that become a recognized part of the personal identity of the recipient. These names and valuables may not be passed from parent to child within the elementary family. They must be conferred by linked relatives at the segmentary level: grandparents, maternal uncles, paternal aunts, and certain affinal and fictive kin who become classified with these relations (parallel cousins are categorized as identical with elementary family members for these purposes and thus, like the spouse-parents, excluded from the circulation of names and valuables to the children of the family). Communal ceremony is chiefly concerned with circulating and conferring these items of value, thus emphasizing the interdependence of fully socialized personal identity and the framework of the extended family segment. What are relatively peripheral relations from the perspective of the elementary family are thus emphasized as the exclusive channels of social identity and value in constituting the social person.

The men's house in the center of the village plaza configures communal institutions and collective ceremonies that schematically reproduce the formation, expansion, and dispersion of the constituent elements of the extended family household and the bilateral kindred. The result is an asymmetrical pattern of differentially weighted transformations of male and female relations to their successive natal and conjugal families. In turn, this gives rise to a patrilateral bias in relations at the middle stages of the developmental cycles of male and female persons and of the families of orientation and procreation to which they belong. Simultaneously, a distinct set of weighted transformations inculcates a counterbalancing pattern of symmetrical unity and equality between the sexes in passing identities and values to children and in the public roles and statuses of both sexes in the final phases of their life cycles and the dispersion of their families of procreation.

For males, the inculcation of this patrilaterally weighted schematic pattern takes the form of separating boys from their natal households, particularly from their biological fathers, by removing them to the men's house under the aegis of a nonkinsman who becomes their "substitute" father. The importance of their attainment of fatherhood in their own right is heavily reinforced in this setting, both as father-husbands in their wives' households and as members of the adult men's age set of "fathers"—their principal social identity as adult men (Turner 1979b, 2002).

The attenuation of males' attachments to their natal households is emphasized in the solidarity of the age sets associated with the men's house. These are recruited by the same rituals of passage that mark a male's transitions through the segmentary household and extended family units. Separation of the men's house—as the domicile of the boys' and bachelors' age sets and the club and meeting place of the "fathers'" age set—from the women's households on the periphery of the plaza is a powerful factor in creating the patrilaterally biased pattern of male relations at the segmentary and communal levels. This bias emphasizes paternity and affinity at the expense of the continuity of male relations as sons and brothers to their natal families and of household units as aspects of adult male identity. The separation of the men's house, in other words, enables the segregation of boys from their maternal houses when they join the age set of boys who sleep in the men's house and in due course move on as husband-fathers to attach themselves as residents to their wives' households.

This series of separations and attachments, or dispersions and formations of families and communal sodalities, constitutes the male half of what I have called the pattern of patrilateral bias of the Kayapó system. The complementary female side of the schema of differential weighting of extended family and communal group relations assumes a different form. Women, who remain members of the households into which they are born for their whole lives, also go through a public ceremony of separation from their biological mothers (genetrixes) and natal families, which like the boys' ceremony takes the form of adoption by a "substitute mother" (mater). This takes place, however, at a much later stage in the life cycle of a woman: the point at which, sometime after she reaches puberty, she is judged to be ready for motherhood, and hence for the consummation of marriage in Kayapó terms. This normally leads more or less rapidly to courtship, pregnancy, and marriage to a young man who thereupon takes up residence with her in her mother's household (Turner 1979b).

The separation from her mother represented by the ceremony of adoption by the "substitute" mother has the effect of opening up a separate space within the household in which she and her husband can set up a new elementary family of their own, with the father-husband playing a strong role from the outset. The ceremony also initiates the young woman into membership in the young women's age set, which consists essentially of young mothers and wives—called initially "the black-thighed ones" after the recruitment ceremony in which the "substitute mother" paints black stripes on the women's thighs, and then "mothers of few children" when the women actually bear children. This young women's age set is also collectively designated "wives of the men's house," meaning that it consists of women married to the younger subset of the "fathers'" age set to which their husbands belong. Even though women have no women's house of their own, they do have a collective age set attached to the men's house that carries out its own naming ceremony as a symmetrical equivalent of the men's naming ceremonies. The stock of personal names and *nêkrêtch* (valuables) is symmetrically gendered, passing between donors and recipients of the same sex.

A woman eventually transitions to membership in the senior women's age set of "mothers of many children" when her family of procreation is beginning to disperse and she is about to become a mother-in-law and grandmother. This transition has some of the same social significance as the young man's passage at marriage into the adult men's age set: it marks a woman's attainment of full adult status. It stands in the same relationship of complementary opposition to her ritual of adoption and the painting of her thighs by her "substitute mother" as the young man's marriage and accession to membership in the adult men's ("fathers'") age set stands to his earlier ritual of adoption by the "substitute father" who also paints him with a black design (on the chest) and thus inducts him into the men's house. A major difference, of course, is that the two women's rites of passage occur at the formation and dispersion of her elementary family of procreation, whereas the two men's rites take place at the dispersion of their natal families and formation of their families of procreation—a difference corresponding to one elementary family cycle, or in Kayapó terms, one generation.

This asymmetrically staggered pattern of transformations of male and female family status and household attachments means that the male completes his transformation one generation or family cycle ahead of the female. During the entire developmental cycle of their joint family of procreation, the male spouse-parent counts as a social adult (as a father in his own right), and the female spouse-parent counts only as a formal minor. She remains the "substitute daughter" under the aegis of her "substitute mother" even as a member of the young mothers' age set and a mother with her own family of procreation until the dispersion of that family. Marriage and fatherhood for a man thus formally advances him to social adulthood one generation or family cycle ahead of his spouse, whereas marriage and motherhood for a woman brings a continuation of her tutelary status as social minor for another generation, until the dispersion of her family of procreation (Turner 2002).

This gendered pattern of generational transitions creates an overlap between the prolonged natal family/household connection of the female spouse and the new affinal family/household attachment of the male spouse. The result is the fusion of the overlapping sets of elementary family relations in a bifamilial extended family, composed of the wife's parents and same-sex siblings and the new husband and the family of procreation he establishes with the wife, as the residential core of a matri-uxorilocal household. The interconnection of the successive elementary families also establishes the framework of the bilaterally symmetrical kindred, which encapsulates the new elementary family of procreation within a network of exchanges of social identities (names and "valuables") between the peripheral, indirectly linked senior and junior members (MM, FM, FZ to DD, SD, and BD; FF, MF, MB to SS, DS, and ZS). Conferring social identity by these acts of socialization simultaneously defines the social identity and value of the segmentary extended family as a social unit, as they bring about the closure (reversal) of the transformations that comprise its structural framework.

Note that these relations are differentially gendered but also symmetrical: they represent the final transformations, in this case the redistribution of attachments, between the senior and junior peripheral relatives of the extended family segment, which corresponds to the final, symmetrical attainment of full social adulthood by extended family household members of both genders. As such, they constitute the invariant boundary condition that contains and limits the asymmetrical patrilateral bias of the middle stages of the expansion of the extended family segment.

The Schema of Kinship Relations as the Embodied Pattern of Production of the Social Person and as Subjective Epistemological Category

I have presented an account of the objective structure of Kayapó kinship relations, as embodied in the segmentary unit of Kayapó social organization, the matri-uxorilocal extended family household and its extension in the bilateral personal kindred, and at a higher level of organization by the communal age set associations and ceremonies of the men's house. This schema of social activities is objectified as the structure of Kayapó society, not only at the level of communal institutions associated with the men's house but also in the extended family household segment and the personal kindred.

The schema also necessarily has a subjective aspect, as a form of social consciousness that orients and coordinates the activities that produce the relations that objectify its form. It is, in fact, directly involved in the production of the subjective identities as well as the objective forms of Kayapó persons and bodies. These identities are socially constructed by the forms of collective activity and bodily decoration that encode and produce the objective structures of kinship relations and communal groups. The same sexually asymmetrical pattern of transformations of family status and household attachments that comprise the content of these objectified forms of kinship relations, in other words, is visually indexed by the changing patterns of bodily decoration and associated rites of passage that define the changing identities of social persons of both genders (Turner 1980, 1995, 2011).

The social identities thus constructed define the subjective perspective of persons on their kinship relations from the standpoint of their positions within the system. The identification of kinship relations with the embodied schema of the social persons who act to reproduce the objectified form of the system of kinship and domestic group relations is indexed by the terminological classification of kin: a man calls his MB, MF, and FF *i-kran-tum* ("my old head"), and reciprocally calls his ZS, DS, and SS *kran-nu*, or "young head." Both men and women use the word for "hand" (*ikra*), as the kinship term for "my child" (*i-kra*); a man also uses the term for "foot" (*pari*) for his ZS, DS, and SS. The head, hands, and feet figure in the code of Kayapó bodily decoration as the appendages that make contact with external social space and are therefore usually painted red, in contrast with the central trunk of the body, which is painted black (Turner 1980). The schema of personal bodily identity is thus articulated in terms of kinship relations and becomes the reflexive perspective of the actors who continually reproduce those relations. The epistemological perspective of the actors on their fields of kinship relations, in other words, constitutes an embodied form of the schema objectified in those relations.

The Gender Asymmetry of Affinal Relations and Egocentric Generation Skewing: The "Omaha" Pattern of Cross-Cousin Relations

The field of kinship relations as seen from a position within the system is not uniformly composed of elementary families. Rather, it is a stratified system comprising successive levels of distance from ego's position. Each level has its own constituent elements of increasing scale and inclusiveness. The first level comprises the individual elementary family, the minimal structural element of the system, represented by the family of orientation (or natal family) and family of procreation to which ego successively belongs, with its constituent elements, the types of individual family relationships, such as F, B, Ch. The next level has for its structural unit a pair of linked elementary families, such as that which forms the core of an extended family household. The constituents of that unit consist of what I call "cross-family" relations, such as FF, MB, FZ.

A third level is formed by linked pairs of elementary families (units of the second level) linked to each other by an elementary family that forms a part of both pairs. The resulting unit comprises a triad of overlapping pairs of families. An example is the triad consisting of the pair formed by ego's natal family and the natal family of ego's mother, and the overlapping pair constituted by the natal family of ego's mother and the family of procreation of mother's opposite-sex sibling, the mother's brother, that contains MBCh (ego's Xc). There is a second such triad linked to ego's family of orientation at the opposite end, as it were: this consists of the pair of ego's natal family and the family of orientation of ego's father, which is in turn connected by father's cross-sex sibling (FZ) to the latter's family of procreation. The central linking relations connecting the units (family dyads) of the two triads comprise opposite sequences of sexes, as do the linking relations to the central, overlapping family to the two peripheral family units (ego's natal family and the family of the cross-cousins). The asymmetrical pattern of weighting of male- and female-linked transitions from natal to affinal families thus comes to bear in opposite ways on the relations between the elementary families that constitute the two triads.

In the matrilateral triad, the link between mother's family of procreation and her natal family (the central family of the triad) is initiated and consummated a whole family cycle later than her male sibling's (ego's MB's) formation of his family of procreation. She therefore remains attached to her family of orientation in contrast to her brother (ego's MB) who has completed his separation from their mutual family of orientation and has attained adult status as the father-husband in his family of procreation (that of ego's matrilateral cross-cousins). The combination of ego's MB's relative separation from his and ego's mother's common natal family and ascent to a higher (adult) generation in his linking capacity to his family of procreation imply that (in relation to his natal family and his link as a cross-sex sibling to mother within it), he has become the equivalent, as a father in his family of procreation and an adult in his own right, of his father. In this way, MB's family of procreation becomes equivalent to his family of orientation, in contrast to mother (his sister), still formally a minor attached in that capacity to her parental family and still untransformed, as a link to her family of procreation (ego's natal family), to adult generational status on a par with that of her brother (ego's MB). The relation between M's family of procreation and her family of orientation, in other words, is one of child to adult, whereas that of MB is transitively one of adult to child, and the relation between their two families of procreation is classified accordingly.

The triadic structures of relations between elementary family units thus reduce themselves, from ego's perspective, to dyads of linked families, constructed as mirror images of each other. The resulting reduction of the third level of structural distance to the second is logically compelled by the fact that the opposite-sex links between and within the family dyads, when juxtaposed with each other, create a contrast equivalent to an entire generational revolution of the developmental cycle of the family. From ego's point of view, as mediated by combinations of families as the structural units of contrast, this pattern of asymmetrical generation "skewing" is clearly the product of asymmetrical weighting of the transformations of household attachments and family statuses in the developmental cycles of the family and domestic group.

Egocentric Aspects of "Generation Skewing": Cross-Family Relations

At the second level of distance (comprising relations within linked pairs of elementary families), a different pattern of skewing appears. Common to many other central Brazilian societies, this skewing pattern involves the treatment of the children of ego's cross-sex siblings, and conversely of ego's parents' cross-sex siblings and parents (ego's grandparents). This essentially consists in raising the generational status of the parental cross-sex siblings, FZ and MB, to that of their parents (ego's grandparents), while lowering the generational status of ego's cross-sex sibling (♂ZCh, ♀BCh). What is involved here is a shift of ego's subject position and perspective from that of his or her natal family to that of his or her family of procreation. When ego forms a family of procreation, his or her subjective perspective on kinship relations is transferred from the natal family to the new family of procreation. Within this new family, ego's offspring are classified as members of ego's current family. The opposite-sex sibling, as a link to his or her offspring, however, is viewed as a member of a family formed after the family of ego, and therefore a generation later than ego's own children. The two families that serve as the subjective vantage points in the two cases, of course, are objectively different, but for purposes of the egocentric classification of kinship relations, they are considered identical. It is intrinsic to the egocentric point of view that ego does not "notice" ego's objective movements from family to family as consecutive temporal stages, but rather identifies ego's point of view as constant ("synchronic") in terms of social space-time. Accordingly, ego categorizes the opposite-sex siblings of his or her parents (members of the parents' prior families of orientation) as a generation prior to the parents, and thus equivalent in generation to the parents' parents (ego's grandparents), which is logically implied by ego's classification of his or her own parents, egocentrically, as members of his or her own natal family and thus a generation younger relative to the families of the grandparents and parental cross-sex siblings.

The generational skewing of cross-family relations arises from a different cause than that of cross-cousin relations or the affinal relatives considered in the last section. All three cases have a common basis in the composition of the field of kinship relations as a field of linked elementary family units: relations between these units, rather than dyadic relations between individual kin types, constitute the common structural medium of all the instances considered, but the specific causes are located at different levels of structural distance and proceed from different specific relations.

Egocentric "Double Focus": Why the Term for Spouse Is "Descriptive"

The spouse is the pivot of the movement of ego from his or her first elementary family (the family of orientation) to the second (the family of procreation). He or she is the external point of reference of ego's separation from his or her natal family and formation of a conjugal family. Then, in a second major moment of ego's life cycle and successive family cycles, the spouse becomes an internal co-member of ego's conjugal family, and a link to the ex-members of his or her former family of orientation (ego's affines). In the first of the two moments, the potential spouse is a nonrelative; at the moment of marriage, an affine, but as a co-member of the conjugal family, he or she is more like kin. In effect, the spouse collapses distinct perspectival identities associated with successive movements of ego from one family to another. As an egocentric subject, however, ego does not distinguish between his two successive family "moments," or register that his subject position has changed from one moment to the next. All the other categories of kinship or affinal relationship except that of the spouse can be unambiguously identified with the perspective of one moment or the other. I suggest that the spouse is designated by an idiosyncratic term, not because she or he constitutes an unambiguous instance of a "descriptive" category in Morgan's sense, but for precisely the opposite reason.

Summary and Conclusion: Kayapó as Omaha?

Kayapó kinship terminology has diagnostic features of "Omaha" generational "skewing" such as MBS = MB, MBD = MZ (= M), and FZD = male ego ZD, female ego ZD (ego D); FZS = male ego ZS, female ego ZS (ego S). I have pointed out other instances of "generation skewing" in the Kayapó terminology not so clearly associated with Omaha systems, such as FZ = FM, MB = MF, and the reciprocals, ♀BCh = ♀SCh, ♀DCh, and ♂ZCh = ♂SCh, ♂DCh. In the light of these and other ambiguities and idiosyncratic features of the Kayapó case, let me identify those aspects of the Kayapó system that may have general relevance to other cases of Omaha-type classifications of kin. The most important point, in my view, is that the generation skewing of cross-cousin terms is a product of schemas for producing extended family segments of standardized form out of linked elementary families. The specific relations involved in linking elementary families to form the segment may take various forms, such as descent, residence, marriage exchange, or other types of collective grouping, ritual performance, or combinations of these. What is most important is that the linking relations are formed and implemented in the same way. The key issue is that there must be an invariant form of coordinating the transformations of male and female relations involved in the dispersion of their natal families and domestic groups and the formation of their conjugal families, *such that one sex carries out its role in this process one family cycle or generational phase before the other.*

To implement such a regular pattern of relations of production of segmentary extended family units virtually requires that a society possess a superstructure of collective groupings or ritual processes that coordinate the reproduction of segments of the same type by the community as a whole. This is my second general point: societies with Omaha or Crow terminologies will generally be found to constitute hierarchical systems, with a lower level of segmentary units of identical structure, and an upper level comprising a communal framework of collective groups and ritual activities. In its institutional structure and recruitment processes, the upper level replicates the forms of transformation of family and kinship relations that bring about the reproduction of the lower level segmentary units. The same schematic pattern of relations and transformations, formulated at different levels of generality and in relation to different specific relations and groups, will thus be found to constitute the structure of relations and groups at both levels. One aspect of this schema, in societies of the type that possess "generation skewing" terminologies, will consist of the differential staggering of the points in the developmental cycle of the family and domestic group where male and female actors attenuate their relations with their families of orientation and attach themselves to their families of procreation. The result will be that in any set of siblings of opposite sexes, one sex will complete the transformations comprising this transition one generation or full family cycle of formation and dispersion before the other. This asymmetrically weighted pattern of interfamily transitions, articulated with the terms of marriage and the formation of conjugal families, may be seen on analysis to constitute a mechanism for linking successive elementary families on one or the other sexually linked side, so as to form extended-family units (at a minimum pairs of linked families) of a standardized form. These units will form the core of the segments that constitute the lower level of the hierarchical structure of the community (Turner 1979a, 1997).

I suggest that such an asymmetrically weighted pattern of transformations of male and female marriage and family relations—as the structure of a collectively standardized process of producing segmentary extended family units, within the framework of a hierarchical system of communal groups and segmentary units—may constitute a general feature of systems possessing generation-skewing terminologies of the

Omaha and Crow types. This is not to dispute the relevance of specific forms of interfamily linkage and segment formation that have been foregrounded by many attempts to account for generation skewing terminologies, such as forms of descent or prescriptive marriage, demographic fluctuations, or other causes. Rather, it is to supply the need, unmet in a number of existing theories, of a specific social and conceptual mechanism for mediating the effects of such factors to forms of classification.

Approaching the analysis of one aspect of a kinship system, in this case the classification of cross-cousins, through a critical analysis of the total system of relations of which it forms part enables a realization that the feature in question, and the social relations from which it arises, may depend on other aspects of the system that have an equal claim to be regarded as diagnostic features of the type of system in question. In the case of the Kayapó—and I suggest that this point holds for Central Brazilian societies in general—the differential weighting of male and female transitions from the family of orientation to the family of procreation, which directly informs the asymmetrical cross-cousin classification, is dependent on and ultimately encompassed by the sexually symmetrical identification of adults of both sexes with their same-sex nieces, nephews, and grandchildren, over the heads, as it were, of the spouse-parents. In the larger perspective of the Kayapó schema of the family cycle and the construction of the social person, the spouse-parents constitute the raw natural productive power that supplies the indispensable content of the process of reproducing the system. But the encompassing network of symmetrical relations between the peripheral senior and junior categories of the extended family segment and kindred provides the essential attributes of social identity and value that complete the process of reproducing the social person, the segment, and the system of communal groupings. Both the asymmetrical and symmetrical sets of relations have their proper forms of skewed relations. Each depends on the other, and neither should be considered to stand alone as the distinctive feature of the systems of which both function as complementary and equal parts.

Australia

12

Omaha Skewing in Australia
Overlays, Dynamism, and Change
Patrick McConvell

Omaha skewing is found in a number of regions of Australia. This is not widely known, as attention has focused on one system found in the Worrorran family of languages in the North Kimberley (Lucich 1968; Scheffler 1978:385–417). One reason the wider range and variation of skewing in Australia has not been studied is that, as elsewhere, skewing in Australia is often an "overlay" rather than a primary kinship system and is usually invoked contextually and optionally, so it is not apparent to an outside observer without extended ethnographic work.

The contextual variation in skewing is related to diachronic change, which is the theme of the second part of this chapter. The original meaning of a kinship term can become less frequent and eventually be lost, allowing a former skewed meaning to become the core meaning.

Ethnology, concerned with kinship meaning patterns and systems, and historical linguistics, concerned with the etymology of the forms of kinship terms, can work together to trace the development of skewing and reveal its presence at past periods where it has subsequently disappeared (see Allen 1976, where a similar method is used to uncover prior skewing in a Tibeto-Burman branch). Using this method applied to the Pama-Nyungan family of languages in Australia, I show how skewing mediated changes. For instance, terms for "mother's brother" change to "cross-cousin/spouse," and this change is implicated in the transformation from symmetrical (Dravidian/Kariera) to asymmetrical kinship and marriage systems.

Omaha skewing has been linked to patrilineal descent and to marriage systems that disperse alliances (Héritier 1981; McKinley 1971a), and there is evidence for both these factors playing a role in Australia. However, such hypotheses are usually tested in terms of synchronic correlations between skewing and factors such as descent and marriage types, or other demographic factors such as population size. Here it is suggested that skewing may relate rather to diachronic processes in groups that are in an expansion phase.

The hypothesis advanced here is that a common type of spread of language groups (which I call "downstream spread," see McConvell 2001, 2010) is driven by a mechanism of language group exogamy that often goes hand in hand with Omaha skewing in the expanding group. This favors dispersal of marriages and patrilineal inheritance of language as well as land and other rights. The hypothesis is compatible with skewing being one of the mechanisms whereby small hunter-gatherer groups such as those in Australia avoid demographic collapse (White and Denham 2008). In contrast, the cross-parallel neutralization (or "horizontal skewing") discussed by Dousset (this volume) may be associated with a different kind of expansion ("upstream spread").

The hypothesis can be applied to other continents where Omaha skewing appears to accompany language spread, such as parts of North America and New Guinea, which are discussed here in a preliminary way.

Varieties of Omaha in Australia

Omaha skewing was divided by Lounsbury (1964a) into four types (with a parallel set of four for Crow). Australian systems appear to be all of Type I in this scheme (Lounsbury 1964a:220–39). That is, equations of the form MBD = M, MMBD = MM, and (in some systems) FMBD = FM are found; Type II equations like ♀BD = ♀Z, or Type III like ♀B = ♀F are not found, however.

Scheffler (1978:395–404) deals with the Ngarinyin system (and very similar systems found in the other Worrorran languages, see Keen forthcoming; Lucich 1968), and introduces a modification of Lounsbury's Omaha Type I rule to allow for the fact that in the Ngarinyin system skewing affects not only consanguineal kin but also stepkin and in-laws, not accounted for in Lounsbury's rule: for example, FZH is designated as *wuningi* (ZH) (Scheffler 1978:397).

Despite there being only one type in Lounsbury's terms, there are significantly different types of Omaha skewing found. The most salient differences are the following.

1. Variable/obligatory: whether the skewing is an optional/contextual "overlay" and has an alternative nonskewed realization of a kin type; or where skewing is obligatory. In some systems, skewing applies obligatorily to some descent lines (see number 3) but optionally to others.
2. Number of generations: In some systems, whole patrilines have a single term (multigenerational skewing); in others only two generations are affected by skewing (bigenerational skewing). There is an intermediate type, too, with skewing crossing three generations (trigenerational) but not more.
3. Skewed lines: The lines affected by skewing vary, but the following seem to be the only ones found in Australia: (a) M; (b) MM; and (c) FM.

Map 12.1 shows the positions of the areas of skewing referred to, which are discussed in the following sections.

In the region north of the northern Central Australian Omaha systems (Gurindji, etc.) and west of the southeast Arnhem Land and Gulf Omaha systems, there are no Omaha features in the kinship terminologies, which are generally Iroquois in the sense used by Scheffler (1971).

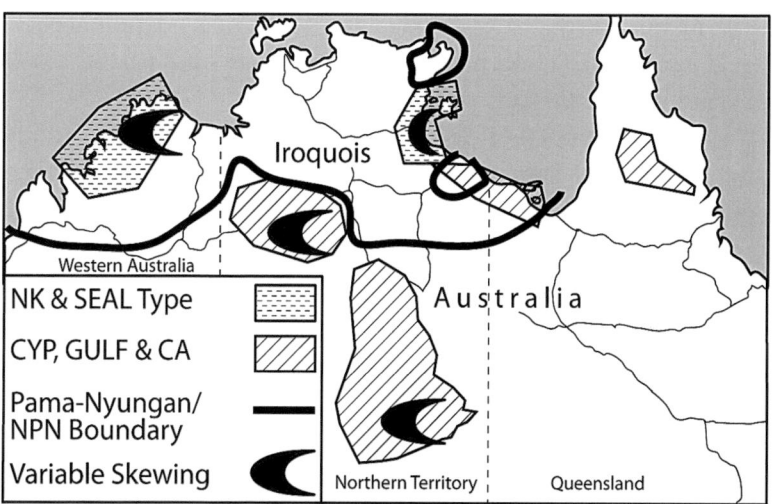

Map 12.1 Omaha skewing in Australia

The interface between the Omaha and Iroquois systems in this region is discussed by McConvell and Alpher (2002) and Avery (2002), and I return to its connections with the dynamics of the Omaha systems later in this chapter.

North Kimberley System

The North Kimberley system, of which Ngarinyin is part, has skewing in three lines: in the M and MM lines it is variable/contextual (to be discussed), but in the FM line, it is obligatory regardless of context (Keen 2004:197). The FM line is the main line from which marriage partners are chosen (as indicated by the affinal meanings of FMBS and FMBSS) so the notion that Omaha skewing is a barrier erected to prevent marriage (see discussion under Cape York Peninsula) cannot be upheld, for this region at least.

The M and FM lines have skewing extending through more than two generations and probably all; the MM line in contrast seems to have it only across two generations. This is shown in table 12.1. The core meaning of the term is in a dark gray box, with arrows indicating the direction of the extensions. The lighter shaded boxes indicate the kin types that have a skewed term, and the white boxes show kin types that have no skewed term as far as we know. The kin types shown are only males in the direct patrilines: sisters of these and parallel cousins are also affected similarly.

Ngarinyin provides a clear case of "overlay" contextual variation in the M and MM lines. Radcliffe-Brown (1931) and Elkin (1932) reported all patrilineal descendants in the MB, MMB, and FMB to be equated in terminology. Frederick Rose (1939–40 fieldnotes) reported

Table 12.1 Omaha skewing in North Kimberley (Ngarinyin)

MF ↑	MMB	FMB ↑
MB	MMBS ↓	**FMBS/WF**
MBS ↓	MMBSS	FMBSS/WB ↓
MBSS ↓	MMBSSS	FMBSSS ↓

the nonskewed terminology only. Rumsey (1981) found that skewed and nonskewed terminologies were used in different discourse contexts.

Skewing is used in talking about *patrimoiety exogamy* (Rumsey 1981: 183–84). In discussion of *maanggarra* (clan estates of the MB patriline), the term *garndingi* (MB) covers all people in the line.

On the other hand, in discussion of interpersonal relations, the non-Omaha more differentiated terms are used. These are *garndingi* (MB and MBSS) and *mamingi* (MF and MBS). These non-Omaha variants are governed by the alternate generation agnatic (AGA) principle in which equations unite kin in alternate generations in the patriline. This AGA principle is commonly found operating in Australian kinship systems.

Southeast Arnhem Land Systems

In southeast Arnhem Land non-Pama-Nyungan languages there are several examples of Omaha skewing. These are similar to the systems of the North Kimberley in that they involve the FM line and have multigenerational equations down through several or all generations (Heath 1981, 1982, 1984; Rose 1960; Turner 1974).

The patterns of variation of Omaha skewing in the southeast Arnhem Land region are shown in table 12.2. The vertical lines in the MBSSS cell refer to contextual variability and may apply to Nunggubuyu only (no data on other languages).

Table 12.2 Omaha skewing in southeast Arnhem Land

Nunggubuyu, Marra, and Anindilyakwa		Marra only	Anindilyakwa only
MF	MMB		
MB	**MMBS** ↓	FZ	
MBS ↓	MMBSS ↓	**FZS** ↓	FZS=MB ↓
MBSS ↓	MMBSSS ↓	FZSS ↓	FZSS=MB ↓
MBSSS ↓	MMBSSS	FZSSS ↓	

Nunggubuyu is the only language in this region of which it is clearly stated that the application of skewing is contextual and variable, as in the North Kimberley case and others that we will encounter later (Heath 1984:223).

Heath (1984:224) also refers to the *junggayi* and *nigararij* relationships (of a clan with its M line patriclan and with its MM line patriclan, respectively) in Nunggubuyu. These have counterparts throughout the area and, as far as *junggayi* is concerned, much more widely. In this area the *junggayi* are referred to as "managers" (as they are called in the local Aboriginal English) and have strong responsibilities for ritual and land matters of their "woman's child" clan. These institutions reinforce the perception of patrilines as united entities. Avery (1985, 2002) puts emphasis on this institution as lying behind the importance of Omaha skewing in this area and the neighboring areas of the southern Gulf of Carpentaria as opposed to the inland groups that have Iroquois kinship.

Central Australian Systems

These systems are found in Pama-Nyungan languages in a belt running from the southern Victoria River District, illustrated here by Gurindji, through Warumungu to the southeast and on south into the Arandic languages of Central Australia. Because these systems are very similar in pattern, they are represented here in one table, table 12.3.

Gurindji is a language of the Ngumpin-Yapa subgroup of Pama-Nyungan, located near the Pama-Nyungan border with non-Pama-Nyungan languages in the west of the Northern Territory. I discovered Omaha skewing when hearing Gurindji people using skewed terms about others in conversation, after I had been in the community several months (McConvell 1982, 1997).

Table 12.3 Omaha skewing in Central Australia

MF	**MMB**
MB	MMBS ↓
MBS ↓	MMBSS
MBSS	MMBSSS

The other eastern Ngumpin languages have Omaha skewing also, but it is absent in the other languages of the subgroup and neighboring non-Pama-Nyungan language groups. The non-Pama-Nyungan groups like Western Mirndi have an Iroquois kinship system in the sense of Scheffler, where, for instance, the children of same-sex cross-cousins are called own children as if the cross-cousin were a same-sex sibling, for example, ♂MBSS is called ♂S. This interface between the Omaha and Iroquois systems in the Victoria River District is strikingly similar to the interface between the southeast Arnhem Land–Gulf Omaha and the Iroquois systems of the interior, which Avery (2002) has called attention to.

In the Gurindji system, skewing only affects two generations directly by use of the same term, M(B) to refer to MBCh, and MM(B) to refer to MMBCh. Other lower generations are indirectly affected by this change by shifting terms down a generation, for example, MBDCh are called by a special term *kanyirri* but are referred to as being "like siblings," as their mother MBD is "like a mother" in the skewing system. Continuing this, MBDSCh are like a man's child as they come from a "brother."

The most commonly used type of skewing among the Gurindji is the calling of some MMBCh by the term MM(B) *jaju*. On eliciting terms, I was given the term *mali* as translating MMBCh. The primary meaning of *mali* is "wife's mother's (brother)" and is an avoidance relationship; if not already actualized by marriage, it implies at least the potential of a "promise" of an MMBBDD as a wife at some later date. The practical effect of using *jaju,* the skewed term, instead of *mali* is to cancel these presuppositions about avoidance and possible marriage with that person's daughter or niece.

Omaha skewing is used consistently although varying with nonskewing usage contextually by speakers of Arandic languages in Central Australia, with some detail supplied for Alyawarre by Denham et al. (1979), Yallop (1977), and Green (1998). Green (1998:60) states that skewing "occurs in the context of broader relations between groups of kin and between land-holding groups."

Skewing is not just a question of marking Omaha "ineligible" for marriage and non-Omaha "marriageable." The interactional usage (whether skewing is reciprocal or nonreciprocal, for instance) between pairs of people is a pragmatic indication of relationships and potential relationships, which may be manipulated by participants as agents, rather than being just determined by a fixed context.

Reanalysis of Denham's field data by Denham and White shows "clear evidence for the asymmetric use of Omaha terminology in that when ego and alter are in potential-spouse genealogical positions, they never shift to a reciprocal use of Omaha terms" (2005:90).

The Gulf of Carpentaria

Extending along the Gulf coast going east from the southeast Arnhem Land region is another area with Omaha skewing. According to Avery (2002), McArthur River people of a patrigroup regard their *junggayi* "managers" who comprise their classificatory women's children ♀Ch/ZCh and cross-cousins FZCh as all being *niyingkara* "brothers" to each other. This obviously fits quite well into the Omaha skewing pattern of effacing generational distinctions.

Avery (2002) contrasts the "Middle Roper" people (e.g., Ngalakan) who have Iroquois systems (separate cross-cousin terms and cross-cousins counting like same-sex siblings as linking relatives) with the "McArthur River" people (e.g., Yanyuwa), who have Omaha skewing. Among the latter, MMBCh and MFZCh are potentially "poison-cousins" (mothers-in-law). The effect of the skewed terminology is to redefine them as close kin rather than affines. This implies that choices are made because both variants are available. The function here is quite similar to that among the Gurindji.

Cape York Peninsula

Omaha skewing is found in several groups most clearly in eastern Cape York Peninsula (CYP), but some traces appear in the southwest, some indicating prior historical skewing, which is mentioned later when we look at the transition to the Yolngu asymmetrical system.

The patterns in some languages seem restricted to the M line and two generations only. However, in Gugu Yimidhirr extensions of the terms around Hopevale in southeast CYP, the oldest generation has at least trigenerational equations: MB = MBS = MBSS (Powell 2002:180).

Gugu Yimidhirr has other nonskewed terms for some of the relatives covered by skewing, so it is likely that this is another variable/contextual system. Close matrilateral cousins and members of close clans are unmarriageable, and this relates to the use of skewing.

To the northwest, Ayabadhu (which Thomson 1972 called Yintjinga) has some skewed equations including *kaali* MyB = MBS, and *paapa* M = MBD. In southwestern CYP, forms related to **tyuwa-y* are found in the meaning of a sibling-in-law term that relates to a presumed previous cross-cousin skewed meaning of the root—the original ♀Ch meaning has been lost. This shift, together with its geographical position closer to the Yolngu where the change to a spouse term has been consolidated, suggests that this is a stepping stone toward the Yolngu system.

Omaha as Contextual Overlay

It is clear from the previous section that many of the cases of Omaha skewing in Australia are what we have been calling "contextually variable"—that is, skewed terms alternate with nonskewed terms (special terms for the kin type like cross-cousins, affinal terms, or other types of equation such as alternate generation merging).

In a number of publications Kronenfeld has outlined a hypothesis that skewing is inherently variable and should be regarded not as another type of kinship system but an "overlay" on other, more basic types. Where skewing occurs it has discourse motivations and may often be better seen as an act of adding meaning by discourse participants than being determined absolutely by external conditions.

The motivations involved, described by Kronenfeld (1991, see also 2009) for Crow skewing in Fanti, are very similar to those in a number of the Australian cases, mutatis mutandis shifting from matrilineal to patrilineal inheritance. Kronenfeld proposes that the Fanti folk explanation for Crow skewing usage based on inheritance is basically correct and shows this by reference to natural conversation.

The other motivation is use of skewing to indicate that a relative or class of relatives are unmarriageable, as we have seen in a number of the Australian cases. Again, this may be a question of an agent adding a meaning, that marriage is not desirable or likely rather than simply reflecting a known state of affairs. Thomson (1955) sees skewing equations in Cape York Peninsula as a mechanism working to ban or minimize close cross-cousin marriage, because an MBD, for instance, is a "mother," prototypically unmarriageable.

Kronenfeld also extends his hypothesis to consider the diachronic dynamics of skewing overlays, seeing them as historically ephemeral. Variation of the type we have been examining is often a prelude to categorical change, with skewing equations disappearing or the skewed meanings being established as categorical. This chapter tries to come to grips with how this happens in particular cases, by examining historical linguistic evidence.

Historical Linguistic Evidence of Change to and from Omaha

As we have seen, there are a number of recently active skewing systems in Cape York Peninsula. There are also relics of previous skewing that can be detected. As Thomson (1955, 1972) noted, the terms *ngama* and *ngami* are found in some languages such as Umpila in eastern CYP, where *ngami* means cross-cousin (MeBCh, FeZCh), but its original meaning (going back to proto-Pama-Nyungan *ngamV) was "mother" (see Alpher 2004). In Gugu Yimidhirr (see CYP section) the mother term is the cognate *ngamu*, which has a skewed meaning MBD.

The hypothesis in this case is that the cross-cousin meaning of this root developed from the entrenchment of the skewed meaning combined with replacement of the "mother" meaning by another root—in the Umpila case, *papa*.

The skewed terms that feature more centrally in the transition to the Yolngu system are **kaala(y)* and **tyuwa(y)*, which originally (probably in proto-Pama-Nyungan) meant MB and ♀Ch/ZCh. They are found in Cape York Peninsula with these meanings, for example, *kaal* MyB in Wik-Mungkan and *thuwi* ♀Ch in Ayabadhu.

Reflexes of both these proto-forms are found also with skewing equations in Cape York Peninsula, for instance, *juway* ♀S with a skewed FZS meaning in Gugu Yimidhirr. In southwestern CYP, forms derived from **tyuwa-y* are found with affinal meanings, such as sister-in-law. This results from prior skewing followed by reinterpretation of the cross-cousin result in terms of cross-cousin marriage—discussed further shortly in relation to the transition to Yolngu.

Before tackling Yolngu specifically, let us look at the overall patterns of distribution of these roots, *kaala-y and *tyuwa-y, in Australia. Both show the following distribution.

1. The earliest meanings, MB (or MyB) and ♀Ch/ZCh, respectively, are found in the northeast of the continent, centered around Cape York Peninsula but extending into inner and southern Queensland.
2. Current or recent attested skewing between MB and MBS (or cross-cousin more generally) and ♀Ch/ZCh and FZCh is found to the southeast of CYP.
3. Full shift to the skewed meanings and loss of the original meaning is found in various locations to the west, some to the far west of the region with the original meaning.
4. Many of the shifted meanings are not only cross-cousin but also a spouse or sibling-in-law or only a spouse or sibling-in-law. In these areas cross-cousin marriage is, or probably was at some stage, practiced.

These distributions are depicted on maps 12.2 and 12.3. The arrows emanating west and south from the northeast present (and presumed earlier wider) area of skewing of these terms indicate the former spread of a skewing pattern for the roots and a subsequent loss of the original meaning. As argued shortly, this may be associated with the spread of Pama-Nyungan languages during the Holocene. See later discussion for the dynamic model involved.

Cape York Peninsula Kariera to Yolngu Asymmetry via Omaha Skewing

In the case of northeast Arnhem Land Yolngu languages the skewed meanings of both the roots *kaala-y and *tyuwa-y are found: *galay* MBCh/MMBDCh and ♂W(Z/B) and *dhuway* FZCh/FFZSCh and ♀H(Z/B) (Shapiro 1981; Zorc 1986) and the original uncle/mother-ling meanings are lost together with skewing. These meanings paired exactly like the original meanings MB and ♀Ch as reciprocals of each other, and retention of the matrilateral and patrilateral property of the

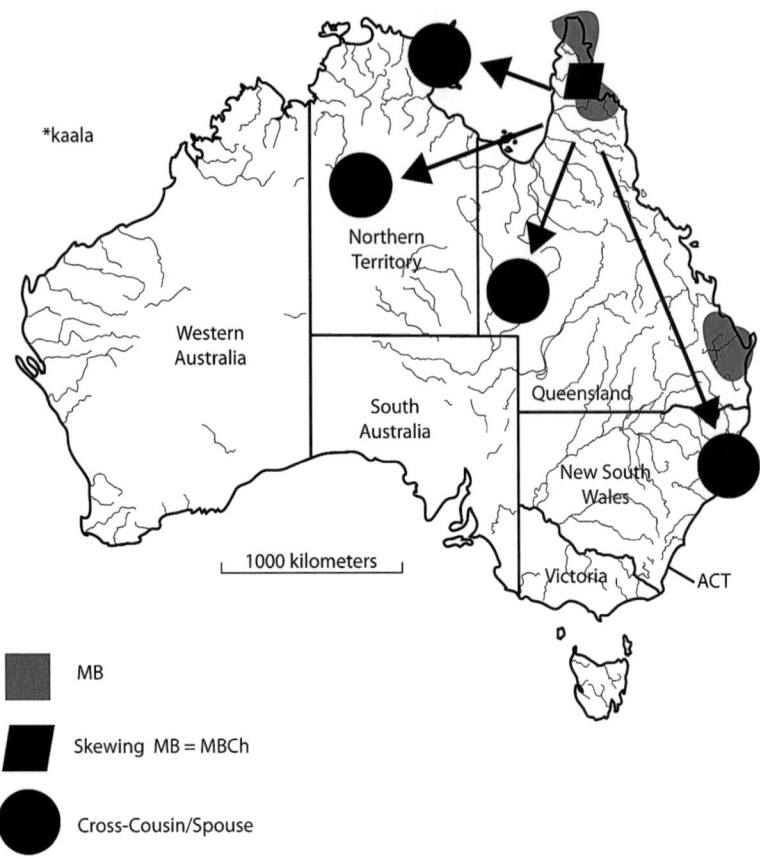

Map 12.2 Proto-terms subject to skewing: *kaala (MB)

cross-cousins, respectively, represent a clear signature of prior skewing paralleling the Omaha skewing found in Cape York Peninsula and the shift to cross-cousin/sibling-in-law terms in southwestern CYP.

The resulting Yolngu asymmetrical cross-cousin/spouse terminology fits exactly with the asymmetrical matrilateral marriage (for a man; patrilateral for a woman) practiced by the Yolngu. There are asymmetrical marriage patterns also in parts of Cape York Peninsula, often matrilateral (for a man), which probably form part of the transition to the Yolngu system.

The original meaning of *kaala* reflexes was probably the mother's classificatory younger brother, who is the wife's father in a junior system such as found in CYP (McConnell 1950). In applying Omaha skewing

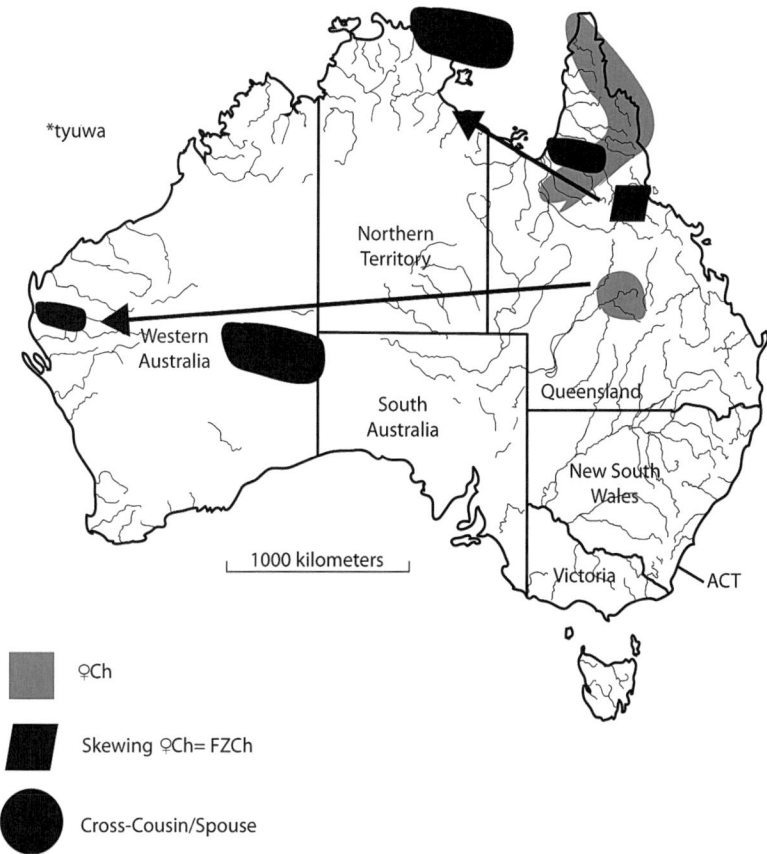

Map 12.3 Proto-terms subject to skewing: *tyuwa (♀Ch/ZCh)

to this term, the result—a MyBD—is a marriageable woman in the junior system, so Thomson's explanation of the Omaha extension of the M term to mark unmarriageability does not apply to this case, only to the unmarriageable MeBD. As the juniority dimension of marriage was lost and matrilaterality alone dominated, *kaalal/galay*, the term for the marriageable cousin for men, was applied to MBD generally.

A Dynamic Account of Omaha Skewing

The arrows going west and south from northeastern Australia in maps 12.2 and 12.3 represent the paths of meaning change of two kinship roots via skewing polysemy (referring to relatives in at least two adjacent generations) to consolidation of the former skewed meaning and loss of the original meaning. This proposal in McConvell and Alpher (2002; see also McConvell and Keen 2011) is not one of diffusion of Omaha skewing. As we have seen, Omaha skewing does not diffuse into contiguous areas with different language groups and kinship systems (e.g., north from Eastern Ngumpin or west from southeast Arnhem Land).

Rather, what may be happening is spread of languages themselves, to which Omaha skewing is an ancillary mechanism. The development of Omaha skewed terms may occur more than once in the expansion of a language family, associated with phases of spread into the territory of other language groups. There are at least two phases of this in the Pama-Nyungan family of languages of which we have evidence:

1. Early Pama-Nyungan spread. It has been proposed that Pama-Nyungan languages spread from northeastern Australia in the mid-Holocene, so the pattern of expansion of the languages may parallel and accompany the early spread of Omaha skewing, which leaves its traces in the terms already discussed. Now for this phase we can only see skewing in the traces it leaves in skewed meanings in outlying western languages and a few peripheral cases of extant skewing around the original homeland.
2. Late Pama-Nyungan spread. The skewing in the Central Australian region does not involve the roots discussed for item 1 in the previous section, but other diverse kinship roots that still have active skewing polysemy. The hypothesis here is that this phase of skewing is also associated with language spread but of a more recent period and less complex and long-distance.

The Phase 2 spreads for which we have most evidence is Eastern Ngumpin going north into the Victoria Basin (represented by Gurindji here; McConvell 1997).

Omaha and Downstream Language Spread

The spread of Eastern Ngumpin languages north into the Victoria Basin has been used as an example of a more general type of language spread that I have called "downstream spread" (McConvell 2001, 2010). This is where a group "moves in on" other groups, usually to get access to better resources in the area, in a process usually involving intermarriage and language shift by the resident group to the language of the incoming group. This process contrasts with "upstream spread," where language groups spread by migrating along a corridor with low resident population or resources, therefore involving little intermarriage with residents or language shift. The example used to illustrate upstream spread is the expansion of the Western Desert language east across a wide area.

As noted, the Eastern Ngumpin languages alone among the languages in the Tanami, Northern Sandy Desert, or Victoria River District either of the same subgroup or of different families, have Omaha skewing. In contrast, the Western Desert dialects have no Omaha skewing but have neutralization of cross-parallel distinctions under certain circumstances (e.g., some cross-cousins referred to as siblings, see Dousset, this volume).

Is there a connection between downstream language spread and Omaha skewing? I begin to develop a hypothesis about what this connection may be. Apart from the Eastern Ngumpin case, an extension of the hypothesis proposes that the earlier history of the spread of skewing (Phase 1) is also linked directly to downstream spread of languages as they moved out from northeastern Australia. That is, language groups encountered other resident groups and moved in on them, intermarrying and causing language shift to the newly arriving languages.

Omaha skewing goes not only with exogamy but also with patrilineal institutions and inheritance, and this is spread and strengthened in the process of language group expansion. This provides strong ownership ties to defined tracts of land. Perhaps the type of arrangement we have encountered as being linked to skewing, in which inheritance of complementary rights via the mother's father (*junggayi* "manager" line) and sometimes MM, plays a role in integrating the residents in a new regime of land rights, as the influence and marital ties of the incoming group increase.

Demographic Models

Hammel (2005:11955–56), in proposing a demographic model of kinship change, refers to the challenges faced in circumstances of population increase or decline that require different strategies of redefining the scope of classes of kin, and this may well relate to the importance of Omaha skewing (or the nonskewing horizontal neutralization in the Western Desert) in shifting people between consanguineal and affinal categories.

White and Denham (2008) also ground their explanation of the "Australian indigenous marriage paradox" in what they call "demographic stress": "stochastic fluctuations in population size or sex ratio," which have been particularly acute in Australia due to the harsh and unpredictable environment and the generally small size of groups. The marriage paradox concerns the ability of so many small groups to survive despite the high levels of such stress.

The solution to the paradox, they propose, lies in various mechanisms that counteract underlying endogamy and enforce group exogamy by imposing restrictions on marriage. One such restriction that allows the integration of outsiders into a local group is Omaha skewing. Here they cite McConvell and Alpher (2002) at length.

A model of demographic stress, producing effects in kinship and marriage practices looks appealing in the case of Omaha skewing.

Skewing and Language Spread outside Australia

North America

Southern Algonquian languages, for instance, Miami-Illinois (Costa 1999:32) have Omaha skewing. Algonquian languages in the north, however, have Iroquois or Dravidian kinship.

Lake Ontario seems still to be supported at least as a staging point of an expansion or migration that started further west (see Goddard 1978:586; Ives 1998:128). In that case, Algonquian would have expanded both north into relatively sparsely populated country (upstream spread) and south into country with denser resident populations (downstream spread). Although in the northern zones there are Dravidian systems with cross-parallel neutralization taking effect (Ives 1998: 128), in this southern area Omaha features emerge, agreeing with the hypothesis proposed.

In California there are a number of societies that have Omaha skewing terminologies. Their languages belong to the proposed macrofamily

Penutian, including Miwok languages in inland central California, and toward and on the coast further north, and Wintu even further north and inland. The proposed proto-language for most of these groups, proto-Yok-Utian, lies to the east in the Great Basin in central Nevada, and they would have moved west in the Holocene (Golla 2007), undoubtedly replacing other languages in the region. They thus fit the pattern described as downstream spread and provide another example where Omaha skewing is found at the leading edge of such an expansion.

New Guinea

O'Brien and Cook (1980:464) note the striking geographical division between Omaha systems in the west of New Guinea and Iroquois systems in the east. Additional sampling of groups outside the areas covered by the chapters in Cook and O'Brien (1980) support this generalization.

The suggestion has been made here that Omaha skewing may develop during expansion of groups and their penetration into new regions at least partially by means of marital alliance. The distribution pattern of Omaha skewing in New Guinea could be related to the same factors in the spread of the Trans New Guinea (TNG) phylum of languages from east to west.

The TNG phylum is a very large grouping of language families, which covers at least half of the continent from the eastern to western ends, most continuously around the central spine, the Highlands. The proposition that TNG spread from the east to west is well supported by linguists (e.g., Ross 2005), in company with archaeologists and geneticists (e.g., Tommaseo-Ponzetta et al. 2002) who propose a movement of population in that direction that could be correlated with the expansion of TNG languages.

In terms of the Omaha language spread hypothesis, the current distribution of Omaha systems in the west would reflect a relatively recent (mid-Holocene) spread. If Omaha had accompanied earlier spreads in the east, these features would have disappeared over time. All or nearly all the groups in the east have varieties of Iroquois systems (Scheffler 1971). The presence of Omaha in the Sepik region might represent an even later expansion as it is thought that this region was probably colonized in the late Holocene because the lower reaches were uninhabitable before then.

Conclusions

Skewing of kinship terms is generally a contextual overlay on another kinship system. The use of the skewing variant signals a discourse about inheritance within a clan/lineage or about interclan/interlineage issues and/or marriage and marriageability. These generalizations seem to apply equally to Crow and Omaha systems.

Variation of this kind can lead to categorical change in systems as one of the variants becomes dominant and the other recedes. This loss of an alternative system may be related to the ending of the downstream spread phase, as already discussed, and consolidation and stability of the language group in a new area. The terminological changes can be studied as change-in-progress, and researchers need to take into account other variable features, such as number of generations covered and different types of reciprocal patterns, as exemplified for Australia. It can also be approached by historical linguistics, for example, where systematic changes in the meaning of terms can flag prior skewing. In the case of the Yolngu languages of Australia, prior Omaha skewing played a role in a change to asymmetrical kinship and marriage.

More generally, skewing systems, at least of the Omaha type associated with patrilineality, are found on the periphery of language groupings and the leading edge of expanding social systems in Australia and elsewhere. It is proposed here that this pattern is associated with downstream spread of language groups.

Omaha skewing is thus a facilitator of dispersed marriage alliances for expansionist groups. This is not in contradiction with another perspective on the function of Omaha skewing, that is, that it counteracts the vagaries of small-group demography, such as loss of population and extinction, particularly acute in Australia, by turning from endogamy to exogamy and recruiting new members. Groups engaging in downstream spread are generally in a difficult environmental and demographic situation, which they are trying to alleviate by marrying into resident groups and obtaining rights to their resources.

13

"Horizontal" and "Vertical" Skewing

Similar Objectives, Two Solutions?

Laurent Dousset

In 1975, Robert Tonkinson presented a paper at a seminar that remained largely unknown and that he unfortunately has never published. In this paper (for which he has provided me with his preparatory notes), he mentions the process called *ngaranmaridi*, explained by Aboriginal informants as "to cut out," which he translates as "splitting," for the Mardu people of the Australian Western Desert. He explains in these notes that *ngaranmaridi* occurs in several contexts and relates closely to what he calls "the riddle of the non-marriageable cross-cousin":

> at the time of ritual introductions of strangers from different areas; would have occurred during big meetings; when the particular kinship links are being determined an element of choice exists as to whether to designate "FZ" as *umari* [WM] or *gundili* [FZ] and thereby differentiate their children accordingly. At the *miljangul*, discussions are held by Ego, if an adult, and others to decide which if any of the stranger women who are initially all related as "spouse" will be "cut out" and thus become *jingani* Z.

We may ask why would people want to reclassify cross-cousins as siblings. Mardu Aborigines themselves provide the most explicit (albeit not complete) answer to the question: "you can't have too many wives." I return to the background to such an answer, of which I have recorded similar versions among the Ngaatjatjarra and Ngaanyatjarra people further to the east. Let me first set the stage for this chapter and explain why "cross-parallel neutralization"—and what I, as a nod to other contributions, label "horizontal skewing" in my title—may possibly be relevant in the discussion of Crow-Omaha types of skewing: both are, I suggest, solutions to similar if not identical problems and objectives. Cross-parallel neutralization is about "cutting out" some potential spouses, and thus reorienting marriages in particular directions. I advance that "cutting out" or "skewing" are not systems but social technologies in the broad domain of resource management.

Background: The Aluridja System

The so-called Aluridja type of kinship system, which is found among Australian Western Desert societies of which the Mardu are one, has considerably occupied kinship specialists since Elkin's publication of *Kinship in South Australia* (1938–40). Indeed, Franklin Tjon Sie Fat explained that "the most intriguing descriptions of anomalous or inconsistent terminological systems combining a variety of Dravidian, Iroquois, and 'Hawaiian' or Generational features with a range of affinal terms and extensive marriage prohibitions pertain to the Western Desert peoples of Australia" (1998b:78). Lévi-Strauss labeled it as "aberrant" (1967:231, 251, and figure 56, p. 249). The lack of section or subsection systems and the presence of what he considered endogamous moieties—more correctly known as merged alternate generational levels—were for him irreconcilable with what he considered "the precision and clarity" of Australian marriage "classes" (1967:461). Similarly to Elkin, Lévi-Strauss thought that the Aluridja system must be in the process of transformation. Another example is Scheffler's (1978) who, discussing the Pitjantjatjara terminology, indicates that an MB marries an FZ and that the cross-parallel distinction is therefore introduced in ego's parents' generation. He nevertheless glosses the term *watjirra* (Xc; some MBCh and FZCh) as "distant sibling" rather than cross-cousin (Scheffler 1978:90–91, table 3.1).

I have discussed elsewhere (Dousset 2003) what I consider a misinterpretation of the Aluridja type of kinship system and here only return to some of its general features. The terminology and social organization of these societies have been described in terms of lack: in particular, the lack of a specific cross-cousin terminology, the lack of local groups as supposedly found elsewhere in Australia, the lack of descent groups, and, last but not least, the lack of section or subsection systems that have been introduced in this area only quite recently (Dousset 2005). Aluridja people, it was thought, were marrying persons they called "brother" and "sister" because they had no other terms to differentiate cross-cousins.

Although it is true that Aluridja kinship terminology is not as extensive as what can be observed in other languages in Australia, it would be erroneous to believe that the cross-parallel distinction is not operated. There are two pieces of evidence here: first, the reconstruction of genealogies predating first contact with the West, which itself dates back to the 1950s among the Ngaatjatjarra people (Dousset 2002b), shows that marriage practices are and were of the cross-cousin type even after contact, with only about 3 percent of irregular marriages (Dousset 1999). Second, there are terms that refer to cross-cousin types of relatives in ego's generation; these relatives are potential spouses or brothers/sisters-in-law(Dousset 2008).

The question that immediately arises is why have so many prestigious anthropologists advanced the lack of cross-cousin terminology when this does not seem to be the case? One must concede that those anthropologists who have advocated the so-called Aluridja aberration based their analysis predominantly on very few and questionable ethnographic records: Elkin's *Kinship in South Australia* (1938–40) and Norman Tindale's later short trips into the area. As Katie Glaskin and I have shown (Dousset and Glaskin 2007), these ethnographies are of very poor and contradictory quality. These anthropologists' fieldwork was of "the short-term survey method" (Burke 2005:212). Elkin and Tindale were in the habit of only staying a few days, at the most a few weeks, in any given field location. As we will see, one legacy of Elkin's rapid ethnography, itself far from the anthropological ideal of prolonged participant observation, is that it resulted in erroneous depictions of Western Desert society that have led many researchers to an ambiguous analysis of the kinship system.

Tindale's most influential publication on the Western Desert (1988 [1972]) is crowded with contradictions and preconceived impressions and generalizations that are scientifically unsustainable and, more important, not in accordance with the data he recorded and on which his paper is supposedly based (Tindale 1935, 1963). For example, Tindale draws (wrong) conclusions about the geographical direction from which the section system arrived in this part of the desert, or he talks of clans without locating them, nor even referring to their nature or names. He also states that Pitjantjatjara, an eastern dialect of the Western Desert language, is rapidly becoming a lingua franca (this has yet to occur) or that it is a rather old Australian language (linguists date the Western Desert language at only 1500 to 2000 BCE; see McConvell 1990). Moreover, again without drawing on any of his field notes, he explains that the Pitjantjatjara are divided into patrilineal totemic descent groups, a formula that is particularly astonishing when one is aware that the only totemic system known in the eastern Western Desert is conception totemism and that, since Frazer and Durkheim at least, one should know that this type of totem is not inherited.

The short-term survey method followed by Elkin and Tindale is directly related to the second explanation that can be provided to elucidate why so many anthropologists considered the Aluridja system "aberrant": Western Desert people do have cross-cousin terms—however, their use is restricted to very particular contexts.

With respect to contextual uses of kinship terminologies, it is necessary to note the importance of alternate generational levels in the organization of everyday life and ritual in the Western Desert. Egocentrically as well as sociocentrically named, they constitute the axes around which behavioral attitudes are shaped. People of the same generational level will sit together during ritual, opposing themselves to the other level sitting on the opposite side. People of the same generational level collaborate in everyday tasks, whereas the relationships toward people of the opposite level are largely dominated by restraint, if not avoidance. This general background is reflected in the contextual usages of the terminology, which I have called egocentric (or egological) and sociological (Dousset 2002a).

A sociological context is one in which speech and practice is articulated around the general opposition between alternate generational levels. In such a context, cross-cousin terminology is avoided and cogenerationals are called "brothers" and "sisters." Furthermore, all members of the other generational level are called "mothers" and "fathers," whether they are actual aunts, daughters, and nieces or uncles, sons, and nephews. In an egological context, on the other hand, when particular persons are addressed or referred to, the cross-parallel distinction is applied and cross-cousin terminology used (but see further nuances, discussed later). People from the other generational level are distinguished as mothers, fathers, mother's brothers, and father's sisters; cogenerationals are distinguished as brothers, sisters, and cross-cousins or brothers- and sisters-in-law. This general picture is, however, not a sufficient description of the usage of the cross-parallel distinction and associated terminology, and we need to further refine the egological context of terminological usage. To do this, we first need to have a closer look at the spatial organization of these groups.

"The Harshest Physical Environment on Earth Ever Inhabited by Man before the Industrial Revolution"

This sentence, taken from archaeologist Richard Gould (1969:273), summarizes well the conditions in which Western Desert people dwelled in the past and still live in today. The mean annual rainfall over the Western Desert, which covers about 600,000 square kilometers (about 230,000 square miles), is less than 200 mm (7.9 inches) per year. However, more critical than the amount of rainfall is its unpredictability in time and space. With a very few exceptions near hilly outcrops, permanent water sources are nonexistent. Local conditions vary, of course, even though only slightly, from one region to another. I thus base the description that follows on the conditions experienced by Ngaatjatjarra-speaking people, a dialectal group of the Western Desert language.

They occupy the area just west of the border between the Northern Territory and West Australia, north and south of the Rawlinson Ranges. Numbering about 500 individuals, they inhabit an area of about 100,000 square kilometers (about 39,000 square miles), the size of continental Greece. The low population density (about 200 square kilometers or 78 square miles per person) is in phase with the low carrying capacity in the Western Desert, dominated by sand hills, plains, dry rivers, dry salt lakes, small amounts of large game, but quite a significant number of reptiles, which constitute the core of the protease diet. Staple food was based on cereals harvested from various grasses, among them wild millet. Today's settled communities have stores and cold rooms that are supplied on a regular basis.

Until the 1970s, the Ngaatjatjarra people were structured into five regional groups, each composed of several extended families. A regional group must be distinguished from the "local group," which has a patrilineal connotation not reflecting territorial organization in the Western Desert. A regional group was an ensemble of several family groups living most of the time in an area in which they traveled, but in which they had neither exclusive rights nor the strict authority to exclude other families from traveling through. They were the guardians of the sites scattered over the area they visited, rather than their absolute owners.

Even though these regional groups were usually exogamous, this rule was based not on corporateness but on the ideal of diversifying social networks. Affiliation to land was and still is established individually through the accumulation of eligible criteria. The place where one was conceived, the birthplace and the place where the umbilical cord fell off, where people live for extended periods, where their parents lived for extended periods, for which one has significant religious knowledge, and so on are criteria each individual accumulates for one or several sites, thus increasing his or her relative power to speak for a particular area. Thus, although individuals, families, and regional groups had strong connections to particular stretches of land because of their knowledge and the uses they made of it, these connections neither were automatically passed on to the following generations nor were exclusive rights.

After contact with white society in 1956, in particular with a government agency responsible for testing nuclear explosions and continental missiles after World War II (Dousset 2002b, 2011), Ngaatjatjarra people migrated into missions and ration depots at the fringes of the desert but returned to their homelands in the 1970s, establishing several settled communities. Although movements between these communities are considerable, they nevertheless broadly reflect the earlier regional groups.

The criteria determining an individual's connection to land have not changed much since then, with the nevertheless significant exception of birthplace. Whereas before the 1970s, children were born at various places, these days pregnant women are usually driven or flown to town hospitals, and so-called bush babies are held in esteem but rare. This practice has standardized the landscape of birthplaces, and with it one of the most important criteria for socially mapping the land. Because one of the explicit ideals is to maintain a large geographical coverage of land affiliation, being born in hospitals is becoming a serious problem for the Ngaatjatjarra people, who now consider the mother's place of residence to be the child's second connection (after the presumed conception site) to a particular site.

One of Western Desert people's explicit ideals is still to maintain a wide geographical coverage of their land affiliations. The reasons are often expressed in religious terms, in which a dispersed social geography is a condition for efficient guardianship of important sites that need to be maintained, ensuring the continuity of the mythical figures associated with them. But the reasons can also be explained in terms of ecological conditions. Diversifying the network of mutual obligations is part of what Gould (1969) called the risk-minimizing mode of hunter-gatherer adaptation, which is particularly appropriate for desert people. Diversifying connections to distant and distinct locations is one answer to the problem of the unpredictability of rainfall in time and space. A strict and bounded system of landownership would be counterproductive in this environment. As Tonkinson (1991 [1978]: 65) wrote, "not surprisingly, considering the great uncertainties of rainfall in their homelands, Mardu local organization is notable for its flexibility and fluidity and a lack of stress on boundaries and exclusiveness of group membership" (see also Myers 1986; Poirier 1992:759; Sackett 1975).

Though I do not wish to advance a causal relationship between environmental conditions and the structure of social organization, it is obvious that these flexible modes of land affiliation and the diversification of these affiliations in time and space is a suited response to particularly unpredictable ecological conditions, because it consolidates mutual and diversified access rights in case of local shortage. This diversification is achieved through the various cumulative criteria enabling each individual to claim a connection to sites. It is also achieved by initiating boys at distant locations and in conjunction with distant families, as initiation also provides rights establishing a strong and lasting community of interinitiates called *ngalunku*. The initiator is himself called *waputju* (WF), even though he may never become the actual father-in-law of the initiated boy. The most visible strategy in this realm, however, occurs during the organization of marriages, which is directly tied to the usage of terminology in which cross-parallel neutralization is, so to say, itself neutralized.

"Horizontal Skewing" in the Light of Marriages

The works that were most helpful in the clarification of the Aluridja type of kinship were those that analyzed Crow-Omaha systems in terms of layered or parallel terminological options rather than independent systems, in particular David Kronenfeld's (1973) work on the Fanti. He distinguishes three terminological subsystems that relate to different behavioral pattern or contexts. The first and central pattern is the one he refers to as being *unskewed,* which is applied in contexts related to parental roling. The second pattern, less commonly used, he refers to as *skewed* terminology. This subsystem concerns contexts of inheritance among semi-localized matrilineages. Finally, the third pattern is the courtesy use of kin terms for nonkinsmen, extending the nuclear family terms according to approximate relative age and aligning behavioral patterns.

There is no direct equivalence between these patterns and those found in the Western Desert. What held my attention was the coexistence of terminological subsystems reflecting distinct behavioral contexts, an idea that is clearly reflected in the Aluridja system: just as the Fanti do not have (only) a "Crow-system" as such, Western Desert people do not have an "Aluridja" system (alone).

The first and most visible usage of the terminology is halfway between the egological and sociological contexts already discussed. It is also the subsystem used among close relatives (and closeness is defined in both genealogical and residential terms) and the terminology one is most likely to observe when visiting and living for only a few days or weeks with these people. It is thus the terminology that gave rise to Elkin's definition of the Aluridja system. In the context of coresidential usages, mothers (*ngunytju*) are distinguished from father's sisters (*kurntili*) and fathers (*mama*) from mother's brothers (*kamuru*). Each fulfills specific roles in the education of children. However, whereas *kurntili* and *kamaru* denote cross-relatives, their children are considered too close to become actual affines and are "cut out," to use Tonkinson's terminology. They are called brothers (*kurta*) and sisters (*tjurtu*). The

Ngaatjatjarra people explain this feature by the expression *kungkankatja, minalinkatja*, of which the confirmed free translation is "children of a sister and of her brother are identical": they are siblings.

The second terminological usage, which I have referred to as being sociological, concerns situations in which the above-mentioned neutralization is extended to all generations. Mother's brothers are called "father" (*mama*), and father's sisters are called "mother" (*ngunytju*). *Mama* and *ngunytju* here are cover terms for all members of the opposite generational moiety, whereas *kurta* and *tjurtu* function as cover terms for all members of one's own moiety. Here again among Crow-Omaha researchers, in particular in Alan Rumsey's (1981) work on the Ngarinyin of northwest Australia, similar situations can be observed.

Rumsey's paper was reconsidering certain claims made for the Ngarinyin. Like the Aluridja system, their terminology had been considered unusual, particularly by Radcliffe-Brown and Elkin, who set it apart as a distinct type among Australian systems. "The feature of the Ngarinyin system which seemed most anomalous is the tendency for all persons within a single agnatic line to be called by the same kin term," Rumsey explains (1981:181). For Elkin and Radcliffe-Brown, the absence of generation differences within the system was due to an emphasis on the solidarity of the local clan as a unit in social integration. Rumsey confirms the important role of patrilineal generation merging, but he also demonstrates the existence of variability in its extent. He emphasizes that terminological usage is context-specific. Quoting the example of a man calling potential wives by the term "mother," Rumsey shows that in the particular context he was investigating, the man was in fact referring to the entire opposite moiety for which "mother" stands as a cover term.

I have arrived at very similar conclusions for Ngaatjatjarra usages of the sociological terminological set. When father's sisters are called "mother," it is not the particular interpersonal relationship that is at stake, but the general principle of the generational moieties, grossly structuring the background of social interaction and role that is the center of attention. This particular use of the terminology is most explicit in ritual contexts, where members of each generational level, called Ngumpaulurru and Tjuntultukultul, sit at opposite places and occupy different roles. Members of the opposite moiety are all called "mother" and "father," whereas members of one's own moiety are called "sister" and "brother." Just as Rumsey writes that generation merging among the Ngarinyin is undertaken in certain discourse contexts (1981:185), we must conclude for the Ngaatjatjarra, and more widely among Western Desert people, that cross-parallel neutralization (combined in some cases with alternate generational level merging) is undertaken in particular situational and discursive contexts as well.

The third terminological set is used by interlocutors when discussing marriage rules or envisioning marriage and setting up alliance strategies. It is also the set that conforms most closely to the genealogical grid and distinguishes all kin categories known by Western Desert people, translating the prescriptive marriage rule: marriageable cross-cousins are distinguished from parallel cousins and some nonmarriageable cross-cousins. When a teenager reaches marriageable age, certain *kurntili* (FZ) and *kamuru* (MB) are "renamed" *yumari* (WM) and *waputju* (WF). Children of *yumari* and *waputju* are *watjirra*[1] (cross cousins) or wives/husbands, *kurri*. Other terms are in use, such as *marutju* for WB/♂MBS/♂FZS and *tjuwari* for HZ/♀MBD/♀FZD, but they usually refer to actual in-laws.

What is important is the passage from *kurntili* (FZ) to *yumari* (WM), and from *kamuru* (MB) to *waputju* (WF), which goes hand in hand with the distinction between cross- and parallel cousins. It does not describe a constriction from a classificatory to a descriptive class because *waputju* (*yumari*) is applied to various men (women) that sit in the MB (FZ) category, whether they are actual fathers-in-law (mothers-in-law) or not. The determination of who sits in this subset is tied to two decisional processes. The first is the normative, the second the intentional marriageability of his or her children. In the first process, discussions take place with respect to the normative capacity of a man or a woman to become an actual in-law. The first criteria retained are of a classificatory nature: a *waputju* (WF/HF) is of the *kamuru* class (MB). The other criteria are spatial and genealogical proximity or distance. A potential father-in-law (mother-in-law) should be genealogically removed (their children should be cross-cousins of the third degree at least) and spatially distant. He or she should have a baggage of land affiliations that is distinct from ego's parents' affiliations. Similarly, his or her children (and thus potential spouses to ego), should have distinct affiliations from ego as well. Ideally, he or she should not already be the father-in-law of one's sibling either. Dumont's *alliance de marriage*, the repetition of identical marriages, is not an ideal here. Rather, the processes reflect what Keen (2002) called "shifting webs," the diversification and extension of the marriage network through the prohibition on marrying close "relatives."

These criteria lead to the second decision-making process that takes place: the intention and possibility of getting involved in an affinal relationship with a particular person or family. The strategies discussed are quite explicit and are about the inclusion or exclusion of potential fathers- and mothers-in-law according to political and economic opportunities. The strategies are fairly obvious today with the arrival of the cash economy and the payment of royalties by mining companies crystallizing people's attentions on particular "wealthy" families. There is, however, no reason to believe that these strategic principles were not at work in former days. There are indeed a few examples of religiously and politically important men who, before contact with the Western world, were highly polygynous (more than two wives in an area where the incidence of polygyny is very low) and who were referred to by numerous persons as *waputju*, rather than *kamuru*.

Why Cross-Parallel Neutralization/ "Horizontal Skewing"?

To my knowledge, none of the explanations advanced to elucidate the so-called Aluridja problem or aberration have done anything else than suggest its instability. Elkin had particularly peculiar ideas in this respect and proposed explanations I have summarized under the idea of the "rucksack theory" (Dousset 2003). He thought of the Aluridja system as being the result of a transformation. In an attempt to explain this transformation, he quickly evacuated the obviously uncomfortable presence of the cross-cousin term *watjirra*, declaring it the consequence of an influence from systems with sections and subsections, such as from Luritja-speaking people in Central Australia. Elkin further maintained that most affinal terms known by Western Desert people were imported during the many migrations of these groups to the south and southwest in response to droughts and Western colonization. Particularly puzzling is his following intriguing question: why did the southern Aluridja groups not adopt all affinal terms, such as wife's brother *marutju* or husband's sister *tjuwari*, even though they were in contact with the same groups as the Spinifex people to the west who had embraced them? His answer is fairly straightforward: the groups migrating southward did so for ecological reasons and were thus isolated from "new" forms of social organizations and kinship terms. This kind of isolation theory had already been used in similar contexts to account for "inconsistent" or "anomalous" systems elsewhere, for instance, by Alfred Howitt, who tried to explain what at that time was the "strangeness" of the Kurnai kinship system, which is in fact very similar to the Aluridja's (see in particular Howitt 1996 [1904]:170, 134–36, 169ff, and 269ff). Elkin, however, goes further and adds to the isolation theory another astonishing idea: "as a result only a minimum number of kinship terms was taken by migrating groups, just sufficient to distinguish generation, sex and marriage relationships. There were no other needs" (1938–40:305). This is thus Elkin's scenario on how "his" southern Aluridja system originated and spread: groups, pushed by harsh ecological conditions, rapidly packed their cultural baggage with some minimal kinship terms, those necessary in a Hawaiian system, leaving behind all other terms, and went off to find a better land. Let us call this transformational theory the "rucksack theory" and leave it behind us.

As I have tried to show, this apparent aberration is in fact not much more than a reflection of Elkin's incapacity to elaborate on contextual uses of kin terms. This incapacity is the consequence of the short-term survey method he applied to collect terminologies in his surveys. Contextual terminologies can only be observed during their actual uses, as Kronenfeld's and Rumsey's work demonstrates. There is no way Elkin could have observed anything other than a limited terminological set used among coresidents, with its mixture of bifurcation in G^{+1} and neutralization in G^0.

I have shown that there are three terminological sets among Ngaatjatjarra-speaking people and more widely in the Western Desert: one is generational, one is a mixture of generational and bifurcation (Elkin's Aluridja), and one is fully bifurcate-merging. Though I do not wish to suggest a direct dependency between ecological conditions and kinship terminology, it is nevertheless significant that the use of the three terminological sets can be seen as a response to such conditions. Using a generational terminological set among people characterized by their genealogical and spatial proximity and inversely applying a bifurcate-merging terminological set to genealogically and spatially distant people contribute to the diversification of affiliations to land and accesses to resources. The core system of the Western Desert is of the bifurcate-merging type. Cross-parallel neutralization is a social technology that is deployed in fairly explicit ways in contexts where marriages need to be politically and economically oriented.

Is the Western Desert Again an Exception?

One further question needs to be asked: is the so-called Aluridja system, now understood as having coexisting terminological sets, still an exception in the Australian landscape? McConvell (this volume) shows that the coexistence of subsets, in particular in terminological systems that have Crow-Omaha features, seems to be a quite well-distributed feature. What about cross-parallel neutralization (see map 13.1 and table 13.1)?

Very similar cases are those in the Western Desert and the Kija north of it because both associate the cross-parallel neutralization with distant marriage. It may be that the Kurnai represent a similar case, even though they do not have a cross-cousin terminology. G^{+1} distinguishes cross-relatives and marriages need to take place between third cousins at least, which are interesting facts in this respect. Kattang and Arrernte are other interesting cases because they seem to combine cross-parallel neutralization with skewing. Little can be said yet about the contexts of neutralization among the other groups, but cross-parallel neutralizations seem to have taken place in other places in northern New South Wales.

Irrespective of the amount of additional investigation or reconstruction that is still needed, we may advance that the Western Desert terminological system is not an exceptional form and that other groups have or had similar features. Despite the general bifurcate-merging "substructure" of the continent, actual terminologies testify to variability and adaptability that reflect the importance of considering terminological systems in the light of their contextual uses.

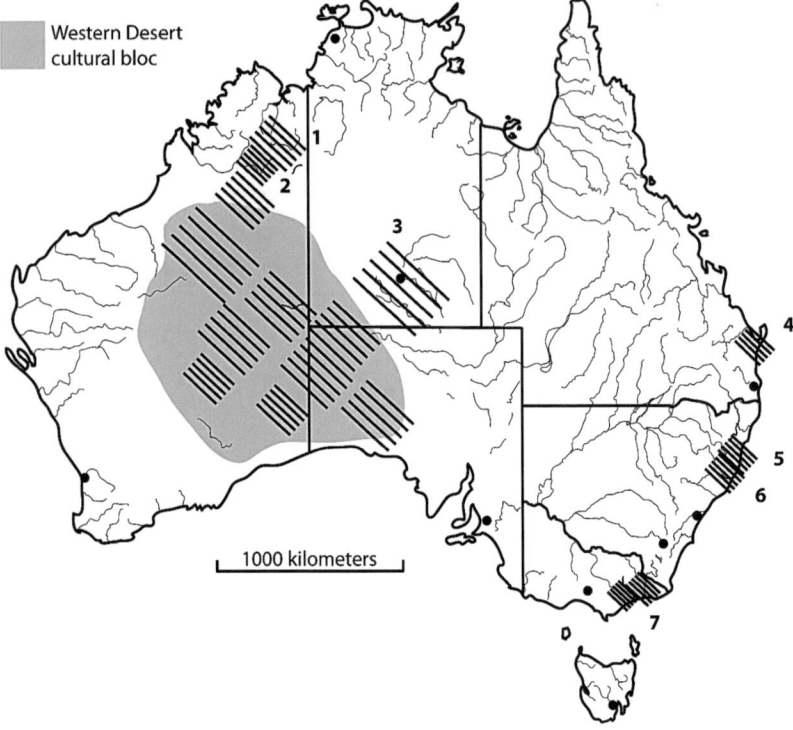

Map 13.1 Cross-parallel neutralizations in Australia

Conclusion

Barnes (2012) recalls how "Godelier (2011:179–180) notes that there are some anthropologists who refuse to recognize Crow-Omaha systems as a separate type, and he is right about this. Needham (1971:14) commented that nothing of any real elucidatory value has come out of the comparative attention to the 'Omaha' type." Kronenfeld, Rumsey, and others have shown that skewing is articulated within strata of layered terminological usages against particular contextual backgrounds. This is also what characterizes the Aluridja system. The definition of sameness through cross-parallel neutralization and the marking of otherness through the use of cross-terminology are a way of orienting alliances toward individual and collective objectives. In this sense, my approach to the Aluridja problem has definitely been materialist; but it

Table 13.1 Cross-parallel neutralizations in Australia

	Language/tribe	G^0	G^{+1}	Marriage
	Western Desert (generic, but in particular, from north to south: Kukatja, Martu Wangka-Mardu, Mandjildjara, Ngaatjatjarra, Ngaanyatjarra, Pitjantjatjara, Yankunyutjatjara, Spinifex people, Kokatha)	B = MBS = FZS (1st and 2nd degree and co-residents) Z = MBD = FZD (1st and 2nd degree and co-residents)	F ≠ MB M ≠ FZ	At least 3rd cross-cousin, local exogamy
1	Kija (McConvell 1997)	B = MBS (close) Z = FZD (close) = MBD (close)	F ≠ MB M ≠ FZ	Preferred: 2nd cross-cousins; 1st cross-cousins possible but not preferred.
2	Gooniyandi (McGregor 1990)	B = MBS = FZS (close) Z = MBD = FZD (close) Merging also when mothers of cross-cousins are countrywomen	F ≠ MB M ≠ FZ M = MMBD when countrywomen	Merging "when distance is small." Merging also when mothers of cross-cousins are from the same geographical area

(continued)

Table 13.1 Continued

	Language/tribe	G^0	G^{+1}	Marriage
3	Arrernte (Aranda) (Henderson and Dobson 1994)	♀B = ♀MBS = ♀FZS = ♂Z = ♂MBD = ♂FZD	F ≠ MB M ≠ FZ	2nd cross-cousin and other conditions
4	Gubbi Gubbi (Mathew 1887)	Z = FZD = MBD	F ≠ MB M ≠ FZ	?
5	Dunghutti (Holmer 1967)	B = MBS Z = MBD	F ≠ MB M ≠ FZ	?
6	Kattang (Holmer 1967)	B = MBS [= MB] [and W = D]	F ≠ MB	?
7	Gunnai (Kurnai) (Fison and Howitt 1991 [1880], Keen pers. comm.)	B = FZS = MBS Z = FZD = MBD	F ≠ MB M ≠ FZ	At least 3rd cousin (no indication as to whether they are cross or parallel or both), exogamy of patrifilial "flesh" totem.

has been so because Aboriginal elucidations of their own practices are congruent with these conclusions.

Despite the layers of contextual applicability of terminologies, the underlying principle of calculating relatedness among Western Desert people remains of the bifurcate-merging type. Lévi-Strauss's superficial depiction of the Aluridja "aberration" is thus in contradiction with his own project of crystallizing the deep structures of kinship (and the human mind). It may be that the identification of a "Crow-Omaha problem," and the existence of semi-complex systems, may well be a similarly fallacious program, at least in those cases where skewing is a social technology rather than reflecting actual cognitive processes and deep structures.

Afterword

14

Crow-Omaha, in Thickness and in Thin
Thomas R. Trautmann and Peter M. Whiteley

Morgan's astonishment in finding that among some peoples the son of an uncle is equally an uncle inaugurated a discussion that this book continues. Since Morgan, the discussion of the Crow-Omaha problem, understood in the simple sense of the problem of explaining skewing, did not have an even forward trajectory. Insofar as explanation of skewing focused only on descent the phenomenon seemed easily understood. We could say that in those narrow terms it had reached a certain kind of resolution in the time of Radcliffe-Brown. But analysis of skewing has also prompted the study of the forms of marriage with which it is associated, since at least the times of Rivers (1914) and Gifford (1916) and continuing with Lowie (1934), Murdock (1949), Lane and Lane (1959), Eyde and Postal (1961), and Lévi-Strauss (1966, 1969). In this wider field of vision Crow-Omaha was and remains a tough nut.

In hindsight we can see why this should have been so. Evidently if the son of an uncle is an uncle, a kinship category is being transmitted to a descendant; it did not take long to discover that skewing had two varieties as the statuses in question were being transmitted unilineally, either matrilineally (Crow) or patrilineally (Omaha). This was a solid gain, even though the exact nature of the transmission was debated. The gain is not lost but it is substantially obscured when the focal point shifts from descent to marriage alliance. Skewing is associated with at least two different regimes of marriage, the one, which we can call dispersed alliance (McKinley 1971b), prohibiting marriage within the clan of the father and the mother and perhaps others, and the other, prescribing asymmetrical cross-cousin marriage. Lévi-Strauss, in the *Elementary Structures*, devoted a great deal of attention to asymmetrical prescriptive marriage, following the extensive work of Marcel Granet, but scarcely mentioned skewing. When he did address Crow-Omaha, in the 1965 Huxley Lecture, his strategy was to identify it exclusively with dispersed alliance, which he theorized as semi-complex marriage alliance midway between elementary and complex forms, and vigorously separated this from asymmetric-prescriptive alliance as whales from fish. Now undoubtedly the concept of semi-complex marriage has been very fruitful for anthropology, as we shall explain further shortly, though attended by much debate and skepticism, not least by Godelier who declines to consider Crow-Omaha kinship as a transition to something else. But with the benefit of all the work done since then, we have to conclude that this move by Lévi-Strauss put the unitary explanation of skewing beyond reach. Marriage alliance being the focus, the explanatory principle came in two very different kinds, so that explanations of skewing based on semi-complex marriage alliance would necessarily cancel those based on asymmetrical prescriptive marriage and vice versa. The Crow-Omaha problem became more complicated, paradoxically, by cutting the phenomenon in half and throwing away one of the halves.

Recognizing that this turning may lead to an impasse is a step forward, for it serves to reopen the question of the relation of descent and marriage to skewing. But not to solve it, for we cannot simply return to the formulations of Radcliffe-Brown and others in his line of explanation and evade the association of skewing with specific types of marriage. Of course, the field of discussion has changed its shape and enlarged its dimensions since Lévi-Strauss because of subsequent theoretical advances and the thickening and widening of the ethnographic record. We have tracked some of the steps that have gotten us from then to now in chapter 1. Let us now draw the balance of these pages and state how a classic problem appears to us at their end.

We begin with the object of study: Crow-Omaha something-or-other. Across the chapters of this book, the search for the right something-or-other has moved in a definite direction.

What is the substantive to which the Crow-Omaha modifier attaches? Is it a kinship system? A terminology type? A dimension of kinship terminology, namely, skewing? Moving across the options from left to right we go from a rich, complex, more thing-like object to the thinnest of abstractions. The tendency of the chapters herein has been toward the right end of this series, impelled not so much by a positive preference for abstraction as by an unwillingness to reify the object of study. Barnes (chapter 4) shows in detail reasons to doubt that Omaha is viable as a kind of kinship system or that the Omaha people have an Omaha system in the Lévi-Straussian sense. All the authors assembled here share this tendency to some degree, none perhaps in so strong a form as Barnes. Nevertheless, the movement away from a thick conception of Crow-Omaha does not dissolve the object; it only acts to make it more precise. What Morgan found exists in the world, and continues to do so, among neighboring peoples with closely related languages and similar social structures, and also, as this book attests, across continents and among the most distant peoples. The net of the vectors, away from reification and toward the affirmation of Morgan's perception, has been in the direction of a thinned, abstract, and formal concept of Crow-Omaha per se. This gain in precision permits critical associations with other structural features, like marriage practices, that make for more effective explanations overall. This, we feel, is the present volume's major analytical contribution.

Thinning down the object of study has had the paradoxical effect of enlarging the field of vision in which we now view it. The authors of this book are unanimous on the point that Crow-Omaha skewing is invariably connected with crossness. In a very real sense, as Coelho de Souza has said (in seminar discussion), "Crossness is the underlying problem" for the study of Crow-Omaha. From this vantage point, the problem of Crow-Omaha becomes the problem of the relation of skewing to crossness.

Overlays and Contexts

A fundamental datum we must take into account in our approach to the problem is that terminologies with skewing also always have crossness, but terminologies may have crossness without skewing. This leads us to Kronenfeld's conception of skewing as an overlay, an idea that has resonated widely in this book. We may show the relation through ethnography and through formal analysis.

Kronenfeld's ethnography of the Fanti of West Africa shows that they have two kinship terminologies, the main one having crossness, and the secondary one a transformation of the first, having skewing and used only in limited contexts. This rich finding (the details of which we do not recite here) has many consequences for the Crow-Omaha problem. In the first place it gives empirical evidence of the relation between crossness and skewing already stated. In the second place it raises the possibility that skewing may elsewhere—perhaps everywhere—accompany an unskewed terminology having crossness. That would help make intelligible how children learn skewing. After all, if one recognizes that the son of an uncle is also an uncle, one works from a prior understanding of what an uncle is to generate the posterior, new understanding of the category of uncle. These last two points are not certain, however, and require further study. Whiteley holds that the Hopi's skewed terminology is not optative, and Godelier that a full-fledged Crow-Omaha system cannot be understood as an overlay. Furthermore, Leach (1945) offers a demonstration of how Jinghpaw children could learn a skewed system directly from clan affiliations and without benefit of an unskewed system; this resonates directly with how Hopi children, among others, learn kin terms, rather than as "extensions" from a nuclear family. In the third place, the overlay concept posits different levels of structural depth, that is, a distinction of deep structure and surface structure, and situates skewing at the higher of the levels. Finally, it prefigures the concept of *kinship contexts* which Dousset articulates in chapter 13, implying that "the" unitary kinship terminology of a people must give way to a terminology the surface features of which vary by kinship context. All these consequences of the overlay concept are good evidence that terminologies having skewing are built on terminologies with crossness.

Lounsbury's formal analysis shows this in another way. Terminologies having crossness have a rule of same-sex sibling merging, which defines parallel kin and, in so doing, the cross-kin (who are the residue not touched by the rule). By virtue of this rule the father's brother is a father, and the mother's brother is untouched by the rule and remains an uncle. Terminologies having skewing also have same-sex sibling merging. The skewing rule acts on cross-kin (such as the uncle), renaming them in such a way that crossness is partially or wholly obscured in the surface structure.

In connection with the distinction between deep structure and surface structure, Dousset (in seminar discussion) has this to say, using Lévi-Strauss's (and Allen's) project as a way of mapping the structural location of skewing in relation to crossness:

Lévi-Strauss's ambition, his idea, not just for Crow-Omaha, but in general, was to go into the *deep structure* of things, of systems. Responding to empiricist critiques of his work (as by Hiatt at the *Man the Hunter* conference), for example, he said that he was absolutely not interested in people's *practice*, but in the deep structure lying behind it, beyond it. In this context, from what we have heard about Crow-Omaha systems, the underlying deep structure, if you will, remains *crossness*, in one way or another. Crossness is in fact rather a simple algorithm easily learned by children in local settings: there are emic relative-product models that actually allow you to do that. So it appears to me that *skewing is a breaking of this rule* (of crossness), and, of course, you can only break this rule, or this crossness, if you have the crossness in mind.

In this sense, the Crow-Omaha problem is not in the realm of Lévi-Strauss's ambition because it is not of the deep structure. It involves something that is breaking that deep structure, in order to allow for social morphology to be a process. So the Crow-Omaha question is not of the same order as Dravidian crossness or Iroquois crossness: it is something that comes on top of these. I am not quite sure if we should say it is an overlay, but it is something that belongs in the realm of social process and social history, rather than being a profound, deep structure. In this sense, I quite agree with Allen's tetradic model, not as a historical model, but as an underlying cognitive process of apprehending and learning the way you can locally construct relatedness.

Valuable as Lévi-Strauss's vision may be as a way of locating the object of study, the deep structure is only available through the close examination of the surface structure. Lévi-Strauss, of course, regarded Crow-Omaha systems as *the* problem requiring solution before grappling with complex structures, so it is not likely he thought of them as *only* surface-structural. Yet Dousset has put his finger on something fundamental regarding Crow-Omaha and underlying crossness. As Godelier says, the matter of crossness in the deep structure of Crow-Omaha leads us to the problem of visibility and invisibility. "At the surface level, the distinction between crossness and parallelness may not be visible, but it is present in the deep structure. So, it is possible in different contexts to see the deep structure creating new things which then (ultimately) become visible" (seminar discussion). The variation in surface structure is how we detect the contents of the deep structure.

If crossness is the larger context in which Crow-Omaha skewing is to be understood, perhaps to deepen our understanding of Crow-Omaha we need to attend to contexts in which crossness, while existing in the deep structure, is suspended; it may be that our understanding of crossness will be broadened and deepened thereby. Dousset (chapter 13) speaks of *horizontal skewing*, by which he means the suspension of crossness in ego's generation, such that all cousins become siblings—what has been called elsewhere the Cheyenne type. Kronenfeld (chapter 8) speaks of the rule of *cross-parallel neutralization* in Iroquois, not present in Dravidian. Barbosa de Almeida (2010) speaks of a *rule of forgetting* that suspends the cross-parallel distinction among grandparents and grandchildren in most Dravidian systems of South India. (His formal analysis of Dravidian is extended to Crow-Omaha in Barbosa de Almeida forthcoming.) The surface-structural facts to which these formulations speak have sometimes been characterized as "Hawaiianization," and all of them represent the further assimilation of cross-kin to parallel kin. Hawaiianization is not a good term, in our opinion, because it implies a connection of Hawaiian-type kinship terminology with crossness that has not been demonstrated. We need to examine whether fully blown terminologies of the Hawaiian type are akin, at the level of deep structure, to crossness. If that were so, it would confirm the significance of the "classificatory" kind of terminologies that Morgan took to be deeply different from nonclassificatory ones.

Marriage Alliance, Semi-Complex and Prescriptive Asymmetric

Identifying crossness within the deep structure of Crow-Omaha systems, subject to variable surface manifestations, may be especially resonant for the Amazonian Gê, as characterized by Coelho de Souza (chapter 10) and in Turner's "schemas" generating Kayapó social categories and processes (chapter 11). This perspective appears heuristic for several other ethnographic regions represented as well: the Pueblo Southwest (Whiteley, chapter 5), northeast Africa (James, chapter 7), Nilo-Saharan cases through time (Ehret, chapter 9), the India-Myanmar borderland (Trautmann, chapter 2), Tibeto-Burman speakers of Nepal (Allen, chapter 3), and northern and northeastern Australia (McConvell, chapter 12). In all these cases, there is simultaneously an additional trend: the variant manifestations consistently articulate with marriage rules and practices. Wherever skewing exists ("horizontal," as for Dousset [chapter 13], as well as vertical), the primary social ground appears to be marriage preferences and strategies. Only for the Fanti case (Kronenfeld, chapter 8) is it suggested that inheritance may be the best explanation for skewing and that marriage alliance plays no role. Yet even here, Fanti statements of a former preference for matrilateral cross-cousin marriage (Kronenfeld, personal communication), the same as recorded for the closely related Ashanti, suggest that further historical investigation is warranted. As noticed elsewhere (pointed out, for example, in Australian cases by McConvell [seminar discussion]), the Fanti situation may involve cultural lag, where skewing itself persists beyond an earlier association with a marriage rule. In general, a correlation between Crow-Omaha skewing and unilateral cross-cousin marriage has long been noticed, and sometimes posited as causal (Eyde and Postal 1961; Lane and Lane 1959), even before Lévi-Strauss's invention of "semi-complex" alliance.

Given that marriage everywhere appears important to Crow-Omaha variations, it follows that considering skewing only from a terminological or a descent-and-inheritance perspective is not sufficient. If we are to put Crow-Omaha and asymmetric-prescriptive systems back together, semi-complex alliance and asymmetric-prescriptive marriage rules must be seen less as fish and whales and more as alternate speciations in the same ocean kingdom governed by underlying crossness. The different routes taken appear to manifest consistent regional flavors, with Crow-Omaha strongly associated geographically and culturally with proximate Iroquois systems in the Americas, Africa, and Australia, and asymmetric-prescriptive systems in Asia and Oceania proximate to Dravidian systems (though Dravidian systems of south India are notably lacking in Iroquois and Crow-Omaha cases in their near vicinity). If in both cases the skewing variations *emerge from* Iroquois and Dravidian, respectively, and if furthermore—as appears to be the case from related geographic and adaptive propinquities in North America (Wheeler et al., chapter 6)—Iroquois systems in turn emerge from Dravidian, what may we conclude about the covariance with marriage practices? Dravidian crossness foregrounds an explicit correlation with affinity: MBCh = FZCh = spouse/sibling-in-law (see Dumont 1953). If this represents the deep structural form for Iroquois and Crow-Omaha manifestations, both should retain echoes in their respective marriage practices. It should be remembered that although Crow-Omaha is the archetype for semi-complex alliance in Lévi-Strauss's and Héritier's formulations, in passing gestures they also include Iroquois in this category.

Lévi-Strauss's signal contribution to kinship studies was to restore marriage practices to center stage. Marriage had belonged to kinship-system study from the beginning: J. F. McLennan (1865), Morgan's contemporary and sometime disputant (e.g., Trautmann 1987), provided an early impetus with his book on the evolution of marriage systems, and Morgan's own clear attention was to "affinity" as well as "consanguinity." But the balance among the three legs of the kinship tripod—terminology, descent, and marriage—shifted, and by the mid-twentieth century, under the aegis of structural-functionalism, descent predominated, to the virtual exclusion of marriage and, to a lesser extent, terminology. Unilineal descent was heralded as the structural engine of nonstate societies, the mechanism for organizing and perpetuating corporate groups that formed the building blocks of social order. Seen through this prism, Crow and Omaha skewing was aligned to corporate matrilineal and patrilineal descent groups, respectively, and presented by White (1939) and Murdock (1949) as exemplifying "stronger" versions than were possible with Iroquois terminology. As Barnes (chapter 4) points out, a narrowly construed emphasis on descent channels ethnographic interpretation in a particular direction and constrains explanation. Perhaps the chief shortcoming of this approach was to frustrate diachronic analysis, of either a historical or an evolutionary sort (see later discussion). Social structures depicted under its method were frozen in synchronic time, and social processes and changes were sidelined.

Although many kinship groups may be seen as constituted by a descent principle, what these groups *do*, in addition to passing on jural, political, and economic rights, is to arrange—often via deliberate strategy—their own reproduction via marriage alliance with other like groups. Structurally, marriage practices are intrinsically transitive, the primary means of social reiteration through time, a fundamentally diachronic social force. With this in mind, Lévi-Strauss insisted on reconnecting "affinity" back to "consanguinity." His principal project showed how "elementary" systems of kinship, associated with terminologies having broadly Dravidian crossness, were predicated on marriage alliance—of "sister-exchange" between groups (and see James, chapter 7). In elementary systems, marriage was prescribed with a particular group or category, whereas in "complex" structures—like the West—marriage rules were only proscriptive, prohibiting marriage within a small circle of kin. When Lévi-Strauss belatedly turned his attention to Crow-Omaha systems as, he thought, transitional between elementary and complex systems, he felt the need to invoke a new category, "semi-complex," characterized by combined prescriptive-proscriptive rules, which produced "aleatory" patterns of alliance that were only probabilistic rather than regularly repeating.

Héritier's (1981) refinement of the semi-complex category argued that alliances were not in fact aleatory but recycled through descent lines connected in cognatic assemblages. Ranges of cognatic kin prohibited by an existing marriage from repeating the alliance in one generation were rechanneled into marriageable classes after several generations. Semi-complex systems like Samo (Omaha) were thus better explained by examining cognatic assemblages regularly repeating via marriage rather than by unilineal lineages seen as closed structures (e.g., Héritier 2000:28–29). Dispersal and retention of alliances were thus the conjoint principles of semi-complex marriage systems (see McKinley 1971b).

Opinions on the value of the semi-complex category among our seminar's members were mixed. Allen (seminar remarks) argued for its continuing usefulness within Lévi-Strauss's elementary-complex typology, particularly as the discussion of several systems in the present volume suggests their transitional status. In keeping with his general antipathy to Crow-Omaha, Barnes (chapter 4; see also Barnes 1982) takes an opposing view, based in part on dissimilarities among Omaha proper and Samo marriage rules. Héritier's defense (e.g., 2000:29) against the charge Samo is a "hapax," or unique case, invokes comparable West African examples (see Copet-Rougier 1990). James (chapter 7) shows that sister-exchange variations in northeast Africa show continuities with some marriage regimes conceived as semi-complex by Héritier and colleagues working in west Africa. With modifications for ethnographic context, Whiteley (chapter 5) concludes that Hopi (Crow) diachronic marriage practices are better explained by Héritier's model of semi-complex alliance, as considered through cognatic "houses," than by existing descent-theory models. The general value of Héritier's model seems to be confirmed by these approaches, especially insofar as they include ethnographic regions far beyond its primary applications to date. Fully testing Héritier's hypotheses requires extensive long-term marriage data, which tend to be rare in the ethnographic record. One path ahead on the Crow-Omaha question, however, in keeping with Tjon Sie Fat's (1998a) recommendation, should lead to comparing Héritier's conclusions in detail against other systems with Crow and Omaha skewing.

In keeping with the deep structure/surface structure discussion, the general sense of the Crow-Omaha seminar was that semi-complex alliance will retain significant explanatory value more broadly if it can be shifted—similarly "elementary" and "complex"—away from "system" status and more toward "social technology," in Godelier's terms: "Crow-Omaha systems . . . may represent a social technology that can be used like an overlay or superstructure imposed on different kinds of basic kinship systems. But I don't like the word 'overlay' or superstructure; I prefer 'social strategy' or 'social technology' insofar as its purpose is to resolve certain societal problems" (seminar remarks). Godelier thus sees Crow-Omaha skewing primarily as a "strategy of using kinship terms and kinship relationships" to produce certain social outcomes. Where the social technology is not directed at (re)producing alliance, as with Fanti (chapter 8), skewing does not create a "full-fledged" Crow-Omaha system: "So it seems to me that you get a full-fledged Crow-Omaha system when the skewing or another aspect of the system is used for organizing marriage alliances. If you use some terminological aspect for managing the dispersal of people, controlling ritual sites, or preventing problems pertaining to strategic resources, it is not really embedded into a strategy of alliance: it is not going into the deep aspect of things" (seminar remarks).

Coelho de Souza (chapter 10) develops the idea of semi-complex alliance as a social technology the farthest, casting new light on the profusion of Gê surface-structure variations. Drawing on Viveiros de Castro's (1998) notion that a terminologically underspecified Dravidianate lies in the deep structure of Amazonian social forms, she suggests redefining complexity, elementarity, and semi-complexity "not as characterizing types of systems or societies, but as specifying regimes or conditions under which an ever-changing alliance structure could be seen to unfold its many versions" (chapter 10). This seems an important advance, shifting the emphasis from structure toward dynamic agency. Reconceiving semi-complexity as a social technology for producing alliances, as one Dravidianate strategy among others that might or might not be mobilized to produce Crow or Omaha alignments—thus a set of conscious social choices (Godelier, seminar remarks; see Héritier 2000:29)—moves semi-complexity out of its status as the intermediate stage of a macro-structural opposition. As a result, it is de-reified and becomes more supple for the explanation of diachronic social processes. As Coelho de Souza points out, this also provides a route toward reapproximation with asymmetric-prescriptive alliance: no longer whales and fish, Crow-Omaha and asymmetric-prescriptive systems disclose substantive common ground in the realm of alliances as well as in their lineal terminological equations. In turn, this necessarily calls for loosening the elementary/semi-complex boundary, particularly in regard to Lévi-Strauss's restriction of asymmetric-prescriptive to the former and Crow-Omaha to the latter.

To bring this full circle—back to Morgan's starting point—we noted allusions by both Lévi-Strauss and Héritier to Iroquois systems as semi-complex. If semi-complexity is reconceived as a social technology, what then of the ethnographic Iroquois, the spark for Morgan's great study of classificatory kinship, and thus the origin and anchor for all kinship system typologies ever since? Might there be lability in actual Iroquois kinship that suggests it, too, is a surface manifestation with proximate Crow-Omaha potentialities? Seen in the light of this volume's advances, there are some intriguing clues. Though not mentioned in *Systems of Consanguinity and Affinity*, Morgan's earlier discussion of Seneca-Iroquois kinship, in his ethnography *League of the Ho-de-no-sau-nee, or*

Iroquois, suggests a former practice of strict moiety exogamy (Morgan 1851:75–79). The eight Iroquois matrilineal clans are divided into two groups of four. Morgan notes the Seneca tradition that each group derived from a single original moiety pair, Bear and Deer. Within a moiety, the four clans were "brothers" (i.e., parallel cousins) to each other and were prohibited from marrying (in the Iroquois communities of upstate New York, both in Morgan's time and in the present, intramoiety marriages occur without apparent restriction). The opposite moiety's clans, however, were "cousins" (i.e., cross-cousins) and could—inferentially, by the context, *should*—marry (Morgan 1851:79). The apparent similarity of this purported former practice to a Dravidian system is striking (and even more reason, albeit unconscious, for Morgan's collocation of Seneca with Tamil). In effect, Morgan infers there had been a historical transition to "Iroquois" (or Type B) crossness: "In process of time, however, the rigor of the system was relaxed, until finally the [marriage] prohibition was confined to the tribe [clan] of the individual, which, among the residue of the Iroquois, is still religiously observed. They can now marry into any tribe [clan] but their own" (Morgan 1851:79).

Eggan (1972:5–6) was thus led to suggest the Iroquois had formerly practiced prescriptive bilateral cross-cousin marriage, a view supported by several Iroquois accounts recorded since Morgan (Shimony 1961: 30–32). Cross-cousin marriage was more than merely historical: 1950s research among conservative communities at Six Nations Reserve in Ontario (Myers 2006) showed that such marriages remained common. Moreover, as well as a person's own matriclan, the *father's matrilineage* remained an important Iroquois group, referred to as "people of my father's sister"—a phrase that might be applied to any individual member of that lineage (Eggan 1972:5). Eggan thus concluded: "One important question has been: Why didn't the Iroquois develop a Crow system of kinship? The answer is that they did in part, since members of the father's lineage might be addressed as 'father's sisters,' symbolizing the jural unity of the father's matrilineage" (Eggan 1972:6).

In short, Iroquois kinship, the cornerstone of Morgan's *Systems*, may be seen as one surface-structure crystallization of an underlying Dravidianate. "Iroquois" and "Crow" variations may thus be the result of the same semi-complex social technology for which there is in fact ethnographic and ethnohistoric evidence for the living Hodenosaunee—"people of the longhouse," the Iroquois self-designation.

Transformations of Kinship Systems

Let us turn now to the problem of locating Crow-Omaha skewing and crossness in the large processes of history and evolution. Evolutionary transformations have been part of kinship system analysis from the start, notably with Morgan's (1871) proposed sequence of terminological stages. More recent efforts to model kinship system evolution have offered a variety of perspectives (e.g., Allen et al. 2008; Dole 1972; Hage 1999; Kryukov 1968). This is a vast question, and we can only give a brief indication of how the problem can be approached.

We need to start from a sense of how kinship systems are transformed from one to another. It is useful to think of this in two steps. The first step is to get a fix on the patterns of transformation; the second is to ask whether such patterns have an overall directionality.

As to pattern, the null hypothesis is that any kinship system can turn into any other—which, we venture to say, no one believes. There are a limited number of such transformations, and they form patterns. We have identified two of them that are strongly grounded ethnographically (Trautmann, chapter 2; see also Wheeler et al., chapter 6, on the first of them):

$$\text{Dravidian} \leftrightarrow \text{Iroquois} \leftrightarrow \text{Crow-Omaha}$$
$$\text{Dravidian} \leftrightarrow \text{AXCM} \leftrightarrow \text{Crow-Omaha}$$

Other patterns are argued for by Ehret (chapter 9) for Nilo-Saharan languages of Africa, on the basis of historical-linguistic comparison:

$$\text{Iroquois} (\to \text{Crow}) (\to \text{Iroquois}) (\to \text{Omaha} \leftarrow) \to$$
$$\text{Hawaiian or Sudanese or Eskimo}$$

As a general matter, Ehret concludes from his material that change from Iroquois to other systems is unidirectional, with one exception: Crow can reverse back to Iroquois (see also McConvell, chapter 12, for Australia). All of these findings are of course subject to further testing and analysis, but for present purposes we need only assent to the notion that there exist patterns of transformations among kinship systems, which, taken together, are less than the transformation of each system into every other—the word *pattern* indicating that we are dealing with a definite, real subset of all imaginable transformations.

As to directionality, then, the question is whether such patterns tend in a certain direction (irreversibility) or not (reversibility), yielding an overall net direction over the course of time. The double-headed arrows in the formulas indicate reversibility; single-headed arrows would imply irreversibility. Which is more true to the ethnographic record? This is a thorny question, which we may expect to be a point of contention for a long time to come. We cannot do justice to it in the few pages remaining to us, but we can briefly pose the problem.

As moderns, the ambient ideology through which we move every day is one of directional growth. Growth of what? We may argue over what exactly gives our world this sense of directionality for us, but we would probably agree it includes growth of the human population as a species, of the size and complexity of political aggregations, of complexity and scale of social forms, of economies. This is not mere imagination, of course; we have very good reasons for thinking so, reasons that include well-developed evidence and well-tested arguments. Because this is our mental world, we are strongly inclined at the outset to think that the arrows of change point in only one direction, on the whole. That powerfully conditions our attempts to find the true location of Crow-Omaha within larger processes of change. This is a capital fact, and we can best put it to work for us, not by opposing this tendency, but by recognizing that arguments for irreversibility have an unearned advantage and they need to be rigorously and skeptically tested.

Within that frame, grand theory—whether of Lévi-Strauss, Kryukov, Allen, Godelier, or even Morgan—is virtually unanimous that the starting point of long-term change, the type of the elementary or simplest form of kinship, is something like Dravidian (which of course determines the place of Crow-Omaha). Here we see two problems for the before and the after of the process. As to the before, the formation of an originary Dravidianate structure out of which later forms evolve is a kind of leap from nature into culture; it is a discontinuity narrative that does not connect with the story of the long, incremental evolution of the species and its highly elaborate kinship practices, so very different from the severely limited kinship practices of our primate cousins. As to the after, the Dravidian-speakers of south India with their dense populations of agriculturalists, their monumental architecture, their large-scale political structures, and their software engineers, are not cooperative witnesses in making the case. These are not reasons to reject existing theories, of course, but to test them.

We know of no Crow-Omaha cases coterminous with the state (as opposed to less complex sociopolitical formations) and infer that an interplay of structural and demographic factors is the cause. As Lévi-Strauss suggested, and as Allen (seminar remarks) confirmed, population size in Crow-Omaha systems has upper limits: we might hazard the typical range as from 600 to 10,000 (though larger in west African cases like Samo). Crow-Omaha skewing occurs in comparatively few "band" societies of foragers, and these are always associated with higher relative population densities, richer resources, or both. For the Australian cases, McConvell (chapter 12) shows that these patterns correlate further with historically known "downstream" territorial expansion of social groups with Omaha terminologies. Whiteley (chapter 5) and Wheeler et al. (chapter 6) suggest that for North American societies kinship system distribution corresponds systematically with forms of social and economic adaptation, with Crow-Omaha corollaries in increased sedentism, density, hierarchy, and dispersal of alliances (see also Ives 1998). Crow-Omaha alliance technologies may thus enable specific forms of dispersed social solidarity that offer a competitive advantage in certain social and adaptive environments. Crow-Omaha systems generally correlate with "middle-range" economic adaptations of one form or another and where adaptation permits higher population thresholds often with emergent or established hierarchical formations that lie somewhere in the "tribe-chiefdom" nexus of political anthropology's standard types. Comparable patterns in widely dispersed global regions suggest that evolutionary change is a plausible explanatory element for at least some cases of the emergence and spread of systems with Crow-Omaha skewing.

Kryukov (1998), it should be said, has well-developed arguments (based on methods pioneered not by Morgan but by a Russian contemporary of his, P. A. Lavronski), for the irreversibility of large-scale historical change of kinship, from Rome and from ancient China, which are based on documentary evidence over thousands of years. These historical cases give badly needed empirical weight to the stated directionality of change in kinship, and Godelier's book further develops the Kryukovian argument. More work of this kind would be very helpful.

It would help, also, to have well-developed counterarguments to test this structure of argumentation. In the peoples we discuss in this volume, we can point to the Ojibwa of North America, who have Dravidian and Iroquois crossness in northern and southern ranges of their population, as if they were different phases of one and the same substance that could go from the one to the other as circumstances (of ecology, of economy, of population density) may require. We have also the Fanti, who simultaneously hold a main system with crossness and a Crow system for special purposes, another particular case that shows reversibility, here as a steady state, it seems. Finally, we may mention that among the Hopi, new village formations have often involved two matriclans (see Whiteley 2008): where these remain the only constituents (as for a long time at Supawlavi on Second Mesa) and retain both village endogamy and clan exogamy, the Crow structure of their mother village (Songòopavi in this case) is no longer possible, clearly pushing them toward a dual (i.e., Dravidian) system of bilateral cross-cousin marriage. We need to develop, through microstudies, a sense of not only the circumstances under which reversibility occurs but its limits, if any. Given their relatively shallow time depth (ca. 3,000 years—chapter 10) and the profusion of surface typological manifestations, societies of the Gê language family may provide a particularly interesting test case.

Final Thoughts

At the last, the strategically thinned-down conception of Crow-Omaha returns to the socially thick social system from which it has been abstracted to make it intelligible. It bears repeating that this book is about kinship, but not only kinship. Kinship structures are part of the multiple ways human beings imagine themselves in the world. They are the means by and through which people transact with each other, producing and reproducing themselves socially and biologically from one generation to the next. Maurice Godelier reminded us of this larger context in seminar discussions. Responding in part to Turner (chapter 11), he said that the Crow-Omaha discussion opens not only kinship problems but also the problem of "the place of kinship in constituting society as an encompassing whole." Here is Turner's perspective on the thin and the thick of it:

> I do think that Crow-Omaha is a meaningful category, but I think we have to take more seriously the question of exactly what it is a category *of*. I would urge that we are not just talking about a category of *terminological* systems or categories, we are talking about systems of *social* categories. In my theoretical jargon, the patterns or schemas of social production are not primarily terminological at all. They are patterns of *social activity*, social processes which have certain results. They produce certain kinds of social solidarities. They generate not only family alignments or marital relations, but collective social groupings. They are systems that have collective social, and even political, dimensions to them, and certain features of these dimensions relate to the asymmetry of the underlying social processes that generate them. That is a long and awkward way of describing what a Crow or Omaha type might be, but I do think that with more attention to not just the terminological expressions or manifestations of these systems of categories, but the underlying social nature of the schemas—of the categories that generate the terminology—we might find ourselves attempting to describe a rather different kind of animal. (Seminar remarks)

Our concerns with this animal—neither whale nor fish!—originated with the classical Crow-Omaha problem but, for the reasons suggested by Godelier and Turner, have necessarily led us to pursue Crow-Omaha through the actual societies and long-term processes in which it lives. In the end, we have deconstructed Crow-Omaha as a type, but made it more effective by making it more exact. This gives us better means to locate Crow-Omaha socially and historically and to make it available for better comparative analysis. Our proposals for ways forward argue strongly for the value of renewing kinship studies in anthropology and beyond.

Notes

Preface

1. Amerind Foundation Advanced Seminar "Transformative Kinship: Engaging the Crow-Omaha Transition," held 27 February–3 March 2010 at the Amerind Foundation, Dragoon, Arizona; National Science Foundation grant, "Workshop on Transitions in Human Social Organization," BCS-0938505.

2. Maurice Godelier participated in the seminar by telephone and contributed comments that are discussed in the concluding chapter of this book. Laura Fortunato presented a paper on residence patterns in Indo-European cultures but decided to publish elsewhere.

Chapter 2

1. I do not like these ethnic labels because they suggest too much when what is wanted is precision. Previously I have called these Type A and Type B crossness. However, the Dravidian and Iroquois labels are too entrenched in usage to be dislodged. My way of controlling the semantic sprawl of these terms is to refer to the abstracted aspect of Dravidian and Iroquois *kinship terminologies* I intend as Dravidian and Iroquois *crossness*.

2. Burling and Lounsbury got together over these terminologies in 1965 at the University of Michigan. Lounsbury elicited Jinghpaw from La Raw Maran, a native speaker and linguist, in connection with a field methods class he was teaching. Burling got Maru kinship terms from fieldwork in Burma (Burling 1971, n 7, and personal communication). This excellent and unusual case of structurally identical kinship terminologies is hidden away in a paper devoted to untangling the historical relations among certain Tibeto-Burman languages, in a difficult-to-find publication.

Chapter 3

1. Suggestions bearing on these (usually) patrilineal types apply mutatis mutandis to the (usually) matrilineal Crow types, so for brevity the latter are ignored here.

2. Even in modern Western society, the divergence is not complete: statistically, a social class is endogamous, and ego's children belong within it.

3. This is not invariable: for instance, a conservative substrate culture may overwhelm an innovation brought by immigrants.

4. The affinal equations *mem* EF = EeB and *iwi* EM = EeZ are interesting because in related languages the roots mean only PF and PM.

5. Sherpa retains at least one prescriptive equation, *ani* FZ = MBW, but although I looked for it, I found no clear evidence of a previous period of matrilateral prescription.

6. FFZSD marriage is mentioned several times in Tjon Sie Fat (1990), for example, pp. 114–15 (theory), 139 (ethnography), but the five-line version receives no special attention.

7. Admittedly, the full set of prohibitions applies only to males: a female marries into the line of her FM.

8. The pointer "plenty" covers fecundity, prosperity, health, or large number.

Chapter 5

Author's Note: Research for analyses and conclusions in this chapter was supported in part by a National Science Foundation grant, "Explaining Crow-Omaha Kinship Structures with Anthro-informatics," BCS-0925978.

1. Gould's symbol variants are modified here to conform to our standard notation (in particular, ♂ for µ, ♀ for φ, and Ch for C).

Chapter 6

Author's Note: Research for analyses and conclusions in this chapter was supported in part by a National Science Foundation grant, "Explaining Crow-Omaha Kinship Structures with Anthro-informatics," BCS-0925978.

1. Even extinct lineages can be thought of as leaves, if at a lower section of the tree.

2. It is hypothetical because we can never "know" if we have observed an ancestor and such a mathematical point need not have ever existed in nature.

3. For n taxa $\geq 3: \dfrac{(2n-4)!}{(n-2)!2^{n-2}}$ (Schröder 1870).

4. This class of problems is referred to as NP-complete in the computer science literature (Karp, 1972).

5. For each tree of n taxa, $\binom{n}{2}-(2n-3)$.

6. This approach was pioneered by Platnick and Cameron (1977).

7. For Seminole, null values were recorded in the EA data set for variables 1–5. Rather than leaving these blank and unanalyzable, values from Creek were substituted, on the grounds that Creek and Seminole represent branches of the same society and culture historically: ethnographic present for the Creek data is 1750, whereas that for Seminole is 1940. Creek data values assigned to Seminole thus represent a hypothetical approximation.

8. As with the culture areas, we adhere to the EA's classification of language families for the present purpose; these differ somewhat from the *Handbook of North American Indians* classification (e.g., Goddard 1997).

Notes 301

Chapter 8

Author's Note: The arguments in this chapter are developed from a long-term inquiry into Fanti kinship and formal analysis. I have presented some of the ethnographic and theoretical context in detail in other sources (see Kronenfeld 2009). Short background passages from those sources (reproduced in Kronenfeld 2009:introduction, chapters 1 and 2) are reproduced largely unchanged here within the following sections: introduction (from chapter 2), Kinship Terminologies as Semantic Systems (from the introduction), the Fanti Context (from chapter 2), Fanti Kin Terminology (from chapter 1), and Formalist Approaches to Kin Terminologies: Gould's System (from chapter 2).

1. "Real" according to Fanti informants. The issue here is "real" versus extended (whether genealogically or metaphorically). Normally "real" is presumed (as a default) to be biological and social (biological father married to biological mother), but in practice it means whatever is accepted as socially real. A "real" spouse is the one that one is (or was) actually married to.

2. This approach was suggested by Tjon Sie Fat (1998b).

3. Note that *mother's sibling* reduces to (maternal) *uncle* or *mother*, depending on the sibling's sex.

4. The lexeme here refers only to a male's sister.

Chapter 10

1. Before the HCBP, the ethnography of Curt Nimuendajú (1942, 1946, 1967 [1939]) was almost the only source available on the Gê. HCBP researchers paved the way for the rich ethnographic tradition on which this chapter is based. Space prevents me from acknowledging the contribution of all those who provided the elements and inspiration for the picture presented here.

2. This description does not apply to the Panará, the most distant offshoot of the northern branch.

3. Apart from the consanguineal and affinal, Crocker lists the name set transmission, formal friendship, informal friendship, and mortuary terminological systems, among others.

4. The Ramkokamekra notion of *hapàà*, "bridge," refers to the way the opposition between two terms is mediated by a third.

Chapter 12

Author's Note: This research was supported under the Australian Research Council's Discovery Projects funding scheme (project number DP0878556), the Australian National University (ANU), and the Centre National de la Recherche Scientifique (CNRS) through the Centre de Recherche et de Documentation sur l'Océanie (CREDO). The software for this project was developed by Laurent Dousset of CREDO and uses a geospatial interface developed by the Research

School of Humanities at ANU using the AUSTLANG (http://austlang.aiatsis.gov.au/disclaimer.php) coordinates and language list developed by Kazuko Obata of the Australian Institute of Aboriginal and Torres Strait Islander Studies). Thanks to the editors, Laurent Dousset, and other participants in the Crow-Omaha seminar, Arizona, February 28–March 1, 2010, for comments on an earlier version presented there. Thanks to Mark Donohue for facilitating New Guinea mapping and presentation at the Papuanist workshop, ANU, 2009.

Chapter 13

Author's Note: Part of this research was supported under the Australian Research Council's Discovery Projects funding scheme (project number DP0878556); the Australian National University (ANU), and the Centre National de la Recherche Scientifique (CNRS) through the Centre de Recherche et de Documentation sur l'Océanie (CREDO). The software for this project was developed by Laurent Dousset of CREDO and uses a geospatial-interface developed by the Research School of Humanities (RSH) at ANU using the AUSTLANG (http://austlang.aiatsis.gov.au/disclaimer.php) coordinates and language list developed by Kazuko Obata of the Australian Institute of Aboriginal and Torres Strait Islander Studies (AIATSIS). The database is hosted at the following address http://austkin.pacific-credo.fr. Full access to the database is however currently only available to team members.

1. I do not go into the details of the usage of *watjirra* generally in the Western Desert, because it has slightly different connotations in different dialectal groups. For example, among northern groups it denotes all cross-cousins, whereas among southern groups it is used only to refer to same-sex cross-cousins (other-sex cross-cousins are in this case called husband/wife). Those groups that do not know *watjirra* seem to be using *marutju* (brother-in-law) and *tjuwari* (sister-in-law) in a classificatory, rather than only in a descriptive way.

Glossary

AFFINES: kin by marriage, in-laws.

AGNATES: relatives linked via a line of males only (see also patrilineal descent).

ALLIANCE/MARRIAGE ALLIANCE: institutional ties between groups linked by marriage(s); see also asymmetric-prescriptive system, elementary, complex, and semi-complex structures.

ASYMMETRICAL CROSS-COUSIN MARRIAGE: pattern stemming from a rule prescribing marriage with either father's sister's child (FZCh) or mother's brother's child (MBCh), but not both.

ASYMMETRIC-PRESCRIPTIVE SYSTEM: system requiring opposite-sex siblings to marry into different groups, preventing direct exchange of marriage partners of the same sex. For example, Group A gives its women to Group B, and Group B gives its men to Group A, but the sexes cannot be reversed. Three groups are thus minimally required (A → B → C → A). Also known as a system with indirect or generalized exchange.

BIFURCATE-MERGING: type of kin terminology in which F and FB are "merged"—called by the same term—and both are distinguished from MB, who is called by a different term (reflecting "bifurcation" between "parallel" and "cross"-kin); M and MZ are similarly merged, and distinguished from FZ. Primarily used for Iroquois and Dravidian systems, secondarily for Crow and Omaha.

BILATERAL KINDRED: group based on ties through both F and M, and lacking a rule of unilineal descent.

BRIDEWEALTH: prescribed marriage payment from the groom's kin to the bride's.

CHEYENNE: type of kinship terminology in which crossness is recognized in above and below generations but not in one's own.

CLASSIFICATORY SYSTEMS: kinship terminologies merging lineal kin (e.g., F, M) with collateral kin (e.g., FB, MZ).

COGNATIC KIN: relatives on one's mother's and father's sides with no distinction made between male or female links.

COLLATERAL KIN: kin linked to ego outside a direct line of descent (e.g., FB, FMB, MMZ, BD, ZS).

COMPLEX STRUCTURE: a system of kinship whose only rules for marriage are negative, that is, proscribing marriage within a narrow circle of consanguines.

CONSANGUINES: kin by "blood," that is, descendants of a common ancestor.

CROSS-COUSINS: MBCh, FZCh.

CROSS-KIN: kin to ego via an opposite-sex link to a collateral relative (e.g., FZCh, MBCh, FFZS, MMBD).

CROSSNESS: differentiation of all relatives as either cross or parallel (via bifurcate-merging terminology). The two basic types of crossness are Dravidian (Type A) and Iroquois (Type B).

CROSS-PARALLEL NEUTRALIZATION: a rule or practice eliminating terminological differentiation of cross- and parallel kin, typically in one generation, for example, in ego's generation in a Cheyenne system.

CROW: a terminological type characterized by "lineal equations" that skew identifications of kin through generations down a matrilineal descent line (e.g., FZ = FM = FZD = FZDD, F = FMB = FZS = FZSS).

DESCENT GROUPS: social action groups comprised by a common principle of descent, typically unilineal, that is, patrilineal or matrilineal.

DESCRIPTIVE SYSTEMS: kinship terminologies that distinguish lineal kin (e.g., F, M) from collateral kin (e.g., FB, MZ). Morgan's category "descriptive"—as opposed to classificatory—is principally applied to Eskimo and Sudanese terminologies.

DISPERSED AFFINAL ALLIANCE: type of marriage alliance associated with semi-complex systems, that disperses marriages among kin groups in a changing, generally nonpredictable pattern from one generation to the next.

DOUBLE DESCENT: system in which kin relationships through both a matriline and a patriline are emphasized for different purposes.

DRAVIDIAN: a terminological type characterized by crossness that equates cross-kin with affines (MB = FZH, ♂MBD = ♂FZD = ♂W, etc.) typically associated with a rule of prescriptive cross-cousin marriage.

DRAVIDIANATE: underlying system of Dravidian pattern.

EGOCENTRIC: specification of kinship relationships relative to a particular person, an "ego"; regarding kinship systems, typically associated with cognatic groups, and contrasted with sociocentric.

ELEMENTARY STRUCTURE: a system of kinship with rules that prescribe marriage with a specific category of relative, for example, typically, a cross-cousin.

ESKIMO: a terminological type characterized by distinctions of lineal kin (e.g., F, M) from collateral kin (e.g., FB, MZ) that lacks crossness. Globally a widespread type, typical of contemporary North American and European societies.

GENERATIONAL MOIETIES: groupings that link all relatives of alternate generations for certain purposes, distinguishing them from those of intermediate generations. Thus one's parents' generation belongs to the same moiety as one's children's, and one's own generation is in the same moiety as one's grandparents and grandchildren.

HAWAIIAN (GENERATIONAL): a terminological type characterized by distinctions only of gender and generation, lacking both crossness and lineality (e.g., F = MB = FB, M = MZ = FZ, MBCh = MZCh = FBCh = FZCh, ZCh = BCh = Ch).

HAWAIIANIZATION: elimination of a distinction of cross- versus parallel relatives, typically for one generation; also known as cross-parallel neutralization.

HOUSE SOCIETIES (*sociétés à maison*): societies in which significant social groups are not based on a distinctive kinship rule, but include relatives by descent or affinity or often both; following the model of European noble houses, Lévi-Strauss coined the term to describe northwest coast cultures like Kwakwaka'wakw and Salish that lack a principle of unilineal descent.

HYPERGAMY: marrying "up," in a ranked or stratified society.

IROQUOIS: a terminological type characterized by crossness (e.g., F = FB ≠ MB, M = MZ ≠ FZ), that allows marriage with cross-kin but does not prescribe it, and makes no terminological equations between cross-kin and affines (so, unlike Dravidian, MB ≠ FZH, ♂MBD ≠ ♂W, etc.)

LINEAL KIN: kin linked to ego through a direct line of descent (e.g., F, FF, M, MM, DS, DDS, SDS).

MATRILINEAL DESCENT: a rule that relatives are traced through a line of women (e.g., M-MM-MMM). May be the basis for corporate groups known as matrilineal descent groups.

MATRILOCAL: postmarital residence with or near the bride's parents.

MATRI-UXORILOCALITY: postmarital residence with the wife's mother.

MOIETIES: a division of society into two halves, often but not always composed by a rule of descent.

NIBLINGS: nephews and nieces.

OMAHA: a terminological type characterized by "lineal equations" that skew identifications of kin through generations down a patrilineal descent line (e.g., MF = MB = MBS, MZ = MBD = MBSD).

PARALLEL KIN: kin to ego via same-sex links to a collateral relative (e.g., FBCh, MZCh, FFBCh, MMZDCh).

PATRILINEAL DESCENT: a rule that relatives are traced through a line of men (e.g., F-FF-FFF). May be the basis for corporate groups known as patrilineal descent groups.

PATRILOCAL: postmarital residence with or near the groom's parents.

POLYGYNY: a man's marriage with more than one woman at the same time.

PRESCRIPTIVE: used of kinship systems with a rule that marriage must be with a specific category of relative, for example, a cross-cousin.

SEMI-COMPLEX STRUCTURE: a system of kinship combining elementary (positive) and complex (negative) marriage rules. Marriage is not prescribed with a specific category of relative, but in these small-scale societies, a substantial proportion of potential mates are off-limits (as classificatory "consanguines"): the effect is an almost positive rule, allowing marriage within a limited remaining class. Prohibitions shift with each generation, depending on the specific alliance created by the parents' marriage. Thus no predictable system of exchange (either direct, indirect, or generalized) is involved.

SISTER-EXCHANGE: a system of marriage in which two groups arrange marriages between brother-sister pairs: sister A marries brother B; sister B marries brother A. Often associated with moieties composed by a rule of descent.

SKEWING/LINEAL EQUATIONS: the merging of kin down a unilineal descent line, as in terminologies of Crow or Omaha type.

Glossary

SOCIOCENTRIC: specification of kinship relationships relative to a particular group (e.g., one's clan, as related to other clans), and its place within the society as a whole, rather than from the perspective of individual relationships. Regarding kinship systems, typically associated with unilineal descent groups, and contrasted with egocentric.

SUDANESE: a terminological type that distinguishes lineal kin (e.g., F, M) from collateral kin (e.g., FB, MZ) and assigns each kinship position its own separate term, with no "classificatory" merging of categories (so F ≠ MB ≠ FB, M ≠ MZ ≠ FZ, MBD ≠ MZD ≠ FBD ≠ FZD).

UNILINEAL DESCENT: a rule that relatives are traced through a same-sex line, either of men (e.g., F-FF-FFF)—patrilineal—or of women (e.g., M-MM-MMM)—matrilineal. May be the basis for corporate groups known as unilineal descent groups.

References

Allen, Nicholas J.
- 1975. Byansi Kinship Terminology: A Study in Symmetry. *Man* 10:80–94.
- 1976. Sherpa Kinship Terminology in Diachronic Perspective. *Man* 11:569–587.
- 1982. A Dance of Relatives. *Journal of the Anthropological Society of Oxford* 13:139–146.
- 1986. Tetradic Theory: An Approach to Kinship. *Journal of the Anthropological Society of Oxford* 17:87–109.
- 1989. The Evolution of Kinship Terminologies. *Lingua* 77:173–185.
- 1998a. The Prehistory of Dravidian-Type Terminologies. In *Transformations of Kinship*. Maurice Godelier, Thomas R. Trautmann, and Franklin E. Tjon Sie Fat, eds. Pp. 314–331. Washington: Smithsonian Institution Press.
- 1998b. The Category of Substance: A Maussian Theme Revisited. In *Marcel Mauss: A Centenary Tribute*. Wendy James and Nicholas J. Allen, eds. Pp. 175–191. Oxford: Berghahn.
- 1999. Hinduism, Structuralism and Dumézil. In *Miscellanea Indo-Europea*. E.C. Polomé ed. Pp. 241–260. Washington: Institute for the Study of Man.
- 2000. Primitive Classification: The Argument and its Validity. In *Categories and Classifications: Maussian Reflections on the Social*. Nicholas J. Allen, ed. Pp. 39–60. Oxford: Berghahn.
- 2004. Tetradic Theory: An Approach to Kinship. In *Kinship and Family: An Anthropological Reader*. Robert Parkin and Linda Stone, eds. Pp. 221–235. Oxford: Blackwell.
- 2005. Thomas McEvilley: The Missing Dimension. *International Journal of Hindu Studies* 9:59–75.
- 2007a. The Pāṇḍavas' Five Journeys and the Structure of the Mahābhārata. *Religions of South Asia* 1(2):165–181.
- 2007b. The Heimdall-Dyu Comparison Revisited. *Journal of Indo-European Studies* 35:233–247.
- 2008. Tetradic Theory and the Origin of Human Kinship Systems. In *Early Human Kinship: From Sex to Social Reproduction*. Nicholas J. Allen, Hilary Callan, Robin Dunbar, and Wendy James, eds. Oxford: Blackwell.

Allen, Nicholas J., Hilary Callan, Robin Dunbar, and Wendy James, eds.
- 2008. *Early Human Kinship: From Sex to Social Reproduction*. Malden, MA: Blackwell.

Alpher, Barry
 2004. Pama-Nyungan Etyma. Appendix 5.1, CD ROM. *Australian Languages and the Comparative Method.* Claire Bowern and Harold Koch, eds. Amsterdam: John Benjamins.

Apoio AER de Colider (MT) e Coordenação de Educação
 2007. *Atlas dos territórios Mebêngôkre, Panará e Tapajúna [Mebêngôkre me Panará me Tapajúna nhô puk Krô neja].* Programa de formação de professores Mebêngôkre, Panará e Tapajúna. Brasília: Fundação Nacional do Indio.

Atkinson, Ronald R.
 1994. *The Roots of Ethnicity: Origins of the Acholi of Uganda before 1900.* Philadelphia: University of Pennsylvania Press.

Avery, John
 1985. *The Law People: History and Initiation in the Borrolola Area.* Ph.D. diss., University of Sydney.
 2002. Jura Conjugalia Reconsidered: Kinship Classification and Ceremonial Roles in Adjacent Aboriginal Populations in the Northern Territory of Australia. *Anthropological Forum* 12(2):221–232.

Barbosa de Almeida, Mauro William
 2010. On the Structure of Dravidian Relationship Systems. *Mathematical Anthropology and Cultural Theory* 3(1). www.MathematicalAnthropology.org
 forthcoming. The Structure of Dravidian, Iroquois and Crow-Omaha Kinship Terminologies: A Unified Approach. *Mathematical Anthropology and Cultural Theory.* www.MathematicalAnthropology.org

Barnard, Alan
 2008. The Co-Evolution of Language and Kinship. In *Early Human Kinship: From Sex to Social Reproduction.* Nicholas J. Allen, Hilary Callan, Robin Dunbar, and Wendy James, eds. Pp. 232–243. Malden, MA: Blackwell.

Barnes, Robert H.
 1974. *Kédang: A Study of the Collective Thought of an Eastern Indonesian People.* Oxford: Clarendon Press.
 1975. Editor's Introduction. In Josef Kohler, *On the Prehistory of Marriage: Totemism, Group Marriage, Mother Right.* Robert H. Barnes, ed., Robert H. Barnes and Ruth Barnes, trans. Chicago: University of Chicago Press.
 1976. Dispersed Alliance and the Prohibition of Marriage: Reconsideration of McKinley's Explanation of Crow-Omaha Terminologies. *Man* 11(3): 384–399.
 1980. Marriage, Exchange and the Meaning of Corporations in Eastern Indonesia. In *The Meaning of Marriage Payments.* John L. Comaroff, ed. London: Academic Press.

1982. Kinship Exercises. *Culture* 2(2):113–117.
1984. Two Crows Denies It: A History of Controversy in Omaha Sociology. Lincoln: University of Nebraska Press.
2005 [1984]. *Two Crows Denies It: A History of Controversy in Omaha Sociology.* New edition with introduction by R. J. DeMallie. Lincoln: University of Nebraska Press.
2012. What Is Left Out in Kinship. In *The Scope of Anthropology: Maurice Godelier's Work in Context.* Laurent Dousset and Serge Tcherkézoff, eds. Oxford: Berghahn.

Barry, Laurent S.
2008. *La parenté*. Paris: Gallimard.

Beattie, John H. M.
1957. Nyoro Kinship. *Africa* 27:317–340.
1958. Nyoro Marriage and Affinity. *Africa* 28:1–22.

Borgerhoff-Mulder, Monique
2001. Using Phylogenetically Based Comparative Methods in Anthropology: More Questions than Answers. *Evolutionary Anthropology* 10:99–111.

Borgerhoff-Mulder, Monique, Charles L. Nunn, and Mary C. Towner
2006. Macroevolutionary Studies of Cultural Trait Variation: The Importance of Transmission Mode. *Evolutionary Anthropology* 15:52–64.

Bowden, Ross
1983. Kwoma Terminology and Marriage Alliance: The "Omaha" Problem Revisited. *Man* 18(4):745–765.

Bruce, James
1804. *Travels to Discover the Sources of the Nile, in the Years 1768–1773*, 2nd rev. ed. Edinburgh: Constable.

Burke, Peter
2005. *Law's Anthropology: From Ethnography to Expert Testimony in Three Native Title Claims*. Ph.D. diss., Australian National University.

Burling, Robbins
1971. The Historical Place of Jinghpaw in Tibeto-Burman. *Occasional Papers of the Wolfenden Society on Tibeto-Burman Linguistics* 2:1–54.

Callan, Hilary
2008. Reaching across the Gaps. In *Early Human Kinship: From Sex to Social Reproduction*. Nicholas J. Allen, Hilary Callan, Robin Dunbar, and Wendy James, eds. Pp. 247–258. Oxford: Blackwell.

Carneiro, Robert
1970. A Theory of the Origin of the State. *Science* 169:733–738.

Carsten, Janet, and Stephen Hugh-Jones
1995. Introduction. In *About the House: Lévi-Strauss and Beyond*. Janet Carsten and Stephen Hugh-Jones, eds. Pp. 1–46. New York: Cambridge University Press.

Chapais, Bernard
- 2008. *Primeval Kinship: How Pair-Bonding Gave Birth to Human Society.* Cambridge: Harvard University Press.

Christensen, James Boyd
- 1954. *Double Descent among the Fanti.* New Haven: Human Relations Area Files.

Collard, Mark, Stephen J. Shennan, and Jamshid J. Tehrani
- 2006. Branching, Blending, and the Evolution of Cultural Similarities and Differences among Human Populations. *Evolution and Human Behavior* 27:169–184.

Copet-Rougier, Élisabeth
- 1987. "L'antilope accouche toujours de l'éléphant" (devinette Mkako): Etude de la transformation du marriage ches les Mkako du Cameroun. In *Transformations of African Marriage.* David Parkin and David Nyamwaya, eds. Pp. 75–92. Manchester: Manchester University Press for the International African Institute.
- 1990. Le clan, le lieu, l'alliance. In *Les complexités de l'alliance I: Les systèmes semi-complexes.* Françoise Hériter-Augé and Élisabeth Copet-Rougier, eds. Pp. 193–231. Paris: Éditions des Archives contemporaines.

Costa, David J.
- 1999. The Kinship Terminology of the Miami-Illinois Language. *Anthropological Linguistics* 41(1):28–53.

Crocker, William H.
- 1990. *The Canela (Eastern Timbira). I. An Ethnographic Introduction.* Washington: Smithsonian Institution.

Da Matta, Roberto
- 1979. The Apinayé Relationship System: Terminology and Ideology. In *Dialectical Societies: The Gê and Bororo of Central Brazil.* D. Maybury-Lewis, ed. Pp. 83–127. Cambridge: Harvard University Press.
- 1982. *A Divided World.* A. Campbell, trans. Cambridge: Harvard University Press.

Darwin, Charles R.
- 1859. *On the Origin of Species.* London: John Murray.

Denham, Woodrow W., Chad McDaniel, and John R. Atkins
- 1979. Aranda and Alyawarra Kinship: A Quantitative Argument for a Double Helix Model. *American Ethnologist* 6(1):1–24.

Denham, Woodrow W., and Douglas R. White
- 2005. Multiple Measures of Alyawarra Kinship. *Field Methods* 17:70–101. DOI: 10.1177/1525822X04271610.

Distefano, John Albert
- 1985. *The Precolonial History of the Kalenjin of Kenya: A Methodological Comparison of Linguistic and Oral Traditional Evidence.* Ph.D. diss., University of California, Los Angeles.

Dole, Gertrude E.
   1972. Developmental Sequences of Kinship Patterns. In *Kinship Studies in the Morgan Centennial Year*. Priscilla Reining, ed. Pp. 134–166. Washington: Anthropological Society of Washington.

Dorsey, J. O.
   1884. *Omaha Sociology.* Third Annual Report of the Bureau of American Ethnology (1881–82). Pp. 205–370. Washington: Government Printing Office.

Dousset, Laurent
   1999. L'alliance de mariage et la promesse d'épouses chez les Ngaatjatjarra du Désert de l'Ouest Australien. *Journal de la Société des Océanistes* 108:3–17.
   2002a. Accounting for Context and Substance: The Australian Western Desert Kinship System. *Anthropological Forum* 12(2):193–204.
   2002b. Politics and Demography in a Contact Situation: The Establishment of Giles Meteorological Station in the Rawlinson Ranges. *Aboriginal History* 26:1–22.
   2003. On the Misinterpretation of the Aluridja Kinship System Type (Australian Western Desert). *Social Anthropology* 11(1):43–61.
   2005. *Assimilating Identities: Social Networks and the Diffusion of Sections*. Monograph 57. Sydney: Oceania Publications.
   2008. The "Global" versus the "Local": Cognitive Processes of Kin Determination in Aboriginal Australia. *Oceania* 78(3):260–279.
   2011. *Mythes, missiles et cannibales: Le récit d'un premier contact en Australie*. Paris: Société des Océanistes.

Dousset, Laurent, and Katie Glaskin
   2007. Western Desert and Native Title: How Models Become Myths. *Anthropological Forum* 17(2):127–148.

Dumont, Louis
   1953. The Dravidian Kinship Terminology as an Expression of Marriage. *Man* 54(1):34–39.

Durkheim, Emile
   1898. Zur Urgeschichte der Ehe. Prof. J. Kohler. *L'Année Sociologique* 1:306–319.

Dziebel, German Valentinovich
   2007. *The Genius of Kinship: The Phenomenon of Human Kinship and the Global Diversity of Kinship Terminologies*. Youngstown, NY: Cambria.

Eggan, Fred R.
   1937a. The Cheyenne and Arapaho Kinship System. In *Social Anthropology of North American Tribes*. Fred R. Eggan, ed. Pp. 35–98. Chicago: University of Chicago Press.
   1937b. Historical Changes in the Choctaw Kinship System. *American Anthropologist* 39(1):34–52.

1937c.   Ed., *Social Anthropology of North American Tribes*. Chicago: University of Chicago Press.

1950.   *Social Organization of the Western Pueblos*. Chicago: University of Chicago Press.

1964.   Alliance and Descent in a Western Pueblo Society. In *Process and Pattern in Culture: Essays in Honor of Julian Steward*. Robert A. Manners, ed. Pp. 175–184. Chicago: Aldine.

1972.   Lewis Henry Morgan's *Systems*: A Reevaluation. In *Kinship Studies in the Morgan Centennial Year*. Priscilla Reining, ed. Pp. 1–16. Washington: Anthropological Society of Washington.

Ehret, Christopher

1983.   Population Movement and Culture Contact in the Southern Sudan, c. 3000 BC to AD 1000. In *Culture History in the Southern Sudan*. John Mack and Peter Robertshaw, eds. Pp. 19–48. Nairobi: British Institute in Eastern Africa.

1993.   Nilo-Saharans and the Saharo-Sudanese Neolithic. In *The Archeology of Africa: Food, Metals and Towns*. T. Shaw, P. Sinclair, B. Andah, and A. Okpoko, eds. Pp. 104–125. London: Routledge.

2006.   Linguistic Stratigraphies and Holocene History in Northeastern Africa. In *Archaeology of Early Northeastern Africa*. Marek Chlodnicki and Karla Kroeper, eds. Pp. 1019–1055. Posnan: Posnan Archaeological Museum.

2008.   Reconstructing Ancient Kinship in Africa. In *Early Human Kinship: From Sex to Social Reproduction*. Nicholas J. Allen, Hilary Callan, Robin Dunbar, and Wendy James, eds. Pp. 200–269. Oxford: Blackwell.

2010.   Reconstructing Ancient Kinship: Practice and Theory in an African Case Study. In *Kinship, Language, and Prehistory: Per Hage and the Renaissance in Kinship Studies*. Doug Jones and Bojka Milicic, eds. Salt Lake City: University of Utah Press.

Ehret, Christopher, T. Coffman, L. Fliegelman, A. Gold, M. Hubbard, D. Johnson, and D. E. Saxon

1974.   Some Thoughts on the Early History of the Nile-Congo Watershed. *Ufahamu* 5(2):85–112.

Elkin, Adolphus P.

1932.   Social Organization in the Kimberley Division, Northwestern Australia. Oceania 2(3):296–333.

1938–40.   Kinship in South Australia. *Oceania* 8(4):419–452; 9(1):41–78; 10(2):196–234; 10(3):295–349; 10(4):369–389.

Ensor, Bradley

2002.   Disproportionate Clan Growth in Crow-Omaha Societies: A Kinship-Demographic Model for Explaining Settlement Hierarchies and Fissioning in the Prehistoric U.S. Southeast. *North American Archaeologist* 23(4):309–337.

Evans-Pritchard, Edward E.
  1965. *Theories of Primitive Religion*. Oxford: Oxford University Press.
Eyde, David B., and Paul M. Postal
  1961. Avunculocality and Incest: The Development of Unilateral Cross-Cousin Marriage and Crow-Omaha Kinship Systems. *American Anthropologist* 63(4):747–71.
Fardon, Richard
  1984–85. Sisters, Wives, Wards and Daughters: A Transformational Analysis of the Political Organization of the Tiv and their Neighbours. Parts I and II. *Africa* 54:2–21 and 55:77–91.
  1993. Alliance et ethnicité: Un système régionale de l'Adamawa. In *Les complexités de l'alliance*, vol. 3. Françoise Héritier and Élisabeth Copet-Rougier, eds. Paris: Editions des Archives Contemporaines.
Farris, James S.
  1982. The Logical Basis of Phylogenetic Analysis. In *Advances in Cladistics*. Norman I. Platnick and V. A. Funk, eds. Proceedings of the Second Meeting of the Willi Hennig Society, vol. 2, pp. 7–36. New York: Columbia University Press.
Feinberg, Richard, and Martin Oppenheimer, eds.
  2001. *The Cultural Analysis of Kinship: The Legacy of David M. Schneider*. Urbana: University of Illinois Press.
Felsenstein, Joseph
  1973. Maximum Likelihood and Minimum-Steps Methods for Estimating Evolutionary Trees from Data on Discrete Characters. *Systematic Zoology* 22:240–249.
Firth, Raymond
  1957. A Note on Descent Groups in Polynesia. *Man* 57(2):4–8.
Fischer, Michael
  n.d. Ethnographic Atlas Cross-Tabulations: The Standard Cross-Cultural Sample. Centre for Social Anthropology and Computing. Canterbury: University of Kent at Canterbury (http://stirling.kent.ac.uk/sac/bt68/The%20final%20cross%20tabulation.html).
Fison, Lorimer, and Alfred W. Howitt
  1991 [1880]. *Kamilaroi and Kurnai: Group-Marriage and Relationship, and Marriage by Elopement, Drawn Chiefly from the Usage of the Australian Aborigines, also the Kurnai Tribe: Their Customs in Peace and War*. Canberra: AIATSIS.
Fletcher, Alice C., and Francis La Flesche
  1911. *The Omaha Tribe*. Twenty-Seventh Annual Report of the Bureau of American Ethnology (1905–1906). Pp. 17–654. Washington: Government Printing Office.
Fortes, Meyer
  1950. Kinship and Marriage among the Ashanti. In *African Systems of Kinship*

and Marriage. A. R. Radcliffe-Brown and Daryll Forde, eds. Pp. 252–284. London: Oxford University Press.

Forth, Gregory L.
  1981. *Rindi: An Ethnographic Study of a Traditional Domain in Eastern Sumba.* Verhandelingen van het Koninklijk Instituut voor Taal-, Land- en Volkenkunde 93. The Hague: Nijhoff.
  2008. Miwok Mysteries: The Question of Aymmetric Prescriptive Marriage in Aboriginal North America. *Ethnology* 47(1):61–83.

Fortunato, Laura, Clare Holden, and Ruth Mace
  2006. From Bridewealth to Dowry? A Bayesian Estimation of Ancestral States of Marriage Transfers in Indo-European Groups. *Human Nature* 17: 355–376.

Fortunato, Laura, and Ruth Mace
  2009. Testing Functional Hypotheses about Cross-Cultural Variation: A Maximum-Likelihood Comparative Analysis of Indo-European Marriage Practices. In *Pattern and Process in Cultural Evolution.* Stephen J. Shennan, ed. Pp. 235–249. Berkeley: University of California Press.

Foster, Michael
  1997. Language and the Culture History of North America. In *Handbook of North American Indians*, vol. 17, Languages. Pp. 64–110. Washington: Smithsonian Institution.

Fox, Robin
  1967. *The Keresan Bridge: A Problem in Pueblo Ethnology.* L.S.E. Monographs on Social Anthropology 35. London: Athlone.
  1972. Some Unsolved Problems of Pueblo Social Organization. In *New Perspectives on the Pueblos.* A. Ortiz, ed. Pp. 71–85. Albuquerque: University of New Mexico Press.
  1994. The Evolution of Kinship Systems and the Crow-Omaha Question. In *The Challenge of Anthropology: Old Encounters and New Excursions.* Robin Fox, ed. Pp. 215–245. New Brunswick: Transaction.

Franklin, Sarah, and Susan McKinnon, eds.
  2000. *Relative Values: Reconfiguring Kinship Studies.* Durham: Duke University Press.

Freire-Marreco, Barbara
  1914. Tewa Kinship Terms from the Pueblo of Hano, Arizona. *American Anthropologist* 16(2):269–287.

Fürer-Haimendorf, Christoph von
  1964. *The Sherpas of Nepal: Buddhist Highlanders.* London: John Murray.

Gell, Alfred
  1975. *Metamorphosis of the Cassowaries: Umeda Society, Language and Ritual.* London: Athlone.

Gifford, Edward Winslow
 1916. *Miwok Moieties*. University of California Publications in American Archaeology and Ethnology 12:4. Berkeley: University of California Press.
Gilhodes, Charles
 1913. Mariage et Condition de la Femme chez les Katchins (Birmanie). *Anthropos* 8:363–375.
 1922. *The Kachins, Religion and Customs*. Calcutta: Catholic Mission Press.
Goddard, Ives
 1978. Central Algonquian Languages. In *Handbook of American Indians*, vol. 15, Northeast. Bruce Trigger, ed., William Sturtevant, general ed. Pp. 583–587. Washington: Smithsonian Institution.
Goddard, Ives, ed.
 1997. *Handbook of North American Indians*, vol. 17, Languages. Washington: Smithsonian Institution.
Godelier, Maurice
 1986. *The Making of Great Men: Male Domination and Power among the New Guinea Baruya*. Cambridge: Cambridge University Press.
 2004. *Métamorphoses de la parenté*. Paris: Fayard.
 2011. The Metamorphoses of Kinship. New York: Verso.
Godelier, Maurice, Thomas R. Trautmann, and Franklin E. Tjon Sie Fat, eds.
 1998. *Transformations of Kinship*. Washington: Smithsonian Institution Press.
Golla, Victor
 2007. Linguistic Prehistory. In *California Prehistory: Colonization, Culture and Complexity*. Terry L. Jones and Kathryn A. Klar, eds. Pp. 71–82. Lanham, MD: AltaMira Press.
Good, Anthony
 1991. *The Female Bridegroom: A Comparative Study of Life-Crisis Rituals in South India and Sri Lanka*. Oxford: Clarendon.
Goody, Jack
 1961. The Classification of Double Descent Systems. *Current Anthropology* 2(1):3–25.
Gould, Richard A.
 1969. Subsistence Behavior among the Western Desert Aborigines of Australia. *Oceania* 39(4):253–274.
Gould, Sydney H.
 2000. *A New System for the Formal Analysis of Kinship*. David B. Kronenfeld, ed. Lanham, MD: University Press of America.
Granet, Marcel
 1939. Catégories matrimoniales et relations de proximité dans la Chine ancienne. *Annales sociologiques*, Série B, *Sociologie réligieuse,* fasic. 1.

Gray, J. Patrick
    1999. A Corrected Ethnographic Atlas. *World Cultures* 10:24–136.
Green, Jennifer
    1998. *Kin and Country: Aspects of the Use of Kinterms in Arandic Languages*. Master's thesis, University of Melbourne.
Greenberg, Joseph H.
    1966. *Language Universals with Special Reference to Feature Hierarchies*. Janua Linguarum no. 59. The Hague: Mouton.
Haeckel, Ernst
    1866. *Generelle Morphologie der Organismen: Allgemeine Grundzüger der organischen Formen-Wissenschaft, mechanisch begründet durch die von C. Darwin reformirte Decendenz-Theorie*. Berlin: G. Reimer.
Hage, Per
    1999. Marking Universals and the Structure and Evolution of Kinship Terminologies: Evidence from Salish. *Journal of the Royal Anthropological Institute* 5:423–441.
    2001. Marking Theory and Kinship Analysis: Cross-Cultural and Historical Implications. *Anthropological Theory* 1(2):197–211.
    2006. Dravidian Kinship Systems in Africa. *L'Homme* 177–78:395–408.
Hage, Per, and Frank Harary
    1998. Applications of the Minimum Spanning Tree Problem to Network Analysis. In *Kinship, Networks and Exchange*. Thomas Schweizer and Douglas R. White, eds. Pp. 251–260. New York: Cambridge University Press.
Hallowell, A. Irving
    1928. Recent Changes in the Kinship Terminology of the St. Francis Abenaki. *Atti del XXII Congresso Internazionale degli Americanisti, Roma 1926 (I)*: 97–145. Rome: Riccardo Garroni.
    1930. Was Cross-Cousin Marriage Practised by the North-Central Algonkian? *Proceedings of the Twenty-third International Congress of Americanists, New York 1928:* 519–544. Lancaster, PA: The Science Press.
    1937. Cross-Cousin Marriage in the Lake Winnipeg Area. In *Contributions to Anthropology: Selected Papers of A. Irving Hallowell*. Chicago: University of Chicago Press, 1975. Pp. 317–350.
Hamberger, Klaus, Michael Houseman, and Cyril Grange
    2009. La parenté radiographiée: Un nouveau logiciel pour l'analyse des réseaux matrimoniaux. *L'Homme* 191:107–138.
Hammel, Eugene A.
    1965. An Algorithm for Crow-Omaha Solutions. *American Anthropologist* 67(5, part II):118–126.
    2005. Kinship-Based Politics and the Optimal Size of Kin Groups. *Proceedings of the National Academy of Sciences USA* 102(33):11951–11956.

Hanson, Ola
    1913. *The Kachins, their Customs and Traditions.* Rangoon: A. B. M. Press.

Hasegawa, Masami, Hirohisa Kashina, and Taka-aki Yano
    1985. Dating the Human-Ape Splitting by a Molecular Clock of Mitochondrial DNA. *Journal of Molecular Evolution* 22:160–174.

Heath, Jeffrey
    1981. *Basic Materials in Mara: Grammar, Texts and Dictionary.* Canberra: Pacific Linguistics. C60.
    1982. *Nunggubuyu Dictionary.* Canberra: AIAS.
    1984. *Functional Grammar of Nunggubuyu.* Canberra: AIAS.

Héran, François
    2009. *Figures de la parenté: Une historie critique de la raison structurale.* Paris: Presses Universitaires de France.

Héritier, Françoise
    1974. Systèmes Omaha de parenté et d'alliance: Étude en ordinateur du fonctionnement matrimonial réel d'une société africaine. In *Genealogical Mathematics.* Paul Ballonoff, ed. The Hague: Mouton.
    1975. L'ordinateur et l'étude du fonctionnement matrimonial d'un système Omaha. In *Les Domaines de la parenté.* Marc Augé, ed. Pp. 95–117. Paris: Maspero.
    1976. Contribution a la théorie de l'alliance: Comment fonctionnent les systèmes d'alliance Omaha. *Informatique et Sciences Humaines* 29:10–46.
    1981. *L'Exercice de la parenté.* Paris: Gallimard, Le Seuil.
    1999. *Two Sisters and Their Mother.* Jeanine Herman, trans. New York: Zone Books.
    2000. Articulations et substances. *L'Homme* 154–155:21–38.

Héritier-Augé, Françoise, and Élisabeth Copet-Rougier, eds.
    1990–94. *Les complexités de l'alliance.* 4 vols. Paris: Editions des Archives Contemporaines.

Hertz, Henry F.
    1915. *A Practical Handbook of the Kachin or Chingpaw Language etc. with an Appendix on Kachin Customs, Laws and Religion.* Rangoon: Government Printing Office.

Hodson, Thomas C.
    1925. Notes on the Marriage of Cousins in India. *Man in India* 5:163–175.

Holden, Clare J., and Ruth Mace
    2003. Spread of Cattle Led to the Loss of Matrilineal Descent in Africa: A Coevolutionary Analysis. *Proceedings, Royal Society of London, Biological Sciences* 270(1532):2425–2433.
    2005. "The Cow Is the Enemy of Matriliny": Using Phylogenetic Methods to Investigate Cultural Evolution in Africa. In *The Evolution of Cultural Diversity: A Phylogenetic Approach.* Ruth Mace, Clare J. Holden, and

Stephen Shennan, eds. Pp. 217–234. London: University College Press.

Holden, Clare J., Andrew Meade, and Mark Pagel
  2005. Comparison of Maximum Parsimony and Bayesian Bantu Language Trees. In *The Evolution of Cultural Diversity: A Phylogenetic Approach*. Ruth Mace, Clare J. Holden, and Stephen Shennan, eds. Pp. 53–66. London: University College Press.

Holmer, Nils M.
  1967. *An Attempt towards a Comparative Grammar of two Australian Languages. Part II. Indices and Vocabularies of Kattang and Thangatti*. Number 5. Linguistic series 3m part II. Canberra: Australian Institute of Aboriginal Studies,

Honigmann, John Joseph
  1954. *The Kaska Indians: An Ethnographic Reconstruction*. Yale University Publications in Anthropology 51. New Haven: Yale University.

Howitt, Alfred W.
  1996. [1904] *The Native Tribes of South-East Australia*. Canberra and London: Aboriginal Studies Press, Macmillan.

Ives, John
  1998. Developmental Processes in the Pre-Contact History of Athapaskan, Algonquian and Numic Kin Systems. In *Transformations of Kinship*. Maurice Godelier, Thomas Trautmann and Franklin Tjon Sie Fat, eds. Pp. 94–139. Washington: Smithsonian Institution Press.

James, Wendy
  1975. Sister-Exchange Marriage. *Scientific American* 233(6):84–94.
  1979. *'Kwanim Pa: The Making of the Uduk People: An Ethnographic Study of Survival in the Sudan-Ethiopian Borderlands*. Oxford: Clarendon Press.
  1986. Lifelines: Exchange Marriage among the Gumuz. In *The Southern Marches of Imperial Ethiopia*. Wendy James and Donald Donham, eds. Pp. 119–147. African Studies Series 51. Cambridge: Cambridge University Press.
  2003. *The Ceremonial Animal: A New Portrait of Anthropology*. Oxford: Oxford University Press.
  2008. Alternating Birth Classes: A Note from Eastern Africa. In *Early Human Kinship: From Sex to Social Reproduction*. Nicholas J. Allen, Hilary Callan, Robin Dunbar and Wendy James, eds. Pp. 83–95. Oxford: Blackwell.

Jin, Guohua, Luay Nakhleh, Sagi Snir, and Tamir Tuller
  2006. Maximum Likelihood of Phylogenetic Networks. *Bioinformatics* 22: 2604–2611.

Johnson, Leroy, Jr.
  1994. Reconstructed Crow Terminology of the Titskanwatits, or Tonkawas,

with Inferred Social Correlates. *Plains Anthropologist* 39(150):377–413.

Jukes, Thomas H. and C. R. Cantor
1969. Evolution of Protein Molecules. In *Mammalian Protein Metabolism*. Hamish N. Munro, ed. Pp. 21–132. New York: Academic Press.

Karp, Richard M.
1972. Reducibility among Combinatorial Problems. In *Complexity of Computer Computation*. R. E. Miller and J. W. Thatcher, eds. Pp. 85–104. New York: Plenum Press.

Keen, Ian
1985. Definitions of Kin. *Journal of Anthropological Research* 41:62–90.
2002. Seven Aboriginal Marriage Systems and Their Correlates. *Anthropological Forum* 12(2):145–157.
2004. *Aboriginal Economy and Society: Australia at the Threshold of Colonisation*. Oxford: Oxford University Press.
Forthcoming. The Evolution of the Yolngu and Ngarinyin Kinship Terminologies: Models of Cumulative Transformations. In *Kinship Change and Reconstruction*. Patrick McConvell, Ian Keen, and Rachel Hendery, eds. Salt Lake City: University of Utah Press.

Kirchoff, Paul
1932. Verwandtschaftsbezeichnungen und Verwandtenheirat. *Zeitschrift für Ethnologie* 64:41–72.

Kohler, Josef
1897. *Zur Urgeschichte der Ehe: Totemismus, Gruppenehe, Mutterrecht*. Stuttgart: Ferdinand Enke.
1975 [1897]. *On the Prehistory of Marriage: Totemism, Group Marriage, Mother Right*. Robert H. Barnes, ed., Robert H. Barnes and Ruth Barnes, trans. Chicago: University of Chicago Press.

Kroeber, Alfred Louis
1909. Classificatory Systems of Relationship. *Journal of the Royal Anthropological Institute of Great Britain and Ireland* 39(1):11–22.
1917. Zuni Kin and Clan. *Anthropological Papers of the American Museum of Natural History* 18(2):39–204.
1954. Critical Summary and Comments. In *Method and Perspective in Anthropology: Papers in Honor of Wilson D. Wallis*. Robert F. Spencer, ed. Pp. 273–299. Minneapolis: University of Minnesota Press.

Kronenfeld, David B.
1973. Fanti Kinship: The Structure of Terminology and Behavior. *American Anthropologist* 75(5):1577–1595.
1980. Particularistic or Universalistic Analyses of Fanti Kin-Terminology: The Alternative Goals of Terminological Analysis. *Man* 15(1):151–169.

1989. Morgan vs. Dorsey on the Omaha Cross/Parallel Contrast: Theoretical Implications. *L'Homme* 29(1):76–106.

1991. Fanti Kinship: Language, Inheritance, and Kingroups. *Anthropos* 86: 19–31.

2001. Using Sydney H. Gould's Formalization of Kin Terminologies: Social Information, Skewing, and Structural Types. Theme issue, "Kinship," David B. Kronenfeld, guest editor. *Anthropological Theory* 1:173–196.

2009. *Fanti Kinship and the Analysis of Kinship Terminologies.* Urbana: University of Illinois Press.

Kryukov, Mikhail V.

1968. *Historical Interpretation of Kinship Terminology.* Moscow: Institute of Ethnography, USSR Academy of Sciences.

1998. The Synchro-Diachronic Method and the Multidirectionality of Kinship Transformations. In *Transformations of Kinship*. Maurice Godelier, Thomas R. Trautmann and Franklin E. Tjon Sie Fat, eds. Pp. 294–313. Washington: Smithsonian Institution Press.

Kuper, Adam

1982. African-Omaha: A Review Article. *Bijdragen tot de Taal-, Land- en Volkenkunde* 138:152–160.

Ladeira, Maria E.

1982. *A troca de nomes e a troca de cônjuges: Uma contribuição ao estudo do parentesco timbira.* Dissertação de mestrado, Universidade de São Paulo.

Lane, Robert, and Barbara Lane

1959. On the Development of Dakota-Iroquois and Crow-Omaha Kinship Terminologies. *Southwestern Journal of Anthropology* 15:254–265.

Larget, Bret, and Donald L. Simon

1999. Markov Chain Monte Carlo Algorithms for the Bayesian Analysis of Phylogenetic Trees. *Molecular Biology and Evolution* 16:750–759.

Lave, Jean

1979. Cycles and Trends in Krinkatí Naming Practices. In *Dialectical Societies: The Gê and Bororo of Central Brazil*. D. Maybury-Lewis, ed. Pp. 16–45. Cambridge: Harvard University Press.

Lea, Vanessa

1986. *Nomes e nekrets Kayapó: Uma concepção de riqueza.* Tese de Doutorado, Museu Nacional/UFRJ.

1995a. Casa-se do outro lado: Um modelo simulado da aliança mebengokre (Jê). In *Antropologia do Parentesco: Estudos Ameríndios*. E. B. Viveiros de Castro, ed. Pp. 321–359. Rio de Janeiro: Editora UFRJ.

1995b. The Houses of the Mebêngôkre (Kayapó) of Central Brazil—New Door to Their Social Organization. In *About the House: Lévi-Strauss and Beyond*. Janet Carsten and Stephen Hugh-Jones, eds. Pp. 206–225. Cambridge: Cambridge University Press.

2004. Aguçando o entendimento dos termos triádicos Mebêngôkre via os aborígenes australianos: Dialogando com Merlan e outros. *Liames (UNICAMP), Campinas* 4:29–42.

Leach, Edmund R.
- 1945. Jinghpaw Kinship Terminology: An Experiment in Ethnographic Algebra. *Journal of the Royal Anthropological Institute of Great Britain and Ireland* 75:59–72.
- 1951. The Structural Implications of Matrilateral Cross-Cousin Marriage. *Journal of the Royal Anthropological Institute* 81:23–55.
- 1957. Aspects of Bridewealth and Marriage Stability among the Kachin and Lakher. *Man* 57(59):50–55.
- 1961. *Rethinking Anthropology*. London: Athlone Press.

Lesser, Alexander
- 1929. Kinship Origins in the Light of Some Distributions. *American Anthropologist* 31(4):710–730.

Lévi-Strauss, Claude
- 1949. *Les structures élémentaires de la parenté*. Paris: Presses Universitaires de France.
- 1966. The Future of Kinship Studies. The Huxley Memorial Lecture. *Proceedings of the Royal Anthropological Institute*. Pp. 13–21. London: Royal Anthropological Institute.
- 1967. *Les structures élémentaires de la parenté* (2nd ed.). Paris: Mouton.
- 1969 [1949]. *The Elementary Structures of Kinship* (translation of *Les structures élémentaires de la parenté*). Rev. ed. Rodney Needham, ed. James Harle Bell and John Richard von Sturmer, trans. London: Eyre and Spottiswoode.
- 1982. *The Way of the Masks*. Sylvia Modelski, trans. Seattle: University of Washington Press.
- 1983. Histoire et ethnologie. *Annales: Histoire, Sciences Sociales* 38(6):1217–1231.

Lounsbury, Floyd G.
- 1964a. A Formal Account of the Crow- and Omaha-Type Kinship Terminologies. In *Explorations in Cultural Anthropology*. Ward H. Goodenough, ed. Pp. 351–393. New York: McGraw-Hill.
- 1964b. The Structural Analysis of Kinship Semantics. In *Proceedings of the Ninth International Congress of Linguists*. Horace G. Lunt, ed. Pp. 1073–1093. The Hague: Mouton.
- 1965. Another View of Trobriand Kinship Categories. *American Anthropologist* 67(5, part II):142–186.

Lowie, Robert H.
- 1912. Crow Social Life. *Anthropological Papers of the American Museum of Natural History* 9(2).
- 1917. *Culture and Ethnology*. New York: McMurtrie.

1928. A Note on Relationship Terminology. *American Anthropologist* 30(2): 263–267.

1929a. Hopi Kinship. *Anthropological Papers of the American Museum of Natural History* 30(7):361–388.

1929b. Notes on Hopi Clans. *Anthropological Papers of the American Museum of Natural History* 30(6):303–360.

1934. The Omaha and Crow Kinship Terminologies. *Verhandlungen des XXIV Internationalen Amerikanisten-Kongresses, Hamburg 1930:*103–108. Hamburg: Friederichsen, de Gruyter.

Lowie, Robert H., with Curt Nimuendajú

1943. A Note on the Social Life of the Northern Cayapo. *American Anthropologist* 45:633–636.

Lucich, Peter

1968. *The Development of Omaha Kinship Terminologies in Three Australian Aboriginal Tribes of the Kimberley Division, Western Australia.* Canberra: AIAS.

Lussier, Dominique

2000. *The Interpretation of Moral Inequality among the Kunama-speaking Communities of Western Eritrea.* Ph.D. thesis, Oxford University.

Malinowski, Bronislaw

1913. *The Family among the Australian Aborigines.* London: University of London Press.

Mallory, James P., and Douglas Q. Adams

2006. *Oxford Introduction to Proto-Indo-European and the Proto-Indo-European World.* Oxford: Oxford University Press.

Mathew, John

1887. Mary River and Bunya Bunya Country. In *The Australian Race: Its Origin, Languages, Customs, Place of Landing in Australia and the Routes by which it Spread Itself over that Continent.* Edward M. Curr, ed. Pp. 152–209. Melbourne: J. Ferres, Govt. Printer.

Maybury-Lewis, David, ed.

1979. *Dialectical Societies: The Gê and Bororo of Central Brazil.* Cambridge: Harvard University Press.

McConnell, Ursula

1950. Junior Marriage Systems: Comparative Survey. *Oceania* 21:107–145.

McConvell, Patrick

1982. Neutralisation and Degrees of Respect in Gurindji. In *Languages of Kinship in Aboriginal Australia.* Jeffrey Heath, Francesca Merlan, and Alan Rumsey, eds. Pp. 86–107. Oceania Linguistic Monographs 24. Sydney: University of Sydney Press.

1990. The Linguistic Prehistory of Australia: Opportunities for Dialogue with Archaeology. *Australian Archaeology* 31:3–27.

1997. Long-Lost Relations: Pama-Nyungan and Northern Kinship. In *Ar-*

chaeology and Linguistics: Aboriginal Australia in Global Perspective. Patrick McConvell and Nicholas Evans, eds. Pp. 207–236. Melbourne: Oxford University Press.

    2001. Language Shift and Language Spread among Hunter-Gatherers. In *Hunter-Gatherers: Social and Biological Perspectives.* Catherine Panter-Brick, Peter Rowley-Conwy and Robert Layton, eds. Pp. 143–169. Cambridge: Cambridge University Press.

    2010. The Archaeolinguistics of Migration. In *Migration History in World History: Multidisciplinary Approaches.* Jan Lucassen, Leo Lucassen, and Patrick Manning, eds. Pp. 155–190. Leiden: Brill.

McConvell, Patrick, and Barry Alpher

    2002. The Omaha Trail in Australia: Tracking Skewing from East to West. *Anthropological Forum* 12(2):159–176.

McConvell, Patrick, and Ian Keen

    2011. The Transition from Kariera to an Asymmetrical System: Cape York Peninsula to North-East Arnhemland. In *Kinship, Language, and Prehistory: Per Hage and the Renaissance in Kinship Studies.* Pp. 99–132. Douglas Jones and Bojka Milicic, eds. Salt Lake City: University of Utah Press.

McGee, W. J.

    1897. Introductory Note. In *Siouan Sociology: A Posthumous Paper by James Owen Dorsey.* Fifteenth Annual Report of the Bureau of American Ethnology (1893–94). Pp. 205–244. Washington: Government Printing Office.

McKinley, Robert

    1971a. A Critique of the Reflectionist Theory of Terminology: The Crow-Omaha Case. *Man* 6(2):228–247.

    1971b. Why Do Crow and Omaha Kinship Terminologies Exist? A Sociology of Knowledge Interpretation. *Man* 6(3):408–426.

McLennan, John F.

    1865. *Primitive Marriage: An Inquiry into the Origin of the Form of Capture in Marriage Ceremonies.* Edinburgh: Adam and Charles Black.

Mekonnen, Berihun Mebratie

    2004. *The Past in the Present: The Dynamics of Identity and Otherness among the Gumuz of Ethiopia.* Ph.D. thesis, Norwegian University of Science and Technology.

Melatti, Julio César

    1976. Nominadores e genitores: Um aspecto do dualismo krahó. In *Leituras de Etnologia Brasileira.* E. Schaden, ed. Pp. 139–148. São Paulo: Cia. Editora Nacional.

    1979. The Relationship System of the Krahó. In *Dialectical Societies: The Gê and Bororo of Central Brazil.* D. Maybury-Lewis, ed. Pp. 46–82. Cambridge: Harvard University Press.

Morgan, Lewis Henry
   1851. *League of the Ho-de-no-sau-nee, or Iroquois.* Rochester: Sage and Brother.
   1871. *Systems of Consanguinity and Affinity of the Human Family.* Washington: Smithsonian Institution.

Muller, Jean-Claude
   1980. Straight Sister-Exchange and the Transition from Elementary to Complex Structures. *American Ethnologist* 7:518–429.
   1997. A Crow Patrilineal System. The Dii of Mbe (Adamawa, North Cameroon): Essay in Methodological Triangulation. *Anthropologie et sociétés* 21(2/3):125–141.

Murdock, George Peter
   1949. *Social Structure.* New York: Macmillan.
   1967. *Ethnographic Atlas: A Summary.* Pittsburgh: University of Pittsburgh Press.
   1970. Kin Term Patterns and Their Distribution. *Ethnology* 9:165–208.

Murdock, George Peter, and Douglas R. White
   1970. Standard Cross-Cultural Sample. *Ethnology* 8:329–369.

Myers, Fred R.
   1986. *Pintupi Country, Pintupi Self: Sentiment, Place and Politics among Western Desert Aborigines.* Washington: Smithsonian Institution Press and AIAS.

Myers, Merlin G.
   2006. *Households and Families of the Longhouse Iroquois at Six Nations Reserve.* Lincoln: University of Nebraska Press.

Nakhleh, Luay, Guohua Jin, Fengmei Zhao, and John Mellor-Crummey
   2005. Reconstructing Phylogenetic Networks Using Parsimony. *Proceedings of the 2005 IEEE Computational Systems Bioinformatics Conference* 93–102. Stanford, CA: IEEE (Institute of Electrical and Electronics Engineers) Computer Society.

Needham, Rodney
   1962. *Structure and Sentiment: A Test Case for Social Anthropology.* Chicago: University of Chicago Press.
   1964. Descent, Category, and Alliance in Sirionó Society. *Southwestern Journal of Anthropology* 20(3):229–240.
   1967. Terminology and Alliance: II. Mapuche; Conclusions. *Sociologus* 17:39–54.
   1971. Remarks on the Analysis of Kinship and Marriage (Introduction). In *Rethinking Kinship and Marriage.* Rodney Needham, ed. Pp. xiii-cxvii. ASA Monographs 11. London: Tavistock.

Needham, Rodney, ed.
   1971. *Rethinking Kinship and Marriage.* ASA Monographs 11. London: Tavistock.

Nelson, Gareth J., and Norman I. Platnick
   1981.   *Systematics and Biogeography: Cladistics and Vicariance.* New York: Columbia University Press.
Neyman, Jerzy
   1971.   Molecular Studies of Evolution: A Source of Novel Statistical Problems. In *Statistical Decision Theory and Related Topics.* Shanti S. Gupta and James Yackel, eds. Pp. 1–27. New York: Academic Press.
Nimuendajú, Curt
   1942.   *The Sherente.* R. Lowie, trans. Los Angeles: Frederick Webb Hodge Anniversary Publication Fund.
   1946.   *The Eastern Timbira.* R. Lowie, trans. Berkeley: University of California Press.
   1967 [1939]. *The Apinayé.* R. Lowie, trans. The Netherlands: Oesterhout N.B.
Nixon, Kevin C.
   1993.   *CLADOS, Computer Program for Cladistic Character Analysis.* Ithaca: L.H. Bailey Hortorium.
O'Brien, Denise and Edwin A. Cook
   1980.   Patterns in Highland New Guinea Kinship. In *Blood and Semen: Kinship Systems of Highland New Guinea.* Edwin A. Cook and Denise O'Brien, eds. Pp. 463–474. Ann Arbor: University of Michigan Press.
Pagel, Mark
   2009.   Human Language as a Culturally Transmitted Replicator. *Nature Reviews Genetics* 10:405–415.
Pagel, Mark, Quentin D. Atkinson, and Andrew Meade
   2007.   Frequency of Word-Use Predicts Rates of Lexical Evolution throughout Indo-European History. *Nature* 449:717–720.
Pagel, Mark, and Andrew Meade
   2005.   Bayesian Estimation of Correlated Evolution across Cultures: A Case Study of Marriage Systems and Wealth Transfer at Marriage. In *The Evolution of Cultural Diversity: A Phylogenetic Approach.* Ruth Mace, Clare J. Holden, and Stephen Shennan, eds. Pp. 235–256. London: University College Press.
Parkin, David
   1997.   *Kinship: An Introduction to Basic Concepts.* Malden, MA: Blackwell.
Parkin, Robert
   1998.   Dravidian and Iroquois in South Asia. In *Transformations of Kinship.* Maurice Godelier, Thomas R. Trautmann, and Franklin E. Tjon Sie Fat, eds. Pp. 252–270. Washington: Smithsonian Institution.
Parry, Jonathan P.
   1979.   *Caste and Kinship in Kangra.* London: Routledge.
Platnick, Norman I., and H. Donald Cameron
   1977.   Cladistic Methods in Textual, Linguistic, and Phylogenetic Analysis. *Systematic Zoology* 26:380–385.

Poirier, Sylvie
   1992. Nomadic Rituals: Networks of Ritual Exchange between Women of the Australian Western Desert. *Man* 27(4):757–776.

Popper, Karl
   1959. *The Logic of Scientific Discovery.* London: Routledge.

Pospisil, Leopold
   1959–60. The Kapauku Papuans and Their Kinship Organization. *Oceania* 30:188–205.

Powell, Fiona
   2002. Transformations in Guugu Yimithirr Kinship Terminology. *Anthropological Forum* 12(2):177–192.

Radcliffe-Brown, Alfred R.
   1931. *The Social Organization of Australian Tribes.* Melbourne: Macmillan.
   1941. The Study of Kinship Systems. *Journal of the Royal Anthropological Institute* 71(1):1–18.
   1952. *Structure and Function in Primitive Society: Essays and Addresses.* London: Cowen and West.

Rannala, Bruce, and Ziheng Yang
   1996. Probability Distribution of Molecular Evolutionary Trees: A New Method of Phylogenetic Inference. *Journal of Molecular Evolution* 43:304–311.

Rattray, R. S.
   1923. *Ashanti.* Oxford: Oxford University Press.

Read, Dwight W.
   2001. Formal Analysis of Kinship Terminologies and its Relationship to What Constitutes Kinship. *Anthropological Theory* 1(2):239–267.
   2007. Kinship Theory: A Paradigm Shift. *Ethnology* 46(4):329–364.

Renard-Clamagirand, Brigitte
   1982. *Marobo: Une société ema de Timor.* Langues et Civilisations de l'Asie du Sud-est et du Monde Insulindien No. 12. Paris: SELAF.

Rexová, Kateřina, Daniel Frynta, and Jan Zrzavý
   2003. Cladistic Analysis of Languages: Indo-European Classification Based on Lexicostatistical Data. *Cladistics* 19:120–127.

Rivers, William H. R.
   1914. *Kinship and Social Organization.* London: Constable.

Rogers, J. Daniel, and George Sabo, III.
   2004. Caddo. In *Handbook of North American Indians*, vol. 14, Southeast. Raymond D. Fogelson, ed. Pp. 616–631. Washington: Smithsonian Institution.

Romney, A. Kimball
   1965. Kalmuk Mongol and the Classification of Lineal Kinship Terminologies. In *Formal Semantic Analysis.* E. A. Hammel, ed. American An-

thropologist special publication. Washington: American Anthropological Association.

Rose, Frederick
   1960. *Classification of Kin, Age Structure and Marriage amongst the Groote Eylandt Aborigines: A Study in Method and a Theory of Australian Kinship*. Berlin: Akademie Verlag.

Ross, Malcolm
   2005. Pronouns as a Preliminary Diagnostic for Grouping Papuan Languages. In *Papuan Pasts: Cultural, Linguistic and Biological Histories of Papuan-Speaking Peoples*. Andrew Pawley, Robert Attenborough, Robin Hide, and Jack Golson, eds. Pp. 15–66. Canberra: Pacific Linguistics.

Rumsey, Alan
   1981. Kinship and Context among the Ngarinyin. *Oceania* 51:181–192.

Sackett, Lee
   1975. Exogamy or Endogamy: Kinship and Marriage at Wiluna, Western Australia. *Anthropological Forum* 4(1):44–55.

Salt, Henry
   1814. *A Voyage to Abyssinia*. London: Rivington.

Scheffler, Harold W.
   1971. Dravidian-Iroquois: The Melanesian Evidence. In *Anthropology in Oceania*. Lester Richard Hiatt and Chandra Jayawardena, eds. Pp. 231–254. Sydney: Angus and Robertson.
   1972. Systems of Kin Classification: A Structural Typology. In *Kinship Studies in the Morgan Centennial Year*. Priscilla Reining, ed. Pp. 113–133. Washington: Anthropological Society of Washington.
   1978. *Australian Kin Classification*. Cambridge Studies in Social Anthropology 33. Cambridge: Cambridge University Press.
   2001. *Filiation and Affiliation*. Boulder, CO: Westview Press.

Scheffler, Harold W., and Floyd G. Lounsbury
   1971. *A Study in Structural Semantics: The Sirionó Kinship System*. Englewood Cliffs, NJ: Prentice Hall.

Schneider, David M.
   1984. *A Critique of the Study of Kinship*. Ann Arbor: University of Michigan Press.

Schröder, Ernst
   1870. Vier combinatorische probleme. *Zeitschrift für Mathematik und Physik* 15:489–503.

Seeger, Anthony
   1975. *By Gê out of Africa: Ideologies of Conception and Descent*. Paper presented at the annual meeting of the American Anthropological Association, San Francisco, November 1975.

1981. *Nature and Society in Central Brazil: The Suyá Indians of Mato Grosso.* Cambridge: Harvard University Press.

Seeger, Anthony, Roberto Da Matta, and Eduardo B. Viveiros de Castro
1979. *A construção da pessoa nas sociedades indígenas.* Boletim do Museu Nacional 32. Rio de Janeiro: Editora Fon-Fon e Seleta.

Shapiro, Warren
1981. *Miwuyt Marriage: The Cultural Anthropology of Affinity in Northeast Arnhem Land.* Philadelphia: ISHI.

Shimony, Annemarie Anrod
1961. *Conservatism among the Iroquois at the Six Nations Reserve.* Yale University Publications in Anthropology 65. New Haven: Yale Univeristy Press.

Spier, Leslie
1925. The Distribution of Kinship Systems in North America. *University of Washington Publications in Anthropology* 1(2):69–88.

Spoehr, Alexander
1942. Kinship Systems of the Seminole. *Field Museum of Natural History Anthropological Series* 33(3):117–150.

Standard Cross Cultural Sample
2006. *Standard Sample Database. By George P. Murdock and Douglas R. White.* (http://eclectic.ss.uci.edu/~drwhite/worldcul/sccs.html)

Steel, Michael, and David Penny
2005. Maximum Parsimony and the Phylogenetic Information in Multistate Characters. In *Parsimony, Phylogeny, and Genomics.* Victor A. Albert, ed. Pp. 163–180. Oxford: Oxford University Press.

Swanton, John Reed
1908. *Social Condition, Beliefs, and Linguistic Relationships of the Tlingit Indians.* Twenty-Sixth Annual Report of the Bureau of American Ethnology (1904–1905). Pp. 391–486. Washington: Bureau of American Ethnology.

Tax, Sol
1937. The Social Organization of the Fox Indians. In *Social Anthropology of North American Tribes.* Fred Eggan, ed. Pp. 243–284. Chicago: University of Chicago Press.

Tehrani, Janshid J., and Mark Collard
2009. On the Relationship between Inter-Individual Cultural Transmission and Population-Level Cultural Diversity: A Case Study of Weaving in Iranian Tribal Populations. *Evolution and Human Behavior* 30:286–300.

Thelwall, Robin
1981. *The Daju Language Group: Systematic Phonetics, Lexicostatistics and Lexical Reconstruction.* Ph.D. thesis, New University of Ulster.

Thomas, Lynn L.
- 1980. Crow-Type Skewing in Akan Kinship Vocabulary and its Absence in Minangkabau. *American Ethnologist* 1980:549–566.

Thomson, Donald
- 1955. Two Devices for the Avoidance of First-Cousin Marriage among the Australian Aborigines. *Man* 55(44):39–40.
- 1972. *Kinship and Behaviour in North Queensland.* Canberra: Australian Institute of Aboriginal Studies.

Tindale, Norman B.
- 1935. *Journal of the Anthropological Expedition to Warburton Range, Western Australia, July–September 1935, and, Sociological Cards. Fieldnotes.* South Australian Museum, Adelaide.
- 1963. Journal of Visit to the Rawlinson Range Area in the Great Western Desert, 24 October–25 November 1963, and, Rawlinson Ranges Genealogies, November 1963. Fieldnotes. South Australian Museum, Adelaide.
- 1988 [1972]. The Pitjandjara. In *Hunters and Gatherers Today: A Socioeconomic Study of Eleven such Cultures in the Twentieth Century.* M. G. Bicchieri, ed. Pp. 217–268. New York: Waveland Press.

Titiev, Mischa
- 1938. The Problem of Cross-Cousin Marriage among the Hopi. *American Anthropologist* 40:105–111.
- 1944. Old Oraibi: A Study of the Hopi Indians of Third Mesa. *Papers of the Peabody Museum of American Archaeology and Ethnology* 22:1.
- 1956. The Importance of Space in Primitive Kinship. *American Anthropologist* 58(5):854–865.

Tjon Sie Fat, Franklin
- 1990. *Representing Kinship: Simple Models of Elementary Structures.* Ph.D. thesis, University of Leiden.
- 1998a. Local Rules and Global Structures: Models of Exclusive Straight Sister-Exchange. In *Kinship, Networks, and Exchange.* Thomas Schweizer and Douglas R. White, eds. Pp. 261–276. New York: Cambridge University Press.
- 1998b. On the Formal Analysis of "Dravidian", "Iroquois", and "Generational" Varieties as Nearly Associative Combinations. In *Transformations of Kinship.* Maurice Godelier, Thomas R. Trautmann, and Franklin E. Tjon Sie Fat, eds. Pp. 59–93. Washington: Smithsonian Institution Press.

Tommaseo-Ponzetta, Mila, M. Attimonelli, M. De Robertis, F. Tanzariello, and C. Saccone
- 2002. Mitochondrial DNA Variability in West New Guinea Populations. *American Journal Physical Anthropology* 117(1):49–67.

Tonkinson, Robert
   1975. The Riddle of the Non-Marriageable Cross Cousin. Seminar presented at the Department of Anthropology, Australian National University, Canberra.
   1991 [1978]. *The Mardu Aborigines: Living the Dream in Australia's Desert*. Case Studies in Cultural Anthropology. New York: Holt, Rinehart and Winston.

Trautmann, Thomas R.
   1981. *Dravidian Kinship*. Cambridge: Cambridge University Press.
   1987. *Lewis Henry Morgan and the Invention of Kinship*. Berkeley: University of California Press.
   2001. The Whole History of Kinship Terminology in Three Chapters: Before Morgan, Morgan, After Morgan. *Anthropological Theory* 1(2):268–287.
   2008. *Lewis Henry Morgan and the Invention of Kinship,* new ed. Lincoln: University of Nebraska Press.

Trautmann, Thomas R., and Robert H. Barnes
   1998. "Dravidian", "Iroquois", and "Crow-Omaha" in North American Perspective. In *Transformations of Kinship*. Maurice Godelier, Thomas Trautmann, and Franklin Tjon Sie Fat, eds. Pp. 27–58. Washington: Smithsonian Institution.

Trautmann, Thomas R., Gillian Feeley-Harnik and John C. Mitani
   2011. Deep Kinship. In *Deep History: The Architecture of Past and Present*, Andrew Shryock and Daniel Lord Smail, eds., pp. 160–188. Berkeley, Los Angeles, London: University of California Press.

Tuffley, Chris, and Michael Steel
   1997. Links between Maximum Likelihood and Maximum Parsimony under a Simple Model of Site Substitution. *Bulletin of Mathematical Biology* 59:581–607.

Turnbull, Colin
   1965. *Wayward Servants: The Two Worlds of the African Pygmies*. New York: American Museum of Natural History.

Turner, David
   1974. *Tradition and Transformation: A Study of the Groote Eylandt Area Aborigines of Northern Australia*. Canberra: AIAS.

Turner, Terence
   1966. *Social Structure and Political Organization among the Northern Kayapó*. Ph.D. diss., Harvard University.
   1979a. The Gê and Bororo Societies as Dialectical Systems: A General Model. In *Dialectical Societies*. D. Maybury-Lewis, ed. Pp. 147–178. Cambridge: Harvard University Press.
   1979b. Kinship, Household and Community Structure among the Northern Kayapo. In *Dialectical Societies*. D. Maybury-Lewis, ed. Pp. 179–217. Cambridge: Harvard University Press.

1980. The Social Skin. In *Not Work Alone.* J. Cherfas and Roger Lewin, eds. Pp. 111–140. London: Temple Smith.
1995. Social Body and Embodied Subject: The Production of Bodies, Actors and Society among the Kayapo. *Cultural Anthropology* 10(2):143–170.
1997. Social Complexity and Recursive Hierarchy in Indigenous South American Societies. Theme issue, "Structure, Knowledge, and Representation in the Andes: Studies Presented to R. T. Zuidema on the Occasion of His Seventieth Birthday," Gary Urton, ed. *Journal of the Steward Anthropological Society* 24(1–2):37–60.
2002. Lo bello y lo común: Desigualdades de valor y jerarquia rotativa entre los kayapo. *Revista de Antropologia Social*, 11(1):201–118. English version: The Beautiful and the Common: Gender and Social Hierarchy among the Kayapo, *Tipiti: The Journal of the Society for the Anthropology of Lowland South America* 1(1):11–26 (September 2003).
2011. The Body beyond the Body: Social, Material and Spiritual Dimensions of Bodiliness. In *A Companion to the Anthropology of the Body and Embodiment.* Frances Mascia-Lees, ed. New York: Wiley Blackwell.

Turton, David
1980. The Economics of Mursi Bridewealth: A Comparative Perspective. In *The Meaning of Marriage Payments.* John L. Comaroff, ed. London: Academic Press.

Ubelaker, Douglas H.
2006. Population Size, Contact to Nadir. In *Handbook of North American Indians*, vol. 3, Environment, Origins, and Population. Pp. 694–701. Washington: Smithsonian Institution.

Urban, Greg
1994. The Social Organization of the Southeast. In *North American Indian Anthropology: Essays on Society and Culture.* Raymond J. DeMallie and Alfonso Ortiz, eds. Pp. 172–193. Norman: University of Oklahoma Press.

Varón, Andrés, Le Sy Vinh, Illya Bomash, and Ward C. Wheeler
2008. *POY 4.0.* American Museum of Natural History. http://research.amnh.org/scicomp/projects/poy.php.

Varón, Andrés, Le Sy Vinh, and Ward C. Wheeler
2010. POY Version 4: Phylogenetic Analysis Using Dynamic Homologies. *Cladistics* 25:72–85.

Vidal, Lux
1977. *Morte e Vida de uma Sociedade Indígena Brasileira.* São Paulo: HUCITEC/EDUSP.

Viveiros de Castro, Eduardo B.
1990. Princípios e Parâmetros: um comentário a l'Exercice de la Parenté. In *Antropologia Social: Comunicações do PPGAS* 17. Pp. 1–106. Rio de Janeiro: PPGAS/Museu Nacional/UFRJ.

1998. Dravidian and Related Kinship Systems. In *Transformations of Kinship*. Maurice Godelier, Thomas Trautmann, and Franklin Tjon Sie Fat, eds. Pp. 332–385. Washington: Smithsonian Institution Press.

Wagner, Roy
   1977. Analogic Kinship: A Dabiri Example. *American Ethnologist* 4:623–642.

Wehrli, Hans J.
   1904. *Beitrag zur Ethnologie der Chingpaw (Kachin) von Ober Birma*. Supplement to Internationales Archiv für Ethnographie, vol. 16. Leiden: Brill.

Wheeler, Ward C., and Kurt M. Pickett
   2008. Topology-Bayes versus Clade-Bayes in Phylogenetic Analysis. *Molecular Biology and Evolution* 25:447–453.

White, Douglas R., and Ulla C. Johansen
   2005. *Network Analysis and Ethnographic Problems: Process Models of a Turkish Nomad Clan*. New York: Lexington Books.

White, Douglas, and Woodrow Denham
   2008. The Indigenous Australian Marriage Paradox: Small-World Dynamics on a Continental Scale. Manuscript (http://eclectic.ss.uci.edu/~drwhite/pub/Paradox07b.pdf).

White, Leslie A.
   1939. A Problem in Kinship Terminology. *American Anthropologist* 41(4): 566–573.

Whiteley, Peter M.
   1988. *Deliberate Acts: Changing Hopi Culture through the Oraibi Split*. Tucson: University of Arizona Press.
   1992. *Hopitutungwni*: "Hopi Names" as Literature. In *On the Translation of Native American Literatures*. Brian Swann, ed. Pp. 208–227. Washington: Smithsonian Institution Press.
   2008. *The Orayvi Split: A Hopi Transformation*. Anthropological Papers of the American Museum of Natural History 87. New York: American Museum of Natural History.

Winter, Edward H.
   1956. *Bwamba: A Structural-Functional Analysis of a Patrilineal Society*. Cambridge: Heffer.

Yallop, Colin
   1977. *Alyawarra: An Aboriginal Language of Central Australia*. Canberra: Australian Institute of Aboriginal Studies.

Zorc, R. David
   1986. *Yolngu Matha Dictionary*. Batchelor: School of Australian Linguistics.

About the Contributors

NICHOLAS J. ALLEN, emeritus Reader in the Social Anthropology of South Asia, Institute of Social and Cultural Anthropology, University of Oxford

R.H. BARNES, Professor, Institute of Social and Cultural Anthropology, University of Oxford

MARCELA COELHO DE SOUZA, Professor, Department of Anthropology, University of Brasilia

LAURENT DOUSSET, Associate Professor, Centre for Research and Documentation on Oceania (École des Hautes Études en Sciences Sociales), University of Provence

CHRISTOPHER EHRET, Professor of History, Department of History, University of California at Los Angeles

WENDY JAMES, emerita Professor, Institute of Social and Cultural Anthropology, University of Oxford

DAVID B. KRONENFELD, emeritus Professor of Anthropology, University of California, Riverside

PATRICK MCCONVELL, Research Fellow in Linguistics, School of Language Studies, Australian National University

THEODORE POWERS, Postdoctoral Fellow in the Human Economy Program at the University of Pretoria, South Africa

THOMAS R. TRAUTMANN, emeritus Professor of History and Anthropology, University of Michigan

TERENCE TURNER, emeritus Professor of Anthropology at the University of Chicago, Visiting Professor of Anthropology at Cornell University

WARD C. WHEELER, Curator of Invertebrate Zoology, American Museum of Natural History

PETER M. WHITELEY, Curator of North American Ethnology, American Museum of Natural History

Topics Index

Adamawa, 138
affinal relations, 208, 215, 224, 233–235
affines (i.e., kin via marriage), 16, 20, 25, 56, 61, 63, 95, 96, 99, 100, 101, 105, 108, 126, 170, 211, 216, 220, 227, 236, 250, 268, 303, 304, 305
affinity (i.e., relationship via marriage), 3, 31, 47, 100, 108, 216, 220, 229, 288–289, 291, 305
Africa, 9, 17, 18, 23–24, 25, 33, 40, 41, 49, 69, 72, 93, 133–203, 283–284, 286, 287, 289–290, 293, 295
agnates/agnatic, 95, 247, 269, 305
Algonquian (language family), 74, 91–92, 93, 107, 121–126, 258
alliance/marriage alliance
    asymmetric-prescriptive, 10, 11, 13, 14–16, 20, 22, 27, 35, 41–48, 77–79, 95–96, 107–108, 221, 254, 260, 281–282, 286–293, 303
    complex, 15–17, 24, 89, 135, 152, 221, 282, 285, 289, 290, 303, 304
    dispersed (affinal), 17, 20, 21, 48, 93, 102–107, 129, 243, 244, 260, 281, 289, 295, 304
    elementary, 13–16, 24, 61, 89, 94–96, 99, 135, 152, 221, 282, 289, 290, 291, 294, 303, 305
    matri-houses, 210, 212
    semi-complex, viii, 10, 11, 15–17, 20–21, 22, 23, 24, 61, 70, 72, 93–97, 99, 107–108, 137, 221, 277, 281–282, 286–293, 303, 304, 306
    See also Omaha alliance
alternate generation equations, 247, 251
alternating birth classes. *See* generation moieties
Aluridja (type). *See* kin terminology types, Aluridja
Amazonia, 9, 25, 93, 99, 203–241, 286, 291
ancestor cult (India), 64
Arnhem Land, 245, 247–248, 249, 250, 253

asymmetrical cross-cousin marriage. *See* marriage, cross-cousin, asymmetrical
asymmetric-prescriptive systems. *See* alliance/marriage alliance, asymmetric-prescriptive
Australia (aboriginal), 12, 13, 16, 22, 24–26, 33, 49, 51, 61, 93, 241–277, 286–287, 293
    (Central), 248–249, 271
avoidance, in-law, 215–216, 220, 249

Bantu languages, 149, 198
Bayesian analysis, 115–116
bifurcate-merging, 12, 186, 272–273, 277, 303
bilateral cross-cousin marriage. *See* marriage, cross-cousin, bilateral
bilateral kindred, 206, 227–228, 303
Blue Nile, 23, 139–141, 191
bridewealth, 80, 148–151, 303
Bunyoro (kingdom), 149
Burkina Faso, 17, 96, 137

Caddoan (language family), 91, 126
California (Native), 78, 86, 89, 258–259
Cape York Peninsula, 250–251, 252–254
cattle, 140, 174, 176, 198
Central Australia. *See* Australia (aboriginal), central
Cheyenne (type). *See* kin terminology types, Cheyenne
child exchange, 52
Choctaw (type). *See* kin terminology types, Choctaw
clade-posterior analysis, 116
classificatory systems, 3, 12, 32, 33, 54, 62, 77, 160, 162, 163, 215, 270, 286, 291, 302, 303
cognatic kin, 54, 80, 96, 99, 100, 101, 105, 108, 207, 226, 289, 290, 303, 305
collateral relatives, 2, 12, 31, 32, 72, 159, 304
complex structure. *See* alliance/marriage alliance, complex

Congo, 138, 149, 197
Congo-Nile watershed, 197
consanguines (i.e., kin by "blood"), 15, 25, 156, 157, 165, 167, 170, 181, 182, 219, 220, 244, 255, 258, 301, 304, 306
consanguinity (i.e., relationship via "blood"), 3, 31, 47, 221, 222, 288–291
corporate groups, 8, 80, 288
Critique of the Study of Kinship, 19
cross-cousins, 3, 4, 52, 54–57, 105, 146, 148, 150–151, 159, 161, 180, 181, 207–208, 211, 217–220, 223, 233, 234, 236, 239, 243, 249–251, 253–254, 257, 261–265, 270–271, 273, 292, 302, 304. See also marriage, cross-cousin
cross-kin, 2, 4, 11, 221, 304
crossness, 2–3, 6–7, 14, 18, 22–26, 31–50, 93, 107, 108, 125, 136, 137, 148, 152, 186, 195, 197, 283–287, 289, 293, 296, 299, 304
  Dravidian (Type A), 22, 23, 24, 26, 35–40, 42, 43, 45, 46, 48–50, 93, 107, 125, 137, 197, 285, 287, 289, 296, 299
  Iroquois (Type B), 2–3, 18, 22, 23, 35–41, 42, 46, 47, 49, 50, 93, 107, 125, 127, 137, 148, 197, 285, 292, 296, 299
  Kuma, 35, 39
  Ngawbe, 35
  Yafar, 35
cross-parallel neutralization, 40–41, 47–48, 143, 164–165, 257–258, 261–275, 286, 304
cross-transmission rule, 209–210
Crow (type). See kin terminology types, Crow
Crow systems, viii, 83–93, 97–108, 153–172, 173–202, 292, 296
Crow-Omaha
  marriage arrangements, 66, 95
  "problem," viii, 1–21, 74, 83, 281–297
  subtypes, 12, 85, 87–88
  systems, viii, ix, 3, 10, 16, 17, 33–35, 39, 70, 73, 75, 83–108, 118, 129, 221, 268, 285, 295
  terms as optative overlay, 18, 20, 24, 97, 108, 153, 164, 168–169, 172, 222, 243–260, 283–286, 290
cultural lag, 287

Dakota (-Siouan, language/cultural group), 40, 171, 172
deep structure/surface structure, 34, 284–286, 290–291
demography, 93, 118, 120, 131, 135, 146, 243, 244, 257–258, 260, 295
descent groups, 8, 9, 12, 74, 79, 80, 81, 94, 97, 140, 226, 262, 288, 304
descriptive systems, 3, 32, 33, 77, 143, 236–237, 270, 302, 304
diachronic change, 222, 243–244, 252
dispersed affinal alliance, 17, 20, 21, 48, 93, 102–107, 129, 243–244, 260, 281, 289, 295, 304
double descent, 80, 97, 304
downstream/upstream spread, 26, 244, 256–259, 295
Dravidian crossness. See crossness, Dravidian
Dravidian (type). See kin terminology types, Dravidian (Type A)
Dravidianate, 186, 205, 217, 221, 291, 294

egocentric, 22, 51–54, 61, 65, 233–237, 264, 305. See also sociocentric
elders, 140, 142, 151, 155, 193, 194, 199, 200, 201
elementary family, 224, 227, 228, 230–238
elementary structure, 7, 13–16, 24, 61, 89, 94–96, 99, 135, 152, 282, 289–291, 305
Elementary Structures of Kinship, The, 7, 13, 15
equations, terminological, 6, 22, 35, 36, 55, 61, 74–75, 78, 82, 84–88, 118, 150, 157, 166, 167, 179, 180, 189, 198, 210, 242, 247, 250–252, 291, 299, 300
  counter-tetradic, 22, 54
  Crow, 74, 85, 85–88, 138, 166, 167, 179, 180, 189, 198, 210
  lineal, 20, 56, 74–75, 85–88, 291, 306
  major types of, 54
  Omaha, 8, 20, 54, 56, 57, 63, 66, 74–75, 85–88, 140, 143, 149, 198, 210, 212, 218, 244, 247, 250–252
equivalence rules, 11, 48, 84–85, 158–165
  merging (of same-sex siblings), 34, 35, 38, 45, 46, 165, 284
  skewing, 11, 84–85
Eritrea, 150–151

Topics Index 339

Eskimo (type). *See* kin terminology types, Eskimo
Ethiopia, 138, 140–141, 145, 148
Ethnographic Atlas, 12, 25, 35, 118, 120–127
evolution, kinship system, vii, 3, 9, 12, 19, 22, 27, 33, 46, 48, 49, 82, 117–131
evolutionary processes, 109–131
exchange (marriage), 7, 13–14, 16, 19, 24, 52, 54, 60, 77, 82, 93, 95–97, 100, 104, 107–108, 135–152, 237, 289–290
  direct, 13–14, 16
  generalized, 13–14, 16, 95–96, 107–108
  See also sister-exchange
exogamy, 7, 14, 16, 37, 52, 57, 59, 62, 95, 97, 101, 102, 150, 206, 207, 244, 247, 257, 266, 275–276, 292, 296
extensionist analysis, 84, 156

formal(ist) analysis, vii, 8, 10, 11, 18–19, 33–35, 36, 38, 46–47, 51–66, 84–88, 153, 158–165, 283–284, 283, 284, 301
formal friendship, 207–208, 220

Gê (language family), 9, 25, 99, 205–222, 223, 224, 226, 286, 291, 296, 301
genealogy, 69, 71, 72, 77, 78, 99, 101, 105, 142–144, 154, 217, 221, 250, 263, 268, 270, 273, 301
generation (as concept), 4, 12, 32, 34, 43, 44, 45, 52–54, 60–64, 135–152, 157, 171, 179, 180, 223, 231, 233–239, 245, 247, 250, 262, 264–265, 269–270, 272–273
Generational (type). *See* kin terminology types, generational
generation moieties, 52, 136, 269
gift of life, 136
Gould's formalist system, 84–88, 158–163, 169, 300, 301
Gulf of Carpentaria, 248, 250

Hawaiian (type). *See* kin terminology types, Hawaiian
Hawaiianization, 57, 143, 286, 305
hierarchy, social, 89, 295
Hindu philosophy, 63
historical linguistics, 24, 173–202, 243, 253–260

HKY (Hasegawa, Kishino, and Yano) model, 116
Holocene, 253, 256, 259, 260
Hopi kinship, 10, 16–17, 85–86, 97, 99–108, 117, 120, 284, 296
  affines, 95, 100–101, 105–108
  clans and clan-sets, 94, 95, 99
  marriage practices of, 101–106, 285
    Hano perspective on, 101–102
  marriage rules, 16–17, 95, 99–101
  relationships, 99–101
  terminology, 85–86, 88, 284
"house" (house societies, *sociétés à maison*), 89, 105, 141, 142, 144, 206, 210, 212, 290, 305
household, 99, 100, 101, 206, 224–235
hunter-gatherers, 149, 196–197, 244, 267
hypergamy, 64, 305

Ice Age, 174
incest, 19, 51, 52, 220
inheritance, 8, 100, 124, 143, 155–158, 169, 171, 244, 251, 257, 260, 268, 287
initiation, 101, 102, 230, 267
Iroquoian (language family), 92, 126, 127
Iroquois (type). *See* kin terminology types, Iroquois (Type B)
Iroquois crossness. *See* crossness, Iroquois

Jukes-Cantor model, 121

Kariera (type). *See* kin terminology types, Kariera
Kenya, 189, 191, 202
kernel kin types, 156–158, 170–171
Kimberley, 243, 246–247, 248
kin terminology types
  Aluridja, 262–277
  Cheyenne, 18, 26, 40–41, 97, 127, 160, 161, 162, 164, 286, 303, 304
  Choctaw, 6, 8, 10, 69
  Crow, 3–12, 23, 24, 25, 33, 69, 74, 79, 84–88, 89, 90, 91, 97, 99, 101, 108, 117, 118, 120, 124, 126, 127, 138, 140, 143, 148, 151, 153–172, 173, 179–181, 186, 188–201, 208–211, 213, 218, 221, 238, 239, 244, 293, 296, 299, 304

kin terminology types (*continued*)
  Crow-Omaha, 3–4, 8–11, 16–21, 27, 31–50, 83–88, 93, 96–97, 107–108, 118, 129, 136, 170, 172, 199, 205, 207, 210–212, 221–222, 268, 273, 274, 281–297
  Dakota (-Iroquois), 126
  Dravidian (Type A), vii, 3, 20, 22, 35–50, 52, 55, 56, 57, 77–78, 93, 97, 99, 107, 108, 118, 120, 125, 137, 144, 148, 150, 160, 186, 243, 258, 262, 285–296, 299, 304, 305
  Eskimo, 12, 19, 32, 33, 34, 48, 118, 125, 196, 197, 200, 293, 304, 305
  Generational, 12, 32, 54, 97, 124, 125, 127, 161, 262, 305
  Hawaiian 12, 32, 33, 34, 40, 54, 118, 120, 181, 189–201, 205, 262, 272, 286, 293, 305
  Iroquois (Type B), vii, viii, 1–12, 18–21, 22, 23, 31–50, 56, 78, 93, 97, 99, 107–108, 118, 120, 125, 126, 127, 137, 148, 160, 181, 182, 186, 188, 191–202, 245–250, 258, 259, 262, 285–288, 291–293, 296, 299, 303, 304, 305
  Kariera, 63, 205, 243, 253–255
  Omaha, 3, 5–12, 17–18, 20, 26, 33, 47, 51–66, 69–82, 84–94, 97, 99, 117–120, 124–129, 137–138, 140, 143, 149, 153, 160, 169, 172, 173, 189–192, 195–199, 205, 208–212, 218, 223, 226, 233, 237–239, 243–260, 274, 283, 293, 295, 306
  Sudanese, 12, 19, 32–34, 189, 192–201, 293, 304, 307
kin terms, 51, 56, 61, 84, 97, 99, 118, 151, 156–160, 166, 169–172, 269
kin type, 55, 84, 159, 160, 164, 245, 251
kin graph, 160–163
kinship system (broadly considered), 1, 13, 22, 27, 33, 42, 53, 83, 153, 239, 243, 249, 251, 260, 262, 263, 272, 282, 283, 291, 293, 295
kinship terminology, vii, 1, 3–4, 8–12, 15, 16–23, 24, 26, 27, 31–48, 51, 53–57, 61, 63, 65–66, 69, 74–79, 82, 83–93, 96, 99, 100, 121, 125–127, 135–149, 153–172, 173, 182–202, 205–222, 226, 233, 236–238, 246–247, 243–260, 262–265, 268–277, 282–297, 299, 301, 303–307
kinship typology, 10, 32, 40, 52, 61, 69, 169–171, 291, 296
Koman languages, 139, 148, 149

laterality, 32, 34, 40,
likelihood, statistical, 111, 115–116, 117, 120, 121, 123, 127, 129, 130–131
lineage (type of descent group), 8, 12, 14, 17, 43, 44, 59, 61, 76, 80, 104, 135, 149, 150, 154, 155, 156, 168–172, 206, 260, 268, 289, 292, 300
lineality, 12, 31, 48, 152, 305. *See also* matriliny; patriliny, patrilines
lineal kin, 2, 303, 304, 305, 307

Maison Suger conference, vii, viii, ix, 7, 19
"managers"/*junggay*i, 248, 250, 257
marking (Greenbergian), 168–171
marriage
  classes, 7, 13, 262
  cross-cousin, 7, 9–11, 13–16, 18, 20–22, 36–38, 41–48, 50, 55, 101, 104, 105, 125–126, 135, 170, 181–188, 252–253, 275–276, 281, 287, 292, 296
  asymmetrical, 11, 13–16, 20, 22, 43–48, 239, 254, 281
  bilateral, 10, 37, 43, 45, 52, 54, 57, 137, 141, 143, 292, 296
  matrilateral, 9–10, 14, 42, 57, 170, 207, 254, 255, 287
  patrilateral, 101, 104, 105, 108, 135, 170
  symmetrical, 14, 16, 43, 45, 47–48, 50, 57, 95, 125, 182, 186, 243
  direct exchange, 14, 203
  generalized exchange, 14
  prescriptions, 14, 57, 58, 70, 71, 78, 82, 95, 96, 126, 149, 300
  prohibitions/proscriptions, 17, 57, 58, 61, 66, 70–72, 76, 82, 95, 99, 101, 105, 108, 126, 137, 138, 144, 146, 262, 271, 292, 300, 306
  rules, 10, 13, 14, 15, 17, 18, 20, 27, 36–37, 38, 46, 47, 55, 56, 70, 82, 94, 221, 270, 287
  strategies, 267, 271, 287, 290

Topics Index

marriage alliance. *See* alliance/marriage alliance, matri-houses, 210, 212
matrilineage, 150, 155, 168, 169, 268, 292
matrilineal descent, 8, 9, 10, 94, 97, 108, 179, 182, 190, 226, 304
matriliny, 97, 100, 138, 146, 150, 189, 191, 192, 193, 198, 200
matrilocal. *See* residence (post-marital), matrilocal
matri-uxorilocality. *See* residence (post-marital), matri-uxorilocal
Metamorphoses of Kinship, The (*Métamorphoses de la parenté*), 19, 77
Middle Nile Basin, 197
moieties, 7, 14, 52, 58, 82, 97, 136, 137, 150, 205, 206, 207, 209, 247, 262, 269–270, 292, 305. *See also* generation moieties
Murngin system, 13, 14
Muskhogean (language family), 92, 126, 127

names (personal), 97, 100, 102, 105, 206, 208–220, 228, 230, 231
    exchange, 216–219
    identity. *See* onomastic identity
    naming relations, 207–218
    transmission, 208, 209, 211, 218
negative marriage rules, 15, 17, 47, 70, 304, 306. *See also* marriage, rules
Nepal, 43, 49, 55, 286
networks, phylogenetic, 114–115
New Guinea, 137, 244, 259, 302
Nilo-Saharan languages, 24, 138, 173–202, 293
no-common-mechanism (NCM), 117, 120, 121–130
North America (Native), 10, 19, 22, 23, 25, 26, 39, 40, 41, 42, 47, 49, 69–131
Northeast Africa, 138, 286, 290

Omaha (type). *See* kin terminology types, Omaha
Omaha alliance, 63, 72–74
Omaha genealogies, 71, 77
Omaha systems, 9, 10, 51–66, 69–82, 173–202, 243–260, 283
Omotic languages, 148
onomastic identity, 209, 210, 212, 213, 218

optimality, 115–121
Orayvi (Hopi) marriages, 102–107
overlay (terminological), 18, 20, 24, 26, 97, 108, 153–172, 222, 243–260, 283–286, 290

Pama-Nyungan (language family), 243, 248, 252, 253, 256
parallel kin, 2–4, 26, 31–41, 46–48, 143, 146, 161, 163–165, 181, 209, 219, 226, 227, 228, 244, 246, 257, 258, 261–265, 268, 270, 271–276, 284–286, 292, 303, 304, 306
parsimony (phylogenetics principle), 111, 115–117, 121–122, 124, 126, 128–129
patrilineal descent, 17, 74, 81, 140, 146, 192, 198, 243, 288, 303, 306
patriliny, patrilines, 57, 59, 191, 197, 198, 245, 246, 248
patrilocal. *See* residence (post-marital)
patrimoiety, 96, 247
pentadic theory, 62–64
Penutian (language family), 259
phylogenetic analysis, viii, 23, 109–131
polygyny, 271, 306
Polynesian societies, 80
polysemy, 255–56
population size/density, 39, 49, 70, 89, 107, 118, 120, 224, 243, 257, 258, 260, 265, 294–296
positive marriage rules, 54, 55, 69, 70, 82, 306. *See also* marriage, rules
posterior probability, 111, 115–116, 129
prescriptive marriage alliance. *See* alliance/marriage alliance, asymmetric-prescriptive; alliance/marriage alliance, elementary
proto-Ateker, 192–193
proto-Central-Kalenjin, 191
proto-Daju, 189, 194
proto-Didinga-Murle, 194–195
proto-Luo, 188, 191, 194
proto-Nilo-Saharan, 174–182
proto-Saharan, 174
proto-Saharo-Sahelian, 179, 189
proto-Sahelian, 174, 175
Pueblo Indian social structures, ix, 10, 23, 83, 86, 89–108, 120

reclassification, 210, 213, 220, 221, 261
regular sound correspondence, 177–178
relationship terminology. *See* kinship terminology
reproduction
    social, 24, 96, 136, 137, 138, 140, 222, 226, 238, 288
    theories of, 19
residence (post-marital), 9, 12, 51, 118, 124, 148, 202, 224, 230, 237, 306
    matrilocal, 9, 193, 202, 230, 306
    matri-uxorilocal, 224–227, 231, 232, 306
    patrilocal, 9, 306
Rift Valley, 191

Sahara, 173–74
same-sex sibling merging rule. *See* equivalence rules
sections (Australianist), 13, 51, 52, 65, 262, 263, 271
segmentary unit, 200, 202, 224, 226, 227, 228, 229, 232, 238
semi-complex alliance. *See* alliance/marriage alliance, semi-complex
Sepik, 259
sheep, 174
siblings, 8, 36, 39–41, 61, 95, 136–140, 143, 154, 181, 186, 208–210, 213, 216–217, 231, 235, 236, 238, 249, 250, 257, 261, 269, 286, 303
Siouan (language family), 10, 40, 72, 74, 91, 126
sister exchange, 24, 135–152, 289–290
skewing, 4, 6, 7, 8, 11, 15, 16, 18, 20, 21, 22, 25, 26, 31, 33, 34, 42– 50, 53–55, 84–86, 100, 135–152, 161, 163, 164, 169, 171, 172, 210, 213, 217–219, 220, 221, 223, 233–236, 237–239, 243–260, 261–277, 281–290, 293, 306
    as overlay. *See* overlay (terminological)
    Crow, 4, 18, 23, 47, 84–86, 101, 108, 165, 172, 210, 238–239, 251, 281, 288, 290, 306
    Crow-Omaha, 4, 7, 9, 16, 17, 20, 22, 23, 24, 25, 31, 33, 40, 41, 42, 46–50, 84–86, 211, 283, 286, 287, 290, 295
    horizontal, 26, 261–277
    Omaha, 5, 6, 26, 46, 47, 53–55, 84–86, 210, 223, 233–236, 238–239, 243–260, 281, 288, 290, 306
    rules. *See* equivalence rules
social technology, 26, 136, 273, 277, 290–292
sociocentric, 22, 51–54, 61, 65, 146, 155, 264, 305
    vs. egocentric, 22, 51–54, 61, 65, 235–237, 264, 305
Standard Cross-Cultural Sample, 12, 118
substance (kinship), 19, 150, 209, 214
"substitute" parents, 209, 212, 213, 226, 230, 231
Sudan, 138, 189, 195
Sudanese (type). *See* kin terminology types, Sudanese
Sudanic
    Central, 178, 180, 181, 188
    East Central, 181, 182, 188, 197
    Northern, 198
    proto-, 175, 189
    proto–East Central, 181, 189, 195
    proto–Northern, 174, 176, 177, 178
    West Central, 188
Systems of Consanguinity and Affinity of the Human Family, 3, 31, 47, 291

Tanzania, 191
terminological rule, 153, 154, 172
tetradic model, 51, 53, 54, 136, 150
tetradic theory, 22, 24, 51–66
Tibeto-Burman language family, 12, 20, 43, 48, 55, 57, 243, 286, 299
totemism, 6, 264
trade, 141, 202
transformation (of relations), 212–222, 228–238
transformations, kinship-system, vii, 19, 20, 27, 38, 53, 55, 78, 93, 108, 109–131, 262, 271, 272, 283, 293–296
    reversibility/irreversibility, vii, 19, 54, 78, 294–296
Transformations of Kinship, 7, 22, 38, 293
Trautmann-Barnes hypothesis, 23, 39, 49, 93, 107, 108, 125, 126
trees, phylogenetic, 109–131
    as explanations, 111–114
    rooted (directed), 110, 111, 114, 121, 122, 123, 128, 130–131

Topics Index 343

strict majority consensus, 118
unrooted (undirected), 110, 118
triadic terms, 208
Two Crows Denies It, 18, 22, 69, 72

Uasingishu plains, 191
Uganda, 138, 140, 149
unilineal descent, 7, 8, 9, 13, 18, 20, 74, 79, 80, 81, 198, 226, 281, 288, 289, 303, 304, 305, 306, 307
Uto-Aztekan (language family), 91, 118

Victoria River District, 248, 249, 256, 257
warfare, 149
West Africa, 93, 137, 147, 283, 290
Western Desert (Australia), 257, 258, 261–277
Worrorran (language family), 243, 244

Yok-Utian (proto language), 259

Zur Urgeschichte der Ehe (*On the Prehistory of Marriage*), 8, 69

Peoples Index

Acholi, 189, 191, 195, 199
Acoma, 91
Agaw, 141
Algonquian, 40, 91–92, 93, 107, 118–131, 258
Alyawarre, 249
Amba, 139, 140, 143, 149, 150, 151
Apinajé, 205, 208, 209, 210, 211, 216, 220
Aranda, 54, 276
Arapaho, 40, 122–124
Arikara, 6, 91, 126–131
Ashanti, 155, 170, 287
Assiniboine, 126–131
Astaboran, 178
Ateker, 192
Attawapis, 122–131
Ayabadhu/Yintjinga, 251–252

Baka, 180, 189
Bantu, 149, 198
Barabaig, 191, 192, 195, 196, 199
Bari, 189–199
Baruya, 137
Blackfoot, 122–131
Blood, 122–131
Bungi, 122–131
Bunyoro, 149
Burushaski, 42
Byansi, 55–56

Caddo, 126–131
Canela, 205, 208, 213, 216
Catawba, 126–131
Cherokee, 6, 10, 92, 119–210, 126–131
Cheyenne (proper), 40, 122–131
Chickasaw, 6, 92
Chinese (ancient), 13
Choctaw, 6, 8, 10, 69, 92, 126–131
Coast Salish, 89, 305
Cochiti Pueblo, 97, 99, 107
Creek, 6, 92, 126–131, 300
Crow (proper), 6, 10, 69, 74, 86, 91, 126–131

Daju, 188, 189, 194
Delaware, 122–131
Didinga, 188, 189, 194, 195
Dongolawi, 177, 195, 200

Eastern Cree, 122–131
Endo, 191, 195, 199

Fanti, 18, 24, 40, 41, 88, 153–172, 251, 268, 283, 287, 290, 296, 301
For, 193, 195, 196
Fox (Meskwaki), 9, 10, 47, 74, 91, 93, 118–131

Gaam, 191, 192, 196, 199
Ganza, 148
Gilyak, 13, 42, 77
Gros Ventre, 122–131
Gugu Yimidhirr, 250, 251, 252
Gumuz, 140–146, 149, 150, 188, 192, 193, 195
Gurindji, 245, 248–249, 250, 256

Haida, 86, 89, 91
Hano (Hano-Tewa, Hopi-Tewa), 86, 91, 101, 102, 117–120
Hasinai, 126–131
Hidatsa, 6, 91, 126–131
Hopi, 8, 10, 16, 23, 83, 85–86, 88, 91, 94–95, 97, 98, 99–108, 117–120, 284, 290, 296
Huron, 125, 126–131

Ik, 188, 195, 199
Illinois, 92, 258
Iowa, 6, 91, 126–131
Iroquois (proper), 1–3, 8, 9, 31, 36, 39, 78, 125, 126–131, 291–293

Jinghpaw, 20, 22, 42–47, 77, 284, 299
Jyang (Dinka), 192, 195, 201

Peoples Index   345

Kachin, 12, 13, 14, 15, 16, 18, 42, 77–78
Kalenjin, 191
Kangra, 56, 66
Kansa, 91
Kanuri, 195, 200
Kapauku, 35
Karen, 22, 42–47
Kaska, 86, 92
Kaskaskia, 92
Katikiteg, 122–131
Kaw, 6
Kayapó, 25, 205, 208, 209, 212, 213, 219, 220, 223–239, 286
Kédang, 69, 75
Keresan Pueblos, 10, 91, 97, 99
Khoesan, 196, 197
Kickapoo, 91
Kija, 273, 275
Kĩsêdjê, 205, 208, 209, 219, 220
Komo, 146–148
Krahô, 205, 209, 210, 213, 220
Krinkati, 205, 208, 210, 211
Kunama, 139, 140, 150–151, 177, 178, 181, 182, 188, 192, 193, 195
Kurnai, 272, 273, 276
Kwakwaka'wakw (Kwakiutl), 89
Kwama, 148
Kwegu, 177, 200

Laguna Pueblo, 86, 91
Lamalera, 75
Lang'o, 189, 199
Latin (-speakers), 87
Lotuxo, 189, 195
Lugbara, 188, 200
Luo, 188, 191, 194, 202

Majangir, 177, 200
Mandan, 91, 126–131
Mao, 148
Mardu, 261, 262, 267, 275
Maru, 42–46, 299
Mbay, 195, 200
Mbuti, 149
Menominee (Menomini), 91, 118–120, 125–131
Meskwaki (*See* Fox)
Miami (-Miami, Miami-Illinois), 92, 122–131, 258

Micmac, 122–131
Midob, 177
Minangkabau, 171
Mirndi, 249
Missouri, 6, 91
Mistassini, 122–131
Miwok, 78, 79, 87, 92, 107, 259
Montagnais, 122–131
Murle, 188, 189, 194, 195

Naath (Nuer), 192, 195, 201
Nandi, 191, 195, 199
Nara, 178, 192
Naskapi, 93, 121–131
Nasupo, 20
Natchez, 126–131
Ngaatjatjarra, 261, 263, 265–273, 275
Ngalakan (Middle Roper), 250
Ngarinyin, 244, 246, 269, 270
Ngumpin, 248, 249, 256, 257, 269
Nilotic, 188, 189, 192
  Eastern, 189, 192, 194
  Southern, 191, 192
  Western, 189, 192
Nipigon, 122–131
Northern Saulteau, 122–131
Nubian, 177, 195
Nunggubuyu, 247, 248

Ocolo, 195, 201
Ojibwa, 6, 38, 93, 122–131, 296
  Eastern, 93
  North-central, 118–119
  Northern, 118–20
Old English (-speakers), 87
Omaha (proper), 6, 18, 22–23, 69–82, 87, 91, 97, 118–120, 126–131, 283, 289
Osage, 6, 91
Oto (Otoe), 6, 91, 126–131
Ottawa, 93, 122–131

Panará, 205, 207, 301
Pawnee, 6, 88, 91, 126–131
Pekangeku, 125–131
Penobscot, 122–131
Peoria, 92
Piankashaw, 92
Piegan, 122–131
Pitjantjatjara, 262, 264, 275

Plains Cree, 122–131
Plains Siouans, 10
Pok, 195, 201
Pomo
    Eastern, 92
    Northern, 92
    Southern, 91
Ponca, 6, 71, 91, 126–131
Potawatomi (Potawotamie), 91, 122–131
Pueblo, ix, 10, 23, 83–108, 118, 120, 286

Quapaw, 6, 91

Rainy River, 122–131
Rub, 188, 194

Samo, 17, 21, 72, 76, 77, 96–97, 99, 101, 137, 140, 146, 147, 149, 152, 289, 295
Santee, 126–131
Sapiny, 195, 201
Sauk, 91
Seminole, 6, 86, 88, 126–131, 300
Seneca, 118–120, 160, 291, 292
Senufo Fodonon, 117–120
Shangalla, 141
Shatt, 195, 200
Shawnee, 91, 122–131
Sherpas, 55–57, 65, 300
Shyita, 148
Sirionó, 35, 78, 117–120, 221
Songay, 178, 180, 188, 193, 195
Soo, 194, 195
Southern Paiute, 118–120
South Valley Yokuts, 92
Spinifex, 272, 275
Sungor, 178, 179, 180
Surmic, 188
Swampy Cree, 93

Tama, 178, 179
Tamil, 160, 292
Taos Pueblo, 118–120
Teso, 195, 201
Teton, 126–131
Tibu, 1951
Timucua, 92, 126–131
Tlingit, 86, 89, 91, 117–120
Toba Batak, 77
Tonkawa, 86, 92
Trobriand, 88
Trukese, 117–120
Tsimshian, 89
Turkana, 195, 201
Tzotzil, 87

Uduk, 23, 140, 146–148, 149, 151, 189, 192, 193, 195
Umeda, 137

Wappo, 91
Warumungu, 248
Wea, 92
Wichita, 6, 126–131
Wik-Mungkan, 252
Winnebago, 6, 91, 126–131
Wintu, 92
Wintu-Nomlaki, 92
Witihama, 75

Xikrin, 208

Yanyuwa, 250
Yi, 20
Yolngu, 250, 251, 252, 253, 254, 260
Yuchi, 9, 91, 92
Yulu, 189, 195

Zhu, 197
Zia, 91
Zuni, 86, 91, 117–120

Persons Index

Allen, Nicholas, J., 21, 22, 24, 43, 48, 51–66, 136, 148, 152, 197, 284, 285, 286, 289, 294, 295

Barbosa de Almeida, Mauro, 286
Barnard, Alan, 49
Barnes, Robert H., 18, 22, 23, 24, 41, 47, 53, 69–82, 83, 93, 96, 107, 108, 125–126, 138, 274, 282, 283, 288, 289
Beattie, John, 149
Bruce, James, 141
Burling, Robbins, 42–46, 299

Carneiro, Robert, 89, 131
Coelho de Souza, Marcela, ix, 9, 25, 205–222, 283, 286, 291
Copet-Rougier, Élisabeth, 137–138, 289

DaMatta, Roberto, 209, 211, 212, 213, 214, 216, 217
Darwin, Charles, 109
Dorsey, James Owen, 7, 10, 70, 72, 77
Dousset, Laurent, 24, 26, 66, 143, 222, 244, 261–277, 284, 285, 286, 301, 302
Dumézil, Georges, 62
Dumont, Louis, 71, 271, 288
Durkheim, Émile viii, 8, 62, 69, 74, 264
Dziebel, German Valentinovich, 54

Eggan, Fred, 10, 92, 95, 97, 99, 101, 107, 124, 127, 131, 292
Ehret, Christopher, 24, 41, 138, 140, 173–202, 286, 293
Elkin, Adolphus, 246, 262, 263, 264, 268, 269, 271, 272
Evans-Pritchard, Edward Evan, 73

Fardon, Richard, 93, 138, 140
Firth, Raymond, 80
Fison, Lorimer, 276
Fletcher, Alice, 70
Fortes, Meyer, 81, 155
Forth, Gregory, 78, 107

Fortunato, Laura, 116, 299
Fox, Robin, 10, 97–99, 107
Freire-Marreco, Barbara, 101
Fürer-Haimendorf, Christoph von, 55

Gilbert, William, Jr., 10
Godelier, Maurice, vii, viii, ix, x, 7, 19–20, 26, 48, 75, 77, 80, 83, 107, 136, 137, 274, 282, 284, 285, 290, 291, 294, 296, 297, 299
Good, Anthony, 57
Goody, Jack, 80, 82
Gould, Richard, 265, 267
Gould, Sydney, 11, 84, 85, 87–88, 153, 158–164, 169, 300, 301
Granet, Marcel, 13, 42, 46, 48, 62, 281

Haeckel, Ernst, 109
Hage, Per, 11, 41, 115, 137, 293
Hallowell, A. Irving, 39
Héran, François, 57
Héritier, Françoise, viii, 16, 17, 18, 21, 23, 58, 70, 72, 76, 93, 96, 99, 101, 105, 107, 137, 138, 146, 243, 288, 289, 290, 291

James, Wendy, 23, 41, 135–152, 286, 289

Keesing, Roger, 80
Kirchoff, Paul, 32
Kohler, Josef, viii, 8, 10, 22, 69, 73, 74
Kroeber, Alfred Louis, 73, 74, 77, 86
Kronenfeld, David B., 10, 11, 18, 19, 20, 24, 40, 41, 66, 84, 97, 108, 153–172, 222, 251, 252, 268, 272, 274, 283, 286, 287, 301
Kryukov, Mikhail V., viii, 10, 20, 32, 48, 78, 108, 293, 295, 296
Kuper, Adam, 138

Ladeira, Maria Elisa, 212, 217
La Flesche, Francis, 70–72
La Flesche, Frank, 71

La Flesche, Joseph, 72
Lea, Vanessa, 212, 217, 220, 226
Leach, Edmund R., 42, 43, 46, 73, 81, 284
Lesser, Alexander, 9, 10, 91–92
Lévi-Strauss, Claude, viii, 7, 10, 13–17, 19, 20, 22, 23, 24, 42, 46, 47, 48, 53, 57, 70–71, 72, 73, 74, 78, 82, 83, 89, 93–96, 99, 107, 111, 129, 135, 137, 205, 206, 262, 277, 281–285, 287–291, 294, 295, 305
Lounsbury, Floyd G., 1, 5, 11, 33–35, 42–46, 48, 78, 84–85, 158, 164, 168, 169, 171, 212, 244, 284, 299
Lowie, Robert H., 10, 12, 31, 32, 73, 77, 85, 89, 99, 101, 226, 281
Lussier, Dominique, 150

Malinowski, Bronislaw, 11, 12, 48–49
Mallory, James, 63
Mauss, Marcel, 62
Maybury-Lewis, David, 9, 25, 205, 207, 209
McConvell, Patrick, 24, 26, 129, 222, 243–260, 264, 273, 275, 287, 293, 295
McKinley, Robert, 17, 18, 83, 93, 96, 105, 107, 129, 243, 281
McLennan, John F., 288
Mekonnen, Berihun Mebratie, 141, 144
Melatti, Julio Cezar, 209, 210, 212, 213
Morgan, Lewis Henry, viii, 1, 3, 5–6, 7, 8, 10, 12, 13, 19, 21, 24, 31, 32, 37, 39, 47, 48, 49, 53, 69, 73, 74, 77, 86, 126, 160, 171, 172, 237, 281, 283, 288, 291–292, 293, 294, 295, 304
Murdock, George Peter, 9, 12, 25, 32, 35, 40, 73, 78, 91–92, 97, 118, 120, 126, 127, 281, 288

Needham, Rodney, 70, 73, 75, 77, 78–79, 81–82, 83, 107, 274
Nimuendajú, Curt, 226, 301

Parkin, David, 107
Parkin, Robert, 42

Parry, Jonathan, 56, 64, 66
Pospisil, Leopold, 35
Powers, Theodore, ix, 23, 49, 109–131

Radcliffe-Brown, Alfred R., 8, 12, 74, 79, 80, 246, 269, 281, 282
Read, Dwight, 84, 158
Rivers, William H. R., 12, 73, 281
Rumsey, Alan, 247, 269, 270, 272, 274

Salt, Henry, 141
Scheffler, Harold W., 35, 78, 81, 243, 244, 245, 249, 259, 262
Schneider, David M., 19
Spier, Leslie, 10

Tax, Sol, 9, 10, 47, 74
Teclehaimanot, Macca, 150
Theophrastus, 109
Thomson, Donald, 251, 252, 255
Tindale, Norman, 263–264
Titiev, Mischa, 9, 94, 99, 101
Tjon Sie Fat, Franklin E., vii, viii, ix, 7, 17, 35, 96, 108, 146, 147, 262, 290, 300, 301
Tonkinson, Robert, 261, 267, 268
Trautmann, Thomas R., vii-x, 1–27, 31–50, 51, 78, 83, 93, 107, 108, 125, 126, 129, 137, 281–297
Turner, Terence, 25, 208, 213, 216, 223–239, 286, 297
Turton, David, 80

Viveiros de Castro, Eduardo, ix, 35, 93, 210, 214, 221, 291

Wheeler, Ward C., viii, ix, 23, 49, 109–131, 287, 293, 295
White, Leslie, 9, 288
Whiteley, Peter M., viii, ix, 1–27, 49, 73, 83–108, 109–131, 281–297
Winter, Edward, 149